All Rise

All Rise

The high ambitions of the International Criminal
Court and the harsh reality

Tjitske Lingsma

Ipso Facto, Utrecht

Copyright © Tjitske Lingsma, Amsterdam 2017
Published by: Ipso Facto, Utrecht 2017
First published in Dutch, December 2014

Graphic design: Helma Timmermans
Portrait: Katrien Mulder
ISBN: 978-90-77386-20-0
NUR: 600

www.if-publishers.com
www.tjitske-lingsma.nl

Contents

PREFACE

'You mean … where Mladić and Karadžić are being prosecuted?' Often conversations about the International Criminal Court start with this kind of question. Many people confuse the court with the International Criminal Tribunal for the former Yugoslavia (ICTY), which, although also located in the Dutch city of The Hague, is a completely different institution. There, indeed, the Bosnian Serb former general Ratko Mladić and politician Radovan Karadžić were put on trial.

All Rise tells the story of the International Criminal Court (ICC), founded by 120 nations in 1998, when their governments signed the Rome Statute. Four years later, in 2002, sixty nations had ratified the treaty, which meant the institution could start operating. The ICC is the first permanent international court tasked with prosecuting individuals responsible for genocide, crimes against humanity and war crimes. Its mandate is not restricted to a specific country or region, such as the ICTY or the International Criminal Tribunal for Rwanda (ICTR), and its jurisdiction covers large parts of the world.

My specific interest in the ICC arose when, in 2010, I followed several classes of the Masters programme in international crimes and criminology at the Vrije Universiteit in Amsterdam. For the first time in many years I was a student again, studying the basics of international criminal law and finding myself preparing for exams. After the theory I wondered: how do international courts and tribunals function in reality, how do cases develop, what is the mood, what are the problems and results? So, being a journalist, I started to cover the ICC for media such as the Dutch newspaper Trouw, the magazine De Groene Amsterdammer and the online International Justice Tribune. While reporting, the idea surfaced for All Rise, in which I describe the functioning of the court in its raw reality, complexity and drama.

The book consists of five thematic chapters (introduction, investigations, detention, witnesses and victims) and five chapters about cases related to conflicts in Kenya, Côte d'Ivoire, the Central African Republic, Libya and the Democratic Republic of Congo, plus a chapter about asylum seekers. As several cases developed into trials, those chapters became bigger than others. The book was largely written while the ICC was still located in its temporary offices. Most descriptions will be about the court functioning in the old building, as the ICC only moved to its permanent premises at the seaside in The Hague in December 2015.

All Rise is based on court hearings, interviews, filings by prosecutors, defence lawyers and legal representatives of victims, decisions by judges, conferences, media reports, studies by academics and human rights organisations, and my own observations. For the descriptions of the exchanges in the courtroom, I extensively and gratefully made use of the official transcripts.

This book was first published in Dutch in December 2014, after which I translated All Rise into English. For this purpose I also updated the text. The last reference date is March/April 2017. Developments at the ICC are slow and trials usually take many years, but sometimes things can suddenly change. I like to compare the court to a turtle, which is not known for its speed. But when you don't pay attention to it for a few minutes, the animal has moved and you find yourself looking for it.

I am very grateful to the people who contributed to the book by sharing their knowledge and expressing their views: court officials, lawyers, academics, human rights activists, observers, politicians, journalists and visitors at the public gallery. I will be eternally indebted to my friends and colleagues for their time and efforts to give me feedback and advice. The first draft – in Dutch – went to Linda Polman and Arita Baaijens, whose critical evaluation helped me to adjust the manuscript. This resulted in deleting paragraphs and reshuffling chapters. My professors Joris van Wijk (director of the Center for International Criminal Justice at the Vrije Universiteit, Amsterdam) and Alette Smeulers (professor international criminology at the Rijksuniversiteit Groningen and Tilburg University) looked at the first version, which felt a bit like doing exams. ICC expert Thijs Bouwknegt, researcher at NIOD and lecturer at Amsterdam University, read and commented on the Dutch text as well. His suggestions and adjustments were so valuable. He knows the subject, the institution and its inhabitants inside out. I have very fond memories of meetings with Tia Lücker, who edited the Dutch version. I would like to thank Minka Nijhuis for her support during the whole process from writing to translating and publishing.

Rohan Jayasekera of Vivarta encouraged me to go ahead with the English translation and gave me the confidence to push forward. Where would I be without the help of my editor Janet Anderson, who edited my English.

It was great to work with Helma Timmermans, who made the impressive cover and book design. My agent Maartje Wildeman assisted me with the promotion and thus finding you, the reader. I would like to thank my dear friends who contributed so generously to the inner-crowd-funding. I am extremely lucky to be publishing All Rise with Ipso Facto. This publishing house, set up by photographer Jan Banning, is developing into an inspiring collective of photographers and journalists who combine forces in publishing their work.

The ultimate responsibility for All Rise lies with me. But without the help, support and contributions of these persons, and so many others, this book would never have seen the light of day. It was a fantastic journey. Thank you all.

1

ENTRANCE

Three crucial words were written on the small white sign near the public entrance of the International Criminal Court (ICC): 'Pas Op! Schrikdraad.' Despite its importance, the vast majority of the visitors, however, would overlook the text. Not only because of its inconspicuous size and location on the fence, but also because of the language that was used. As most of the court's guests are from abroad, they simply wouldn't be able to understand the words in Dutch that warned them about the risk of an electric shock if one touched the trellis-work surrounding the court. A version in English or French – the working languages of the ICC – seemed to be absent. So, over the years, I had started to wonder how serious I actually had to take that warning.
Until autumn 2014.
Just outside the court, right next to the public entrance, a colleague working for international media was having her cigarette during a break in the hearings. She inhaled with the enviable sense of joy of an addicted smoker, and blew out the smoke. With every inhalation her head would bend dangerously backwards, almost touching the fence. For many years she had been covering the ICC. On that same spot near the entrance, oblivious of the risk, she had smoked numerous cigarettes. So I pointed at the sign and translated the words. We laughed about the absurdity of the situation in case she might be electrocuted by the ICC's fence. But then a tall young man, clearly in a hurry, came sprinting to the court's entrance. When he saw my colleague inhaling, he stopped and shouted in panic: 'Be careful! A few weeks ago a friend touched the fence. He got a terrible shock, which blew him metres away!'
Welcome to the ICC, that forgot to properly inform its visitors about the dangers of its trellis-work. Only when I examined the fence, I saw a glimpse of an English text: 'Warning High Voltage Security Fence.' It was written on tiny notices, few in number and attached to the inside of the trellis-work, invisible to arriving guests.
Numerous visitors have entered the ICC headquarters, which was located, from 2002 until Christmas 2015, in an uninviting part of the Dutch

city of The Hague amidst highways, railways, offices and a run-down industrial harbour area. They would take the revolving door into a hall, where uniformed guards with stern faces checked the arrivals. Obediently, guests and court officials would put their coats, bags and other belongings on the X-ray belt. Then they stepped into the walk-through gate detector, as if they were checking in for a flight. Indeed, appropriate security measures for an organisation that is tasked with prosecuting warlords, presidents, ministers, officials, military, militia leaders, rebels, politicians, professionals and other powerful persons suspected of being responsible for gruesome atrocities that deeply shock humanity's conscience.

With professional politeness, the personnel in the lobby show visitors the way to the coat racks and lockers, where they can store their belongings. Signs warn the guests that taking photos and filming is forbidden. The atmosphere is one of formal courtesy and sometimes even unease.

While the court is a prominent international institution, which can be visited by anyone, the public spaces are often oases of silence. Everyday hearings hardly attract visitors. An exception is formed by the small group of supporters of the former vice president of the Democratic Republic of Congo (DRC), Jean-Pierre Bemba Gombo. They have been making efforts to visit all hearings in his long trial, which started back in 2010. During lunch breaks they would push together the small wooden table blocks in the lobby to form a large table, and arrange the red modest armchairs in a circle around it. Under the photo gallery with portraits of the court's judges, they would display plastic bags with soft bread rolls, packs of sliced cheese and meats, and cans with soft drinks. Then lunch could start. Acquaintances and other familiar faces would be invited to join in, grab a sandwich and enjoy a drink.

But the large public – diplomats, journalists, legal experts, observers, human rights activists, representatives of think tanks, professors, students and politicians – mainly visits the court during highlights such as initial appearances, the start of trials, closing statements and verdicts, or when prominent suspects like the Kenyan president and deputy president were forced to be present. These are the only moments the public galleries are truly packed.

On ordinary days the silence is just disturbed by the clicking of shoes of court officials crossing the lobby on their way to another meeting. Sometimes judges or prosecutors, in their judicial robes, could be spotted. Others would be wearing smart suits and stylish combinations, while the interns are dressed to impress. In their dashing outfits, balancing on high heels, some women would do very well on the catwalk. This legal branch is not only considered noble and important, but also cool, hip and hot. Many staff are notably young. Just like international criminal law itself, that only started to flourish in the last decades.

In atmosphere and distance, though, this squeaky-clean building and its well-paid personnel are so remote from the areas where the crimes that are prosecuted here, were committed. The contrast couldn't be bigger between the headquarters and the hellish areas where terrified people were killed, slaughtered, maimed, tortured, burned, raped, enslaved, deported, persecuted and robbed of all things they loved and cherished.

A moment of Utopia

In the court building strict rules apply. Not only in the public spaces, but also in the well protected office areas. When I arrive for an interview, autumn 2011, a press officer navigates me through the building. Every time she gets to the next electronic lock, she presses her security pass against the device. Arriving at the last door, she takes out her hand-phone and calls for a final okay. She then pushes the heavy door that gives access to the protected wing, enters the corridor and walks to the room of Gilbert Bitti, an amiable Frenchman who works as senior legal advisor for the judges of the pre-trial division, that handles cases in the entire phase before the trial. In his appearance – spectacles with a light metal rim – he resembles a professor who's passionate about his subject. When he is present during hearings in the courtroom, he is recognizable because of his full beard. But now, after some drastic razor blade action, suddenly his shaven jaws are visible.

Bitti has been involved since ICC's conception. In fact, he was present even before the 'midwives' arrived on the scene, he tells with a friendly smile. 'It was a bit of a miracle,' the legal expert says about the birth of the court, speaking with his typical high voice, in an English that is lifted up by a charming French accent. With satisfaction he remembers the 'nineties' when he, as a young lawyer, was part of the French diplomatic delegation at the United Nations.

It was a special time. The campaign by human rights organisations and a large group of 'like-minded' countries, dedicated to establish the first permanent international criminal court in history, had reached its climax. World politics were still caught up in large disputes, but there were opportunities as well. 'We experienced that moment of Utopia. Between the end of the Soviet Union and the attack on the World Trade Centre in New York,' recalls Bitti, who, as a true French intellectual, enjoys with visible delight a more contemplative discourse. It was a period with political leaders on the world stage who were positive about the idea of international justice. Tony Blair had just been elected, and was still fresh as the new prime minister of the United Kingdom. In France, the government was led by the socialist prime minister Lionel Jospin. The Democrat Bill Clinton was president of the United States of America. The basics were in place. The United Nations had – after a vacuum of forty years since the war tribunals of Nuremberg and Tokyo – established two new ad hoc tribunals to punish suspects of international crimes committed during the wars in Yugoslavia and the genocide in Rwanda. 'We were about to change the world,' says Bitti, with such animation that his voice almost goes off the rails. 'Interestingly, many persons dedicated to the International Criminal Court were still young. I was 32 years old. Still a boy. But one needs that naivety and youthful enthusiasm to get things done.'

The Netherlands was keen on getting the ICC to The Hague. While lobbying, the government had chosen a softly-softly approach in order to prevent attracting too much attention of rivals, whose interest in hosting such a prestigious institution might otherwise be awoken. Much to its surprise, there was no resistance nor competition. When the Dutch suggested to put 'The Hague' behind the word 'seat' in the draft version of the Rome Statute, nobody objected. And so The Netherlands succeeded in fulfilling its ambition.

In the summer of 1998 the moment was there. An enormous feeling of relief was felt when 120 countries were prepared to put their signature under the Rome Statute during that unique diplomatic conference in the Italian capital city. The International Criminal Court – in French la Cour Pénale Internationale (CPI) – was born. The ICC was thus not established by the UN, but by a large group of countries, while supported and pushed by a global human rights movement. 'It was a very emotional moment: when you have diplomats, usually very serious people, dancing and crying and kissing each other on that Friday 17 July 1998. It was a great moment of achievement,' Bitti says. But the writing was on the wall. The USA, at the peak of its power, had tried to obstruct the project and finally would not participate.

For Bitti, it was the result that counted. 'We offered this present to humanity,' the French lawyer says poetically. Not many people are able to talk with such a mix of seriousness, involvement and mild derision about the most terrible things as Bitti does. 'This court goes against the entire history of mankind,' he explains. 'For centuries human beings have been killing each other with a lot of delight. In fact, I am still surprised that humankind has managed to survive. People love to kill each other so much, that I couldn't imagine they would renounce one of their big pleasures. Especially those in power have always been able to kill whoever they wanted. Nobody would ever bother them. Because you are in power, you can kill. It is part of the power. But this is changing and the ICC is part of that process. Now you can't kill, simply arrange an amnesty and forget about it. The court reflects that change in the history of mankind.' The Rome Statute, a document containing 128 articles, spells out the most important rules and principles that govern the ICC. Its preamble reminds us of the horrors of the twentieth century, where it says that 'millions of children, women and men have been victims of unimaginable atrocities that deeply shock the conscience of humanity.' The signatories affirm that these grave and most serious crimes 'threaten the peace, security and well-being of the world,' are of 'concern to the international community as a whole' and 'must not go unpunished.' Therefore the court is tasked to investigate and indict perpetrators, 'to put an end to impunity' and 'to contribute to the prevention of such crimes.'
The court prosecutes individuals (not states, organisations or companies) who are accused of committing international crimes: genocide, crimes against humanity and war crimes (Appendix III). The ICC might also go after persons suspected of the crime of 'aggression' (the use of armed force by a state against the sovereignty, territorial integrity or political independence of another nation). But the prerequisite was that first a minimum of thirty states that are members of the court, had to ratify the amendments in the Rome Statute on this crime. This condition was met with Chile and The Netherlands doing so in September 2016, bringing the number of ratifications to 32. This means that the member states are in the position to take a decision on activating that jurisdiction. Before that happens, the court won't be able to prosecute the crime of aggression. It is considered an innovation that victims have been given a special position before the court. Previously, in proceedings before other international criminal courts and tribunals, their role was limited to

testify as witnesses. But the ICC recognizes that victims have their own rights. Groups of victims can be represented by a lawyer in court cases. If judges have given permission, at specific moments, victims themselves can address the court. They are also entitled to reparations. These rights and privileges, however, come with serious limitations as well (see chapter 10). The ICC is a court of last resort. Following the principle of 'complementarity', the court only comes into action when national authorities are unable or unwilling to investigate and prosecute international crimes that fall under its jurisdiction. The ICC will only intervene if genuine proceedings in a country are absent. This limitation is important. 'National prosecutions are always better,' says Bitti, 'because these are close to the victims, to the persons holding the evidence, to the people who understand the situation and speak the language. But it is good to have an international legal institution as a backup. To remind perpetrators that if no action is taken on the national level, you won't be free from prosecution for ever.'

There is however an important restriction in time. The ICC can only deal with crimes that have taken place after 1 July 2002, when sixty countries had ratified the Rome Statute (sooner than expected) and the institution could get started.

But compared to 1998, when the treaty was signed, the mood had changed very much, says Bitti. With the terrorist attacks of 11 September 2001, against the USA, the world had entered a new phase of conflict. The Zeitgeist had changed. The optimism of the nineties – 'that little window' – when many hoped that mankind was able, despite itself, to establish a better world, had been followed by an era characterized by concern, fear, anger, revenge, violence and war.

The Netherlands

Immediately after the green light for the start of the ICC was given, the Dutch legal expert Sam Muller, who was called in to be part of the advance team, went to the place where the court was going to be located. It was summer 2002. With the keys in his hands, he stood on the pavement before a huge empty office building previously inhabited by telecom giant KPN in The Hague. One of his first priorities as he entered was to make sure there was at least a person to pick up the phone, in case calls would be made to the court. Intensive renovation works had adapted the two white office towers to accommodate the ICC. Courtrooms, public galleries, a meeting room and a media centre were created where once the indoor carpark had been. The grey concrete ceilings of the lobby and the pillars that limited the view from the public gallery into the courtroom, reminded the visitor of the building's previous destination. This was the temporary housing of the ICC. The Dutch government had promised to pay its annual rent of 6 million euros during the first decade, starting in 2002. But the honeymoon between the host state and the court would not last forever. When the ten years were over, while the permanent premises still needed to be built, the government said it had fulfilled its promise. In July 2012 the Dutch authorities announced they would stop paying the building's rent. Behind the scenes a huge row erupted between The Netherlands and the ICC. Marc Dubuisson, director of the division of court services, told me in an interview in 2011: 'We expected some flexibility from the host state, and that it would continue to pay for the rent for a few more years.' But the authorities behaved like 'real Dutch', he said, referring to a renowned national characteristic: being stingy.

His remarks were not appreciated by all court officials, and even less so by the Dutch government, but at least the row was in the open. His comments yielded results. The Dutch parliament pressured the minister of foreign affairs to be a better host, after which he agreed to pay the rent for another six months, until the end of 2012. For the time being the issue was settled. His successor then offered to pay 9 million euros for the following three years until the new premises would be ready in 2015 (this amount was half of the total rent, the other 9 million euros were paid by the member states). In a letter to parliament, the new minister of foreign affairs pointed out that the Dutch were not only contributing to the institution. He referred to figures provided by the ICC itself, which claimed that the economic benefits for The Netherlands in hosting the court amounted to 66 million euros per year.

Apart from the financial frictions, other problems would surface as well. In 2011 Dubuisson said it had become 'extremely difficult' to get emergency visas for potential witnesses who had to be evacuated from their countries urgently, as they were in danger. Other international courts and tribunals prosecuting crimes in former Yugoslavia, Sierra Leone and Lebanon, experienced similar problems with the Dutch authorities. The institutions decided to combine their efforts to request The Netherlands for a more smooth handling of visa.

When Dutch members of parliament visited the ICC, early 2013, they were told that witnesses were often provided with short stay visa with very limited validity. This created difficulties for court officials in scheduling their testimonies before the judges. Because if the previous witness would take longer or hearings were postponed, the visa of the next witness might no longer be valid. Again, the ICC had requested the host state for more flexibility. Together with several colleagues, the Dutch MP Sjoerd Sjoerdsma asked the cabinet about the matter. But the minister of foreign affairs responded he was 'not aware' of the problem.

Getting started

After the official birth of the ICC, Bitti would remain committed to the new institution. He still knows the exact date. It was 14 October 2002 when he participated in his first meeting at the court. 'We were with eight persons, and we only had one floor at our disposal: the third floor.' Currently, more than eight hundred staff members, originating from a hundred countries, are working at the ICC. The court is divided in four organs. First, there is the presidency, consisting of three judges (currently all female), which is responsible for the administration of the court and represents the institution to the outside world.

Secondly, there are the chambers. A total of eighteen judges are assigned to the pre-trial, trial and appeals chambers. They supervise and oversee the court's cases, making sure that the rules are applied correctly, that the rights of suspects, victims and witnesses are respected, and that the accused gets a fair trial. The judges come from all parts of the world, and half of them are women.

The third organ is the office of the prosecutor (OTP), which is tasked with analysing situations where serious human rights violations are committed, investigating atrocity crimes, collecting evidence, selecting suspects and leading the prosecutions for genocide, crimes against humanity and war crimes. The first chief prosecutor was the Argentine lawyer Luis Moreno-Ocampo, who was elected by the member states on 21 April 2003. After he had served his nine year term, which ended in June 2012, he was succeeded by Fatou Bensouda, who originates from Gambia. For many years she had been Moreno-Ocampo's deputy.

The fourth organ is the registry, which is responsible for the non-judicial aspects of the administration of the court. Life at the court is not always a perfect co-habitation between the different organs. There have been tensions within divisions as well. In private, for instance, guards complain about the work atmosphere and the authoritarian way the security unit is run, resulting in stress and conflicts. Recently the ReVision project, initiated to reorganise the registry that employs 550 staff, caused considerable unrest. The number of women appointed in mid-to-senior level posts has decreased since July 2012, says The Women's Initiatives for Gender Justice in a report published in 2015.

'There are no female heads of division within the registry. Women in professional posts are clustered into the lower professional grades, and no women participate in senior management meetings of the registry where key policy, operational and institutional decisions are made,' the organisation underlines. In another way diversity was dealt a blow as well. The Women's Initiatives for Gender Justice notes that '36 percent of professional posts occupied by those from the Africa region' will be 'abolished in the restructuring of the registry.' A source who wants to remain anonymous, said that staff is complaining about the power of 'the Benelux-mafia' within the registry – western men deciding on matters.

The members

Currently 124 countries (of a total of 195 nations) have adopted, ratified and acceded to the Rome Statute. These members of the court play a crucial role. Together they form the Assembly of States Parties (ASP), which is the management oversight and legislative body of the ICC. Their governments decide on the adoption of legal texts, the election of judges, the prosecutor and the deputy prosecutor and pay for the budget of the ICC, that amounted to 145 million euros in 2017.

Member states have the obligation to cooperate with the court – which does not have its own police force to arrest suspects, for instance – and to give authorisation for wide-ranging matters such as criminal investigations and outreach on their territory. Support for the ICC has been stagnating, however. In 2011 six countries joined. But in 2012 only one country became member: Guatemala. The same goes for 2013, with just Ivory Coast joining. 2014 saw no new membership. However in 2015 an important nation joined: Palestine, which might give a new dynamic to the court. In 2016 El Salvador became member of the ICC.

The list of member states is unbalanced. Mainly countries in Africa (Senegal was the first to ratify the Rome Statute in 1999), Europe and Latin America have joined the ICC. A little over a dozen Asian countries (including Japan, Bangladesh, East Timor, Afghanistan) and three nations in the Middle East (Tunisia, Jordan, Palestine – although the first is categorized by the ICC as African and the other two as Asian-Pacific) are members. Big powers such as the USA (that signed the Rome Statute, but did not ratify, later unsigned, campaigning against the court), Russia (signed, no ratification and recently unsigned), China and India refused to join.

When the court started operating, the USA initiated a diplomatic offensive against the new institution. The government went on a campaign pressuring countries to sign bilateral agreements promising never to hand over an American to the ICC. In Dutch media cynical and giggly editorials and opinion pieces appeared about the idea of Americans landing on the beaches when the 'American Service-Members' Protection Act' was signed into law by US president George Bush on 3 August 2002. This act, nicknamed 'The Hague Invasion Act', envisages the possibility of US military force to liberate any American who is detained by the court in The Hague. A 'bizarre law', commented American diplomat and professor David Scheffer in 2012 in an interview with 'Wordt Vervolgd', the magazine of the Dutch branch of Amnesty International. 'It gives the president the largest powers to go to war ever in the history of the USA. He doesn't even have to inform the Congress, but can directly send troops to The Hague.'

But in terms of rejecting the court, one of the biggest crises erupted in October 2016, when three African countries said they pulled out of the ICC. The procedure to withdraw requires an official notification to the secretary general of the United Nations, after which it will take a year before the withdrawal takes effect. After its parliament had voted to pull out, the president of Burundi signed legislation to leave the ICC on 18 October. One day later, on 19 October, South Africa followed by sending a notification to New York. Then Gambia announced it would withdraw. It was feared that towards the end of 2017, the number of member states would have dwindled to 121 or even less.

The three governments had different – not always very clear – reasons. South Africa was in conflict with the court after it had been criticized for not arresting the president of Sudan, who is wanted by the ICC. Burundi seemed to try to escape justice as the prosecution is looking into accusations that the government and security services are committing atrocities such as torture, rape, executions and forced disappearances.

The move to withdraw, left the ICC with just a year to decide whether it should start full investigations into crimes in Burundi. Under the previous government led by president Yahya Jammeh, Gambia had developed a shocking human rights record, but as the ICC was not considering investigations the motive was less obvious.

Although South Africa and the new president of Gambia revoked the decision to withdraw, there are still countries that threaten to leave. This it is a serious development, not only because pulling out could set an example for governments that fear the ICC might start investigations against them, but also because international cooperation is vital for the functioning of the ICC. Court officials are continuously contacting member states, other countries, embassies, the UN, European Union, African Union, law enforcement agencies, experts and non-governmental organisations. These contacts are ranging from witness protection to information gathering, investigations, arrest warrants, detention possibilities or outreach to affected communities. Even powerful nations that formally don't accept the ICC, can decide to cooperate.

How the ICC gets its cases

The court has been conducting criminal investigations with regard to ten different 'situations' in a total of nine countries: Uganda, Democratic Republic of Congo (DRC), the Central African Republic (CAR), Sudan, Kenya, Libya, Ivory Coast, Mali and Georgia. (Because the ICC is dealing with two situations in the CAR, that country appears twice on its list: CAR-I and CAR-II). The court is bound by rules in deciding where to investigate.

There are three ways the ICC can become active in a country. First, a member state can refer a situation on its own territory to the court: a state referral, usually called a self-referral. Members that have accepted the ICC's jurisdiction can officially invite the court to come and conduct an investigation. In the past experts were sceptical whether this option would ever be applied. But the first prosecutor, who actively sought these self-referrals, succeeded in his strategy. In December 2003 Uganda made such a request. A few weeks later, on 29 January 2004, prosecutor Moreno-Ocampo and the Ugandan president Yoweri Museveni organised a press conference in London where they announced that the ICC would investigate atrocity crimes in northern Uganda with the aim of prosecuting the leaders of the Lord's Resistance Army (LRA).

In 2004 the neighbouring countries DRC and CAR, and many years later Mali (and to a certain extent also Ivory Coast), urged the court to go after perpetrators of violence. After a civil war had broken out, the CAR government asked in 2014 for a second time the ICC to come and investigate crimes.

The reality of these self-referrals though is that they are initiated by states and – so far – have led to cases prosecuting one side. In these conflict situations the ICC has been charging militia leaders, rebels, opponents and politicians who lost power struggles, while individuals who are part of the official agencies (government, army, police, intelligence services and their militia) and are suspected of international crimes, walk free.

The second route goes via the Security Council of the United Nations (UNSC), which can refer a situation when there is a threat to international peace and security. The advantage of this option is that the ICC can investigate crimes committed in countries which are not members of the court. The flipside is that the international community will only take such action with regard to nations that are internationally isolated, have no friends to rely on and are considered pariahs (although over the years such a status can change). So far the UN Security Council – of which three of the five permanent members have declined to become member of the ICC – has referred two situations to the court: Sudan/ Darfur and Libya.

The third possibility lies in the hands of the prosecutor, who can start an investigation on her own initiative – known by its Latin term 'proprio motu' – with the limitation that the judges of the pre-trial chamber will have to give permission for such action. Another restriction is that the prosecutor can use this option only with member states (and their nationals) or countries that accept the jurisdiction of the court. On this basis, the prosecutor charged six persons – three politicians, two officials and a broadcaster – with crimes against humanity that were committed during the post-election violence in Kenya in 2007 and 2008. The prosecutor took the opportunity to hold national authorities to account, even if they are respected as leaders by the world community. But it also shows the difficulties of prosecuting powerful officials in office, as the cases against all six suspects have collapsed.

The Ivory Coast case – former president Laurent Gbagbo and minister/ youth leader Charles Blé Goudé are on trial – is also a proprio motu case. So far, however, the prosecution hasn't managed to start proceedings against the current authorities. The investigations in Georgia, where the judges on 27 January 2016 gave the prosecutor permission to go ahead, is a proprio motu case as well.

Suspects in numbers

The ICC has indicted 40 persons: 33 for international crimes and 8 for offences against the administration of justice which mainly involves cases of witness interference. One person, Bemba, is charged for both categories. It is possible that the court still keeps some arrest warrants under seal, which haven't been published yet.

Since its start, the ICC has convicted four persons of crimes against humanity and war crimes, while the cases against nine suspects failed. Apart from these international crimes cases, the ICC convicted five persons of bribing and coaching witnesses.

In the special ICC detention centre, which is part of in the international section of the prison in The Hague, currently six suspects are detained on charges of international crimes. Most defendants however aren't staying here.

First of all, suspects like the Kenyans (the so-called 'Ocampo Six') were never detained because they agreed to abide by summons to appear. This means they travelled to The Hague when the judges demanded their presence in court.

The rules also offer the possibility of granting suspects interim release, as happened with the five persons accused of bribing defence witnesses during the Bemba trial. They had been detained for almost a year, when four were released on certain conditions before their trial started. (Bemba himself remained in detention all the time.)

Third, charges don't necessarily result in convictions. After the prosecution had presented its evidence (at the confirmation of charges hearings, or during trial), the judges decided in nine cases there was not enough proof, so the suspects (six Kenyans, a Congolese, a Rwandan and a Sudanese suspect) walked free.

Then there is death. Being involved in international crimes is a dangerous lifestyle, as proved by the fate of at least four suspects whose death has been confirmed. The Libyan leader Muammar Gaddafi was murdered in 2011. Two (but likely three) members of the Ugandan LRA militia and a Darfur rebel leader are dead as well.

Fifth, there are countries that refuse to hand over suspects. Ivory Coast, that initially had encouraged the ICC to investigate, insisted it wanted to prosecute former First Lady, Simone Gbagbo, before a national court. During a first trial she was sentenced to twenty years in prison. In spring 2016 she faced a second trial in Ivory Coast for international crimes, which resulted in an acquittal. Libya refused to hand over Saif Al-Islam Gaddafi to the ICC. While the son of the former dictator was held by rebels, he was prosecuted in absentia in Tripoli under fierce international criticism that he didn't receive a fair trial. He was given the death penalty on 28 July 2015, although that sentence hasn't been carried out.

Last but not least, there are another twelve persons at large. Nine supects of international crimes (one Congolese warlord, two LRA-commanders, a Libyan and five Sudanese suspects); and three Kenyans charged with witness interference. The best known is the Sudanese president Omar Al-Bashir, charged with genocide and other international crimes in Darfur. The ICC is depending on governments to arrest these fugitives when they arrive on their territory. Although such arrest warrants are not always carried out, they do limit suspects in their movements. 'Certain people now hesitate to go to a hospital in Germany or in France. Voilà, they are extremely annoyed about that,' says Bitti about high profile individuals who are at large. In 2011 Malawi was told off by the ICC after it had received Al-Bashir. The next Malawi president, however, decided to do it differently. She openly said her government would not receive the Sudanese president if he would come to visit a summit of the African Union, which was hosted by Malawi. The AU then decided to move the meeting to the Ethiopian capital of Addis Ababa. Between the ICC's first arrest warrant in 2009 against Al-Bashir and early 2016, he made 74 international trips, according to the Coalition for the ICC. These included travels to member states such as Uganda, Chad, DRC, Djibouti and Nigeria. He seems to go on hajj to Mecca a fair bit as well.

The biggest outcry, however, came when Al-Bashir visited ICC's member state South Africa for an African Union summit, in June 2015. The government was well aware of its obligation to arrest him, but decided otherwise. A regional NGO, the Southern Africa Litigation Centre, filed a suit with the South African judiciary against his presence. While the nation's High Court decided that Al-Bashir was not allowed to leave the country, the government helped the Sudanese leader to flee, like a thief in the night. Several hours after his departure, the High Court decided that Al-Bashir should have been arrested. A few months later the ICC started proceedings on a possible finding of non-cooperation. In a reaction, South Africa's ruling party ANC threatened to leave the ICC.

The following year, on 19 October 2016, the government officially announced its withdrawal, citing the fact that the Rome Statute clashes with domestic laws granting immunity to sitting heads of state. The move sparked a fierce debate in the country between supporters and adversaries, about the legality of the decision as the parliament was not consulted, and about the reasons behind it. The government faced huge domestic and international pressure to change its position and stay with the court.

On 22 February 2017 a judge of the South African high court blocked the withdrawal saying the move was unconstitutional without prior approval of the parliament. Two weeks later, on 8 March, the government revoked its decision to pull out.

Observers point to the Al-Bashir case as proof that the ICC is a weak institution, which can be further weakened if countries like South Africa decide to leave. 'We have limited power,' Bitti agreed in the interview in 2011. 'It is very difficult or almost impossible to exert power over the powerful, while it is usually them who are responsible for organising large-scale violence.'

Hunting Africans

Many people in Africa are criticising the ICC because so far the court has been prosecuting only persons from that continent. In international forums such as the African Union and the UN Security Council, several African governments have been vehemently protesting against what some call the 'hunt' for Africans. This campaign against the court started when Al-Bashir was indicted in 2009, but grew louder when the court decided to prosecute the six Kenyan suspects, which included politicians and top officials. Although Kenya has threatened to leave the ICC, so far it hasn't realised its threat. When Gambia announced on 24 October 2016 it would withdraw from the court, its information minister, Sheriff Bojang, said the ICC was 'an International Caucasian Court for the persecution and humiliation of people of colour, especially Africans.' Burundi decided to leave the ICC citing similar reasons. President Pierre Nkurunziza called the court an instrument of powerful countries singling out leaders who do not comply with the West.

The fact that heads of state can be the subject of prosecutions, has been met with fierce resistance in Africa. When the Assembly of States

Parties held its annual meeting in November 2013 in The Hague, the delegations devoted a special session on the issue. It appeared that one of the cornerstones of the Rome Statute – the principle that no one is immune before the law – is less sacrosanct than when the court's text was formulated in the nineties. With Kenya in the lead, several member states managed to change a part of the Rules of Procedure and Evidence, an important document spelling out the workings of the court. A paragraph was added to rule 134 saying that if a suspect fulfils 'extraordinary public duties at the highest national level', he or she can write to the judges asking to be excused from attending his or her trial.

But there is also support – in Africa – not only among victims groups and human rights organisations, but indeed among governments. Some are truly committed, others just pragmatic. As stated earlier, half of the African conflict situations under investigation by the prosecution have been referred by these African countries themselves (Uganda, DRC, CAR, Mali and to a certain extent also Ivory Coast). These governments have invited the ICC to investigate international crimes on their territory. Recently, in September 2016, Gabon also made such a request, urging the ICC to go after the opposition. The prosecution is looking at the case.

Preliminary examinations

The court not only invites states, but the public as well, to inform the prosecution about grave situations that deserve its attention. So far, the OTP has received more than 10.000 communications requesting the court to take action. In several cases information (from governments and civil society) has led to official 'preliminary examinations.' This is a stage where the prosecution analyses the crimes, the gravity and whether the court has jurisdiction. Potentially such an examination can lead to a decision to conduct full criminal investigations.

Currently the prosecutors are conducting preliminary examinations in ten situations where serious human rights violations have been reported – Afghanistan, Colombia, Nigeria, Guinea, Iraq/UK, Ukraine, Palestine/Israel, vessels of Comoros/Greece/Cambodia, Burundi and Gabon. Six situations are out of Africa. If the circumstances don't improve, or if there are no proper national investigations, the ICC prosecutor might start full criminal investigations. Several countries, such as Colombia, have been on this list for ages. In the case of Afghanistan – a member since 2003, under ICC examination since 2007 – the prosecution says the office has 'a reasonable basis to believe' that crimes against humanity and war crimes were not only committed by the Taliban and Afghan government forces, but by international forces as well. In its latest report on preliminary examinations, the prosecution specifically mentions American military deployed in Afghanistan and the secret detention centres run by the Central Intelligence Agency (CIA) in countries such as Lithuania, Poland and Romania.

The prosecution will 'imminently' take a final decision whether to start full investigations. It is likely that it will be difficult to conduct cases in Afghanistan. In April 2016 Human Rights Watch (HRW) and the Transitional Justice Coordination Group (TJCG) wrote they are concerned about 'the possible role of the US and other foreign forces to influence the scope of Afghanistan's cooperation with the ICC.'

With the strong possibility that international crimes were committed in secret CIA detention centres in three European countries that are members of the ICC, the prosecution might make a strategic choice to focus its initial criminal investigations in this case on Europe.

The list of preliminary examinations includes other Western countries as well. For many years, human rights organisations have been trying to get the ICC involved in developing a case against high profile officials and military in the United Kingdom related to crimes during the invasion of Iraq in 2003 and its violent aftermath. These allegations focus on atrocities committed by British forces against Iraqi detainees and terror suspects. Iraq is not a member state, but the ICC has jurisdiction with regard to international crimes on Iraqi soil when committed by nationals of a member state, such as the UK.

On 10 January 2014 two human rights organisations, the European Center for Constitutional and Human Rights (ECCHR) and the Public Interest Lawyers (PIL), requested the OTP to investigate British troops for their alleged involvement in the 'systemic abuse' of hundreds of prisoners in Iraq. Since then the organisations sent new information to the ICC, expanding the list of allegations, which include torture, ill-treatment, killings, rape and other sexual abuse.

The UK government, however, says the ICC doesn't need to get involved since its own national prosecutor is looking into the matter. The Iraq Historic Allegation Team, set up by the UK ministry of Defence in 2010, is analysing more than 1500 allegations of abuse, torture and murder by its soldiers. In short, the national authorities claim they are willing and able to investigate these crimes themselves, which means the ICC doesn't need to step in.

But on 13 May 2014 ICC prosecutor Bensouda opened a preliminary examination into possible war crimes by British officials. In her latest report she said that 'PIL provided a total of 1390 victim accounts, out of which 1071 related to alleged ill-treatment of detainees and 319 to alleged unlawful killings attributed to British personnel in Iraq from 2003-2008.' (In a public letter, dated 9 February 2006, former prosecutor Moreno-Ocampo explained he had declined to investigate similar allegations because the crimes didn't meet the 'gravity threshold,' though he added that this 'conclusion could be reconsidered in the light of new facts or evidence.')

Formally Ukraine is not a member state. But when its ambassador paid an official visit to the ICC on 17 April 2014, he deposed a declaration from his government in Kiev acknowledging the court's jurisdiction covering the revolutionary days from 21 November 2013 until 22 February 2014. More than a hundred persons were possibly killed by police and snipers during those dramatic months when people took to the streets to demonstrate against the then government, which was pushed out of power. Former officials, such as the ousted president Viktor Yanukovych, are accused by Ukraine of being responsible for those deaths.

On 25 April 2014, prosecutor Bensouda announced she would open a preliminary examination. The following year, on 8 September 2015, the Ukraine government expanded the mandate of the ICC, allowing it to look into crimes committed since February 2014 as well. This means the court might have the possibility to investigate the Russian occupation of Crimea and the war in eastern Ukraine, including the downing of the MH17 aeroplane, which had taken off from the main airport of The Netherlands and was shot down on 17 July 2014 during the conflict between Ukrainian forces and Russia-backed rebels, killing 283 passengers and 15 crew. The expanded mandate could have large consequences if the prosecution found that Ukrainian or Russian officials are responsible for these crimes.

Harsh Reality

Many potential suspects manage to escape justice because of the limited powers of the court. Take the regime of the Syrian leader Bashar Al-Assad. A considerable group of countries, such as France and The

Netherlands, have repeatedly underlined the importance of prosecuting Syria's head of state, government officials, security services, militia and rebel groups. They could likely be charged with crimes against humanity and war crimes for atrocities such as mass killings, illegal imprisonment, persecution, sexual violence, starvation, torture, enforced disappearances, looting, destruction and attacks with chemical weapons. But – so far – the Syrian leader and his entourage remain untouchable. The ICC has no possibilities to investigate or indict him or other officials who are responsible for international crimes in Syria, nor can the rebel groups be prosecuted. The country is not a member state, which already cuts off two routes: a self-referral (which would be unlikely anyway) and a proprio motu action by the prosecutor. That leaves just one option open: a referral by the UN Security Council. But Russia, being a supporter of the Syrian regime, and China have blocked such a proposal. It seems the only possibility for the ICC to start investigations into the atrocities in Syria, is in case of foreign fighters if they are nationals of a state that is a member of the court.

Human rights organisations, UN rapporteurs and officials have also been calling on the Security Council to refer the situation in North Korea to the ICC. But Pyongyang is out of the court's reach as well, with China likely being prepared to block such an international referral. Groups have also been campaigning for an ICC investigation into the violent oppression of Rohingya, a Muslim minority in Myanmar (Burma). But as the country is not a member, such a referral can only come from the UN Security Council.

Often people wonder why persons like the American ex-president George W. Bush, his vice president Dick Cheney and defence minister Donald Rumsfeld aren't charged in relation to the invasion of Iraq and the hostilities that followed. Here all roads seem to be blocked as well. The USA is not a member of the ICC. The UN Security Council – with the USA being one of its five permanent members – obviously won't be able to request the court to start investigations, which could lead to indicting American officials.

Serious efforts have been undertaken to persuade the ICC to prosecute Israelis for international crimes. Israel is – like the USA, Russia, India, China, Syria, North Korea – no member of the court. The country has strong allies within the UN Security Council. There seemed to be an opportunity when on 14 May 2013 a Turkish law firm, acting on behalf of the Union of the Comoros, presented a referral to the prosecutor with respect to Israeli raids on a humanitarian aid flotilla, which was on its way to the Gaza Strip on 31 May 2010. Nine activists were killed by Israeli forces on the vessel 'Ms Mavi Marmara,' that was sailing under the flag of the Comoros. The attack thus took place on the territory of this African nation, which is a member of the ICC. The referral also extended to the Greek ship 'Eleftheri Mesogios/Sofia' and the Cambodian 'Rachel Corrie' – Greece and Cambodia are members of the court as well.

On 6 November 2014, prosecutor Bensouda decided that, although there is 'a reasonable basis to believe that war crimes' were committed during the raids on the Mavi Marmara, these were not of 'sufficient gravity' to justify further action by her office.[1] In other words, the attack which led to a dozen deaths, was not serious enough to be handled by the ICC. However, on 16 July 2015 the pre-trial chamber requested the prosecutor to reconsider her rejection. (With regard to gravity, the ICC has been prosecuting three rebel leaders from Darfur for an attack on a peacekeeping mission, during which twelve soldiers were killed).

For years Palestinians tried to give the ICC jurisdiction over their territory. In 2009 the Palestine Authority launched a declaration acknowledging the ICC's mandate over crimes committed on its territory since 2002. Former prosecutor Moreno-Ocampo however rejected the request in 2012, because the status of Palestine was unclear. The UN or the ICC's Assembly of States Parties would first need to establish that Palestine is a state, so that its government could sign and ratify the Rome Statute.[2] The Palestinian authorities pursued this avenue. On 29 November 2012 the UN General Assembly granted Palestine the status as non-member observer state.[3] This opened a new array of possibilities. Prosecutor Bensouda met with the Palestine minister of foreign affairs on 5 August 2014. The meeting took place during a short but violent war in Gaza, started a month earlier by Israel against the Palestinian Hamas government and armed groups. Israel was bombing and raiding the territory, while Palestinian militants fired rockets into Israel. In a few weeks more than 2100 people were killed. The majority of the

---

1   'Rome Statute legal requirements have not been met,' OTP statement, 6 November 2014.

2   Report on Preliminary Examination Activities 2012, OTP, November 2012.

3   'General Assembly Votes Overwhelmingly to Accord Palestine 'Non-Member Observer State' Status in United Nations,' United Nations, 29 November 2012

victims were Palestinian civilians. On the Israeli side over seventy people (including six civilians) were killed. More than 11,000 Palestinians and 1600 Israelis were wounded. Huge parts of Gaza were destroyed.

On 2 January 2015 there was a major breakthrough when Palestine acceded to the Rome Statute. Three months later, on 1 April 2015, the Palestinian state became a full member of the ICC. Rules prescribe that the court can only investigate crimes committed after the entry date. That's why the Palestine government lodged a special declaration accepting the jurisdiction of the ICC over alleged crimes committed in occupied Palestinian territory, including East Jerusalem, since 13 June 2014.[4] Currently the prosecutor, cautiously underlining that this is a matter of both policy and practice, is conducting a preliminary examination into crimes committed in Palestine. Although these activities are not criminal investigations, the examinations are creating huge tensions. A human rights lawyer of the Palestinian organisation Al Haq, who has been working on the case handing over materials to the ICC, has received death threats in The Netherlands. The Dutch police was however very slow in its reactions. Only when four NGOs, one being Amnesty International, closed their offices in The Hague as a precaution, were the authorities truly alarmed.[5]

Back to Gilbert Bitti. Over the years the legal advisor started to realise how complex and harsh reality is. 'This court is a beautiful idea. But it is a beautiful idea which has a lot of limitations, because the states wanted the ICC to have a lot of limitations. To change the world, working from a building in The Hague, is not easy,' he admits. But he stresses that, despite the difficulties, the ICC has its significance. 'I have seen on television people in Syria singing: Bye Bye Bashar, have a nice travel to The Hague.' While admitting the UN Security Council hasn't referred Syria to the ICC, Bitti says: 'The simple existence of the court is important for people and it is changing things. From now on people in power will feel the threat that one day they could be held accountable for what they did. That is a very important symbolic function. In my view maybe even more

4   'ICC: Palestine is Newest Member. Court Membership Could Open Door for Justice to Victims,' Human Rights Watch, 1 April 2015
5   'Ze dacht dat Nederland veilig was,' NRC Handelsblad, 10 August 2016.

important than current cases handled by the ICC. It is a change in the history of humankind.'

The permanent premises

Bitti spoke these words during the interview in 2011. Five years later I meet him while he is waiting at the traffic lights for pedestrians on his way to work. The ICC has just moved, in December 2015, to its new and permanent premises, which consist of six block buildings standing in a row along the coastal landscape of The Hague. The tallest, rising 42 metres and holding three courtrooms and the media centre, has grey concrete walls with here and there some thin strings of ivy needing sunlight and warmth to grow before it can become a natural green cover for the building. The five smaller blocks are bedecked with trapezoid windows, meant to reflect the changing daylight and convey a sense of transparency. Bitti's office is in one of them. Electrified high fences, like the old building had, are absent. The sand dunes that protect the Netherlands from the North Sea's high tides are, along with many other measures, ingeniously used to provide security.

In December 2007, the Assembly of States Parties had agreed the court needed newly built permanent premises. The Netherlands had offered a site free of charge on the edge of the city, where at the time the Alexander barracks were still located. Before any building could take place, this military complex needed to be demolished and the area cleared, which was done at the cost of the host state. The Netherlands also provided a 200 million euros loan for the construction of the new permanent premises. In 2009 the Danish firm schmidt hammer lassen won the architectural contest and was chosen to design the complex. On 18 March 2010 the official launch of the project took place. After the construction works had finally started, however, the budget began to creep up. At a closed-door session in June 2015 the member states placed a cap of 206 million euros on construction and transition costs, and called for an urgent audit while the project director suddenly resigned.[6]

While Bitti is about to arrive at the reception building in front of the vast new court complex, he says his previous remarks are still valid: 'The

---

6   'The International Criminal Court: A new building, but is it better?' International Justice Tribune, 15 December 2015

ICC is still developing itself and discovering its possibilities.' In fact, a few minutes later on this Tuesday morning, 1 March 2016, Bitti will be present in the courtroom to assist the judges during the confirmation of charges hearing in the case against Ahmad Al Faqi Al Mahdi. The suspect was part of a radical Islamist group that violently occupied and terrorised the city of Timbuktu, in northern Mali. Al Mahdi was the head of the 'Hisbah', which saw upholding public morals and preventing vice as its task. He was also involved with the Islamic court and participated in carrying out its decisions. Although Al Mahdi is allegedly seen on a video punishing citizens by flogging them, he is prosecuted by the ICC for ordering and participating in hammering down nine mausoleums and destroying a mythical door of a mosque in Timbuktu. These crimes, razing the buildings, are also captured on film.[7]

When Bitti has entered the reception building, he goes through the security check for personnel, while I wait in the separate line for the public. After my passport and media pass are checked, and my belongings and body are X-rayed, the visitors and court staff mix again to cross a broad bridge over a stretch of water. Then we go, one by one, through a heavy bomb-resistant revolving door which is the only one of its kind in The Netherlands. It gives way to a long and spacious hall. Security measures have stepped up in the new premises. To such an extent that in these early days, many court officials prefer bypassing the annoying electronic locks between office spaces by taking the public hall to go from one area to the other.

The new court building is practically located just one kilometre from the detention centre, where suspects in custody are being held. That morning Al Mahdi has been taken by a prison van to a separate court entrance for defendants. Guards have brought him into the courtroom, where the jihadi is sitting in the dock, dressed in a long white Islamic robe with some modest embroidery at the front. When he is responding to the judges, he speaks Arabic. The headphones he wears, necessary to hear the translations as the judges speak English, are unintentionally functioning as a headband, controlling his wild curly hair.

This case has several new features. Not only is Al Mahdi the first Malian suspect brought before the court, he is also the first jihadi to be

---

7   Prosecutor v. Ahmad Al Faqi Al Mahdi, ICC case information sheet.

prosecuted by the ICC. It is also the first time the court charges a person for the war crime of destroying cultural heritage and it's the first ICC case where the accused pled guilty.

A very short trial followed. It started on 22 August 2016 and lasted just a few days. Al Mahdi admitted he was guilty and also showed remorse, calling on Muslims to refrain from destroying monuments because it was wrong and would only lead to misery. On 27 September 2016 the judges found him guilty and sentenced him to nine years in prison.

Adjacent to the courtroom are special detention cells where suspects in custody - such as Al Mahdi - are held during the hearing's breaks. The claustrophobic cells with their fixed furniture, all walls painted in gunmetal grey, seem a marked contrast to the lighter ones with windows the suspects enjoy in the ICC detention centre down the road. Next to these court cells there is an alarm which guards can pull in case of an emergency, for instance when a suspect becomes unruly, sending the building into lockdown.

For people who come to watch the trials, the new design of the courtrooms has its drawbacks. From the steeply-raked public gallery visitors look down, making it more difficult, especially in the huge main courtroom, to grasp the mood among judges, prosecutors, lawyers, legal representatives of victims, court officials and defendants. What's more, some defendants' seats are completely out of the public view. In the old building, because of the smaller set-up and closeness, the public could see how a defendant reacted to testimony and rulings. This is generally deemed an essential part of holding a public trial. 'Some suspects were very uncomfortable in that situation,' a court official explained the changes during a media tour, held before the new court building was officially opened. Compared to the previous situation, guests have to rely much more on the court-controlled images which are broadcast on monitors in the public gallery – and on the Internet.

The premises were also designed to consider the particular needs of witnesses. Many are traumatized, another ICC official said during the media tour, with 80 to 90 percent of the witnesses testifying under protective measures. This means their identity is kept from the public. To prevent recognition, their testimony is broadcast on screens with their image and voice distorted. In the new courtrooms, the witness stand is situated under the public gallery and thus out of direct public view. Even if a witness testifies without any protective measures, the public won't be able to see that person directly.

Before testifying, a witness can choose to sit with a support person (a psychologist, for instance), in a separate room, where a two-way mirror renders him or her invisible to the courtroom. In another discreet location inside the main building, a large, comfortable lounge overlooking the surrounding coastal nature, lets witnesses and victims relax during breaks and prepare themselves for the next part of their testimony.

The permanent premises have other new features too, such as an exhibition area. One of the improvements is the public cafeteria, conveniently situated in the main hall next to the courtrooms and workplaces. In the old temporary complex guests had to help themselves with soft drinks, lousy coffee and snacks from machines. The new cafeteria is selling freshly made cappuccinos and lattes, cakes, chocolate, biscuits, crisps, croissants and even some fresh fruits. During lunchhours a hot meal can be bought – meat or fish, vegetables, salad, potatoes – for 9.50 euros. The main improvement, however, is not so much the menu. Its quality lies more in the communications sphere, as queuing guests will find themselves standing in line with prosecutors, officials, lawyers and experts which can lead to spontaneous chats and remarkable conversations.

2

THE OFFICE OF THE PROSECUTOR
From high ambitions to meagre results

With irritation prosecutor Luis Moreno-Ocampo responded to the question. It was still in the early stages of the interview, and his reaction came abruptly and unexpectedly. The question hadn't been outrageous, I thought. It had seemed a normal thing to ask: what personal characteristics do you need to possess to be a good prosecutor? It was autumn 2011. The Argentine lawyer was into his eighth year leading the Office of the Prosecutor (OTP), the organ of the court tasked with investigating international crimes and prosecuting the main perpetrators. While he slammed with his hand on his desk, he answered my question: 'It is not about personality. It is about duty. The requirement for the job is to have integrity. And integrity is not just about being honest. It means that if you have the evidence and the law says that you should [prosecute], you do it! Integrity is also ignoring applause or criticism.'

Two years before this interview I had seen the prosecutor live for the first time – although from a distance. He was invited as the special guest for the presentation of a documentary about the work of the ICC in general, and more specifically about Moreno-Ocampo's OTP, during the Movies that Matter Festival, organised by Amnesty International in The Hague. A film crew had been following the prosecutor for three years. The result, 'The Reckoning: The Battle for the International Criminal Court,' was shown to the public that evening.

The hall of Theater aan het Spui filled up. The guests, half of whom were ICC officials, climbed the stairs to find themselves a seat. After an introduction the lamps dimmed. On the big screen the first images appeared of a documentary about the court and its mediagenic prosecutor.

After a full hour the lights flipped on again. A table and two chairs had been placed before the screen for an interview between journalist Linda Polman and the main character of the documentary. The two walked to the stage, where Polman invited Moreno-Ocampo to take a seat. The prosecutor ignored her request. He preferred to stand, made a few steps until he was right in front of the audience, raised his arms and with a big smile encouraged his staff: get up, this movie and screening are in honour of you!

Happily surprised, the court officials got up from their seats as they heard Moreno-Ocampo's encouragements to applaud. Soon the staff were standing, clapping joyfully for themselves, while the rest of the audience moved uncomfortably in their chairs – looking around in amazement as the screening had turned into an ICC celebration, in which they didn't participate.

In this festive ambiance, Moreno-Ocampo seemed even less inclined to take part in an interview with a critical journalist. Again he refused to sit down next to the small table. Like an Argentinian cowboy he put his foot on the seat of the chair reserved for him, focused on the audience and reacted with repulsion to Polman and her questions. He did not even want to talk much about the Darfur case, in which he had won a major victory a few weeks before. On 4 March 2009 the judges had honoured his request for an arrest warrant against the Sudanese president Omar Hassan Ahmad Al-Bashir, charged with crimes against humanity and war crimes committed in Darfur.[8]

Moreno-Ocampo had wanted to prosecute the head of state for genocide as well, but the judges ruled he hadn't provided enough evidence to support charges for this crime of crimes. The prosecutor appealed that decision. A year later, on 12 July 2010, the pre-trial judges would issue an arrest warrant for genocide charges as well.[9]

Back in the theatre the prosecutor didn't feel like responding to journalistic questions such as: would the arrest warrants not trigger revenge by the Sudanese regime against the population in Darfur? Moreno-Ocampo was, in fact, looking for a way to cut short the interview. Again he walked to the public, then stood still and asked one of the filmmakers to take his place on the stage.

---

8   Decision on the Prosecution's Application for a Warrant of Arrest against Omar Hassan Ahmad Al Bashir, pre-trial chamber, 4 March 2009

9   Second Decision on the Prosecution's Application for a Warrant of Arrest for Omar Hassan Ahmad Al Bashir, pre-trial chamber, 12 July 2010.

The painful session came to an end. Later in the foyer a concerned organiser of the Amnesty film festival came up to journalist Polman asking: 'What went wrong?' It was anyone's guess. One ICC official briefly approached Polman and suggested the prosecutor did not like being grilled by female journalists. Further down in the foyer the ICC staff were having a great time amongst themselves. Polman and her problematic interview had ceased to exist.

In the following years I would continue to follow and watch Moreno-Ocampo. When there were important announcements, it was the prosecutor himself who would, with his usual assertiveness, address the media during press conferences. He was the director of the show. Without a trace of doubt he would passionately counter critical questions from journalists, in his 'Spanglish' – his English flavoured by a heavy Latino accent. He appeared worldwide on television and thus Moreno-Ocampo became the face of the International Criminal Court. As chief prosecutor he only came to the courtroom for principal hearings, where he would, with great alacrity, present his case against the suspect. But when he was not speaking, he would slump back in his chair and play with an arm of his glasses between his teeth; quasi offhand or sometimes even showing disregard for the opposing party. As if he wanted to demonstrate that the words of the defence did not affect him at all.

Interview with the prosecutor

Already three long minutes his assistant was waiting in the doorway that led to his office. She could see him sitting at his desk, where the prosecutor was completely absorbed by a document he was editing on his computer. She did not dare to step in the room. Her faint knock on the door was hardly making any sound. Until the assistant, after encouragement from a colleague, knocked harder. Finally, her boss raised his head. He got up from his chair, walked up to the interviewer and shook hands. 'I am the chief editor of the whole lot here,' he said smiling elegantly as part of his introduction.

He was wearing a black suit, a black tie and a white shirt with his sleeves rolled up to his elbows. His eyebrows made a wild, hairy impression. As usual he had a three-day beard. The prosecutor opened the interview with some small talk. 'You are coming from Amsterdam? Great city. I am afraid I haven't been there for three years though.' I replied jokingly that I pitied him, because he was living in The Hague, which is considered much more boring than the lively capital city. Moreno-Ocampo explained he was also travelling a lot for his work and visited his family in Buenos Aires every two weeks.

He got 'the best job in the world' without even having to apply for it, Moreno-Ocampo said. He was invited. Towards the end of 2002 he received a phone call and heard that his name was on top of the list with candidates to be elected as the first prosecutor of the new International Criminal Court. 'But we don't know whether you want the position,' he was asked. Moreno-Ocampo was due to teach at Harvard University in the United States. 'And now I am here,' he said laconically.

As a young prosecutor Moreno-Ocampo had been involved in trials against the Argentine military junta. 'It was a massive change for a country that for sixty years had witnessed coups, when we indicted the generals. Of course I was criticized for it. My mother was furious with me. My uncle did not want to talk to me anymore. Half of my family was military. But I said: I just do my job as a prosecutor.' Later in his career again he met with fierce opposition, this time from the 'other' side as well. 'The political leaders who had been victims of the dictatorship were happy when I did the junta trials. But they were very unhappy with the corruption cases I did after that.' But Moreno-Ocampo persisted and targeted massive fraud. He also starred in the TV program 'Fórum, la corte del pueblo' in which he mediated between citizens. He was standing out – although he did not have much of an international profile, yet.[10]

After he was elected by the member states on 21 April 2003, he left for The Hague to start his new job. A man with a mission – to uphold the law in a largely lawless world. 'The Netherlands were the first republic in the world. In the last few centuries you have built a constitutional state. The law is like air for you. It is invisible because it ís there. But internationally the law was never applied. Never. This is the first time. This is totally new,' he stressed. When he arrived in The Hague there weren't yet many persons working at the OTP. His main mission – certainly at the start – was to build the organisation. 'Now I have three hundred staff from eighty countries. In the beginning it was terribly difficult. But we found our identity.' As the ICC's first chief prosecutor he laid the basis for how the OTP would be functioning. 'I have to do my

---

10 Curriculum Vitae Luis Moreno-Ocampo, ICC, 2012

normal job: selecting the most serious cases, investigate and conduct trials properly. But each decision was and is strategic. Because if we would, in the beginning, select the wrong cases, or present bad cases with no evidence, we would not just lose one case, we could jeopardize all efforts. That is why the first cases were so critical.'

During his term Moreno-Ocampo would pull off investigations in no less than seven 'situations': Uganda, the Democratic Republic of Congo (DRC), the Central African Republic (CAR), Sudan/Darfur, Kenya, Libya and Ivory Coast. After he left, Mali and Georgia were added to the list. The eighth and ninth country. The CAR would call on the court for a second time, referring the latest civil war to the ICC. That's why the court is now investigating ten situations, in nine countries.

For years the list contained only African countries. That exclusive focus on the continent often yielded strong criticism. Although Moreno-Ocampo said he didn't take verbal attacks personally, he did talk about it in that manner. 'The idea that it is wrong to be in Africa is a campaign that was promoted by Bashir,' he said with a sharp voice. While the prosecutor was referring to the Sudanese head of state, it sounded as if he was involved in a personal vendetta with the president. He added: 'After that, even some NGOs said I should not do a new case in Africa. But when we opened an investigation in Kenya, everyone was clapping. And then when we opened in Libya, everyone was saying: "Yes! Go for Libya!" And now we opened Côte d'Ivoire, everyone is saying that we should do it.'

Apart from the countries where his office was conducting criminal investigations, there were also conflict situations in Afghanistan, Colombia, Nigeria and – at the time also – Georgia that were subject to 'preliminary examinations.' These nations were in a sort of waiting room. The OTP was constantly checking whether circumstances were improving, whether investigative measures were being taken by national authorities so that Moreno-Ocampo would not need to start a case himself, or whether the opposite was taking place: a deteriorating situation with continuing impunity that would force the prosecutor to act. Hence the journalistic question: why had he not taken a decision to open a case in Afghanistan – a member country that isn't located in Africa, where the court has jurisdiction and which, with massive human rights violations taking place, by then must have qualified for an intervention by the prosecutor. 'Afghanistan is such a mess,' Moreno-Ocampo sighed. 'We are trying to identify what are the groups committing different crimes. It is very difficult now. I know there are no national proceedings against warlords. But the Taliban are saying to us that they are doing national proceedings themselves. And NATO countries are doing their own national proceedings as well. And ... so it is highly complex ...' When Moreno-Ocampo noticed the expression of disbelief on my face, he reacted: 'Exactly – you don't believe the Taliban. But what happens is that they are doing cases. So, should I respect them or not?' The prosecutor was referring to the fact that the ICC is a court of last resort and only acts when national authorities are not able or willing to prosecute international crimes themselves.

During the interview I saw Moreno-Ocampo as a man of alternating temperaments. He could be friendly and elegant, before turning assertive or even intimidating. When he felt questions were too critical, he would counter them vehemently and defend himself with sentences such as: 'My decisions are based on the law! And no one can say that what I do is legally wrong!' As if a simple interview with a journalist was a case he had to win.

Criminal investigations

The ambitious Moreno-Ocampo had worked hard to make sure the spotlights were turned on the ICC. He had been successful in that respect. The institution had become an important player on the world stage, being much in the news. Most of the work, though, lies outside the public sphere. Criminal investigations, one of the main tasks of the OTP, are by their nature done behind the scenes. During this complex trajectory the office analyses a conflict situation, selects the main crimes and suspects, formulates charges and finds conclusive evidence. These activities take place in secrecy.

While Moreno-Ocampo was the public face, the investigators are shielded. Their identities remain hidden to the audiences. For their own safety, but also for the protection of witnesses and victims who had better not be seen with prosecution staff. Even the head of investigations – Michel de Smedt, whose name and photo are publicly known – remains a figure in the background and doesn't give much interviews. The reticence also has to do with the strategic interest of the prosecutor – by exposing as little as possible about the internal state of affairs and keeping his cards as long as possible to his chest – to present as strong cases as possible in court.

How do criminal investigations work? Hans Bevers was previously an official of the Dutch ministry of justice and involved in the legal preparations of the establishment of the ICC in The Netherlands. After he had 'been bricklaying the court from the outside,' he wanted to see what it was like inside. Since 2006 he has been working as general legal advisor with the OTP, a few doors away from Moreno-Ocampo's office. Bevers explains that every case starts with general research. The staff studies the conflict situation in broad terms. Not only do they analyse confidential information, but also open sources such as newspaper articles, magazine features, TV stories, academic studies and reports by human rights organizations and institutions such as the United Nations.

In the early stages it is crucial to know whether the human rights violations committed fall under the jurisdiction of the court. If that is the case, and the decision to start investigations is taken, a joint team is formed consisting of staff of three divisions of the OTP (Investigation; Prosecution; Jurisdiction, Complementarity and Cooperation) to take the lead in the investigative process.

Evidence not only comes from witness testimony and documents, but also from computers, cell phones, log books, satellite images, photos, audio, videos, phone taps and other materials. While information is being gathered, the data are registered and analysed. The material will be modelled in a matrix showing crimes, incidents and suspects, from which the prosecutors select the persons and crimes they will investigate further and prosecute. This implies there will always be potential suspects who escape justice.

As easy as this process seems on paper, in reality it is a hugely complex job. Often there are difficulties in getting access to evidence, which usually is located abroad. The powers of the court have been significantly constrained by the founding fathers. Contrary to what many believe, investigators can't just go and investigate on foreign soil. The rules and regulations prescribe that the court first has to ask permission from countries where crucial information and persons might be located. 'We never in our life went to a country to investigate without informing the authorities and having consensus,' Moreno-Ocampo told me.

A member state is obliged to cooperate. But not all countries are warm-heartedly willing to assist the court. It can happen that national authorities inform the OTP that the prosecutor should formulate his questions, after which officials of that state will do their own investigations, Moreno-Ocampo explained. At a certain moment the authorities will provide the OTP with their answers and possible evidence. In such instances, with the government largely in control, the prosecutor doesn't have much grip on the process. It is questionable how independent such an investigation will be and whose interests are served. At the other end of the spectrum are the states that invite the court to come and investigate – with or without the involvement of national authorities. Every situation is different, Moreno-Ocampo said. 'Each country decides in its own way. Sometimes countries refuse. There are also countries that say: "Prosecutor, send your investigators, but don't tell me you are coming".'

Contrary to what many might assume, the OTP had not been setting up whole branches in countries where investigations took place. According to the Strategic Plan 2012-2015 the office had 'mainly relied on a limited field presence, given the often difficult environment in which it operates, in combination with the development of protection strategies and capabilities.'[11] But that was changing. In the following Strategic Plan 2016-2018, the prosecution said the office has been 'systematically' implementing 'longer term or permanent field presence of investigators' in Mali, Côte d'Ivoire, Central African Republic and Uganda.[12]

When the OTP is dealing with obstructive countries, investigators have to be creative to get the information they need for their cases. Moreno-Ocampo knew for instance his staff would never get permission from the Sudanese regime – the president and several ministers are charged with crimes in Darfur – to do on the spot investigations. Let alone guarantees for their safety. That's why the prosecution tried to do investigations among Darfur refugees, who had crossed the border and stayed in camps in Chad.

But such operations can be quite dangerous as well. In this case the investigators decided it would be better to not do the interviews inside the refugee camps, but outside, in the city of Abéché, some sixty kilometres west of the border with Darfur/Sudan. 'It was a huge operation to move the witnesses individually,' Moreno-Ocampo explained, so they would not share their experiences and possibly influence one another. The

11   Strategic Plan 2012-2015, Office of the Prosecutor, 11 October 2013.
12   Strategic Plan 2016–2018, Office of the Prosecutor, 6 July 2015.

prosecutor sent four of his staff. 'But that same night, the rebels who were working for the government of Sudan, took Abéché. They said they would respect the life of international workers. But that would not count for my workers, of course. So we acted swiftly to evacuate them immediately.' Much to his relief the emergency operation succeeded and his investigators could be brought into safety.

Local intermediaries

Security is an issue in all cases. The ICC is prosecuting powerful persons who are suspected of being implicated in organized crime. Many perpetrators will not hesitate to prevent the truth coming out. The prosecution will have to weigh carefully whether or not it is too risky to send its staff to a (former) conflict area and whether their protection is sufficient. Caution is not only required for the court's officials. For witnesses, victims and informers it can also be risky to been seen talking to the court. 'So we are not going with two big UN cars to people and knock on their door. When we want to interview someone and if the situation is dangerous, we send a local intermediary,' Moreno-Ocampo explained.

These intermediaries can be local aid workers, human rights activists and journalists, but sometimes even agents of the secret service. 'Intermediaries are often the first responders,' reads the summary of a conference on the relationship between NGOs and the ICC, organized by the International Refugees Rights Initiative (IRRI) and Open Society Justice Initiative (OSJI) in the Tanzanian city Arusha in 2014. The report points out that intermediaries, sometimes being on the spot when atrocities take place, are capable of 'gathering evidence and working with witnesses long before the court is able to start its own investigations.' They are low-cost, too, as the ICC didn't pay salaries but surprisingly only reimbursed expenses. Take for instance the total annual 108 million euros budget in 2012, of which the ICC spent only 5490 euros on intermediary remuneration. The modest transaction may help avoid 'corruption allegations,' says the Arusha report, though it also notes that 'many intermediaries carried out the work for the court voluntarily while struggling financially.'

There are also concerns about the quality of their work. Intermediaries are not professional investigators and 'may lack the skills and expertise to investigate and preserve evidence,' the report warns. And even though security factors are one of the reasons to deploy these go-betweens, their safety was a 'paramount concern' at the Arusha conference as well. The report notes that working for the ICC exposes intermediaries to 'security threats and retaliatory attacks.' NGOs from Ivory Coast complained that after the ICC issued arrest warrants against suspects of the previous government, including president Laurent Gbagbo, OTP officials left their local counterparts to fend for themselves, providing no security or information on potential threats.

There are other risks as well involving local go-betweens, who can have their own agendas or can be pressured by other parties. On 8 July 2010 the judges of the ICC ordered the stay of proceedings against the Congolese warlord Thomas Lubanga and decided he should be released. A fair trial had become impossible, the chamber said, as the prosecution refused to obey its orders to disclose to the defence the identity of intermediary code-named '143', who was suspected of having forced witnesses to give false statements against Lubanga. Three months later the appeals chamber decided however that both the judges, who should have applied sanctions first, and the prosecution, that should have carried out the order to disclose, were wrong. On 8 October the appeals chamber ordered the resumption of the trial.[13]

When I raised the intermediary issue during the interview with Moreno-Ocampo, he got irritated: 'There was one case where we found an intermediary was cheating. We informed the defence and the judges. Of course the defence took the opportunity to turn it into a big thing. That is normal, because that's the defence's role.'

Nevertheless, in their verdict in the Lubanga trial the judges harshly criticized the prosecution who 'should not have delegated its investigative responsibilities to the intermediaries.' Due to 'unsupervised actions' of three intermediaries, the evidence of nine witnesses was deemed unreliable (see chapter 4).

In the case against the Kenyan deputy president William Samoei Ruto and broadcaster Joshua Arap Sang, the court faced serious problems with an intermediary allegedly changing sides. Walter Barasa had been contacting witnesses for the OTP. But in 2013 the ICC charged him with harassing and bribing witnesses to weaken the prosecutor's case. However,

---

13   'Appeals judges rule that Lubanga will not be released,' International Justice Monitor, 8 October 2010.

interference in this case allegedly also might have gone the other way. On 2 May 2016 Karim Khan, defence counsel for deputy president Ruto, filed a notice to the ICC judges detailing his suspicions that two Kenyan intermediaries had pressed witnesses, bribed them and fabricated evidence that would be in support of the prosecutor's case (see chapter 3).

Initially, NGOs were eager to work with the ICC. But since the Lubanga scandal in particular, their 'enthusiasm has waned' due to 'attacks on the credibility and motivations of intermediaries' in court, and 'threats and physical attacks on NGOs on the ground,' IRRI notes in the Arusha report.

Fatou Bensouda

After a term of nine years Moreno-Ocampo's dream job came to an end. The woman who had been his deputy since 2004 would replace him: Fatou Bensouda. What had been his best moments, I asked Moreno-Ocampo in the interview, that took place a few months before he left. 'I have them each day. Also now, having your questions,' he said. Then he bowed towards me. 'Each day you have to make one or two difficult decisions. And when you have made a decision, you have a new challenge waiting. Every day is fascinating.'

When I asked him what his worst moments were, he responded with a remarkable long silence. I thought about the accusations against the prosecutor for sexual misbehavior towards a South African journalist who, after the incident, called in distress with his staff, as a source who didn't want to be named, had told me.[14] Or the repeated exoduses of well-known prosecutors and lawyers who left the OTP, reportedly after rows with their boss. But Moreno-Ocampo did not refer to those moments. His voice sounded softer. He almost whispered. 'I can't say there was a worst day. I like …,' he started his answer, but reformulated his sentence. 'I am trained to have conflicts. So I have conflicts every day. A big conflict is not a problem for me. It is normal. I am Argentinian. I am used to chaos.'

He was proud of the effect the ICC was having. 'In the club of world leaders there is no room for génocidaires[15] anymore. If you want to be

14 'International court plagued by in-fighting,' NRC Handelsblad, 19 November 2008.
15 Génocidaire: a person who is guilty of genocide.

in power today, you need some kind of legitimacy. And if the court investigates you for crimes against humanity or genocide, you have no legitimacy. Whether you are a rebel leader or president, you can't gain or retain power by committing atrocities. Because then you are out.'

The interview was almost over when he spontaneously referred to an old master. 'You know what Machiavelli said? He said: "Building new public institutions will create two enemies. Those who lose power, will realize that and will oppose you. Those who win, don't realize they won, and also they will attack you." Think about that. People will need to learn how important it is what we do here at the ICC.'

It is 15 June 2012 when Fatou Bensouda is taking her oath during an official ceremony in the courtroom. Afterwards there's a reception in the lobby where diplomats, politicians and friends congratulate the new prosecutor. Women in breathtaking African robes – from elegant wide flowing models to tight dresses with wasp waists – draw everyone's eyes. Friends and acquaintances want to be in the photo with the new chief. When most guests have finally left, I approach Moreno-Ocampo together with a colleague from the Dutch news agency ANP.

'What will you be doing next? To the FIFA?' we ask. There are rumors the prosecutor might run the ethical committee of the discredited soccer federation.

'That hasn't been decided yet,' he says.

'What then? Writing a book?'

'No, no,' Moreno-Ocampo laughs.

'Lecturing at a university, to transfer the knowledge you acquired here?' we continue. 'Oh no, that pays so badly,' he answers. 'I have been asked by private law firms in New York,' says Moreno-Ocampo. He is considering saying 'yes' to their offers. 'You can make so much money there in just a few weeks' time.'

That's it. The lobby is deserted. Only Bensouda and Moreno-Ocampo, who look like a couple who have seen the guests out, are still present. Together they stroll to the secured door, for which they will have to use their security passes giving access to their offices. Thus pass the last moments of Moreno-Ocampo's reign.

Tarnished image

The image of the OTP had been tarnished long before Moreno-Ocampo left. The judges had been highly critical of the errors made during the criminal investigations against the Congolese warlord Lubanga. The case would be halted twice as the judges deemed that due to the behaviour of the prosecution, a fair trial had become impossible. In 2010 the prosecutor had lost his case against Bahar Idriss Abu Garda. This rebel leader from Darfur had been accused of war crimes for attacking African peacekeepers, but was let off because of lack of evidence.[16]

There was also the failed case against Callixte Mbarushimana, the executive secretary of the Forces Démocratiques pour la Libération du Rwanda (FDLR), a militia group of Hutus accused of extreme violence against the population creating a 'humanitarian catastrophe' in the Congolese region of Kivu. Mbarushimana, arrested by France on 11 October 2010 and transferred to the ICC on 25 January 2011, was charged with a list of war crimes and crimes against humanity.[17] But when the judges evaluated the evidence, they were shocked about the 'utterly inappropriate' techniques some investigators had applied.[18] The chamber reminded the OTP it has the obligation to establish the truth by 'investigating incriminating and exonerating circumstances equally.' While studying the interviews with witnesses the judges were 'repeatedly left with the impression' that some investigators were so attached to their 'theory or assumption' that they didn't 'refrain from putting questions in leading terms and from showing resentment, impatience or disappointment whenever the witness replies in terms which are not entirely in line with his or her expectations.' The judges noted that certain investigators complained 'about having "to milk out" from the witness details which are of relevance to the investigation, lamenting that the witness does not "really understand what is important" to the investigators in the case, or hinting at the fact that the witness may be "trying to cover" for the suspect.' Such a way of investigating seems 'hardly reconcilable with a professional and impartial technique of witness questioning,' the judges concluded.

As a consequence, the chamber stated that 'the probative value of evidence obtained by these means may be significantly weakened.' The judges found the case against Mbarushimana not convincing as they did not see

---

16   'Pre-Trial Chamber I declines to confirm the charges against Bahar Idriss Abu Garda,' ICC press release, 8 February 2010.
17   Case Information Sheet, ICC, 15 June 2012
18   'Decision on the confirmation of charges.' Pre-Trial Chamber, 16 December 2011.

proof 'that the suspect encouraged the troops' morale through his press releases and radio messages.' In their 16 December 2011 decision they declined, by majority, to confirm the charges. Just before Christmas, on 23 December 2011, the Rwandan was released. (Mbarushimana, who had been a UN employee for years, had escaped justice before. The International Criminal Tribunal for Rwanda had investigated him for his alleged role in the Rwandan genocide in 1994, but would not indict him because of a lack of evidence.)

Exactly one month later, on 23 January 2012, the judges decided in the cases against six Kenyans, charged with organizing political-ethnic violence that erupted after the elections of 2007, during which at least 1100 people died. The judges had studied the materials that were presented during the confirmation of charges hearing, and decided there was no evidence against two of the suspects. The charges against Kenyan member of parliament Henry Kiprono Kosgey and police chief Mohammed Hussein Ali were not confirmed.[19]

Half a year after Moreno-Ocampo's departure, the OTP would face another blow. On 18 December 2012 the judgment was pronounced in the trial against the Congolese warlord Mathieu Ngudjolo Chui, accused of war crimes and crimes against humanity during an attack by his militia group on 24 February 2003 on the village of Bogoro in the eastern Congolese district of Ituri. The judges concluded that the OTP failed to show that he was the commander of the combatants during the attack.[20] So the case collapsed. While the presiding judge was reading the verdict, the prosecutors looked utterly devastated. They had lost their legal battle against the Congolese man sitting opposite them, who was spending one of his last moments in the dock. The decision was even more shocking because the magistrates added that if an accused is found 'not guilty,' this didn't necessarily mean that he was 'innocent.' Apparently something had gone terribly wrong during the criminal investigations.

There seemed to be no end to the bad news. In a dramatic video message prosecutor Bensouda announced on 11 March 2013 that she withdrew the case against another Kenyan suspect: Francis Muthaura. She didn't have enough evidence against the top official, who had been the secretary

19   Weekly Update, ICC, 30 January 2012.
20   'ICC Trial Chamber II acquits Mathieu Ngudjolo Chui,' ICC press release, 18 December 2012.

of the cabinet and head of public services. Bensouda suggested this wasn't the fault of her office. The prosecutor insisted that witnesses had been too frightened to talk and some were even dead, while the Kenyan government in Nairobi 'failed to provide my office with important evidence, and failed to facilitate our access to critical witnesses who may have shed light on the Muthaura case.'[21] The final blow crushing the investigation had been a crucial witness who had recanted his statement and admitted that he had been bribed. From the original 'Ocampo Six' now three suspects were off the hook and only three were still being prosecuted. The nightmare was not over though. There was more to come. On 3 June 2013 the judges decided that the evidence against the former president of Ivory Coast, Laurent Gbagbo, was too thin to refer the case to trial.[22] In their report the magistrates painted a picture of a weak investigation, leading to 'serious concern' that the prosecutors had 'relied heavily on NGO reports and press articles.' Even though this kind of information can be used when describing the historical context, 'such pieces of evidence cannot in any way be presented as the fruits of a full and proper investigation by the prosecutor,' the judges said. But because it was such a complex and serious case, the OTP were given a second chance. This process would take a whole year. On 12 June 2014 the judges ruled that now the evidence was sufficient to start a trial against the former president, who had been detained in The Hague since November 2011. The decision was taken with a narrow margin though. One of the three judges disagreed with her colleagues. She still wasn't convinced about the evidence against Gbagbo.[23]

Scorecard

What is the state of affairs? Judges decide on evidence in four major instances. The first evaluation takes place before issuing an arrest warrant, followed by a more thorough analysis during the confirmation of charges phase, when the prosecution has presented its first findings in court. In this interim phase the judges decide whether the evidence is strong enough to admit the case to trial. The third instance is after the trial,

---

21 Statement by ICC Prosecutor on the Notice to withdraw charges against Mr Muthaura, ICC, 11 March 2013.
22 Decision adjourning the hearing on the confirmation of charges, ICC, 3 June 2013.
23 Dissenting Opinion of Judge Christine Van den Wyngaert, ICC, 12 June 2014.

which can last for years and can end in a conviction or acquittal. The fourth evaluation takes place during the appeal phase.

So far judges have issued arrest warrants or summons to appear against 33 persons for international crimes, which are the core business of the ICC. (Possibly there are also some confidential arrest warrants out). They ruled - ranging from confirmation of charges, trial to appeal – on the evidence presented in court against nineteen individuals. Nine of these cases – which is almost half – have failed because of lack of evidence. In the fourteen years since its actual start in 2002, the ICC has convicted four perpetrators for international crimes.

The Congolese warlord Thomas Lubanga Dyilo was the ICC's first convict. In 2012 he was found guilty of war crimes for recruiting and using child soldiers, and sentenced to fourteen years in prison. Germain Katanga, another Congolese militia leader, was convicted in 2014 of war crimes and one crime against humanity for the attack on the village of Bogoro in Ituri. He received a twelve year prison sentence. In 2016 the Congolese politician/warlord Jean-Pierre Bemba Gombo was found guilty of crimes against humanity and war crimes committed by his militia in the neighbouring Central African Republic and sentenced to eighteen years in prison. Ahmad Al Faqi Al Mahdi, an Islamic jihadi from Mali, was convicted in 2016 for the war crime of attacking religious and cultural heritage in Timbuktu, and sentenced to nine years imprisonment. Currently four suspects of international crimes are on trial: the Ivorian ex-president Laurent Gbagbo and his co-accused Charles Blé Goudé; the former Congolese warlord Bosco Ntaganda; and a former commander of the Ugandan Lord's Resistance Army, Dominic Ongwen. However another trial against two Darfuri rebels couldn't start because one suspect, Abdallah Banda Abakaer Nourain, is still at large, while his colleague Saleh Mohammed Jerbo Jamus has died.

The court is increasingly busy with cases involving the offense of perverting the course of justice and charged a total of eight individuals. In 2016 the judges convicted five suspects for corruptly influencing defence witnesses in the case against Bemba (see chapter 5). Three Kenyans, who have been charged with witness tampering, are at large. The prosecution accused other suspects of such activities as well, but didn't charge them. The OTP's record – 33 persons charged for international crimes, resulting in 4 convictions and 9 failed cases – compares rather bleakly to other international tribunals and courts. 'I have pointed out earlier that the scorecard of the prosecutor is not very impressive,' William Schabas, professor in international law at Leiden University and Middlesex University London, said in an interview in 2013. He referred to a study by Alette Smeulers, professor in international criminology. In 'Sixty-five years of international criminal justice' she compares the records of the nine international criminal courts and tribunals that have been set up after the Second World War.[24] Smeulers concludes: 'The overall conviction rate of international criminal courts and tribunals is 87 percent, with only 9 percent of the defendants who were acquitted.' (Smeulers' latest data are from May 2012).

Why is it that the ICC seems much more ineffective? For Schabas it remains a guess. Many professionals working for the ICC have come from institutions such as the International Criminal Tribunal for the former Yugoslavia (ICTY), where 83 of a total of 161 suspects have been convicted and sentenced, while 19 persons have been acquitted and 37 cases were withdrawn or stopped because suspects died. Also 13 cases were referred to a national court. 'Why did those professionals do better there than at the ICC?' Schabas wonders. He points out there is not 'one single' explanation for their lower performance. But one obvious difference is the selection of conflict situations. For other tribunals and courts the territory was defined: former Yugoslavia, Rwanda, Sierra Leone, East Timor, Germany, Japan. Besides, both the ICTY and the Rwanda Tribunal (ICTR) were established by the UN Security Council, which obliged all nations to cooperate.

ICC's jurisdiction potentially covers large parts of the world. With their combined powers, the member states, the UN Security Council and the ICC prosecutor theoretically can call for criminal investigations in all countries. Schabas is critical though of Moreno-Ocampo's selection of cases: 'The prosecutor also could have aimed at investigating torture in Iraqi prisons or the situation in territories occupied by Israel. But he didn't want to take a risk because that could have been politically sensitive with, for instance, the United States. He thought: let's go where it is easiest, let's go Africa.' That, says Schabas, was a miscalculation. It appears to be very difficult to do prosecutions on the African continent. Another

---

24 'Sixty-five years of international criminal justice,' Alette Smeulers, B. Hola and T. van den Berg. Published in: International Criminal Law Review, 2013.

issue is that the OTP has a relative small budget. Of the ICC's total budget of 145 million euros for 2017, some 45 million euros went to the prosecution, compared to 77 million euros for the registry.

Strategic choices

The War Crimes Research Office (WCRO) of the Washington College of Law of the American University also studied the work of the OTP. In October 2012 the institute published a sharp analysis: 'Investigative management, strategies, and techniques of the International Criminal Court's Office of the Prosecutor.'[25] The academics were very familiar with this organ of the court as they had been advising the prosecutors for several years. They had withdrawn from that position and wrote their analysis as independent scientists, based on public sources. The WCRO acknowledged that the OTP is facing problems which it hardly can influence, such as countries that refuse to cooperate, safety and security issues, cultural and linguistic barriers that play a role during interviews with witnesses and the mixed staff hailing from different legal systems. All true, says the WCRO, but the OTP itself made questionable strategic choices as well. Take the budget for 2013, when Bensouda asked funding for just 46 'professional staff members' for the Investigations Teams to guide the investigations in, at the time, seven conflict situations. Another matter was the deliberate choice by her predecessor Moreno-Ocampo to adopt a 'small team approach' because it was assumed that with such units the work could be done faster, and cheaper. The reality was that investigators hardly had time to research the crimes under investigation in all their dimensions. Another complication was that the investigators not only came from different countries, but professionally were a diverse lot (policemen, military, human rights activists, lawyers, young legal professionals). The academics suggested: 'The most important point in terms of composition is that the OTP should prioritize the recruitment and retention of experienced investigators, including those with specific experience investigating international crimes.'

The WCRO wrote that the OTP decided too quickly to focus attention on certain suspects and crimes, which meant that others were never

---

25   'Investigative management, strategies, and techniques of the International Criminal Court's Office of the Prosecutor.' War Crimes Research Office, American University, 2012.

investigated. Sexual crimes, used as a weapon in war but difficult to prove, were not successfully prosecuted (until recently, in the trial against Bemba, who was convicted in 2016). The work pressure and dissatisfaction lead to a burn out of staff and a flow of experienced professionals leaving the OTP.

Other experts blame the inadequate performance of the office to the oppressive work environment when Moreno-Ocampo was leading the place. In an interview, an ex-official, who only wanted to talk on the condition of anonymity, explained how difficult it was to work under the Argentine prosecutor. Moreno-Ocampo distrusted people working for him, the official said. He was suspicious and subjected his staff to strict control. Even when he was with his family in Buenos Aires, he would keep on calling the office in The Hague.

Time was precious, but 'there were so many conflicts' at the headquarters 'that investigative missions to conflict zones sometimes even had to be postponed,' the anonymous ex-staff said. Officials who went abroad to do investigations on the spot, had to report immediately about the interviews they had conducted with witnesses, and were often obliged to wait for further instructions from The Hague before they could continue. This could result in such delays that sometimes they even lost potential witnesses, who did not accept to stay in such insecurity for so long. The smallest details needed to be discussed at meetings. The climate was so paranoid and oppressive that the ex-official speaks of 'a dictatorship.'

The discontent led to a dramatic exodus of top professionals, which was reported by media and institutions such as the WCRO as well. Among the people who left were international big shots. Top prosecutor Andrew Cayley came in 2005 and left in 2007. He became defence lawyer of a suspect at the ICTY and of the Liberian ex-president Charles Taylor who was indicted by the Special Court for Sierra Leone, before getting his post as co-prosecutor with the Extraordinary Chambers in the Courts of Cambodia. Currently he is director of service prosecutions in the UK (and now dealing with the ICC in the Iraqi torture case). Deputy prosecutor Serge Brammertz, hired by the ICC in 2003, wanted to put heavyweights on the criminal investigations. According to the anonymous source Brammertz soon was 'sidelined and dumped.' The deputy formally left in 2007, but in reality he had departed earlier when he accepted an assignment to become commissioner with the United Nations International Independent Investigation Commission (later: Special

Tribunal for Lebanon), which investigates the murder of the Lebanese prime minister Rafiq Hariri. Other qualified professionals didn't stay long either.

'The OTP, hurt by its strict management, was suffering from a lack of quality,' the former staff member said. The source pointed out that all too often, vacated positions were filled by ambitious young men and women with little experience, but who looked up to the prosecutor. 'There were young people who worshiped him. Some girls who had never been a prosecutor, were allowed to run cases,' the ex-official noted.

Catching thieves with thieves

Joris van Wijk, director of the Center for International Criminal Justice (CICJ) of the Vrije Universiteit (VU) in Amsterdam, was flabbergasted when he heard the OTP had requested a budget for only 46 senior investigators for the year 2013. 'Even for a murder investigation in Groningen [a provincial capital city in the north of The Netherlands] usually more detectives are being deployed, while the ICC is doing very complex and huge cases that are extremely difficult to investigate,' Van Wijk states. He stresses that the court is basically dealing with organized crime comparable to that of the mafia. 'It is important to build up a case by first catching the smaller thieves so you can – with their help as crown witnesses – prosecute the mafia boss. At the ICTY it was done by indicting lower ranking perpetrators and offering them sentence reduction in exchange for a statement against their superiors. In this way they built up cases against the top leadership.' The strategy of the ICC has been different. 'The ICC chose to go straight for the leaders,' Van Wijk explains.

This doesn't mean the court can do without the lower ranking perpetrators. It takes a thief to catch a thief. Instead of prosecuting criminals lower down the hierarchy, the OTP tries to convince these insiders to testify against their former bosses. At the time Moreno-Ocampo defended this approach, saying: 'This is normal when you work on organized crime. These persons are not taking minutes or notes of their decisions. So the only way to show how they decided to commit crimes, is through the inside people. So I am very proud of my investigative team, who got insider witnesses willing to testify. These people are facing a lot of problems.'

Van Wijk points out it is often difficult to encourage insiders, also called dirty hand witnesses, to cooperate with the court. Because they are not indicted or detained, the prosecutors don't have many possibilities to get them on their side. The risks can be extremely high for insiders when they testify against the persons most responsible for the crimes. Their lives can be in danger when networks around suspects and their accessories want to shut them up or take revenge. 'There are efforts to kill or bribe them,' Moreno-Ocampo had explained in the interview. So why would insiders cooperate with the OTP?

The court doesn't stand completely empty-handed, as it has a witness protection programme. In case of peril the ICC will transfer that witness to a safe place, often in another country, where the threatened person and his or her family will be offered housing, education, health services and financial support – all paid for by the court – if necessary, for years. 'The ICC won't be keen to offer this protection to many witnesses, because that will become way too expensive,' Van Wijk says.

The protection programme falls under the Victims and Witnesses Service (VWS), which previously was called Victims and Witnesses Unit (VWU), which is part of the registry. VWS officials do not always agree with requests from the OTP to include people in the program. Prosecutors are more keen to offer people protection, because it helps them in securing a bigger group of potential witnesses for their case. The relatively luxurious protection circumstances also form a risk, says defense counsel David Hooper, who for many years has been defending suspects before international tribunals. People can present themselves as witnesses, to grab this chance of a better life in, for instance, a western country.

'It can be a real encouragement to make yourself attractive to a prosecutor, who is looking for evidence – even if it needs a lie,' explains Hooper, who has been part of the defence team of the Kenyan deputy president Ruto and was lead counsel of the convicted Congolese warlord Germain Katanga. The lawyers of the Kenyan president Uhuru Kenyatta have repeatedly pointed out that some insiders first offered themselves to the defence, but when they found out there wasn't enough to gain for them, they went to the prosecution and presented themselves there as witnesses.

In general, Hooper was not much impressed by the quality of the investigations by the OTP. 'The biggest problem is that the prosecutor is leaning too much on what the witness says without checking that person's account thoroughly. Lying witnesses, or people who are not witnesses at all, are being presented as reliable, while they are not,' the defence lawyer says. False testimony is a risk not limited to insiders, who usually are perpetrators themselves. Hooper says there are also victims who have a deep wish to testify because they want to support justice. They might be willing to tell a little lie, just to get a perpetrator convicted. There are also witnesses who have suffered so much that they want to take revenge and see no problem in juggling with the truth. Hooper calls this: 'Lying for justice.' Some of these witnesses are prepared to testify anything against just anyone, he says.

On the other side, explains Van Wijk, witnesses don't necessarily present false testimony on purpose. Culture plays a role as well. Besides the more general problem that any person will find it hard to remember perfectly all details related to incidents (persons, identities, data, numbers, colors, locations, names, distances, sequences), let alone facts about violent, chaotic and traumatic situations, there are societies where people think differently about concepts such as time. These are exactly the sort of aspects on which defence lawyers focus their cross-examinations of witnesses.

It is a huge strain and difficult to testify without making mistakes. It can happen that witnesses, despite their best intentions, mix up perpetrator and suspect. Witnesses from cultures with a strong oral tradition sometimes retell incidents in a very lively and intense way, as if they had endured these events themselves, while in reality they only heard about it from others who indeed were direct victims and eyewitnesses.

Investigation by lawyers

Formally the prosecutor has the duty to look both for incriminating evidence against the suspect as well as exonerating information. The latter is a myth, concludes Hooper. 'It is pie in the sky, pigs will fly stuff. It will never happen. The only people that will go to that remote village in Congo to look for potential defence witnesses are the suspects' lawyers.' That is what Hooper and his team have been doing. They travel, if necessary, to any spot on the planet to find witnesses that support the case of their client. And so, parallel to the investigation of the prosecutor, there is a contra-investigation taking place by the defence.

Her job starts with many meetings with her client, tells the Dutch lawyer Caroline Buisman who has been part of Hooper's team defending

Katanga. In this case she had to go to the ICC detention centre in The Hague, where the suspect was detained. 'You spend a lot of time with him to go through his case. During those conversations names of persons emerge who could be defending him. You will start looking for these people,' Buisman tells. She often travelled to Ituri, where the crimes of which her client was accused of having committed, had taken place. Buisman always went with a local investigator to find witnesses and information that could exonerate her client.

She is careful. 'You want to take a critical position to your evidence. So you interview persons several times. Again and again you start all over, just to see how consistent a person is. The prosecutor didn't do such double-checks. But we did. It is necessary. It is not easy to find reliable witnesses. Some people want to help you. Or they think they can get something out of it, for instance, a trip or a drink. Sometimes people want to testify out of boredom or loyalty to the client. But that doesn't help. Witnesses have to be reliable.'

During the last few years the lawyer, who speaks Swahili, has also been part of the defence team for the Kenyan broadcaster Joshua Arap Sang. She has often been in the courtroom, but actually prefers her work in the field. Even though the circumstances are not always that easy. 'You will have to be flexible. Sometimes there is no food on the market. But I can handle it to go without food for one day.'

While Buisman was investigating for her client Katanga in Ituri, the ICC watched over her safety. In principle every trip was made in consultation with the court. If a situation was too uncertain, or if there were no hotels or appropriate guesthouses in the area, she would, for instance, stay on a UN compound. 'For investigations in such areas you are provided by the court with a driver and car,' she explains. The lawyer remembers the massive security measures when the judges in the Katanga trial themselves travelled to Ituri to have a look. On the road to the town of Aveba they were supported by a UN unit that included military tanks. 'During the visit to Katanga's father, UN soldiers, armed with guns, were taking position,' she recalls.

But Buisman favours the low-key approach of just herself and the local investigator. 'We take the motorbike to go and interview witnesses. Usually it is not that dicey. If you come on your own, there is not much risk.' Although she once saw how soldiers ransacked houses, and another time it was a bit scary when her tiny team got stuck, in the middle of the night, in some remote area. But she never felt really threatened. In her opinion the prosecution too often refers to security issues when it comes to witnesses. She finds that their inclusion in the protection programme 'often is rubbish.'

New prosecutor, new policy

Prosecutor Moreno-Ocampo stood square behind his approach, when I interviewed him in 2011. 'We never present cases without evidence. We are not doing stupid things. We are not inventing witnesses. We are checking carefully. We never present witnesses that should not be trusted. So we are totally confident.'

It was bravado. One and a half year after his departure in October 2013, his successor Bensouda presented her 'Strategic Plan' that implicitly was a confirmation of the mistakes made by the office during the Moreno-Ocampo era.[26] Although it should not be forgotten that during all that time, Bensouda was head of the prosecution division and thus just as responsible for its output as her boss.

While the report repeatedly stressed that the resources didn't meet the high demand faced by her office, the new policy should lead to more solid cases and better results. 'Due to the higher evidentiary standards and the expectation to be trial-ready earlier, the notion of focused investigations is replaced by the principle of in-depth, open-ended investigations while maintaining focus,' the OTP wrote. Bensouda also indicated she would invest in collecting 'other forms of evidence in addition to witness statements, in particular scientific evidence' such as video, audio, digital data from smart phones, tablets and computers, 3D-scanning and satellite images. She wanted the 'investigative standards' validated 'with a panel of international experts' and 'further training' of her staff. The plan also included hiring 'more senior trial lawyers to lead the investigations and prosecutions.'

But one of the most important changes was that Bensouda indicated that prosecuting the most responsible persons and the evidence that is required in such cases, might force the OTP 'sometimes' to apply a different 'approach due to limitations on investigative possibilities and/or a lack of cooperation.' In those situations 'a strategy of gradually building upwards'

26   Strategic Plan June 2012-2015, OTP, 2013.

might be needed. This meant that the OTP at first might prosecute 'a limited number of mid- and high-level perpetrators in order to ultimately have a reasonable prospect of conviction for those most responsible.' The prosecutor would use such trials against perpetrators positioned in the ranks right below the top, to collect enough evidence against the highest leaders. This is exactly the point Joris van Wijk, associate professor at the Vrije Universiteit in Amsterdam and director of the Center for International Criminal Justice, was making when he compared the ICC to the ICTY. 'We want to build more often cases from below. We will start with perpetrators from the lower echelons and will investigate all the way to the top in order to prosecute the most responsible persons,' confirms OTP's legal advisor Bevers. Besides that, Bensouda decided she would prosecute 'lower level perpetrators where their conduct has been particularly grave and has acquired extensive notoriety.'

Since she took office, Bensouda has drastically slowed down the number of arrest warrants and seems first to want to get rid of the caseload she inherited from her predecessor. As far as is known she has requested the judges to issue arrest warrants against only two suspects for international crimes: the Malian jihadi Ahmad Al Faqi Al Mahdi, who was already in prison in Niger, and Al-Tuhamy Mohamed Khaled, the former head of the Internal Security Agency in Libya who was living in Egypt, but seems to be back in Libya. There might, of course, still be sealed arrest warrants that haven't been made public yet. Bensouda also indicted eight persons for witness interference, of whom she succesfully prosecuted the five suspects of the Bemba bribery case.

So how has the prosecution been doing? The anonymous former official was extremely critical, when I spoke to him a few years back. 'So far the balance is negative. If there aren't quickly a few changes, the court will be a failed project'. But others, like Alex Whiting, now professor at Harvard Law School but previously coordinator investigations and prosecutions at the OTP in The Hague, argued that the current prosecutor needed to be given the chance to show her new approach is working. 'Institutions like the OTP take time to change. It is rather more like turning a super tanker in the ocean than a little speedboat. So it is much, much too early to judge,' he wrote in a piece published in March 2014 by the widely appreciated blog Justice in Conflict (JiC).[27] Bevers agreed: 'We are still in

27   'The ICC's End Days? Not So Fast,' Alex Whiting, JiC, 20 March 2014.

the phase of discovering what the legal possibilities of the whole system are. Although I would like to see some progress as well.'

Two years later Mark Kersten, the creator of the JiC-blog and quite a supporter of the court, wrote a critical comment: 'The institution's ability to deliver on its mandate of ending impunity for war crimes, crimes against humanity, and genocide hasn't gone according to plan. Not even close.'[28] Its achievements 'are modest in comparison to the lofty expectations that its brand of international criminal justice would prevent and deter mass atrocities.' He pointed out that Bensouda had no other option but change her strategy. 'What else can you do when your record on the hardest, yet most important cases, is dreadfully poor but there aren't any obvious signs that it will improve in the future?' he wrote. He noticed 'a turn to the symbolic resonance of the institution.' One of the changes has been that Bensouda 'pumped the brakes' and limited the number of new investigations and trials, while pitching the ICC as an institution that tackles 'crimes that are of the greatest salience to the international community, measured, presumably, by the amount of global attention these crimes receive.' Such as prosecuting the use of child soldiers, sexual and gender based violence, the destruction of cultural and historical property and, more recently, plans to investigate environmental crimes and land grabs. 'The wisdom of this turn to the symbolic can't yet be known,' Kersten stated. But he warned that 'ultimately' the ICC's success will be measured 'by the institution's effects on the ground and its impact on victims and survivors – and not whether it resonates with an abstract international community.'

---

28 'A Turn to the "Symbolic" at the International Criminal Court,' Mark Kersten, JiC, 5 October 2016.

3

KENYA
The dramatic case against the Ocampo Six

'You are not allowed to take cameras or bags to the public gallery. Also your hand phones have to be stored in the lockers.' With a loud voice, a communication officer tries to shout over the noise in the lobby of the ICC. An international crowd of diplomats, politicians, human rights activists, experts, journalists, lawyers and observers is gathering here. They are busy greeting each other and try to make their way through the limited space in the foyer, which characterizes the old court building. Most of the visitors are Kenyans, who have taken the plane to The Netherlands to be present for the initial appearance hearing in the criminal cases against six compatriots, who had received summons from the judges to show up. During this short session the identity of the suspects is checked. They will also be informed about the charges and their rights.

'Please, would you not point at people in the courtroom, when you are seated in the public gallery. And not wave to persons you know either?' the court official shouts the rules to the crowd, while a steady flow of visitors takes the stairs and elevator up. Pen and paper are the only items guests are allowed to bring with them to the public gallery. Once at their destination they select a free place, flip down the seat and put on headphones, necessary to follow the hearing since there is a huge window of thick bulletproof and soundproof glass installed between the public and courtroom. From their vantage point the visitors have a full view over the sea of brown. The furniture in the courtroom is of Scandinavian style wood. Even the walls are covered with wooden panels as if it were a sauna. The carpet is of striped beige.

It is 7 April 2011 and it is by no means definite that today's proceedings will lead to full trials against the six. The appearances will be followed by the confirmation of charges hearings a few months later. During those sessions the prosecution will present its first evidence in court, after which the judges will decide whether they have a case or not. The six Kenyans are suspected of organising large-scale violence after the national elections on 27 December 2007. In large parts of Kenya huge mobs of fighters and civilians, mainly armed with machetes, sticks, spears, bows and arrows but also with guns, attacked defenceless compatriots belonging to other ethnic groups. In a few weeks' time more than 1100 people were killed. Hundreds of thousands fled their homes, fearing for their lives. Kenya was on the brink of a civil war.

Suddenly the buzz stops. The three judges, dressed in their dark blue robes with light blue borders, make their entrance. In a wave visitors and officials get up, only to sit down again when the bench takes its seat. Presiding judge Ekaterina Trendafilova, seated in the middle, takes the floor. 'Unfortunately, we start with three minutes' delay. The judges had been waiting outside the courtroom,' she says with irritation in her voice.[29] All participants are asked 'to respect the start of every hearing and every session, because this chamber is very strict about this.' The tone has been set. Trendafilova just presented herself and her two colleagues as professionals one doesn't mess around with.

Next point. 'You have one minute and a half to take your pictures and no more,' Trendafilova tells the two photographers who have permission to take pictures in the courtroom, which soon will be distributed through the press agencies all over the world. Visitors seated on the second floor of the public gallery are getting up to try to see what is happening a few meters below in the courtroom. A security guard quickly intervenes and tells them to sit down. From their seats the visitors can hardly see the action. They have no other option than to look at the monitors in the public gallery displaying ICC controlled video images of the proceedings in the 'aquarium' below.

On the right is the prosecution section, responsible for the criminal investigations against the Kenyans. Prosecutor Luis Moreno-Ocampo, as usual fashionably unshaven, presents his team in his heavy Spanish-accented English. Three suspects and their legal teams are seated left. Names drawn from nationalities all over the world fill the courtroom again when the defence and registry are presented.

---

29   Official transcript, ICC, 7 April 2011.

When Trendafilova asks the first suspect to expound on his personal details, William Samoei Ruto (born in 1966) is getting up. With hesitation he adds: 'Apparently, I am a member of parliament for Eldoret North Constituency, which is 320 kilometres northwest of Nairobi.' Ruto has been accused of corruption in Kenya and has been suspended as minister for higher education, but the ICC is prosecuting him as an organiser of post-election violence.[30]

He has hardly uttered his last words, when there is the voice of Trendifilova, sounding like a schoolteacher when she makes him a little compliment: 'Thank you, Mr. Ruto, you perfectly well answered the questions that, on behalf of the bench, I posed to you.' In the public gallery people are chuckling. Ruto, at home a powerful politician, is blinking his eyes. He doesn't feel at ease.

Then it is MP Henry Kiprono Kosgey's (born in 1947) turn to present himself. Lastly the judges look at the short man who has his arm in a sling. 'You might not stand up because we were informed about the accident that you experienced some days ago. So you can reply to the chamber seated. Your name, your date and place of birth and your current occupation,' says Trendafilova. The Kenyan presents himself as Joshua Kirwa Arap Sang (born in 1975). 'I am an innocent journalist,' he adds. Trendafilova doesn't waste a second and speeds on. The judge has a warning for these suspects, who are complying with the court's summons to appear, therefore haven't been arrested and are able to move around freely. She points out that the judges have been reading in Kenyan newspapers that 'there are some movements towards re-triggering the violence in the country by way of using some dangerous speeches.' If these incitements continue – she refers to no one in particular – this might prompt the chamber to issue arrest warrants. In that case the suspects will be worse off. However, arrests wouldn't be what the chamber wishes, 'because we would rather that you appear as free persons in this courtroom,' Trendafilova says – a comment many will doubt later on.

Prosecuting both parties

The ICC will handle the Kenyan violence in two separate cases, reflecting the opposing camps during the post-election violence. The men led

---

30 'Accused Kenyan minister William Ruto is suspended,' BBC, 19 October 2010.

before the judges today – Ruto, Kosgey and Sang – are suspected of organising attacks on the ethnic Kikuyu, Kamba and Kisii, who were seen as supporters of the governing Party of National Unity (PNU).[31] The aim of the violence was to chase out these groups from the Rift Valley, an enormous territory northwest of the capital city Nairobi. The people who stayed behind would belong to the Kalenjin-group and be able to vote as one big block for the political opposition, the Orange Democratic Movement (ODM). This seems like a textbook example of ethnic cleansing with the goal of gaining political power. According to the prosecutor, Ruto was positioned at the top of a criminal network of politicians, media, police and military. Kosgey was allegedly second man and Sang did communications, especially through his radio-show.[32] Ruto blinks again with his eyes, now that he hears the charges: crimes against humanity for murder, deportation and persecution. Kosgey is looking straight ahead. Sang nods when he hears the names of the areas where crimes have been committed. At the end of this list Ruto is getting up, angrily because he had tried to get more details about the charges against him, but didn't manage. 'The allegations that have been made here, sound to me like they can only be possible in a movie,' he says, aggrieved. Two young women at the public gallery snigger. 'Mr. Ruto, could I just ask you to sit down and I shall give you some explanations,' Trendafilova responds. The judge lays down the basics of a court case. The prosecutor is the 'triggering force,' she explains. 'So he's going to come with strong evidence, hopefully, and you will, of course, be assisted throughout these proceedings by very competent and highly professional counsel.' She continues telling Ruto that during the upcoming confirmation of charges hearing he will have 'all the opportunities' to make 'extensively' his points. Towards the end of the session Trendafilova explains to Ruto that he 'will be presumed innocent until proven guilty beyond a reasonable doubt at trial – if this case proceeds to trial – with the onus firmly placed on the prosecutor to prove your guilt.' It is unlikely her explanation will satisfy Ruto, who earlier said: 'That an innocent person like me be dragged all the way here, really, is a matter that baffles me.'

---

31   Case Information Sheet, ICC, April 2016
32   Document Containing the Charges, OTP, 1 August 2011

Trendafilova then turns to prosecutor Moreno-Ocampo, who says there is an obstacle, since the Kenyan government has filed an admissibility challenge, arguing that the ICC has no jurisdiction over these cases (which the court rejects on 30 May 2011 because there are no indications that Kenya is willing to start investigations or prosecutions itself). But Trendafilova doesn't agree. She orders the prosecutor to start disclosing evidence to the suspects and their lawyers so they can prepare themselves and build the defence. The judge then settles a few more matters and closes the hearing. 'All Rise,' says the court usher. The judges are the first to leave the courtroom. Then prosecutor Moreno-Ocampo quickly follows in order to prepare himself for his press conference.

Television cameras of the international news agencies and networks are being set up in an office turned media room. With strong tape some journalists fix their microphones to the lectern. A few moments later a self-assured prosecutor steps into the room. 'Today is accountability day,' says Moreno-Ocampo. It is one of those typical one-liners that journalists like to repeat when they want to imitate the prosecutor amongst themselves. 'We serve the Kenyan people,' continues the prosecutor, who clearly loves press conferences.

The Kenyan case is extra important for Moreno-Ocampo because he has started it himself – proprio motu – in contrast to the other cases which were referred to by member states and the UN Security Council. In Kenya the accused persons are therefore referred to as the 'Ocampo Six.' A journalist wants to know whether this is a political case? The prosecutor wipes that suggestion immediately off the table. 'The killing of people can't be part of a political career. Not in Kenya and not in Libya.' Next question. What does he think of Ruto who recently had called him an 'evil' man? 'That is fine,' Moreno-Ocampo smiles with superiority. 'Apparently they continue to incite people to commit again crimes for which they now have been charged.'

A powerful state apparatus

The next day people are jostling at the entrance of the court. More than a hundred visitors want to attend the initial appearance hearing of the second group. It is unclear whether there will be enough room to let everybody in. While people start pushing to get in, some are pressed against the fence with the signs 'Pas Op! Schrikdraad.' Luckily nobody is getting an electric shock. When Kenyans see that some white people are allowed in, several accuse the court of discrimination. A Kenyan hawker stands among the crowd with an impressive tower of caps in the national four colours piled on his head. He seems mainly there for a bit of a show as he doesn't sell much. Kenyan men in smart dark suits are showing placards with texts such as 'Give Kenya a CHANCE to handle the Ocampo Six locally.'

After the opening of the second hearing Trendafilova again keeps the pace. With her direct style the judge, publicly lecturing politicians who were always deemed untouchable, will gain considerable popularity in Kenya. Her strict demeanour, Bulgarian accent and blond modest wavy hair are the key attributes copied when she becomes (just like Moreno-Ocampo) one of the main characters in the ICC episodes of the Kenyan satirical puppet TV show 'XYZ', which, following the British tradition with Spitting Image, makes serious fun of politicians and other celebrities. The three suspects who appear before the court today, present themselves in a less provocative way than their compatriots earlier. The most significant person in this trio is Uhuru Muigai Kenyatta (born in 1961). He is the son of Jomo Kenyatta, who in 1963 became prime minister of Kenya when the nation gained independence. A year later he would become the country's president. The young Kenyatta is continuing the dynasty. At this point, he has made it to deputy prime minister and minister for finance. Rumoured to be a multimillionaire, he is possibly among the richest people of Kenya. With co-defendant Francis Kirimi Muthaura (born 1946), head of public service and secretary to the cabinet, he is being accused of orchestrating a criminal plan to attack – using a criminal gang called the Mungiki – civilians belonging to the ethnic Luo, Luhya and Kalenjin in areas around the cities of Nakuru and Naivasha, northwest to Nairobi.[33] These ethnic groups are seen as supporters of the opposition ODM. The goal of the suspects was to keep the PNU in power. Police chief Mohammed Hussein Ali (born in 1956) is charged by the ICC because he allegedly ordered his men to let the attackers proceed, instead of stopping them. The trio is accused of five counts of crimes against humanity: murder, deportation, rape, persecution and other inhumane acts such as forced circumcision.

---

33   Case Information Sheet, ICC, 13 March 2015.

The two cases seem nicely in balance. With three suspects on each side, the warring parties are being dealt with equally, although this 3+3-approach might also look a little too perfect. Nevertheless, there are significant differences between the two cases. With Kenyatta, Muthaura and Ali, key players of the powerful state apparatus are being charged. The ICC is confronting top officials who occupy central positions in the government, administration and police – institutions that yield immense influence. The suspects in the other case – two MPs and a journalist – have less formal power. Indeed, the secret service of Kenya was prepared to handover information about Ruto to the ICC.

When the identities of today's trio are checked and the charges are explained, Trendafilova declares the hearing over. A chubby woman at the public gallery is fuming with anger. 'It is a disgrace that these people are being charged, because they were the ones who stopped the violence!' To her Kenyatta, Muthaura and Ali are innocent. Following the rhythm of the angry words, the woman next to her – a flashy lady in a little black dress with a deep cleavage, a golden coloured jacket and wearing pumps on her feet with golden high heels – is nodding in agreement. There are several Kenyan beauties present here one would sooner expect to meet in a nightclub than at a court. While the public gallery is being vacated, both women get up from their flip-up chairs and leave the place.

'They must be the concubines who have come along with the suspects,' explains a Kenyan sports teacher who has taken a plane from London to be present, while getting his coat and bag from the locker in the lobby. 'I have come especially here to see the fear in the faces of these men. Even if it would last for just one minute,' he says about the suspects. And, I ask him, satisfied? 'Absolutely,' he responds all beaming. 'It is good that the case is before the ICC. In Kenya they would have drummed up a million people to sabotage the court case with demonstrations and protests,' he adds, quickly taking his belongings before rushing to the airport. Meantime, the supporters of the three suspects have walked to the front of the court buildings to welcome their heroes with cheers. There, on the steps of the ICC and in the evening sun, deputy prime minister Kenyatta will boisterously start singing the Kenyan national anthem.

From Ocampo Six to Ocampo Four

The initial appearances are the overture for two turbulent court cases that will have enormous consequences. Not just for Kenya, but also for the court and even internationally. Five months later – in September and October 2011 – the court has organised the confirmation of charges hearings, during which the prosecution presents its first evidence. For several weeks the judges, prosecutors, suspects and lawyers come together in the courtroom, where tough legal battles are fought. The prosecutors champion the strength of the case, while the defence counsels contest it. Moreno-Ocampo himself cross-examines Kenyatta, which turns out to be a surprisingly weak performance. When the hearings are over, the judges withdraw for deliberations. A few months later, on 23 January 2012, the court decides that the evidence against four suspects is strong enough to start a full trial. The judges however are not unanimous. One of them, the German judge Hans-Peter Kaul (who died of an illness in 2014), is of the opinion that Kenya did indeed suffer large-scale violence, but that the case doesn't fall under the court's definition of crimes against humanity, as he doesn't see proof that the attacks were part of an organizational policy. Kaul says that the post-election violence is therefore not a matter for the ICC, but for Kenya's courts.[34] The judges decline to confirm the charges against police chief Ali and politician Kosgey because the prosecutors couldn't back up their accusations with sufficient evidence. So the Ocampo Six become Ocampo Four. That is just the beginning of a series of setbacks that will continue to haunt the prosecutors for years to come.

Suspects and elections

The big hall of the Catholic University in Nairobi is filled to the brim with elated politicians and enthusiastic supporters. A clip on YouTube shows the man who just heard, on 9 March 2013, that he has won the presidential elections. Greeted with applause and songs, Uhuru Kenyatta is getting ready on stage for his acceptance speech. As soon as he starts to speak the crowd falls silent. Kenya has just seen its most 'free and fair general election' in the history of the nation, he says. 'We dutifully turned out. We voted in peace. We upheld order and respect for the rule of law. And we maintained the fabric of our society,' the statesman proclaims. 'That, ladies and gentlemen, is the real victory today.'
The new head of state refers to his 'brother' on the first row. The 'Honorable Mr William Ruto' will be the new deputy president. It is

---

34   Decision on the Confirmation of Charges, ICC, 23 January 2012.

his finest hour. Ruto, who grew up in a poor family and, as a child, sold peanuts along the Eldoret Highway, and who nevertheless managed to get to university, rose to high positions in the ruling Kenyan African National Union (KANU), became minister and reportedly gained a fortune in business, has now conquered the second most powerful position in Kenya.

The Office of the Prosecutor (OTP) in The Hague must have been following these developments with concern and cynicism, as the two main suspects in the Kenyan cases have been elected to the posts of president and deputy president. How could this happen? While the men were allowed to await their trials in freedom, Kenyatta and Ruto were able to use every opportunity for strategic manoeuvring in Kenya's political landscape. The two opponents, charged with organising the violence against each other's communities, had embraced each other as allies for these elections. Kenyatta, belonging to the Kikuyu, had forged an alliance with the popular Kalenjin politician Ruto. The pair presented (along with two other parties) their Jubilee Alliance as an act of reconciliation. It also was a matter of calculation. With the backing of the Kikuyu and the Kalenjin the two suspects expected to secure a significant number of votes for their political alliance. It turned out to be a brilliant move. The forecasting became true. The pair, known as 'Uhuruto', won the elections of 4 March 2013 – which were marred by 'technical hitches, mysterious delays and mathematical anomalies' according to Michela Wrong in a column for the New York Times[35] – though by the narrowest margin: 50,07 percent of the votes.[36]

While their trials were being scheduled by the ICC, the two rivals had managed by clever political planning to get the highest government posts. In Kenya and beyond the debate focused on whether the charges against them might have actually stimulated Kenyans to vote for Uhuruto as a protest against the ICC. Alongside official approval and high expectations among victims of atrocities, there is also intense revulsion against the 'colonial' institution which so far has only been prosecuting Africans. In her piece for the New York Times journalist Michela Wrong writes she was convinced that the indictments had indeed helped the two politicians

35   'Indictee for President!' Michela Wrong, 11 March 2013
36   'Uhuru Kenyatta wins Kenyan election by a narrow margin,' The Guardian, 9 March, 2013

to win the elections. A political analyst had described her the sentiments within the Jubilee Alliance as: 'Thank God for the ICC!' The charges had provided Kenyatta and Ruto with the fortuitous chance to present themselves as victims of a court that was targeting Africa.

During the campaign the team behind 'Uhuruto' had 'cleverly tapped' into 'scepticism' among people that the court wasn't prosecuting the true culprits (as then president Mwai Kibaki and opposition leader Raila Odinga were seen by many) and into 'a deep well of anti-British, anti-Western sentiment,' the journalist states. The campaigners accused 'foreign powers' of being behind the ICC prosecutions. Wrong had seen it herself: 'In the Rift Valley towns of Eldoret and Nakuru, I heard the same refrain from both Kikuyu and Kalenjin: the ICC prosecutions were attacks on entire communities rather than just on two individuals.' A part of the Kenyan population felt they were being charged as an ethnic group and as a nation.

In her piece Wrong quotes Maina Kiai, the United Nations special rapporteur on freedom of assembly, who explains that the very fact that Kenyatta and Ruto freely and successfully managed to present themselves 'as martyrs' of the ICC, shows the weakness of the institution. 'With any court, if you're accused of murdering five people, you don't get bail. You are remanded in custody,' Kiai said. 'With the ICC you get to go home and mobilize your community. Powerful people have powerful ways of keeping themselves out of court.'

The Bensouda Three

While the implications of the victory of the two suspects are still being assessed, there is breaking news from The Hague. On 11 March 2013 an avalanche of tweets runs over the Internet. Prosecutor Fatou Bensouda has just posted a video message on YouTube. Dressed in a white robe while seated against a blue background, with a deeply serious face, she announces she has had to take a very difficult decision: to withdraw the charges against Francis Muthaura. 'This is an exceptional decision. I did not take it lightly, but I believe it is the right thing to do.'[37] The prosecutor can't continue her case.

---

37   Statement by ICC prosecutor on the notice to withdraw charges against Mr Muthaura, OTP, 11 March 2013.

Bensouda explains that a number of people who might have been able to deliver evidence, are dead, without explaining who they are or how they died. Others are 'too afraid to testify for the prosecution,' she says. Her office was thwarted by the Kenyan government, which had refused to give her investigators access to evidence and witnesses. But what completely destroyed the case was that she was left with no other option than dropping a key witness (known under his pseudonym '4') against Muthaura because he had 'recanted a crucial part of his evidence' and admitted to the prosecution 'that he had accepted bribes.'

The incident shows the problematic context in which the ICC is operating when it is prosecuting key figures in the state apparatus, and how the prosecution itself has been failing by trusting unreliable witnesses. The result is that the original Ocampo Six now had dwindled to the Bensouda Three. On one hand there is still the active case against deputy president Ruto and broadcaster Joshua Sang. President Kenyatta remains as the only suspect in the other, increasingly weak, case where the judges heavily criticized the prosecution for handling its investigations. No fewer than 24 witnesses (of 31 witnesses) were interviewed for the first time after the confirmation of charges hearing.[38] 'In addition, a large quantity of documentary evidence appears to have been collected post-confirmation and to have been disclosed at a late stage,' the judges say. One of the judges, Christine Van den Wyngaert, adds a concurring opinion in which she criticizes the way the prosecution has been handling the Kenyatta-Muthaura case, saying that 'there are serious questions as to whether the prosecution conducted a full and thorough investigation of the case against the accused prior to [the] confirmation [of charges hearing].' She points out that there 'can be no excuse for the prosecution's negligent attitude towards verifying the trustworthiness of its evidence,' as there had been for a long time doubts about the inconsistencies in the story of this particular key witness, who has just been withdrawn. The judge scolds 'there are grave problems in the prosecution's system of evidence review, as well as a serious lack of proper oversight by senior prosecution staff.'[39]

---

38   Decision on defence application, ICC, 26 April 2013.
39   Concurring Opinion of Judge Christine Van den Wyngaert, ICC, 26 April 2013.

Hunt for Africans

Western governments prefer to largely ignore the ICC cases against the two newly elected leaders and want to keep their contacts with the Nairobi government on track. The American president Barack Obama cordially congratulates the pair with their victory. Kenya is a powerful country that is doing well economically. It is seen as a partner in world politics. The nation is involved in international peace operations and participates in the fight against terrorism.

In many African circles there had already been a growing dislike for the court, but since Kenya's highest officials are being prosecuted, the critical voices grow louder. A group of African leaders passionately pledges solidarity with the suspects. During the summit of the African Union (AU) in Addis Ababa, in May 2013, there is no room for subtleties. Hailemariam Desalegn, AU chairman and Ethiopia's prime minister, takes a swing at the court: 'The intention was to avoid any kind of impunity... but now the process has degenerated to some kind of race hunting.'[40]

In a resolution AU leaders express their concern about the risks that the prosecution of Kenyatta and Ruto 'may pose to the ongoing efforts in the promotion of peace, national healing and reconciliation, as well as the rule of law and stability, not only in Kenya, but also in the region.' They 'deeply regret' the ICC judges' dismissal of Kenya's admissibility challenge which meant they 'denied the right of Kenya to prosecute and try alleged perpetrators of crimes committed on its territory in relation to the 2007 post-election violence.'[41]

In the meantime, the ICC judges are repeatedly granting the requests for postponements. The trial against Ruto and Sang is now scheduled for 10 September 2013 (after having been scheduled for 10 April, 28 May and 16 June), while the Kenyatta trial is supposed to start on 12 November. Kenyan politicians are busy too. A few days before the trial against deputy president Ruto finally starts, parliament convenes an emergency meeting about a motion to withdraw Kenya from the ICC. 'Let us protect our citizens. Let us defend the sovereignty of the nation of Kenya,' comments Aden Duale, member of the ruling Jubilee Alliance and presenter of

---

40   'African leaders accuse ICC of "race hunt",' Al Jazeera, 28 May 2013.
41   Decisions, declarations and resolution, AU Assembly, 26-27 May 2013, Addis Ababa.

the motion.[42] After members of the opposition walk out, the motion is passed. The move is – also internationally – big news. However, a parliamentary motion is not enough to have Kenya pull out from the ICC. And for the current trials it won't have consequences at all. As ICC spokesperson Fadi El-Abdallah explains to the BBC: 'A withdrawal has an effect only for the future and never for the past.'[43] In fact, if the Kenyan authorities were to actively pursue this road, it could backfire. In a case of active obstruction, the judges could decide to have the Kenyan suspects arrested.

Start of the trial

The uproar in the Kenyan parliament is still resonating when the big day arrives. With a sky of dark grey clouds above the ICC, the trial against Ruto and Sang starts on 10 September 2013 – half a year after the deputy president has been elected in office. Again dozens of members of parliament, representatives of human rights organisations, diplomats and other ICC watchers go up to the public gallery. The international and Kenyan media have turned out as well. For the first time in the history of international criminal tribunals and courts a deputy president in active service is on trial. Ruto is not a pariah, not a defeated militia leader who is on the run or has been languishing in prison. Ruto is a popular, rich and influential government leader.

It was quite a conundrum for the host state – The Netherlands – to decide how to receive the defendant, a source disclosed. At the ministry of foreign affairs there was great reluctance to apply the full diplomatic protocols, as Ruto was not visiting the country as deputy president, but as a suspect of international crimes. The Kenyan government was however expecting nothing less than first class diplomatic treatment. Apparently some halfway solution was found, between politely handling the delegation while not providing a full official motorcade.

Two women take the front seats on the left of the public gallery, as close as possible to the deputy president and his defence team. Rachel Ruto and daughter June have come along to support their husband and father. Next to them sits the Kenyan ambassador, who explained during a press

---

42 'Kenya votes to leave ICC days before deputy president's Hague trial,' The Guardian, 5 September 2013.
43 'Kenya MPs vote to withdraw from ICC,' BBC, 5 September 2013.

briefing a day earlier, that the trials harm Kenya and are a logistical nightmare for her embassy as well. Her staff is working night and day to make all the necessary arrangements for the suspects and their supporters who are travelling with them.

Sitting in the dock, dressed in a nice grey suit and a red tie, Ruto smiles at his family. The nation's leader is the absolute eye-catcher. His co-accused, Joshua Sang, not only sits further away, but is such a short man that, while seated in a chair, he can barely see over the desk.

Presiding judge Chile Eboe-Osuji opens the hearing. The Nigerian law expert, a man with a distinct heavy voice and an impressive CV with previous posts such as legal advisor to the UN High Commissioner for Human Rights, head legal affairs for the judges of the Rwanda Tribunal, counsel with the prosecution at the Special Court for Sierra Leone and a PhD from the University of Amsterdam, starts to speak. With visible delight he will guide the trial, assisted by two fellow judges. (Trendafilova is a judge with the section that handles cases in the pre-trial phase; but when cases enter the trial phase another set of judges oversees these proceedings). After an introduction describing the history of the case, Eboe-Osuji addresses the Kenyan deputy president. 'Mr Ruto, please rise to take your plea. William Samoei Ruto, you have been charged in count 1 with murder, constituting a crime against humanity,' he says. 'How do you plead, guilty or not guilty?'[44]

'Not guilty,' Ruto answers with a remarkably soft voice.

'In count 2 you have been charged with deportation or forcible transfer of population,' the judge continues. 'How do you plead, guilty or not guilty?'

'Not guilty.'

'In count 3 you have been charged with persecution.'

'Not guilty.'

'Thank you very much. You may resume your seat,' says the judge, who then turns to Sang. The broadcaster – facing the same charges – will also plead 'not guilty.'

As the driving force behind the trial, prosecutor Bensouda is given the floor to start with her opening statement. 'It is difficult to imagine the suffering or the terror of the men and the women and children who

---

44   Official transcript, ICC, 10 September 2013.

were burned alive, hacked to death, or chased from their homes by armed youths,' she recalls the violence that erupted after the elections of December 2007. While Bensouda describes the terrible fate of ordinary citizens, the suspects listen carefully to her address. But when she refers to Ruto and 'his syndicate of powerful allies,' the deputy president is given a note by one of his lawyers and starts to laugh. Undisturbed the prosecutor continues her statement.

Bensouda tells how Ruto allegedly planned and organised the violence to 'satisfy his thirst for political power.' Eighteen months before the elections, he had started building a criminal organisation consisting of community leaders, former military, businessmen and media. Ruto played the key role. He 'assigned responsibilities, he raised finance, he procured weapons and hosted meetings in furtherance of the criminal aims of the network,' Bensouda says. He used the social structure of his ethnic group and gathered 'an army of loyal Kalenjin youth to go to war for him in the event of an election loss.' The main target were the Kikuyu, as they were perceived 'the unwelcome settlers who had misappropriated what the Kalenjin considered to be their ancestral land.' The prosecutor accuses Ruto of stoking 'the flames of anti-Kikuyu sentiment, both personally at public rallies and indirectly through other influential speakers and through the media.' So when the election was lost, Ruto 'gave the order to attack,' Bensouda tells the court.

Broadcaster Sang, who was the 'main mouthpiece', placed his 'prime-time radio show at the disposal of the network.' He not only spread the word of Ruto's rallies, but even helped to coordinate attacks through 'coded' messages. 'In this way, he too contributed to the violence,' the prosecutor explains.

A security guard walks to the first rows of the public gallery where a Kenyan man seems to have fallen asleep. Other visitors chuckle when the guard taps the person on his shoulder and explains it is not allowed to have a nap. The man isn't impressed and remains in the same position. Suprisingly the guard leaves it at that. Usually the security personnel is strict in applying rules of order and decorum.

The names

The prosecutor points out that it wouldn't even have been necessary for the ICC to deal with this case. In fact, her office had waited a long time to see whether Kenya would take steps to prosecute the perpetrators itself.

She underlines that during the violence Kofi Annan had been sent to Kenya to try to end the conflict through mediation. The former secretary-general of the United Nations and chair of the AU's Panel of Eminent African Personalities, had managed to strike a power-sharing deal between the parties. Part of the agreement was the installation of an investigative body. This Commission of Inquiry on Post-Election Violence (CIPEV), led by the Kenyan judge Philip Waki, made an analysis of the conflict. In its final report, published on 15 October 2008, the commission came with an urgent recommendation to the Kenyan authorities to set up a special national tribunal to prosecute those responsible for the political violence between 2007 and 2008.

The CIPEV had produced a confidential list with names of suspects (later it was revealed that Ruto's name was on it), but Waki didn't disclose the names publicly. He gave the records in a sealed envelope to Kofi Annan, in an effort to keep the pressure on the government to set up the tribunal. In July 2009 Annan handed over the list to prosecutor Moreno-Ocampo – together with several boxes full of investigative material that the commission had assembled during its inquiry. When no national tribunal was being set up, it was clear that Kenya was not willing to initiate prosecutions. So Moreno-Ocampo took steps to start these himself. On 5 November 2009 he notified the president of the ICC that he would ask for authorization to open investigations – 'a decision which was fully supported at the time by the Kenya government,' says Bensouda. In other words, the Kenyan leaders owed it to themselves that a trial was now taking place in The Hague. (The suspects had requested the ICC to move hearings to Kenya or Tanzania, but by a tiny majority the judges rejected that option during a plenary session in July 2013. It was deemed too expensive, cumbersome, logistically complex and too unsafe for victims, witnesses and even for ICC staff to hold part of the trials in these countries.[45])

It hasn't been easy for her office to handle this case, Bensouda explains to the judges. Cooperation with Kenya is problematic. Many witnesses and victims are too scared to talk. Others who have given testimony face such heavy intimidation that out of fear they have been pulling out. There are persons who have been offered bribes to force them to change their

---

45   Ruto and Sang case: Trial to open in The Hague, ICC press release, 15 July 2013.

statements or withdraw. 'The very fact, Mr President, that I stand before you at the opening of this trial today, your Honours, is something of an achievement in itself,' Bensouda says before issuing a warning to 'those persons behind the ongoing attempts to intimidate and bribe the ICC witnesses: these are serious offences under the Rome Statute and they carry hefty sentences upon conviction.' The OTP is investigating these signs of witness interference and her office will get to the bottom of it, the prosecutor warns.

Bensouda is coming to the conclusion of her statement. 'This is not a trial of Kenya or of the Kenyan people. It is not about vindicating or indicting one or other ethnic group or political party. It is not about meddling in African affairs. This trial, Mr President, your Honours, is about obtaining justice for the many thousands of victims of the post-election violence and ensuring that there is no impunity for those responsible, regardless of power or position.'

Then she hands over to Anton Steynberg, lead counsel for the prosecution, who will explain in more detail the structure behind the violence. Ruto's network wasn't an official military or government organisation, he stresses. Steynberg: 'It did not have formal ranks, offices, or letters of appointment. It did not keep formal records in the form of cabinet minutes, nor did it report its activities via military situation reports. Rather, this network was a criminal organisation in the style of a mafia group or a triad organisation.' This didn't mean that it was less organised. 'It had a clear hierarchy and chain of command, with Mr Ruto at the apex,' the lead counsel explains. The suspect used his 'political and tribal authority and the tradition of obedience of the Kalenjin to their leaders.' The ultimate goal was: 'to rid the Rift Valley of its political and ethnic opponents.'

The political component of the network was formed by prominent politicians and community leaders. The money was provided by Kalenjin businessmen and Ruto himself, and used for implementing the common plan, 'handing out cash to those who attended meetings and pledging rewards to those who killed perceived PNU supporters or destroyed their properties.'

Militarily the network included former servicemen who coordinated attacks, while divisional leaders were leading 'thousands of Kalenjin youth' who committed the actual violence. Traditional leaders were calling their followers to attend preparatory meetings. They 'exploited traditional circumcision and oathing ceremonies of Kalenjin youth in order to indoctrinate and train large numbers of warriors before the elections,' Steynberg tells the court. To those who refused to participate, the traditional leaders meted out punishments which included 'public humiliation, flogging and forcing them to pay penance in livestock, some of which were used to feed warriors on the ground.' After the violence the traditional leaders 'performed cleansing ceremonies' to absolve youth of any crimes they had committed.

The OTP had found out that the operations had started back in 2006, during a first meeting with a small group of confidants in Ruto's house in Sugoi, on the outskirts of the city of Turbo, in the west of the country. In advance of the elections the organisation would have the complete logistics ready to go to war: leaders, sponsors, perpetrators, money, weapons, transport, food and communication. During the attacks houses and companies were looted. 'Kikuyu who were found, were caught and attacked on sight, with weapons such as arrows, or pangas, and many were killed or gravely injured.'

How many witnesses the prosecution plans to call remains unclear. The list is confidential for the public – also because witnesses keep dropping out. The only specific number Steynberg wants to give is that the prosecution will present up to 22 victims who will come to testify. They are common Kenyan people who will describe what happened during the attacks. Also experts will testify. But Steynberg remains silent about the insiders, who were part of the alleged criminal network, possibly were perpetrators themselves and have knowledge about what happened in the organisation. Prosecutors usually need these witnesses to bring cases to a conviction. Several Kenyan insiders are said to be included in the ICC's witness protection programme and are residing in safe houses abroad. Steynberg does have a message to witnesses who suddenly change their minds and desert the prosecution's camp to join Ruto's defence. 'The prosecution will, if necessary, present evidence as to the true motives behind their actions, and that is, that they have been bribed to do so.'

The suffering of the victims

It is quiet when the legal representative of the victims takes the floor. Although international criminal law is said to be developed in the name of those who suffered, in the legal power struggle between the prosecutor and defence lawyers, victims often have just a supporting role. A new aspect of the ICC is that victims do have their own legal representation. In this case they are represented by Wilfred Nderitu. The Kenyan lawyer, with his deep sonorous voice, takes care of the interests of 628 victims. With his philosophical approach, Nderitu brings a whole new sphere into the courtroom. For a few moments the lawyers don't pass notes to each other. There are no smiles or laughter. Finally, amidst the commotion, there is a moment of calm to think about the fate of the people who directly suffered. A pain that is only really known to persons who endured it, Nderitu says. Victims have been deeply hurt. 'They suffered emotional damage and scarring, physical damage and scarring, financial damage and social damage.' Nderitu experienced pain himself. 'I may say that I know exactly what I'm talking about, being myself a survivor of the 1998 US embassy bombing in Nairobi,' he says, referring in one sentence to the terror attack by a group of jihadis, with a link to Osama bin Laden and Al Qaeda, during which over two hundred people were killed. Nobody in the courtroom can predict, when the lawyer speaks these words, how close Kenya is to this kind of violence again.

The legal representative explains how the victims feel 'stripped of their dignity.' They are sad and angry. They blame themselves and are ashamed. They feel insecure and unsafe because they don't know whether they will be able to trust their neighbours. They have been let down by the government, who didn't do anything to help them or to get justice. Nderitu then focuses especially on the many forgotten children 'whose lives were drastically and brutally affected by their witnessing death, human injury, material destruction and other dangerous conditions.' With their families they were forced to flee their neighbourhoods to 'a life of living in tents, with their parents having to wait for handouts from charitable organisations and well-wishers.' Many children dropped out from school. 'Their trust in the world, in spirituality, in deeply held beliefs about social order, justice, and humanity was fundamentally upset and replaced with cynicism, suspicion, and resentment for humanity,' Nderitu tells the court. 'The emotional scarring to them is lifelong.'

These are words that touch the soul. Judge Eboe-Osuji listens with great attention, his hand before his mouth. Nderitu explains how, in a refined way, people are victimised again by 'subtle silencing.' Politicians and ethnic communities stress that it is 'unfashionable to bear the tag of "victim" and therefore to participate effectively in the criminal justice process.' Every day they hear: 'Kenyans have moved on.' A slogan championed by the media and general public, says Nderitu, telling people there's no sense in looking back and that victims should forget about the suffering, atrocities and justice. But they can't forget, Nderitu underlines. On top of the stigma they bear, victims face an intense pressure to give up. There are reports of witnesses and victims who no longer want to testify, and the Kenyan government trying to withdraw from the ICC. Nderitu brings the court back to the people in whose name these trials are conducted: 'Despite all these setbacks, the victims look up to you with hope – hope that justice will be done in this case.'

This case is rotten

Meanwhile defence counsel Karim Khan can't wait to start his presentation. The successful British lawyer is a whopping rhetorical master, with an attacking style, using rich language, venom and big words. His pleas contain sentences for which one would like to keep a dictionary permanently at hand. The lamps in the courtroom reflect on the bald skull of Khan, a man with small dark alert eyes and a vague grey beard that touches the points of a tiny moustache.

When finally it's his turn, he manages to sound both stately and devastating at the same time. 'Mr President, your Honours, Mr Ruto's waited quite a while to put forward the truth, and we welcome this opportunity to blow away, hopefully, some of the cobwebs of confusion, the deceptions, the errors and the misconceptions that have so woefully befallen the prosecutor in her investigations.' Khan praises his client, whose 'passion, his commitment, his objectives, his spirit has been his testament for a brighter Kenyan future' and who worked for a 'united Kenya, marching forward not as a disparate group of ethnic communities, but as one people under one flag.'

Khan goes on to describe there was 'a lot of press' and a bit of 'excitement' earlier at the start of the trial, because indeed, it is for the 'first time ever in the annals of international criminal law that a serving head of state and deputy head of state have voluntarily, whilst in office, come before the court and bowed his head to justice in the expectation that justice will be done.' However, the defence counsel stresses, 'one cannot escape the reality that this investigation has been exceptionally deficient.' Khan predicts the case will be withdrawn or end in a 'not guilty verdict' and will lead to an inquiry into how it was 'that somebody innocent has come before this court to answer charges that will be shown to be patently false.'

In typical Khan sentences he wipes the floor with the OTP. He doesn't point at the current prosecutor Bensouda alone. It is her predecessor Moreno-Ocampo 'that must take an awful lot of blame for the systemic failings of this office that still bedevil the OTP today,' the lawyer says. 'Your Honours, we say that there is a rotten underbelly of this case. That the prosecutor has swallowed hook, line, and sinker, indifferent to the truth, all too eager to latch on to any version, any account, any story that somehow ticks the boxes that we have to tick in relation to putting forward a summons.'

In the break a Kenyan top official tells me that the deputy president pays his lawyers from his own pocket. There are two British lawyers in Ruto's team with the title of 'Queens Counsel': Karim Khan and David Hooper. There is a considerable price tag attached to hiring defence counsel of this calibre. The Kenyan official doesn't want to say how much money is involved, but even a court appointed and paid defence team receives a monthly sum of 33,000 euros in the trial phase. The costs of Khan's top crew will be much higher.

After his opening shots the lawyer discusses a sensitive matter that has become a major problem of these Kenyan trials. 'We do not want witnesses to withdraw,' Khan starts. 'We want witnesses to come and be free to speak to the prosecution and to the defence, to speak the truth. And those that come to this court and speak the truth, are heroes.'

They have nothing to fear, the lawyer stresses. And if witnesses feel threatened, there is always the ICC's protection programme which can bring them into safety, if necessary, abroad.

Then Khan gets to the point he wants to make. The witnesses who think 'there's a foreign court in a foreign land that can be easily deceived, that they can spin a yarn that will entrap an innocent man, should be aware that this court can arrest and detain anybody who seeks to pervert the course of justice. Your Honour, no system of law anywhere in the world can operate with lying witnesses, with a culture where people feel, as a shortcut to a better life, they may think, they can lie.' He adds that the judges 'will need to be exceptionally vigilant in this case to unravel and unmask what we say is a very clear and glaring conspiracy of lies and woeful inadequacies by the OTP.' But an observer notes that his words, which he has been repeating several times, now increasingly start to sound like a threat to deter people from testifying.

On the Bench

Khan performs his tasks as defence lawyer. He will cast doubt about witnesses, calls the case deficient and rotten, and presents his client as an honourable man who could never have been the organiser of violence because he has been a model leader, and who in fact always had been in favour of the ICC. To visualise this positive image Khan shows video clips of 'On The Bench.' In this popular Kenyan TV program, anchorman Jeff Koinange (previously CNN) conducts interviews with famous people. Ruto has been invited numerous times. On the monitors in the public gallery the images appear of two men on a bench surrounded by a lush garden. In one of the first clips Ruto tells interviewer Koinange that the ICC will get all the support it needs.

After having presented two videos Khan continues his tirade. 'What Mr Ocampo did, is latch on to an infected information stream. It was convenient, it was easy – it may even be described as lazy prosecution, lazy investigations – but he didn't have regard to the source of the information,' says the defence counsel, who is famous for his use of metaphors and symbols. The OTP was 'drawn in an ocean of their own making of errors, relying upon a drip of evidence that selectively they have sought to put out, without any regard for the fact that the source of those drops is from a very polluted spring.' In short: 'They've been fed a lie.' Khan says the prosecution wrongly made use of 'a very convenient box of evidence given by Waki.'

The lawyer speaks mostly without notes. Sometimes, the colleague who is always there to support him, Shyamala Alagendra, sticks a piece of paper with instructions on the screen in front of him. The ridiculousness of the accusations against his client, Khan asserts, is shown by the fact that two sisters of Ruto are married with Kikuyus, the ethnic group that is said to be attacked by his network. His own nephews and nieces have Kikuyu names. 'He pays for those childrens' education,' Khan adds. Now would a man like that say: 'All Kikuyus, out! You're no longer wanted! You'll be kicked out! You'll be killed!'? The charges simply aren't logical. 'My submission to you is that you're getting the truth today from us. With the greatest of regret, you're not getting the truth from the prosecution when it comes to the responsibility of William Ruto.'

The defence counsel tells the judges they carry a heavy burden. 'A man's life, his good name, is in your hands.' Again he shows an 'On The Bench' video clip. This time Ruto tells Koinange how the charges weigh on him.

While the cheesy interview is being shown on the screens, a faint ironic smile appears on Bensouda's face. The accused Ruto laughs about himself. The images are shown to point out what a fine man the deputy president is, but unintentionally the clips function also as short theatre scenes that offer some distraction. They lighten the heavy atmosphere in the courtroom. The Kenyan members of parliament, who travelled with Ruto and sit in the public gallery, are amusing themselves with the clips. Every now and then the ambassador bursts into laughter.

With a lot of emphasis anchorman Koinange pronounces his words when he describes Ruto as a victim of the ICC. 'You are being dragged through the mud,' he says.

'That is an understatement, Jeff,' Ruto answers.

In case anyone still has any doubts about his client, defence counsel Khan points out: Jeff Koinange is a Kikuyu. Just like Ruto's brothers-in-law, the anchor belongs to the ethnic group that, according to the analysis of the prosecutor, has been the target of the supposed network. The OTP's allegations against Khan's client are not only unlikely, but it is a 'false, concocted case,' the lawyer says.

It is counsel's job to present his client in a most favourable way. There is, however, also another story to tell. During some of the bench-talks with Koinange, Ruto is still minister of higher education. But he lost that post after corruption accusations. There were other scandals as well in which his name featured. In fact, just before the start of the ICC trial, Ruto had faced a case before the national courts in which he was accused of land-grabbing. The 70-year old farmer Adrian Muteshi was a victim of the post-election violence. Early 2014 he had fled his farm and land in Uasin Gishu County, one of the worst hit areas. He lost his possessions, that finally ended up in the hands of no one else but William Ruto. Muteshi had the courage to start a court case. The case went up to the High Court, which concluded that Ruto could not present the official documents showing he had lawfully purchased the property. The judges ruled he had acquired the land fraudulently. Ruto was ordered to surrender the land to the farmer and to pay the victim 5 million shilling (42,000 euros) in compensation.[46]

46   'Kenya deputy president loses case linked to poll violence,' Reuters, 28 June 2013.

And so on 28 June 2013 Ruto lost a case that linked him in another unsavoury way to the same violence for which he was being prosecuted at the ICC as an organiser, and from which he had benefitted personally. These are facts that Khan understandably prefers to leave out of his plea.

The Christian broadcaster

The next day it's the other defence team's turn. Broadcaster Joshua Sang, wearing a dark pin-striped suit, is sitting behind his lawyers. 'My client, Mr Sang, does not belong to this court. Indeed, this is because he never belonged, as alleged, to any network,' counsel Joseph Kipchumba Kigen-Katwa kicks off.[47] 'He actually neither incited, nor co-ordinated violence, nor advertised for meetings,' explains the Kenyan lawyer who is very close to the deputy president. In fact, he recently defended Ruto during the land-grabbing case. The lawyer has a calm style, and is in an almost imperceptible manner, sharp in his comments.

To show that Sang is a true man of peace, Kigen-Katwa plays an audio recording from a radio broadcast. When the appeal, made in a local language, has sounded through the courtroom, the lawyer translates the words his client spoke at the time addressing his audience: 'Greetings, Kalenjins, wherever you are today. I would like to proclaim to you Kalenjin listeners a message of peace. That is: Kenya is crying for peace. Everyone is crying for peace. A little child is crying for peace. An adult is crying for peace. A woman is crying for peace. A man is crying for peace. A grandfather is crying for peace. So is a grandmother. Everyone is crying for peace.'

After he has, with a handkerchief, wiped the perspiration from his face, Kigen-Katwa says there is not a shred of evidence against his client. When the prosecution started investigations in Kenya, the office allowed itself to be misled by 'some Kenyan political brokers', 'zealous civil societies' and 'some ethnic-minded individuals who wished to use the ICC to shape Kenya's political future.' These 'opportunists' seized 'the chance to use the ICC process for their own purposes,' the lawyer argues. He blames NGOs of joining in. 'In their desperate desire for donor funding, and strive to find ways to make themselves relevant, [they] exploited the difficult

---

47   Official transcript, 11 September 2013.

situation of victims, and took it upon themselves to protect prosecution witnesses.'

During a press conference human rights activists had explained that their Kenyan colleagues had decided to stay away from the opening of the Ruto & Sang trial. The pressure had been too big. Later a Kenyan journalist would explain to me that in Kenya 'human rights organisations are being accused of working together with the ICC's prosecutor and to have passed on incriminating information about the suspects.' The hostile climate in Kenya against human rights activists, potential witnesses and sympathisers of the ICC was described a few weeks later by Human Rights Watch.[48]

In its report 'Rights defenders under attack' the organisation wrote that a gang had threatened to burn down the house of Maina Kiai, the UN special rapporteur on rights to freedom of assembly and association and former chairman of the official Kenya National Commission on Human Rights (KNCHR), after he was falsely accused of being one of the witnesses against ICC suspect Kenyatta.

Other people were targeted as well. Pro-government bloggers had for instance spread the false news that a certain Rahab Muthoni Kagiri would be testifying against Ruto and published her photo. As a result the woman received death threats and had to go into hiding.

Dennis Itumbi, director of digital communication in the office of the Kenyan president, is named as one of the persons who 'singled out people' such as Kiai on social media. In March 2013 he had 'posted on his personal website a chart of civil society leaders and opposition figures he described as the "evil society" for supporting the ICC,' HRW wrote. (When still a blogger, Itumbi was arrested in 2012 by Kenyan authorities and detained for four days for allegedly hacking an ICC email account and leaking documents.[49] Later he would acquire the important official communications position, but was sacked from that job in June 2016.[50]) HRW described a climate of increasing hostility, which even led to the killing of two human rights activists. While calling upon the authorities to investigate these crimes, the organisation noted that 'Kenya's leaders have failed to prevent – and at times encouraged – hostility toward

48   'Kenya: Rights Defenders Under Attack,' Human Rights Watch, 4 October 2013.
49   'Itumbi wants compensation for 2012 arrest over leaked ICC documents,' Nation, 9 June 2015.
50   'Why members of Uhuru's press team were suspended,' Nation, 30 June 2016.

activists.' This was in line with their previous attitude as Ruto, Kenyatta and 'allied bloggers began to attack civil society soon after the ICC issued its summons for the two men to appear in The Hague in December 2010,' HRW wrote.

In court, defence counsel Kigen-Katwa states that the prosecution did not properly check the motives of its own witnesses, whose 'personal integrity and truthfulness is in question.' Mockingly he refers to their 'superhuman characteristics of being omnipresent and having infinite resources.' He explains that in their statements they 'claim to have travelled extensively to all meetings and rallies' of the alleged criminal network. Apparently these witnesses 'have access to cameras, videos, video equipment, they can use guns, bows, arrows, and seem to listen to Sang's radio programme on Kass FM, despite having expressed disapproval, and on a full-time basis.' This is 'unrealistic,' says the lawyer. In other words, such witnesses are simply unreliable. Again Kigen-Katwa wipes off the sweat from his face. He has started to speak so fast that the judges ask him to slow down, otherwise the interpreters can't keep up with him.

Kigen-Katwa sharply criticizes the proposition that the network used Kalenjin rituals and structures. The lawyer rejects the OTP's analysis that, for instance, traditional circumcision ceremonies were used to initiate youngsters to become warriors, to train them in using arrows and bows, and to follow orders. He denounces this suggested link between Kalenjin traditions and the violence. 'It appears that one becomes a criminal by virtue of being an African Kalenjin. The prosecution has put sinister spin on all aspects of Kalenjin culture.' And he adds that 'what is on trial are not individuals. It is actually a community and its culture.' The quote will be carried by Kenyan media in big headlines.

Sang simply made a radio programme, Kigen-Katwa says. He used typical Kalenjin-proverbs, words and metaphors. 'Such colour to language exists in all cultures.' Sang's expressions have been 'woefully misinterpreted' by the prosecution and have wrongfully been given 'criminal meaning.'

And then one more point. When the violence had reached its climax there was a ban on live broadcasts. How could Sang then have incited on the radio, advertised for planning meetings and co-ordinated violence? 'How could he remain un-arrested and unnoticed?' the lawyer notes. Were the Kenyan police, the criminal investigations department, the national security intelligence service and administration officials 'deaf to his words and unable to stop him?' Kigen-Katwa wonders, before giving his explanation. Sang was not arrested, because there was no reason to do so. The radio journalist is a 'confident Christian', who opposes violence, who was just a junior staff member at the radio and who 'not only preached peace, but mobilised for peace.' Kigen-Katwa states: 'This trial is an insult to the Kenyan government, the Kenyan people, the Kenyan institutions, the Kenyan judiciary and Africa as a whole.'

Seven minutes

When he has almost reached the end of his opening statements the lawyer asks whether his client can say a few words.

'How long would this take?' presiding judge Eboe-Osuji asks.

Kigen-Katwa: 'It should not take more than seven minutes, your Honours.'

Eboe-Osuji: 'You may proceed.'

But prosecutor Steynberg is on his feet: 'I beg your pardon, your Honours. Before we continue with this, I don't recall that my learned friend notified me that the accused would be making statements at this time. Was this discussed in any of the status conferences? Perhaps I might have missed it.'

Eboe-Osuji: 'Is that an objection from you then?'

Steynberg: 'It is, your Honours.'

Eboe-Osuji: 'Mr Kigen-Katwa.'

Kigen-Katwa: 'Your Honour, our recollection is that we were allocated two hours. How would we spend our two hours was up to us and it included the window to have our clients speak. Your Honour, there was no indication that we needed to issue any notice to anybody.'

Judge Eboe-Osuji: 'Fair enough. You may proceed. Mr Sang may make the seven-minute statement.'

Sang is rising from his chair and starts to explain how his life has been affected by the trial. 'I've never stood before any court because I am a law-abiding person. I've lived my life as a Christian, with all the Christian values,' he says. It had been his dream to become a radio broadcaster. A dream that became true. After he had worked for two Christian radio stations he made the transfer to Kass FM, where he is to have made his alleged inflammatory statements. But because of the charges against him, he had to resign. The ICC case ruined his life.

He goes on to explain that it is simply inconceivable that he would have called people to join a criminal network and to attack. During the dramatic days of the violence he had been in Nairobi, but his family was in Eldoret, some three hundred kilometres northwest of the capital city, where the violence had been particularly vicious. The broadcaster questions the logic of the prosecutor's case. Would 'a foolish Arap Sang' be directing attacks on Kikuyus, Kisiis and Kambas at the heart of Eldoret, where his wife and two young children are 'living in a Kikuyu house?' Rhetorically he asks: 'Would I be so silly, so stupid, not to be concerned about my family?' Of course not, Sang adds. 'I'm a caring father and husband. I couldn't do that.'

After the address his lawyer Kigen-Katwa takes over and concludes that Sang is 'innocent' and 'it is an insult to the intentions of the Rome Statute to have presented him to this trial.'

The opening statements are over. In the next phase the witnesses will testify. This most crucial part of the trial can last for months or even years. The OTP's trial lawyer Steynberg gets up from his chair and makes objections to the way the defence has characterized the trial. This case is not about 'ethnic hatred' or indicting the Kalenjin and their traditions, he explains, but about 'a thirst for power' and 'exploiting existing tensions' between groups. 'So the fact that his sisters may be married to a Kikuyu or that he may have had Kikuyu running partners in subsequent ...'

Judge Eboe-Osuji: 'I must stop you on that. This is a matter you can litigate in the course of the case.'

Steynberg: 'As the court pleases, your Honours.' Then he says: 'The first witness is en route.' The woman will have to be familiarised with the court and won't be able to testify before next week. Right at the start the trial is already delayed. The reason why the OTP doesn't have several witnesses ready to testify at the beginning of the case is disclosed by defence counsel Khan: 'The first three witnesses have withdrawn.'

The first witness

Ssst ssst sssssst. Several people are warning the others that the judges are entering the courtroom. It is 17 September 2013. On the first row of the public gallery the wife and daughter of Ruto and the Kenyan ambassador to the Netherlands have taken their places, with, next to them, members of parliament, senators and diplomats from Kenya. The hearing has hardly started before the blinds go down, blocking their view of the courtroom. The sound is also switched off. 'Is this justice in Europe?' a Kenyan MP shouts from the last row. When I turn around to ask him why he is so angry, clearly on purpose, he looks right past me. I repeat my question. Then he begins to speak, but in a Kenyan language that I don't understand. His colleagues think it is utterly funny that he is making a fool of me. They double up with laughter.

When the blinds go up again, two parts in the middle are kept down. Behind these broad strips functioning as a screen, combined with extra curtains on the sides, witness P-536, whose identity has to remain secret for the public, has been seated. But Khan says he can't see her at all, and asks if the curtain could 'be put back a couple of inches.'[51] Judge Eboe-Osuji suggests he switches places with one of his teammates. But the lawyer insists that won't help because his colleagues also might want to put questions to the witness. 'If it's not possible, I'll just crane my neck,' the lawyer says. Eboe-Osuji: 'Thank you for your understanding, for offering to crane your neck, if need be. It seems to be inconvenient for the curtain to be moved back any further than it is, from what I understand.' Jokingly he adds: 'There are times when we have to make these sacrifices, Mr Khan.'

The judge then takes off his large, heavy and rather intimidating glasses. It gives his face a much friendlier impression. That is exactly the purpose. In this way he tries to put the witness at ease, while giving her instructions. Eboe-Osuji speaks slowly to be clear. The judge tells the witness that she will have to listen carefully to the questions the prosecution, defence and the legal representative of victims will put to her. 'Do not try to guess at an answer you do not know,' he says.

Lawyer Khan is standing on his feet and opens his microphone: 'I think it's only fair to the witness that the court informs her that the court has clear powers to look into false evidence. Your Honour, I think it's ....' But Eboe-Osuji cuts him short: 'I'll stop you right there.' The lawyer tries to finish his phrase, but the judge says: 'Excuse me, Mr Khan, please don't. Thank you. I need you to not proceed along that line.'

'I'm grateful,' Khan answers politely.

'Thank you,' the judge replies.

Then Steynberg asks: 'May I proceed, your Honour?'

'Yes,' Eboe-Osuji answers, though it will not be the end of the issue of false testimony.

---

51   Official transcript, 17 September 2013.

'Good morning, madam witness,' says Steynberg, a man with a grey beard and inconspicuous glasses. He is an experienced South African prosecutor who managed complex organised crime and corruption cases in his own country. On the screens in the public gallery the woman's face is being projected in pixelated form – tiny moving blocks that make her unrecognizable and protect her identity. The only thing that is clear, is that she is wearing something dark. Through their headphones, which visitors use to hear what's being said inside the courtroom and to receive translations, the witness' voice sounds distorted.

'Sorry, Mr Steynberg, I've got to stop. This is my fault, not yours, my fault,' Eboe-Osuji interrupts the prosecutor. The judge has forgotten to administer the oath. A few moments later the court officer reads the words repeated by the witness, who speaks Swahili: 'I solemnly declare that I will tell the truth, the whole truth, and nothing but the truth.' When that is done Steynberg can proceed, although he almost immediately asks the judges to turn off the sound to the public gallery so he can go through the witness' personal details.

When the sound is back on, the Kenyan woman starts explaining that the village of Kiambaa, which will be at the epicentre of her testimony, is seven miles from Eldoret.

But then defence lawyer Khan again raises the issue of false testimony. He says that in other trials witnesses have been warned by judges that it is an offence to lie in court and that they even can be imprisoned. Eboe-Osuji asks the witness to remove her earpiece so she won't be able to follow the debate and then explains: 'I do not want to create an intimidating atmosphere for a witness who's testifying.' Such a warning about lies and punishments 'looms large in their mind when they testify,' he says, adding that the oath is sufficient to remind witnesses of their obligation to tell the truth.

Briefly the testimony resumes with the witness telling how the house of her parents was burned down on 30 December 2007. But then there appears to be a technical problem with the voice distortion. It is also 11 o'clock – time for the coffee break.

When the hearing resumes Eboe-Osuji repeats that it is not necessary for the judges to tell a witness that it is an offence to lie in court, as they have been informed about this earlier during their preparations. Khan however suggests that the prosecution should make 'a short pro forma document' that a witness needs to sign on 'every' occasion. 'That would also provide independent documentary evidence that the witness has been informed, clearly and unequivocally, that not only should they tell the truth, but that it is a criminal offence to perjure oneself that may result in imprisonment.'

But Ebou-Osuji says 'the matter' should not be overstretched. Khan is not giving up though. 'Your Honour, it is one thing to be mistaken, to have a hazy recollection. It's quite another to deliberately come and tell lies to the court.'

The judge thinks it is enough, stops Khan and calls in the witness. By now it is noon. In a friendly manner Eboe-Osuji will tell her that lying is an offence. 'Again, please bear in mind that the idea is not that we are suspecting you of not having told the truth or we are suspecting you of coming here to not tell the truth.' It is simply that the rules prescribe that a witness should be informed about this matter, Eboe-Osuji explains, somewhat meeting the objections made by the defence.

Blue jerrycan

Finally the witness can continue her testimony. After Kalenjin youth had attacked the place where her parents lived, she had fled with three of her children and one adult family member to the Kenya Assemblies of God church in Kiambaa. A church that was made of wooden planks and mud on the inside. The roof consisted of corrugated iron sheets. Some two thousand people had sought refuge in the building. When the prosecution asks her what happened when she woke up in the morning of 1 January 2008, the little blocks on the monitor are moving fast. The memories trigger intense emotions. Next to me in the public gallery there is the sound of scornful laughter from Kenyan politicians as they listen to her evidence.

A massive group of a thousand Kalenjin attackers were coming closer to the church from two sides, the witness tells. They were singing. They carried machetes, axes and sticks. 'Most of them were wearing clothing of a khaki colour, while others tied pieces of cloth around their heads,' the witness explains. Their faces were covered with white clay to make them unrecognizable, she says, while her words stir agitation at the public gallery.

Through the holes in a church window the witness saw a man – a local ODM candidate – carrying a blue jerrycan with petrol. 'The church was set alight,' she tells the court. 'The mattresses were burnt and the port was barricaded with bicycles, and then later we were all trying to find a way to escape.' She took one of her children and in a desperate attempt to save the kid, she threw the child out of the window.

Steynberg looks at her and then refers to the judges: 'Your Honour, the witness seems to be visibly upset. We are about to get to a particularly sensitive area of the evidence. I see it is ten minutes before the scheduled adjournment. I wonder whether either we could take a short break so the witness may compose herself.'

Eboe-Osuji also sees she is 'emotionally overcome' and agrees to break. When the hearing is resumed after lunch, he explains to her that the judges fully understand how difficult it is for her to talk about these experiences, but that the questions put to her are necessary 'to help us find out the truth in this matter.'

Responding to questions of the prosecutor, the woman tells how people were trying to get out of the burning building, but were falling over bicycles that were lumped together by the attackers obstructing their escape. Arriving at that traumatic episode, the witness seems to be crying and reaching for tissues next to her. 'When someone would try to leave the church, they would grab the person and push them back in,' the witness tells, explaining that later the women and children were ordered out.

The visitors in the public gallery protest again, when the prosecutor asks for a private session because he wants to discuss matters that might reveal the identity of the witness. During fifteen minutes the sound is switched off. When it is back on and her distorted voice can be heard over the headphones, the witness is continuing her testimony. 'When I left the church and when I was told that the children had been put back in, I just became mad, as if I was mad.' She doesn't offer further explanations, but describes how she saw the attackers holding a woman. 'It's difficult to tell because this was a woman whom I know. She was taken by her legs, one leg on one side, another on the other side, she was raped.' In despair P-536 called a 'notable person', hoping he could stop the violence. But it would all go so very wrong. When the man arrived he was struck with an axe on his neck and injured with spears.

In the midst of the mayhem the witness grew terribly worried about her brother, who was hiding near a fence. He tried to escape, but in vain. He was shot with an arrow and fell amongst the angry crowd. 'When I saw that, I did all I could to save him,' the witness tells. 'I took off all my clothing and there I stood entirely naked,' she says with a big sigh.

'Are you all right to continue, madam witness?' Steynberg asks her.

'Yes, I can keep on going,' the woman replies.

'Thank you very much. Can you explain to the court why it is that you decided to take off all your clothes?'

'First of all, you see, in the Kalenjin custom or way of doing things, when a woman takes off her clothes it is as if – it is as – it is like a curse,' she says.

While at the public gallery visitors burst into laughter, the prosecutor encourages her to continue her statement. 'My purpose was to save my brother's life,' she explains.

The witness succeeded in her attempt. The attackers shoved her brother at her and said: 'Take your trash away.' He was in a very bad condition. 'Someone had shot an arrow at him and it was lodged in the nape of his neck, the throat. You see, his head and his neck were nearly separated.' Finally she managed to find a shortcut through the forest to the road, where a pick-up truck stopped. The driver, who happened to be a Kalenjin, offered help. They reached a hospital. Although doctors would save her brother's life, dozens of people would die in the church incident. When the prosecutor requests again for a private session, I ask the Kenyan politicians why they are laughing all the time. 'The story is not practical,' says a female MP. 'It is war. Would you then stay in such a terrible place, while you have thrown your child through the window, while you have seen how a woman is being raped, a man is killed with a spear and your brother is having an arrow in his body? And then you decide to take off your clothes? Has she been through all this? It just doesn't make sense.' Another politician adds: 'If I had been that woman, after witnessing the rape, I would have fled immediately instead of hanging around at that place.' Behind me an agitated voice is saying: 'The story is made up.' But then the guard is walking towards us. 'You will have to be quiet, otherwise we will have to evacuate the public gallery. If you want to talk you will have to go downstairs, to the lobby.' After that reprimand the audience remains silent and looks at the soundless spectacle in the courtroom, where, not much later, the hearing ends.

Identity disclosed

The next morning a large group of Kenyans is standing on the stairs to the main entrance of the ICC, waiting for the arrival of the two suspects. The Kenyan politicians and media amuse themselves by taking group pictures. A few metres away from the crowd, defence counsel Khan and two members of his team are ready to welcome their client. When four black luxury cars arrive, the crowd rushes to the road. With a broad smile, deputy president Ruto gets out from the vehicle. He is surrounded by politicians, supporters and journalists. After the first greetings, the Kenyans grab each other's hands to form a large circle. Soon a prayer rises up from the pavement. 'Protect us from evil,' they pray. After this biblical call Ruto climbs the stairs and proceeds with his lawyers to the court's revolving main door.

Meanwhile the supporters hurry to the public entrance around the corner. With their cameras in their hands Kenyan TV journalists run ahead of the crowd to be able to get a nice shot of the arriving politicians.

The atmosphere in the public gallery on the second day of the witness testimony resembles that of a lively café, but without the drinks and foods. Mrs Ruto, who made a subdued impression during earlier hearings but is now dressed in a golden coloured skirt suit, is getting up from her seat and stretches herself. Visitors are exchanging pieces of news. There are big salvoes of laughter. A Kenyan wearing large sunglasses and a tight fitting suit that makes him look like a rapper, walks towards his colleagues and starts to shake their hands. 'Why don't they just show the witness? Why would you hide your identity if you tell the truth? If you tell the truth, you will be protected by the truth,' the woman next to me starts complaining. Her odour is that of excellent perfume. Around her neck she is wearing a golden chain combined with a second necklace of massive pearls that look like huge drops. Golden earrings complete the jewellery outfit. When I suggest that security measures aren't just in place for the witness, but also to protect her family, the politician cries: 'But we know who she is!'

It is the talk of the day. While the court has taken every effort to protect her identity, Kenyan blogs and media managed to trace the name of the witness. Her picture circulates on the Internet.

In the media centre of the court I log on to the worldwide web to try to find out who leaked the name of the witness. Kenya has a vibrant media landscape. While Congolese journalists are rarely able to come to The

Hague to report on the cases at the ICC against militia leaders that have been terrorizing the population, the Kenyan trial is directly covered from the court by a large group of journalists. At home developments are closely followed by a massive number of media and blogs. One source that carries the name of the witness is the Kenya Daily Post, a site that is fighting the 'neo-colonial' ICC and offers a mix of news, scandal and gossip. When I continue surfing, I stumble upon the tumult around an anchorman at Citizen TV, who's accused of tweeting the identity of the witness. The presenter says however that his account has been hacked and that he has nothing to do with revealing the woman's name.

A Kenyan journalist approaches me and says that emotions among the politicians escorting Ruto to the ICC, are running high. The MPs are fed up with all the private and closed sessions. This could get out of hand, she explains. It would be good if a person from the ICC could come and start to give some explanations. She then contacts the court's press officers and within an hour there's a solution. The Kenyan group is invited to a large room on the ground floor. After a few minutes the registrar, Herman von Hebel, walks in. He's been given the unhappy task to inform the Kenyans and to try to assuage the dissatisfaction. Several supporters continue to wear their baseball caps in national colours during his talk.

'I understand your frustration,' starts Von Hebel, a Dutch man wearing huge spectacles as a kind of trademark. 'If I would come to a courtroom to find out that a hearing will take place behind closed doors, I would be annoyed as well. Especially if I had come all the way from Kenya. But the witness needs to be protected as well. It is hard for me to predict how often this will happen, but closed and private sessions will take place regularly.' A female parliamentarian wants to know: 'If a witness lies, in a sensitive case, how can this be established as a lie?' Von Hebel: 'If a witness says something about which the defence has doubts whether it is true or not, the lawyers have the right to question the witness about it and to do their own investigations.' But the registrar also warns: 'Let's not draw conclusions right now after the first day of the trial, that will continue for a long time.' 'My problem is,' says a woman, 'that witnesses are being pampered here. If they sneeze only once, then the reaction is immediately: 'Ohhh here is a handkerchief.' Her remark is well received by her compatriots, who are chuckling and laughing. But Von Hebel disagrees. The court takes care of the witnesses of the prosecutor, and equally looks after defence witnesses.

While grumbling, a politician walks away. 'That witness tells lies. The baby she threw through the window, was not her own child. They tear Kenya apart with these trials. Ruto and Sang are no criminals. If they are looking for criminals, they should not be with us.'

A remedy for an exceptional situation

The scandal of the disclosure of the identity of the witness is the central matter of the hearing the next morning, 19 September 2013. Witness P-536 has received messages from family members who tell her they are being intimidated, prosecutor Steynberg discloses. Despite these threats the woman is prepared to continue with her testimony, but only if it takes place fully behind closed doors. The defence opposes the idea. 'Your Honour, there's no risk to this witness in our respectful submission,' says Khan, because she has been relocated.[52] He doesn't see 'why the shutters should come down and the hearing put in closed session.' But Nderitu, the legal representative of victims, agrees with the OTP.

The judges withdraw for a few moments. When they are back in court Eboe-Osuji says: 'It is indeed an exemplary act of courage on the part of this witness that she wants to continue with her testimony undeterred. It shows that the spirit of justice marches on in this case.' He is impressed by her bravery and that of other witnesses. 'That is the only way that we can hope to get at the truth in this case.' The judges decide that the rest of her testimony will be in closed session. Sharply Eboe-Osuji points out there have not only been attempts to intimidate her by revealing her identity, but also 'by calling her extremely unkind names and addressing other manner of threatening language against this witness.' After this statement the sound to the public gallery is turned off. The Kenyans are leaving. Silence reigns when the seats have been flipped up. In the empty space Ruto's wife and daughter, the Kenyan ambassador and a fourth woman are the only ones staying. In the salutary quietness suddenly the sound of the air conditioning becomes audible.

Downstairs in the lobby the Kenyan supporters are having a heated discussion. After a few minutes the group sets itself in motion. They have decided to return to the public gallery. 'To support our deputy president,' one supporter explains.

---

52   Official transcript, 19 September 2013.

Terror attack in a shopping mall

During the weekend Ruto doesn't fly back to Kenya. He stays in The Hague, where he will hear the dreadful news. Around noon that Saturday morning, 21 September, a group of terrorists armed with guns and hand grenades have attacked the fancy Westgate Mall in Nairobi. A death squad of Al Shabaab, a violent jihadi group operating in East Africa, is hunting down personnel, visitors and shoppers, many of whom are wealthy Kenyans and expats. National security forces surround the complex, while attackers are causing a bloodbath inside. Information about what is taking place inside remains scarce. Kenyan authorities say a group of ten to fifteen terrorists have raided the mall. But video clips disclosed later, show just four men. There are also reports about soldiers of the Kenyan army being involved in looting shops. At least 67 people will lose their lives during the onslaught.

The terror attack is still ongoing when on Monday morning at half past eight the three judges leading the Ruto & Sang trial organise a special hearing at the ICC. 'The chamber expresses its deepest sympathy to the victims, their families and friends and to all Kenyans in this most difficult time,' Eboe-Osuji says before allowing Ruto's lawyer to speak.[53] After Khan expresses his condolences, he says that his client asks the court permission to go home. 'The world would have found it intolerable if the president and vice president of the United States were not in the country after 9/11. Well, this is Kenya's 9/11. It is absolutely essential for law and order, for assisting the president to resolve the situation, to prevent recurrences, to give confidence and security and succour to the families of those that have lost loved ones that the deputy president returns home.' Trial lawyer Steynberg also expresses his sympathy with the Kenyan people. He agrees that Ruto needs to be in Kenya. The Kenyan legal representative of victims doesn't have objections either. 'It's a matter that's really ...' Nderitu says. But then his voice lets him down. He is incapable of continuing to speak. For Nderitu the dreadful incident must bring back terrible memories of fifteen years ago when he himself was a victim of the attack with a truck bomb on the American embassy in Nairobi, carried out by jihadis, which killed about two hundred people. Judge Eboe-Osuji addresses him: 'I'm sorry, I see you are overcome as well,

---

53   Official transcript, 23 September 2013

Mr Nderitu, with emotion and that's totally understandable.' Khan quickly intervenes by saying there is a flight at eleven o' clock his client would like to get.

The judge looks at Ruto and tells him that the chamber gives the deputy president permission to be absent from the trial 'for one week only.' The hearing is closed.

Before he travels however, Ruto finds time for a speech. At the steps, right in front of the main entrance of the ICC, flanked by the lead counsels of the two defence teams, the deputy president addresses the Kenyan media. Words matter, especially in such circumstances. After having expressed his sympathy with the victims, he turns the attention to himself. While cameras are clicking and recording, Ruto says: 'It is really unfortunate that this terrorists' attack was timed to coincide with my presence here at the Hague and the visit by his excellency the president of Kenya to New York for the UN general assembly. Meaning that both the president and myself would not have been in the country.' And so Ruto implicitly links the terrorist assault to the agendas of both leaders, and suggests how unfortunate his presence at the ICC has been.

A video clip on YouTube shows how he walks towards an expensive black car and steps in. This time Dutch policemen on motorbikes apparently are provided. They clear the road for the vehicle that speeds off. That same evening the deputy president is landing at the airport of Nairobi.

The Barasa affair

The next morning the Kenyan political gossip site Daily Post not only puts out stories about the dreadful attacks. The blog also carries a remarkable item: ICC judges have issued an arrest warrant against a Kenyan journalist. A certain Walter Osapiri Barasa, who used to write for the newspapers 'The Nation' and the 'People Daily', is accused of intimidating witnesses. It is striking that social media already report the notice while it is still confidential. It will take a week before the court officially announces on 2 October that indeed, since two months, Barasa is wanted by the ICC.[54]

For the first time the court is prosecuting a person for intimidating and bribing witnesses. Or in legal terms: offences against the administration

---

54   Warrant of arrest for Walter Osapiri Barasa, ICC, 2 August 2013.

of justice. Barasa is no stranger to the court. He has been working as an 'intermediary' for the ICC prosecution: a local person who, for instance, contacts witnesses on their behalf. It is not the first time 'intermediaries' have proved to be a weak link.

According to the arrest warrant the first witness P-536, whose identity was illegally disclosed, was one of Barasa's victims. He is suspected of having offered money to the woman and her husband when they stayed in the Ugandan capital Kampala and to have pressured her to withdraw from the trial against Ruto. Similar incidents happened to two other witnesses. Sums of money, amounting to even fifteen thousand euros, have been offered.

In the media, Barasa defends himself with force. In a personal account published on a website, apparently several days before the arrest warrant was made public, the intermediary explains he was approached by ICC's prosecution in 2012.[55] One of his activities had been to hand over a temporary passport to a Kenyan woman so she could travel to Uganda. Here she would be questioned by investigators. According to Barasa's account, the ICC prosecution team had told her to say that she had been a cook at the home of a Kenyan politician where she had witnessed planning meetings for the assault on the Kiambaa church. But when Barasa questioned her about her statement, she allegedly told him it was not true. She had previously been a cook, but not at the time of the planning meetings and violence, as she was a casual worker during those days, planting tree seedlings and harvesting maize.

Barasa claims in this account that ICC investigators had asked the witness to lie. After some time he received calls from the woman from Uganda, Burundi and the Democratic Republic of the Congo (DRC) – where she, for her safety, apparently had been transferred to by the court. The woman was complaining about her living conditions. Barasa writes he did not want to be in contact with her, but she kept stalking him. This woman, so he claims in his account, had been no one other than witness P-536.

In the end, there was a meeting between the Kenyan journalist and ICC investigators on 15 September 2013, according to Barasa. They allegedly accused him of switching sides, from the prosecution to the accused

---

55 'Walter Barasa statement on ICC arrest warrant,' 22 September 2013.

deputy president, and of coercing witnesses. He was given one more chance by his ICC contacts, but only if he himself was willing to testify against Ruto. In that case he would be flown out of Kenya that same evening as his life might be in danger. The Kenyan journalist claims he refused the deal. And so the arrest warrant was issued. If found guilty of intimidating or bribing witnesses, the ICC can punish the Kenyan journalist/intermediary with a fine and/or a prison sentence with a maximum of five years.

Barasa has still not faced up to the allegations by the ICC. He has taken his case to the Kenyan High Court to prevent his transfer. And even though Kenyan judges have agreed he can be handed over, new legal procedures have been initiated to block the surrender.

He would not remain the only person to be accused of such offences. Similar cases would follow. Things would get very murky in both the Ruto & Sang case and the proceedings against president Kenyatta.

The UN Security Council

On the international stage the Kenyan cases continue to stir emotions as well. During the weekend of 11-12 October 2013, the African Union (AU) is holding a meeting in the Ethiopian capital Addis Ababa, dedicated to the continent's relationship with the ICC. Addressing his fellow heads of state, Kenyan president Kenyatta lashed out at the court, accusing it of interference in domestic affairs and of insulting hard fought African sovereignty. 'The ICC has been reduced into a painfully farcical pantomime, a travesty that adds insult to the injury of victims. It stopped being the home of justice the day it became the toy of declining imperial powers,' Kenyatta fulminated.[56]

In a resolution, the delegations declare that sitting African heads of state and other senior officials enjoy immunity. No international court or tribunal has the right to prosecute them during their term in office, the AU said. The organisation therefore expressed its 'concern on the politicization and misuse of indictments against African leaders by the ICC.'[57] The organisation decided to compose a contact group to discuss

---

56 'African Union urges ICC to defer Uhuru Kenyatta case,' BBC, 12 October 2013.
57 Decisions and declarations. Extraordinary session of the Assembly of the African Union, 12 October 2013, Addis Ababa, Ethiopia

with the UN Security Council in New York the relation between the continent and the ICC, including a 'deferral' – the postponement of the trials against Kenyatta and Ruto (and the Sudan cases). It called upon the Kenyan government to send a letter to the council requesting that the trials are suspended. The reason? Kenya is 'a frontline state in the fight against terrorism,' the African states' organisation concluded. Trials would keep the two leaders from their real work – ruling the country – and endanger national and international security, the AU argued.

It is a logical step. The Security Council has the power to have ICC cases postponed if they endanger international security. Article 16 of the Rome Statute says: 'No investigation or prosecution may be commenced or proceeded with (…) for a period of 12 months after the Security Council, in a resolution adopted under Chapter VII of the Charter of the United Nations, has requested the court to that effect.' This article however applies only to exceptional cases. It is doubtful whether the terror attack on the shopping mall in Nairobi and the participation of Kenyan troops in international peacekeeping missions will meet the criteria and conditions.

15 November 2013, voting day. The Security Council turns out to be seriously divided. Seven members – China, Russia, Togo, Azerbaijan, Rwanda, Morocco and Pakistan – vote for a deferral. The other eight countries – France, USA, UK, Argentina, Guatemala, South Korea, Australia and Luxemburg – abstain. The chance of postponement is crushed. Disappointed, the Kenyan foreign ministry speaks of 'clear cowardice in the face of a critical African matter' and a council that 'humiliated the continent and its leadership.'[58]

Meeting in The Hague

The UN says that actually another international body is better suited to deal with this matter: the ICC's Assembly of States Parties (ASP). The timing is perfect. The annual meeting of the countries that are member of the court is about to start. One expensive car after the other arrives at the World Forum conference centre in The Hague, on 20 November 2013. In the dimmed lights of the auditorium, an exclusive party of ministers, ambassadors, (former) heads of state, top diplomats, court officials and

---

58   Africa fails to get Kenya ICC trials deferred at United Nations, Reuters, 15 November 2013

human rights activists gets together. From a little distance on the podium, the ICC's president, South Korean judge Sang-Hyun Song, watches how the distinguished guests greet each other. The complete top of the ICC is present. Prosecutor Bensouda and registrar Von Hebel are busy shaking hands.

When it is almost time to start, the delegations proceed to their designated places and take a seat behind the boards with the names of their countries. The meeting, which will last for a week, starts with a minute's silence for prayer or meditation. A tall African, distinguished elder statesman, Abdou Diouf is the first speaker. It is a masterly move by the organisation. There might be much anger on the African continent, but the former president of Senegal is still a devoted supporter of the ICC. His country was the first to ratify the Rome Statute. In his speech Diouf praises the court as a 'historical step' forwards in the fight against international crimes.

The delegates each take their turn to make a short statement. Frans Timmermans, the then minister of foreign affairs of The Netherlands, expresses his trust in the 'strong preventive' influence of the court. Leaders who commit international crimes must understand they can be prosecuted. 'Be aware, otherwise one can end up in The Hague,' Timmermans warns.

On the second day the members have organised, at the request of the African Union, a special programme: an open discussion about the prosecution of heads of state and government leaders and the consequences for peace, stability and reconciliation. While one top official after the other takes the floor, it becomes clear that quite a number of countries are calling for flexibility. Not that delegations go on a full campaign for immunity for heads of state, but the basic principle that no one is above the law and high officials can be prosecuted by the ICC if there are serious indications that they are implicated in international crimes, feels less firmly grounded than when the Rome Statute was adopted in 1998.

During this annual meeting Nairobi gets its way with regards to one subject. The member states agree with a change to the ICC's Rules of Procedures and Evidence. Rule 134-quater says that an accused who is subject to a summons to appear, but fulfils 'extraordinary public duties at the highest national level,' may request the judges 'to be excused and to be represented by counsel only.' The victory might actually not be that significant since the judges had already been asked to excuse deputy president Ruto and president Kenyatta from attending every session of their trials. The judges had decided that both leaders would only have to be present during important hearings such as the start and end of the trial, the verdict and other special sessions. However, the appeals chamber thought that their colleagues had been too lenient in their decision.[59]

On the other hand, the member states also adopt a text change that is less favourable to the Kenyan suspects, which may have ramifications for arguments in the courtroom about witnesses who change their minds and refuse to testify. The new 'rule 68' permits judges to allow the parties to introduce 'previously recorded audio or video testimony of a witness, or the transcript or other documented evidence of such testimony' in case a witness can't be present in the courtroom because he or she has passed away, has disappeared or has been victim of intimidation, coercion or threats. This rule is seen as a warning not to mess with witnesses. If witnesses change their testimony because they are pressured or no longer testify because they are deceased, the judges can allow earlier statements to become leading evidence.

In the meantime the problems with witnesses in the Ruto & Sang trial are increasing. The prosecutors withdraw an untrustworthy witness. By now there are eight persons who refuse to testify in court or simply don't answer the court's summons. The ones of that group that finally agree to testify, will give their statements through a skype-connection while remaining in Kenya.[60] In their new testimonies many say they had initially been attracted by the advantages the court offers to protected witnesses, but that they had become disappointed because they received less money and services than hoped. That's why they decided to stop cooperating with the court and to withdraw from the case. The repetitions in these new testimonies make them sound like a rehearsed standard answer. It is likely that the judges would want to compare these new testimonies with their original statements.

59   Ruto and Sang case: ICC Appeals Chamber sets criteria for the absence of an accused from trial, ICC press release, 25 October 2013.
60   Decision on Prosecutor's Application for Witness Summonses and resulting Request for State Party Cooperation, ICC, 17 April 2014.

Delay in the Kenyatta trial

At least one thing can be said about the trial against Ruto and Sang: it has started. In contrast, the trial against president Kenyatta has been postponed again and again. On 19 December 2013 there is breaking news. Prosecutor Bensouda announces she doesn't have enough evidence against the Kenyan head of state and therefore has asked the judges for extra time. The reason: huge problems with witnesses.

The most disastrous development for the prosecutor was when a crucial witness, P-12, who was supposed to have given direct evidence that Kenyatta was involved in organising the violence, recently admitted that he had lied. When this witness was questioned for the fifth time by Bensouda's staff, he gave in. He said that, indeed, he hadn't attended himself an important meeting on 30 December 2007 at State House in Nairobi, where Kenyatta was supposed to have participated 'in the organisation and funding of violence that later unfolded against perceived ODM supporters,' the prosecution acknowledges.[61] In reality P-12 hadn't been an eyewitness. He had heard about the meeting from someone else. His statement, which might have contained some elements of truth of what had happened at State House, fell apart.

This was exactly the kind of risk that Kenyatta's lawyers had been pointing at all the time. Several prosecution insider witnesses belonging to a criminal gang, the so-called Mungiki network, which was said to have been paid by Kenyatta and others to fight on behalf of the Kikuyu during the post-election violence, proved unreliable. Already on 10 October 2013 the defence team had requested a permanent stay of proceedings.[62] In their heavily redacted report to the judges, the lawyers painted a picture of crucial Kenyan prosecution witnesses who had been interfering with potential defence witnesses or had otherwise been utterly unreliable providing false evidence. They insist there has been 'a serious and sustained abuse of the process of the current proceedings by a significant prosecution witness and a significant prosecution intermediary, both of whom are responsible for providing the majority of witnesses of fact in this case.'

---

61 Notification of the removal of a witness from the Prosecution's witness list and application for an adjournment of the provisional trial date, OTP, 19 December 2013.
62 Defence Application for a Permanent Stay of the Proceedings due to Abuse of Process, Defence, 10 October 2013.

The defence also explained that prosecution witness P-12 was involved in several attempts to make money from the case. He first offered himself to Kenyatta's lawyers, willing to give exculpatory statements in exchange for money and other benefits. When the defence refused, the witness apparently crossed over to the prosecutor, whom he provided with a 'false incriminatory account.' To the lawyers it is clear – the evidence against their client is simply non-existent. The prosecution 'is presiding over an utterly corrupt and dishonest case that is an affront to justice and amounts to an abuse of process,' the defence said. Now that Bensouda herself had to admit that P-12 had lied, her case has become seriously compromised.

It was not the only witness the prosecution lost. Initially the OTP had indicated it had wanted to call thirty witnesses in the trial against Kenyatta. But in 2013 seven witnesses were withdrawn because they were too scared to testify, had changed their statements or because of other unspecified reasons, writes the International Justice Monitor.[63]

So what went wrong? Did the OTP simply not do its work correctly? Had the prosecutor charged the wrong persons and therefore struggled with evidence and cases? The defence alleges that the investigators believed stories of unreliable and lying witnesses who thought that by participating in a case before the ICC they could improve their lives because the court would protect and take care of them. The prosecution states however that its witnesses are intimidated so heavily that they don't dare to come to give testimony, resulting in the collapse of the case. But could it not be both? Frightened and intimidated witnesses on the one hand, and some calculating and lying witnesses on the other.

Hampering cooperation

The parties are ready and waiting for the judges to enter the courtroom. It is ten o'clock, 7 October 2014. The main theme on the agenda: the cooperation between the OTP and the Kenyan state. Kenya's attorney general, Githu Muigai, has been especially flown in for this session. It is not the first time he is called by the judges. Muigai will prove to be a passionate defender of Kenya's interests. In the benches opposite him sits

---

63 'Prosecutor withdraws seven witnesses in Kenyatta case in past year,' International Justice Monitor, 16 January 2014.

Benjamin Gumpert, the prosecution's trial lawyer who has been leading the Kenyatta case for a year now.

There's a rumour that, after he was appointed in 2013, Gumpert was shocked when he saw the poor evidence against Kenyatta. Witness P-12 was re-interviewed, proven unreliable and taken off the list, which prompted Bensouda to ask for an adjournment of the trial. He is a welcome addition to the atmosphere in the courtroom, having a soothing effect on the tense relationship between the parties. He commands awe and respect with his calm attitude, his control over the multiple files and his strategic insights. His British politeness is razor-sharp.

While searching for evidence during the trial's postponement, the OTP has chosen to intensify its investigations in another direction – in addition to witness statements – but it needs the cooperation of Kenya for that. There is an outstanding request since April 2012 to the Kenyan authorities for eight different categories of materials relating to Kenyatta's conduct: telephone data, bank accounts, tax papers, information on land ownership, vehicle registrations, foreign financial transactions, company shares and reports by the secret service. The judges have given the prosecution and Kenya an extra few months to work out their cooperation issues so that the requested information could become available. This period has now come to an end, hence this status conference. Kenya is being accused of delaying tactics. 'There is a considerable body of material which the prosecution say should have been provided, could have been provided and hasn't been provided,' Gumpert says.[64] The reason the OTP wants to receive these data has to do with the fact that much of the evidence on which it built its case is no longer available. Of the thirty witnesses, only nine are still on the list. They will be able to come forward to give evidence and 'say that they were told by people who approached them to organise violence, that the person who was financing or ultimately coordinating that violence was Mr Kenyatta, and that they would be paid for their work and that they would be protected from the consequences of what they did,' Gumpert explains. The problem for the prosecution is that the statements of these nine witnesses don't provide sufficient evidence against Kenyatta himself.

64   Official transcript, 7 October 2014.

The OTP hopes that the eight categories of data will provide extra support to back up these remaining statements and give a stronger foundation to the case. For this, however, the prosecution has to rely completely on the Kenyan authorities, which have handed over only a small part of the requested items. This information, already in the hands of the prosecution, hasn't resulted in a smoking gun. 'It is fair to say – and I say it openly – that nothing in the 75 pages of material which we have received from the Kenyan government makes the case against Mr Kenyatta any stronger,' Gumpert admits.

That might not mean much, since the OTP hasn't received information and data 'which might be regarded as the truly critical material.' The trial lawyer adds: 'I don't want to rehearse submissions I've made before about the likelihood of somebody who is involved in offences wanting to cover their tracks. But the requests we have made are those which we could best design to uncover Mr Kenyatta's involvement, if there are records which would reveal it.' Thus Gumpert expresses his concern that possible crucial evidence may be withheld.

Judge Kuniko Ozaki asks the trial lawyer whether he wants to ask the Kenyan government 'indefinitely' to handover these materials 'until the cooperation request is fully executed, or do you consider there is or will be a stage at which they are exhausted?' Gumpert: 'That's a hard question.' But indeed, if Kenya remains silent then 'after a reasonable period of time' one has to conclude that the process is 'exhausted.' For now, 'it would appear that we are at a deadlock.' When judge Ozaki asks a clarification of that term, Gumpert responds: 'By that I mean that the Kenyan government is not going to give us what we are asking for and what the chamber has approved our asking for.'

The OTP finds itself with its back against the wall, though it might not yet have completely lost the battle. The hearing today is also about something else: credibility and image. Gumpert says that if the court agrees with the prosecution's arguments 'it should make a finding of non-compliance on the part of the government of Kenya.' With these words he puts the finger on the sore spot, because such a reprimand is exactly what the Kenyan attorney general wants to avoid.

The wrong questions
Judge Ozaki turns to Muigai and asks him: why during the summer was there a 'period of non-communication from the side of the Kenyan

government?' The attorney general quickly explains he hasn't been inactive at all. On the contrary, he sent letters to the Kenyan Registrar of Companies, the Communication Authority, Airtel, Safaricom, the Central Bank of Kenya, the Kenya Revenue Authority, the Ministry of Lands, the National Intelligence Service, the National Transport and Safety Authority. This was all done to comply with the information requests by the prosecution. He prepares himself for the following remark: 'There has been a misconception that by some bureaucratic feat, it is possible for the attorney general sitting in his office ……' But Ozaki stops him there. 'Mr attorney general, please be more focused on my question.'

Muigai explains it has simply been impossible for him to deliver the requested information because the OTP has been asking the wrong questions. Institutions need registration numbers before they can do a search. So the ICC's prosecution would need to send, for instance, the details of a number plate of a motor vehicle. Then the attorney general 'will bring the logbook that tells us who owns that number and I will do it in 72 hours.' But the other way round, searching by name to see how many cars a specific person has, is impossible, Muigai says. The same goes for land ownership and phones. 'If you have a telephone number, we will be able post-2009 to ask the providers to give us the name and the logs of the telephone.'

So the problem lies with the OTP, Muigai argues. Without the correct input, the Kenyan institutions are helpless. He sighs: 'We are put in a most embarrassing and difficult and impossible situation.'

Did Kenyatta have just one phone?

When it is his turn Gumpert explains that his team managed to trace one phone number used by Kenyatta, ending on 891. But the prosecution only partially received the data that go with it: just incoming calls of people who contacted Kenyatta, but not the outgoing calls he himself made. Through that number Kenyatta was in contact with five persons. Obviously there must be more telephones, numbers and contacts. 'We suggest that the idea that the Kenyan government doesn't have records of telephones being used by cabinet ministers, as Mr Kenyatta was at the relevant time, is an unrealistic one,' says Gumpert. If the authorities would do 'a diligent and proper search in their own records, they would come up with the numbers which were being used.' He concludes: 'It is simply a circular argument for the attorney general to say, "I can only give you the records if you give me the telephone numbers," because it's the telephone numbers which we are asking for.'

Muigai is under considerable pressure. With irritation he says that the OTP had insisted for five years that it had a case against Kenyatta. Now that there seems no evidence 'they would like the Kenyan government to help them to find it, because the Kenyan government must be assumed to keep a register of phones used by cabinet ministers. There is no offer of evidence that Mr Kenyatta's phone was a phone assigned to him as a cabinet minister.' Unimpressed, judge Ozaki continues with her questions. But she stops the attorney general when he openly refers to a confidential matter: the efforts by the ICC to freeze Kenyatta's assets in 2012. Two weeks later, Muigai will be reprimanded by the judges on this point.

When Ozaki asks what the state of affairs is with regard to the tax records, Gumpert holds up a form. He explains that the OTP doesn't necessarily want to know how much tax Kenyatta is paying, but that the prosecution is looking for the filled-in forms because 'we want to know what he says about things like his directorships of companies and other financial details which this form will require him to provide.' Muigai answers that the tax authority simply 'doesn't retain the form.'

Gumpert steps in: 'I'm very sorry to interrupt, your Honour.'

Judge Ozaki: 'Yes, prosecution.'

Gumpert: 'But that's a piece of information which I don't believe we've had before.'

Ozaki: 'I'm sorry, could you repeat? I didn't catch that.'

Gumpert: 'Yes. I'm sorry, I interrupted, my fault. But this is a piece of information which I believe is new. It is in fact further purported cooperation, but I just want to be clear: The position of the Kenyan government is that Mr Kenyatta filed tax returns like this one, but they have subsequently been destroyed, so they are not available to be given to us. Have I understood correctly?'

Scornfully Muigai answers the prosecutor: 'I don't know whether my learned colleague wishes the court to believe that he never received the letter that I communicated to him on 26 August, and that he's seen it for the first time this morning, or having received it that he didn't read it, or having read it he didn't understand it, because it says exactly what I am saying. It says we have extracted …'

But again judge Ozaki cuts him short: 'Mr attorney general, I have to confess that this letter is not so clear about whether the revenue authority retains all those documents or not.' And after Muigai has responded, she finishes her argument: 'I don't think the prosecution is saying that he hasn't read the document.'

Stalemate

The bank accounts form another point of controversy. The OTP received copies of accounts from December 2007 until February 2008, when the violence peaked, but had requested more details in order to get insights in Kenyatta's financial status over a period of three years. Steven Kay, the British lawyer representing Kenyatta, is invited to give his opinion. He says that the copies of the bank accounts over those three months 'provided absolutely no support for the prosecution case.' Kay explains that although the defence consented in handing over these financial records – and some telephone data – to the prosecution, it felt it was not respected for its cooperation. 'Less credit was given to us for what we had done,' says Kay, who continues: 'I decided no more evidence would be voluntarily disclosed by me.' He made that decision because he felt 'the court was moving in the direction of a defendant having to prove his innocence.'

But then Judge Ozaki intervenes: 'Mr Kay, please, please confine your submission to my very specific question. How about vehicle records?'

Defence counsel Kay answers: 'Yes, we disclosed the vehicle records and then the request became vehicles used by Mr Kenyatta, but how on earth are we going to –'

Ozaki: 'Thank you very much, Mr Kay.'

But Kay wants to finish his sentence: '– document every vehicle he had a lift in?'

So far the visitors at the public gallery have been listening quietly, but now they chuckle while the Kenyan ambassador bursts into laughter. Judge Geoffrey Henderson points to the fact that the prosecution is accusing Kenya of not fulfilling its obligation as an ICC member to fully cooperate with the court. 'Quite a serious allegation,' Henderson says. The judges are being requested to make a finding of non-cooperation and refer the matter to the Assembly of States Parties, the annual meeting of the ICC member states, to decide on the matter. 'It is totally fallacious and baseless,' Muigai replies, rejecting the idea that 'the Kenyan government is not working with the ICC because Mr Kenyatta is in the office of head of state.'

For today the hearing is nearing its end. The judges would like to know whether the prosecution has changed its mind. Gumpert says there is 'no indication' that the Kenyan state will hand over the requested information and so the case remains 'I would respectfully submit, deadlocked.' But Muigai disagrees. 'It is totally untrue to suggest that we are deadlocked because the government of the Republic of Kenya is failing to do something', or that offices 'are inoperative' or 'non-functional.' He repeats that all the OTP needs to do is give 'actionable' information and then 'we will supply it, whatever you need, within 72 hours.' When judge Ozaki closes the two-hour hearing, one thing has become clear: the impasse is complete.

Respect our Prezo

The next morning a group of Kenyans, who have travelled especially to The Hague to be present for the Kenyatta case, is assembling in front of the public entrance of the ICC. Journalists eagerly turn their cameras and microphones to the men in red overalls who form a 'rescue team' for the man whose photo is on the large banner they are holding up. 'Respect our Prezo – He's Innocent' is written under the portrait of president Uhuru Kenyatta. Some men perform spectacular dances. Then the Kenyan group bursts into singing a gospel song 'Hakuna Mungu Kama Wewe' – though with a slight change in the text. The word Mungu, which means 'God', is replaced by the name of the president. And so the song 'No Uhuru like you' echoes in the street.

While moving on to 'Rivers of Babylon' the group starts swinging to the court's main entrance. Here they join a large crowd of about a hundred Kenyans. Some have draped the national flag around their shoulders, while others are wearing green-red-black-white shawls. A man has put party spectacles in the national colours on his nose. The accused radio broadcaster Joshua Sang is arriving by foot. Like a hero he is hoisted up on shoulders and carried around. 'We hope he will be free soon,' says the Kenyan politician Justina Ndungu about the man the crowd is waiting for. 'They don't have evidence. They have no witnesses. We love him. He is a good man. He is a humble man. He must be acquitted.'

Suddenly everybody rushes to the street where a black car is arriving. Broadly smiling president Uhuru Kenyatta is getting out. While shaking hands he is moving through the crowd. For the first time in history a president enters the ICC building as a suspect. But Kenyatta doesn't want that as any part of his political epitaph. Instead he has officially 'stepped down' for the day and transferred the presidency to his deputy William Ruto – also an ICC-suspect – so that Kenyatta will appear as an ordinary citizen before the judges.

This hearing is international news. Seldom has there been more interest in a status conference. All the seats in the public gallery are taken. The first row is reserved for the family of Kenyatta and the official Kenyan delegation. Most of the other seats are taken by politicians and supporters. They see how, behind the bulletproof window, an apparently self-confident Kenyatta is sitting next to his lawyers in the courtroom.

Again the hearing will be focused on the cooperation issue, but the judges also want to know from the parties what to do with the case. Gumpert is the first to put forward his proposal. 'I submit the best course is to adjourn the case effectively 'sine die' – that is to say: without fixing a date' until Kenya cooperates properly.[65] With an adjournment the OTP wants to keep the pressure on. 'We know that there is evidence in existence,' he says, but the prosecution doesn't know its value, 'because we are being obstructed from doing so.'

Judge Henderson says: 'Ultimately, the exercise is one of carefully balancing the rights of the accused person and also the rights of the victims.' Gumpert replies: 'I don't mean to say that the defendant's rights should be ignored for a moment, but the interests of justice should, I submit, be the most important consideration in your Honours' minds.' He warns for a decision by the judges that will be interpreted as the 'court saying: if a country sticks out for long enough, obstructing proper enquiries being made by the prosecutor, despite the court having made a finding that that obstruction is improper, then the case against the person that country wants to protect, will go away.' Gumpert underlines that as president the accused has 'a specific duty under the Kenyan constitution' to ensure that his government complies with its international obligations and thus cooperates with the ICC which includes handing over evidence that potentially may harm him. 'Although he may bear no personal responsibility, he is constitutionally responsible.'

---

65   Official transcript, 8 October 2014.

Kenyatta's defence counsels are listening with great concentration to the prosecution's exposé, while their client is seen broadly smiling and then again looking slightly worried. Fergal Gaynor, the legal representatives of victims, who is known for his direct style, agrees there has been 'no evidence presented to the court that the accused has specifically taken action to destroy evidence or other acts which would ordinarily fall under the rubric of obstruction of justice.' But his point is that constitutionally Kenyatta controls the government and the attorney general, who are 'unlawfully withholding evidence which your Honours have directed to be provided.' The lawyer continues: 'If the accused were the director of a company, your Honours had ordered that company to deliver evidence to you, and if the accused did not take any action to ensure that that company delivered the evidence to you, in many jurisdictions he would be liable for an obstruction of justice investigation and possible prosecution.' Gaynor concludes that 'the one person who can remove the principal obstacle to progress of this case, is the accused.'

Judge Henderson asks the victims' representative what he thinks of the option to withdraw the charges, while giving the OTP the possibility to continue its investigations, so that when it is ready, the prosecution can file new charges. But the lawyer disagrees. Firstly, he fears that when the case would be reopened, obstruction by the Kenyan government with regard to the evidence would only be worse. Secondly, he fears that the prosecution would prefer to undertake other cases that are more promising and easier to do, thus abandoning the Kenyatta case altogether. 'As victims, we don't have the choice of focusing on an easier case.' Gaynor wants to continue until all means to force cooperation are exhausted. If the prosecution would withdraw the charges now, 'I frankly think that would be the complete end of the justice process for victims in this case.'

Then Steven Kay, lead counsel for Kenyatta, is given time to explain his position. He says there is no evidence, the case should be terminated and Kenyatta should be acquitted.

During the break a Kenyan lawyer, who also is a member of parliament, says: 'If this case is terminated I am happy for Kenya, because it is not good for our image that the country is governed by a suspect. With an acquittal that stigma will disappear.' A man in a pinstriped suit agrees that the case should stop. 'But crimes have been committed in Kenya. We have a lot of victims who haven't seen justice taking place. That's why I want the ICC, after the acquittal of the president, to continue to investigate and prosecute the perpetrators.'

What do the nine witnesses say?

When prosecutor Bensouda is given the floor she refers to the 'balancing act' between the rights of the accused to get an expeditious and fair trial, and those of the victims and the wider interests of justice. 'The scales of justice have to come down one side, or the other,' she says. It is however incorrect to say that the prosecution has no case at all. 'There remains a considerable body of evidence that implicates Mr Kenyatta,' she says. The hearing takes an interesting turn when Gumpert guides the court through the proposed prosecution testimonies. From this overview it becomes clear that most of the key witnesses were indeed members of the criminal Mungiki network that allegedly has received money to buy weapons and to participate in the fighting, allegedly following the suspect's orders.

Witness P-152 was at a meeting in a hotel where Kenyatta 'contributed money to the Mungiki and announced there had been an agreement with the Mungiki that they would fight on the PNU Kikuyu side during the post-election violence,' Gumpert explains. During the violence this witness was approached by a member of parliament with a message from Kenyatta, who wanted to facilitate the Mungiki in protecting the Kikuyu community.

Witnesses P-428 and P-505 each received money and weapons from a former MP acting on behalf of Kenyatta.

Witness P-510 was given money by another parliamentarian, who allegedly coordinated the violence in Naivasha. During a meeting in a hotel this politician not only contributed 200,000 Kenyan shillings (some 2,000 euros) from his personal funds, but also handed over a million shillings (about 10,000 euros) which came from 'Kamwana' ('young man') – Kenyatta's nickname.

P-493 and other Mungiki members were persuaded by an MP to join the fight and later he understood this politician was acting on behalf of Kenyatta.

Witness P-494 heard from a Mungiki leader that in January 2008 he had received large sums of money from Kenyatta for the violence. Both witnesses P-429 and P-430 testified that they went to Kenyatta's house, where they were given a 'significant amount of money.'

When the OTP compared witness statements with the few telephone data it possesses, the prosecution came to a quite remarkable discovery. P-12, the Mungiki member who had been removed from the witness list because he had lied being an eyewitness, appears to have been in contact by phone on six occasions with Kenyatta, between 4 and 21 December 2007. 'What was the government minister and future president talking to the Mungiki member about?' Gumpert is wondering.

One of the MPs who is said to have been involved in contacting Mungiki who became prosecution witnesses, was calling with Kenyatta on 39 occasions in December and January. This might be not unusual, Gumpert admits, but 'what is surprising' is that the contact spikes in the three days before the violence in Naivasha in which the politician allegedly was involved. 'Was that just a coincidence, or was the MP getting instructions on how he should proceed?' Gumpert concludes: 'The prosecution doesn't know the answers to those questions, but they raise uncomfortable suspicions.' And the prosecution can only properly investigate this matter, if it receives all relevant data with regard to Kenyatta's use of phones. 'As a wealthy man and a cabinet minister, he must have had access to many phones.'

Fergal Gaynor, the victims' lawyer, points to another problem. 'One of the most troubling aspects of this case has been intimidation of witnesses. In the meetings I have held with victims, they very frequently raise this issue. They want to know what the court is doing about it, given its potentially devastating impact on the administration of justice.' He repeats his concern that if the judges decide to terminate this case 'others will draw the conclusion that a prosecution at the ICC can be effectively undermined through a combination of bribery, intimidation and unlawful obstruction of access to evidence.'

Gaynor is rounding up. 'Is it really fair to force the victims to pay the price given what they have gone through? They have lost mothers, fathers, brothers, sisters. They have been repeatedly raped. They have been set alight. They have lost their small businesses in Naivasha and Nakuru. They have received next to no compensation from the government of Kenya, and there is no accountability in the Kenyan courts. Is it really fair to force them now to pay the price for obstruction of justice by Mr Kenyatta's government?'

Scandalous misrepresentation

But defence counsel Steven Kay is not impressed. 'Well, everything I've heard in the last 30 minutes confirms my application in the justice of an acquittal being entered on the record in this court. What you heard from the prosecution is a scandalous misrepresentation of the quality of their case as well as the reasons for not pursuing this case.' The lawyer repeats his complaints that his team got 'no credit' when they supplied the OTP with data that revealed that their prosecution witnesses 'were not at the places they had claimed to be' and had been lying. So the defence had 'drawn a line in the sand.' It would not provide any further data to the prosecution. 'I say deliberately there is no evidence because if there was evidence, we would have a trial. Those are my submissions,' Kay concludes. Judge Ozaki takes over: 'Thank you very much, Mr Kay. And that brings us to the end of the matters to be discussed today.'

The blinds are slowly lowered. The view on the courtroom has disappeared. The Kenyan visitors rush downstairs, leave the building and go to the large main entrance at the front of the court. Although it rains harder and harder, they wait on the stairs for Kenyatta to come outside. The supporters brave the water drops. Killing time, people make selfies and group photos. 'Uhuru, Uhuru, Free Uhuru,' they shout. Suddenly the president comes through the revolving door. He walks towards his supporters who have been waiting to honour him. Loudly they sing Kenya's national anthem, just like in spring 2011 when Kenyatta – not yet president then – made his initial appearance before the court.

Using their arms and fists the president's security men push the supporters to the sides to form a narrow passage, and wrestle themselves through the thick of the crowd down the stairs followed by the head of state. Halfway Kenyatta stops at a small girl with tiny hair braids, who is terrified to see this stranger and starts crying loudly. The fans reach out for the president. They all want to touch and feel the power. The pushing and pulling continues until Kenyatta has reached his shiny car. 'We love our president. It is terrible he has to endure all this,' says a woman overcome with emotion, while Kenyatta gets in and is driven away.

It is now up to the judges to take a decision in this case. But before that happens on 21 October 2014 the trial chamber issues a report on a sensitive matter – public disclosure of secret information. The judges say that on several occasions the Kenyan authorities have breached the obligation of confidentiality with regard to the court's efforts since 2011 to trace and freeze Kenyatta's accounts and to seize property and assets. One of the ways this was done, was to include confidential information in filings to the court without applying the necessary redactions. Recently attorney general Muigai spoke in open court about the efforts to freeze assets. The judges caution the Kenyan government that it can sanction such breaches. Separately, the judges note 'with concern' there is 'a pattern of information contained in confidential filings being leaked to the media, in some cases even before the filings have been notified to the chamber, parties or participants.'[66]

The Kenyan case has harmed the image of both parties. It is highly unlikely that a Kenyan attorney general is unable to get access to phone numbers of a person who was a cabinet minister at the time. But the OTP hasn't come out of this affair without bruises either. While it has been investigating the violence in Kenya for five years, the case has dwindled steadily. It is up to the judges to decide on Kenyatta's fate – and that of the reputation of the prosecution.

Bensouda Two

The chamber doesn't need much time. On 3 December 2014 the judges issue two decisions. The first is about the cooperation matter, focusing on the eight categories of material the prosecution requested from Kenya. The judges note that indeed only one request – the intelligence records – has been fully carried out. Ironically, the Kenyan authorities confirm that no relevant intelligence information exists about Kenyatta, so nothing had to be disclosed. Four categories – tax, vehicles, bank and foreign transaction records – have been partially handed over. But when it comes to company, land transfer and telephone records – 'no requested materials have been provided,' the chamber writes.[67] The judges conclude that the Kenyan government 'falls short of the standard of good faith cooperation' that is required from member states. Kenya has breached its international obligations.

But the judges have also 'serious concerns regarding the timeliness and thoroughness of prosecution investigations in this case.' The delay in investigations had particular grave consequences. When one witness

---

66   Order concerning the public disclosure of confidential information, ICC, 21 October 2014.
67   Decision on Prosecution's application for a finding of non-compliance, ICC, 3 December 2014.

withdrew, the prosecution's evidence 'apparently fell below the standard required for trial.' The judges state that the OTP should have raised the cooperation problems with Kenya not handing over materials 'at a much earlier stage.' This could have 'mitigated the impact that the non-compliance has had on the proceedings in this case.' Besides, the judges note, it is 'speculative' as to whether the information requested would have provided enough evidence against Kenyatta.

After weighing all the factors the chamber decides it won't make a finding of non-cooperation, nor refer the matter to the Assembly of States Parties. For now, the prosecution has lost this part of its battle. (The appeals chamber however concluded on 19 August 2015 that the judges handling the Kenyatta case made several mistakes in their decision on cooperation and said they should look at it again.)[68]

In their second decision the judges reject a further adjournment of the trial, as was requested by Gumpert and his team. The judges reiterate their devastating conclusion that the prosecution 'in general' failed 'to take appropriate steps to verify the credibility and reliability of evidence on which it intended to rely at trial,' which is 'the direct reason' why the case is failing at such a late stage.[69] (For the record they state there is no 'substantiation' for the allegation that Kenyatta deliberately interfered in preventing the transfer of information.) There is no certainty there will be evidence against Kenyatta. Or as the judges put it: 'It is apparent that the prosecution does not have any concrete prospect of obtaining evidence sufficient to meet the standard required for trial and to sustain the current charges.' Prosecutor Bensouda is given one week to take a decision: either withdraw the charges or go ahead with a trial because the 'evidentiary basis has improved.'

The prosecution must have seen it coming. Bensouda doesn't need a week to make up her mind. Two days later, on 5 December, she files a notice to the judges. She also issues a press release and a video statement to the public. Dressed in a grey robe and looking quite exhausted, Bensouda explains that 'given the state of the evidence' against Kenyatta she has 'no alternative' but to withdraw the charges.[70] She sums up three reasons that

---

68 Judgment on the appeal against Decision on Prosecution's application for a finding of non-compliance, ICC, 19 August 2015.
69 Decision on Prosecution's application for a further adjournment, ICC, 3 December 2014.
70 Statement of ICC prosecutor on the withdrawal of charges against Kenyatta, OTP, 5 December 2014.

frustrated her investigations – similar to those in March 2013 when she withdraw the case against Francis Muthaura, the former secretary to the Kenyan cabinet, who was charged together with Kenyatta.

Bensouda explains that 'several people' who might have provided 'important evidence' have died, while others 'were too terrified to testify for the prosecution.' Key witnesses withdrew or changed their accounts – especially about their presence at crucial meetings. And last but not least the Kenyan government refused to hand over large parts of requested documentary evidence, which 'compromised the prosecution's ability to thoroughly investigate the charges,' says Bensouda.

The prosecutor understands how hard this decision must be for the victims. 'This is a painful moment for the men, women and children who have suffered tremendously from the horrors of the post-election violence, and who have waited, patiently, for almost seven years to see justice done,' she says. Bensouda draws the bitter conclusion that 'those who have sought to obstruct the path of justice have, for now, deprived the people of Kenya of the accountability they deserve.'

She underlines that the case against Kenyatta is not terminated permanently. It can be reopened if there is new evidence. (Kenyatta's profile remains on the ICC website.) It is her 'firm belief', Bensouda says, that this decision won't be 'the last word on justice and accountability' for the post-election violence in Kenya. But she has to acknowledge that 'today is a dark day for international criminal justice.'

The Ocampo Six have become the Bensouda Two.

The pre-trial brief

A month later the prosecutor releases her 'second updated pre-trial brief', which originally dates from 26 August 2013. The document tells the story of how the OTP sees Kenyatta's role in the crimes against humanity for which he had been charged: murder, deportation, rape, persecution and other inhumane acts. It was the legal representative of victims who had asked for the 'reclassification' of this confidential document, so that it would become public. Kenyatta's lawyers objected because it would 'serve only to proliferate untruths' as it is based, in their view, on witnesses who lied, refused to testify or who are otherwise not credible.[71]

---

71   Defence Response to Victims' Request for Reclassification, 14 November 2014.

It is, the defence alleges, 'premised upon false evidence.' Moreover, the 'reputational damage' suffered by Kenyatta would be 'unduly amplified by the unnecessary further publication of rumours.' But the judges decide otherwise noting, among other matters, 'the principle of publicity.' They order the prosecution to publish a redacted version of the original document.[72]

The pre-trial brief is a shocking account of how Kenyatta, Muthaura and PNU officials – using intermediaries such as an agent of the intelligence service, a reverend and politicians – allegedly managed to make a deal with the outlawed Mungiki gang.[73] The mafia group agreed to support the political party PNU during election time in exchange for the suspension of extrajudicial killings of its members by the Kenyan state, and for allowing the gang to gather publicly without police interference. 'The alliance with the Mungiki provided the PNU with grass roots political support during the campaign and a reserve of manpower in case the PNU lost the election and needed to retain power by force,' the prosecution writes. The political party would use the criminal sect if the 'contest for power moved to the streets.' The pre-trial brief focuses on Kenyatta's activities. While his group would rely on Mungiki and PNU youths, William Ruto had established his network with Kalenjin fighters, according to the prosecution.

Around 30 December 2007 – the day that the election commission announces that PNU candidate Kibaki has won the presidential elections – Kenyatta is leading a crisis meeting at State House in Nairobi. An assistant is summoned 'to bring in a large sum of cash, which was distributed to the Mungiki to mobilise men and purchase materiel for the attacks,' the prosecution writes. Then Kenyatta instructs the coordinators to 'go and organise your people' and get 'prepared for war.' The names of politicians and other crucial persons involved in tasks such as distributing money and organising people are disclosed in the report. More meetings, more cash and more promises follow, while the Mungiki and PNU youth are mobilised.

---

72   Decision on request of the Legal Representative of Victims for a public redacted version of the pre-trial brief, 11 December 2014.
73   Public Redacted Version of "Second updated Prosecution pre-trial brief", 19 January 2015.

The powerful state official Muthaura, who in court had made such a humble impression and had seen the case against him withdrawn, appears no fewer than 26 times in the pre-trial brief. According to the prosecution he 'assured the Mungiki that the police would not interfere in the Rift Valley attacks, a message which was passed down to Mungiki members on the ground.' Muthaura also 'distributed large sums of money' to the mafia group and gave them instructions on the attacks. It was a huge operation. Automatic weapons, ammunition, grenades, camouflage uniforms and police handcuffs were supplied – allegedly authorised by Kenyatta and Muthaura – through intermediaries to the criminal gang. Kenyatta tasked a whole range of people to liaise with the militia on the ground and to coordinate attacks on people who were suspected of having voted for the opposing ODM party. Through these intermediaries, Kenyatta 'directed Mungiki members and pro-PNU youth, dispatched to the Rift Valley, to show no mercy during the retaliatory attacks,' says the pre-trial brief.

To provide a focus for the case, the prosecution had selected two flashpoints: the attacks on people in the cities of Nakuru (24-27 January 2008) and Naivasha (27-28 January 2008), both northwest of Nairobi. The brief describes how the Mungiki and pro-PNU youth were ready to go and chase ethnic groups such as the Luo and Kalenjin and ODM people. The fighters were armed with guns, pangas, swords and metal bars. 'Some wore camouflage uniforms, which made them look like police and enabled them to surprise their victims,' the report says. They went house to house looking for ODM supporters. Unarmed men, women and children were 'shot, cut and burned to death.' Attackers 'pulled a Luo man from his bicycle, bludgeoned him and his children with pangas [machetes] and clubs, poured petrol on them, and set them alight.'

The quarry near Nakuru was used as an execution site. Many women were raped, especially the wives and daughters of known ODM supporters. Houses were set ablaze and property was destroyed. The attackers 'forcibly circumcised non-Kikuyu men using pangas and other sharp objects, such as broken bottles and pieces of glass.' They cut off penises – before killing their victims. In fear people fled their homes. 'The police did not intervene to stop the attackers,' the prosecution writes. In numbers the charges relate to 153 killings, at least 29 (gang)rapes, 8 men being forcibly circumcised with 2 having their genitals cut off and 60.000 people forced to flee Nakuru and Naivasha.

The pre-trial brief details the cruelty of the attacks and details the nature of the allegations against the man who is currently president of Kenya. The report also discloses the story behind the mysterious paragraphs in the prosecutor's public statements about potential witnesses being killed. It refers to Mungiki members who allegedly had dealt personally with Kenyatta and his agents, 'but were systematically eliminated in the aftermath of the violence.'

The brief lists eight names. One of them is Charles Ndungu Wagacha, belonging to the top of the Mungiki and who replaced its founder and leader Maina Njenga, already in prison for firearm and drugs crimes before the political-ethnic violence erupted. According to the prosecutor, Wagacha had liaised with the 'principal' PNU actors to coordinate the Rift Valley attacks and 'in particular' with Muthaura, 'for whom he had a direct channel of communication.' But Wagacha and another Mungiki member were reportedly shot by police in broad daylight. According to Kenyan media they were driving in a car and going to meet with the imprisoned gang leader late April 2008. A few weeks earlier, on 12 April, Njenga's wife and the personal assistant to the Mungiki top leader had been killed under similar circumstances when they were on their way to the prison. Another slain Mungiki was spokesman Njuguna Gitau Njuguna, who 'collected money' from Kenyatta for the Rift Valley attacks. He was killed in Nairobi on 5 November 2009, the pre-trial brief discloses, by 'plain clothes police officers, after expressing an intention to meet with the former ICC prosecutor, who was in Nairobi that day.' Four Mungiki members are listed by the prosecutor as victims of forced disappearances, some after having been arrested by the police.

The prosecutor alleges that these killings and forced disappearances were part of a 'clean up' campaign 'to conceal' the involvement of Kenyatta in the violence. Even if the judges would conclude that these events could not be directly attributed to the accused, the pre-trial brief writes, 'they are nonetheless relevant because of the effect they have had on the witnesses who will be testifying at trial.' Moreover 'at each stage of the judicial process,' the prosecution states, Kenyatta's 'intermediaries have attempted to bribe witnesses to shield' him from 'responsibility' for his role in the violence.

A killing in the Ruto & Sang case

While the proceedings in the Kenyatta case have been terminated, the Ruto & Sang trial is still on. Immediately after the Christmas holidays, on 6 January 2015, the ICC publishes an astonishing statement. The court expresses 'its deep regret at the reported abduction and violent death of Mr Meshack Yebei.'[74] The Kenyan man had last been seen in the town of Turbo, in Rift Valley, on 28 December 2014, when he and his wife went to a clinic because their child had fallen ill. Yebei went out to buy his son some water, but never returned. His body was found dead four days later, floating in a river in Kenya. He had been brutally killed. 'His eyes had been gouged out, his genitals chopped off, his tongue cut out and he had been shot in the head,' the UK newspaper The Guardian wrote.[75]

Yebei had a connection with the court. But in the press release the ICC's registrar underlines that the murdered Kenyan was 'not on the prosecution witness list, nor was he in contact with prosecution staff at the time of his abduction.' So who was Yebei? He must have been a witness, as the ICC acknowledged it had offered him protection, including a safe residency in a new location. For some reason Yebei had returned home and was brutally killed.

Three days later the prosecution comes with a statement in a bid to end 'recent speculation' that its office was involved in the abduction and murder.[76] Such suggestions are 'outrageous and utterly false,' the OTP writes, and 'nothing could be further from the truth.' Yebei had been one of the 'numerous individuals' the prosecution had contacted during investigations in Kenya. But he hadn't made it to its witness list because there were indications that he 'was deeply implicated in the scheme to corrupt prosecution witnesses' in the case against Ruto and Sang. The OTP reminds the public that the witnesses in this trial 'have been under siege.' A network of individuals has been trying to 'sabotage' the prosecution's case by bribing and threats 'to either dissuade witnesses from testifying in this case, or influence prosecution witnesses to recant their testimony.' Possibly Yebei was one of these individuals.

74 'ICC deeply concerned with reported death of Mr Meshack Yebei,' ICC, 6 January 2015.
75 'Discovery of witness's mutilated body feeds accusations of state killings,' The Guardian, 6 January 2015.
76 Statement of the Office of the Prosecutor regarding the reported abduction and murder of Mr. Meshak Yebei, OTP, 9 January 2015.

At first Karim Khan, lead counsel for Kenyan deputy president Ruto, refused 'all requests by the media' to comment on this matter.[77] But when he learns about the prosecution's accusations with regard to Yebei, and the fact that confidential information about his request to the Kenyan authorities to investigate this murder was leaked to the press, the lawyer feels compelled to react. He discloses that Yebei was a 'critical' defence witness. In his statement Khan accuses the OTP of carrying out 'a gratuitous character assassination of an individual not available to defend himself and without regard to the dignity of the family of the deceased.' It is 'highly significant' that despite claims Yebei had been involved in witness interference, the prosecution had not sought to arrest him, the counsel states. Khan reveals that Yebei's first contact with his defence team was in July 2013. The Kenyan man had told the lawyers exactly the opposite of what the prosecution is claiming. According to Yebei's account there was 'a cabal' of prosecution witnesses who had 'deliberately concocted false accounts' against Ruto for 'financial and other benefits.' The prosecution had interviewed Yebei – without the knowledge of the defence – in a third country about his possible involvement in witness intimidation. But he had denied the allegations. Khan reveals that Yebei was actually threatened with abduction by one of the OTP witnesses and that Bensouda's team knew about these threats. It was the lawyer himself who alerted the ICC's Victims and Witnesses Unit (VWU). 'Mr Yebei was referred to the ICC witness protection programme by me,' Khan writes. While Yebei's family is preparing for his funeral, the Kenyan serious crimes unit releases incredible news: the fingerprints retrieved of the mutilated body are not his. National media report that the remains belong to a certain Yusuf Hussein, who had gone missing around the same time. On 22 January the Kenyan Criminal Investigations Department (CID) confirms that DNA results show that the body is that of Yusuf Hussein, who is immediately buried by his family, in line with Islamic rules. While Kenyan police treats Yebei as a case of a missing person, late February his remains are found. A body, which had been in the Moi Voi Hospital Mortuary since 30 December, turns out to be that of Ruto's defence witness. It had been discovered in Tsavo National Park forest (the

---

77   Statement by Karim Khan QC regarding the reported abduction and murder of Mr. Meshak Yebei, 13 January 2015.

killers possibly hoped wild animals would eat the remains), which is 600 kilometres from Eldoret where he went missing. The post-mortem doesn't provide conclusive results on how he met his death.[78]

However, this will not be the only murder connected to this case. On 30 April John Kituyi, a journalist from the Mirror Weekly, is severely beaten when he walks home from work. He dies later in Eldoret Hospital. His family, journalists and human rights activists relate his death to a recent article he wrote about the Ruto & Sang case. The Committee to Protect Journalists spoke to two Kenyan reporters investigating the murder, who believe Kituyi could have been targeted for an unpublished story concerning Yebei, who may have switched sides from being a Ruto witness to supporting the prosecution.[79]

While the Yebei tragedy is still making headlines in the media, the prosecutor confidentially seeks an arrest warrant against two more Kenyans who are suspected of offences against the administration of justice. On 10 March 2015 the ICC orders the arrest of Paul Gicheru, an advocate with the High Court of Kenya, and labourer/farmer Philip Kipkoech Bett.[80] They are accused of bribing and inducing a total of six prosecution witnesses to withdraw from the Ruto & Sang case or recant their prior statements.

Gicheru is alleged to be the manager of the scheme. He is accused of having 'finalised agreements with corrupted witnesses, organised the formalisation of their withdrawal and handled the payment.' Philip Kipkoech Bett worked under Gicheru's direction and contacted witnesses. There are interesting links with other persons. The duo allegedly worked together with Barasa, the former intermediary who has been wanted on similar charges by the ICC since 2013. The very first witness testifying in court against Ruto and Sang, and whose name was leaked after which she was allowed to give her testimony behind closed doors, was offered money by Barasa. He had told her that Gicheru was in charge of this operation. Bett does not play a role in attempts to bribe this woman, but he did interfere with other prosecution witnesses. It is unclear how much further the connections spread, but Bett reportedly was one of Yebei's neighbours.

---

78   'Kenyan body confirmed as ICC witness Meshack Yebei,' BBC, 9 March 2015
79   'Journalists Killed,' Committee to Protect Journalists, 30 April 2015.
80   Decision on the Prosecution's Application under Article 58(1) of the Rome Statute, ICC, 10 March 2010.

There are rumours that the murdered Yebei was a 'potential prosecution witness, particularly in proving allegations of witness interference in the Ruto and Sang ICC case,' writes the well informed blog The Hague Trials Kenya.[81] The three suspects – Barasa, Gicheru and Bett – are still not handed over by Kenya to the ICC.

No case to answer

The prosecution is continuing to face serious problems in the Ruto & Sang trial. There is an 'organised and effective scheme to persuade prosecution witnesses to withdraw or recant their evidence,' Bensouda writes in her confidential request of 21 May 2015.[82] No fewer than 16 of its 42 original witnesses – some 40 percent – have refused to testify. Most of them cite threats, intimidation and fears of reprisals. A dozen were summoned by the judges to testify. Several witnesses who showed up, recanted their statements. Others refused. One of them was a Kenyan national who was given asylum in The Netherlands with his family. He received such serious threats, his Dutch lawyers said, that he did not dare to testify against Ruto, fearing for his life and that of his family. The ICC reacted by sending a request to hear the witness to the Dutch investigative judge in The Hague, who then threatened 'to arrest and detain the witness for as long as he chooses not to give testimony,' the lawyers wrote.[83] The Kenyan witness was so scared he went into hiding.

A month later newspapers in Kenya reported that a Kenyan secret agent, who was on a covert mission, was arrested in The Netherlands when he allegedly tried to trace an ICC witness residing in The Hague.[84] The officer was immediately deported to Kenya.

On 10 September 2015 the prosecution is done with its presentation of evidence. Usually the defence then begin their refutation by calling their own witnesses. Instead the lawyers of deputy president Ruto publish, on 26 October, their long awaited 'request for judgment for acquittal.'[85]

---

81 'Who are the two new Kenyans wanted by Bensouda?', 15 September 2015.
82 Public redacted version of "Prosecution's request for the admission of prior recorded testimony of […] witnesses", OTP, 21 May 2105.
83 'Threatened witness in ICC case against Kenyan vice president Ruto forced to testify by Dutch judge,' press release Prakken d'Oliveira, 24 March 2015.
84 'Why Dutch kicked out our man,' Daily Nation, 21 April 2015.
85 Public redacted version of Corrigendum of Ruto Defence Request for Judgment of Acquittal, Defence William Ruto, 26 October 2015.

Karim Khan and his team argue that the 'underlying foundations' of the case against their client were 'rotten' from the start. Originally, at the confirmation of charges hearing, the case was primarily built on the evidence of six witnesses. But these persons proved to be unreliable, did not show up or were withdrawn. 'The evidence obtained since confirmation is equally unreliable,' the defence says, as it is 'mutually inconsistent, uncorroborated in its material incriminatory aspects and contradicted by other trial evidence.' Further, it is 'almost entirely hearsay or speculation.'

The defence argues that the 'disintegration' of the prosecution's case 'cannot be blamed on extraneous factors, but derives directly from the serious deficiencies in the OTP's investigations from the outset.' The prosecution wrongfully relied on witnesses sourced by the Waki Commission (named after the Kenyan judge who in 2008 had been leading the national investigations into the violence) and failed to 'properly investigate' the accounts of these witnesses themselves. In other words: sloppy investigations. The case has 'completely broken down,' says Ruto's defence, and should 'be dismissed.' The lawyers of radio journalist Sang draw a similar conclusion: there is no evidence that their client had broadcast messages to incite people to commit violence. On 23 October 2015 defence counsel Kigen-Katwa files his 'no case to answer' motion.[86]

A huge Kenyan delegation

The matter is now in the hands of the judges who will make their own assessment. As the trial is not over, and nothing is sure, the Kenyan government itself takes up the battle to save Ruto. The annual meeting of the member states – the Assembly of States Parties – in November 2015 in The Hague offers an excellent opportunity. There is the usual buzz of official delegations, court officials and human rights activists assembling in the big hall of the World Forum. People are shaking hands and politely engage with each other. The stars on stage are the new ASP president, the Senegalese justice minister Sidiki Kaba, as well as the ICC's new president, judge Silvia Fernández de Gurmendi, and prosecutor Fatou Bensouda.

---

86   Public Redacted Version of Sang Defence 'No Case to Answer' Motion, 23 October 2015, Defence, 6 November 2015.

The official Kenyan delegation, headed by minister of foreign affairs Amina Mohamed, hasn't come alone. About one hundred politicians, officials and campaigners have joined her. In the corridors a huge man with a round face, lobbyist David Matsanga of the Pan African Forum, is distributing his magazine. The cover carries the pictures of Ruto and Sang with the ICC building on the background and the text: 'Wrong suspects – Flawed trials.' The magazine reflects the viewpoint of many in the Kenyan delegation as it speaks of 'ICC follies' and the trial being turned into a 'legal circus in international comedy.' Matsanga writes that the witnesses in the Ruto and Sang case were 'fake, procured and evidence was doctored by ICC investigators and with the help of international NGOs like Open Society Foundation of George Soros and other Western Agencies.' The magazine calls for a motion during the ASP to investigate Bensouda and her office 'to bring sanity in the ICC.'

Although the annual meeting is meant to deal with a large number of issues – ranging from the budget, cooperation between the court and states, the permanent premises, reparations for victims, the welcoming of Palestine as its newest member – the week-long conference will be overshadowed by the Kenyan lobby and to a lesser extent to South Africa's problems with the court after Pretoria was slammed for not arresting the Sudanese president Al Bashir when he visited the country a few months ago. The ASP's bureau has allowed an open general debate about both matters.

The focal point in the Kenyan campaign is 'Rule 68' which had been amended by the member states during the annual meeting in November 2013 (two months after the Ruto & Sang trial started) in the very same World Forum. It allows, under strict conditions, the use of early prerecorded statements of a witness. The prosecution had asked the judges to allow such early statements of several witnesses in the case against Ruto and Sang. On 28 August 2015 the judges had partially fulfilled the request by admitting into evidence the prior recorded testimony of five witnesses.[87]

'It's war,' says a human rights activist to describe the tough negotiations behind the scenes of the ASP conference, where the Kenyan delegation

---

87 'ICC admits statements of five witnesses as evidence against Ruto and Sang,' International Justice Monitor, 20 August 2015.

is trying to convince member states to adopt a resolution saying that the amended rule 68 can't be used retroactively in the Ruto & Sang case. The activist discloses that Kenya is making all kinds of promises to other governments in order to get them behind their campaign. The issue has become highly politicized. The idea of the trias politica – separation of powers between politicians and judges – seems far away.

While the assembly is busy with its own issues, the world outside and its harsh reality is never far away. A diplomat whispers to an ambassador that there has just been an attack by Islamist militants on a hotel in Bamako, the capital city of Mali. In their speeches many delegations refer to the tragedy in the French capital of Paris a week ago, where terrorists killed 130 people who were enjoying life in restaurants, on terraces, at the Bataclan theatre and in the soccer stadium. Others recall that in the Lebanese capital Beirut more than forty people were killed during a suicide attack by the terrorist group Islamic State.

When the 'Rule 68' matter is up for a general discussion, a group of international activists have put on white T-shirts with texts such as 'Witness tampering should not pay.' Furiously magazine man Matsanga storms at the protestors and starts shouting: 'This is no time for campaigning! These people have to leave!' Another angry Kenyan delegate plays on the term 'civil society' when he cries out: 'You are evil society!' While slightly perplexed by so much anger, some activists are taking off their protest shirts. An aggressive Matsanga grabs the textile, throws the shirts on the floor and starts to trample the attire with his feet. Until a Kenyan delegate interferes. 'It's enough,' he corrects the big magazine man, who two days earlier had been happily distributing his own lobby material. A Kenyan journalist filming the scenes comments: 'In Kenya, every day it's like this.' (A year later Matsanga will accuse ICC president Silvia Fernández de Gurmendi of having accepted money to bribe witnesses so the ICC could indict the Sudanese head of state. When the court investigated the matter, it turned out that the magazine man had 'forged' documents to 'fix' the judge, as the Daily Nation writes.[88])

The 'Rule 68' debate is in fact a series of government statements. Foreign minister Amina Mohamed kicks off presenting Kenya as a faithful ICC member, that has indeed adopted and integrated the Rome Statute in

---

88 'Ugandan activist Matsanga 'used forged papers to fix ICC president,' Daily Nation, 8 August 2016.

its laws. Then she explains that African countries are starting to feel 'unwelcome' at the ICC. 'Are we a heavy lot that you want to get rid of?' she wonders. All Kenya is asking, she explains, is to reaffirm that the amendment to Rule 68 can't be used retroactively.

While Kenya is supported by Uganda, other countries find the debate inappropriate. Colombia, Liechtenstein and Chile say this is a matter for the judges, and not for governments. The Czech Republic stresses that member states must be 'very careful not to trespass' on matters before the court, which has to be able to function in 'total independence without political interference.' Applause is heard when the Czech official concludes: 'We can't accept the proposal of Kenya.' Only a dozen countries will make a statement and there is not much support for the Kenyan position. This hasn't been the victorious debate Kenya has been hoping for. It seems a display of calculated frustration when foreign minister Mohamed, reacting to a representative of a Kenyan NGO making a statement about Mungiki being eliminated, suddenly loudly shouts: there is a terrorist in the hall. She demands that the person is expelled, but her call has no effect.

In the corridors a group of Kenyan politicians and campaigners is passionately discussing the situation. 'We will withdraw from the ICC if we are not being listened to. Most African countries will follow,' says member of parliament Ferdinand Waititu, who has been arrested several times in Kenya, including for hate speech.

While the Kenyan delegation retreats into a large room, the ICC's Trust Fund for Victims is organising a drink. Officials, NGOs, academics and observers relax with chats, wine and beer, while fried snacks such as typical Dutch 'bitterballen' are being served. When it is time to go home, the Kenyan delegation has just ended its deliberations. A long line of Kenyan participants cross the corridors and make their way to the exit. I meet foreign minister Mohamed when she is leaving the building, and I ask: 'If Kenya doesn't get what it wants, will you pull out of the ICC?' But the minister keeps her cards to her chest and says that she first wants to wait for the outcome of the ASP: 'I will not speculate. We will cross that bridge when we come to it.'

The ASP does adopt a paragraph reaffirming 'its understanding that the amended rule 68 shall not be applied retroactively.' In her contribution to the Justice in Conflict blog, Elizabeth Evenson, associate director in the International Justice Program at Human Rights Watch, writes: 'The language is best described as a dodge on substance, but one that gave Kenya enough room to claim that the Assembly had backed their version of events regarding the rule's history.'[89]

Status Conference

People are standing in queues before the counter of the reception centre which is built in front of the new court complex. A month ago the ICC moved to its permanent premises. Everything is shiny and brand new. The security measures are tighter than previously. The handling of passports and press passes takes ages. New things are not always an improvement. But then unexpectedly an ICC official seems to want to help by pushing me to the front to get my pass, and with a mix of relief and discomfort I am bypassing several people in the queue. The coats, bags and belongings all need to go on the belt for the X-ray, while one by one everybody walks through the metal sensor. Then visitors and officials cross a broad bridge over a stretch of water which leads to the actual court building.

The ICC is organising today, 12 January 2016, its first public hearings in the new building. The sessions, that will take four days, focus on the 'no case to answer' motions by the defence teams of Ruto and Sang, who say there is no proof against their clients, so there is no need for the lawyers to present their case and the suspects should be acquitted. Originally the hearings were scheduled for November 2015, but the judges postponed the sessions so the deputy president could be present during the Pope's visit to Kenya. The question that lies before the court is whether the prosecutor introduced sufficient evidence for the chamber to convict the accused.

Presiding judge Eboe-Osuji welcomes everybody in the premises.

The main courtroom is spacious, with extremely high ceilings and an austere interior. The gleaming white desks and sombre liver coloured walls create a businesslike atmosphere. The judges oversee the hearings from a heightened platform at the back of the room. The setting has changed compared to the old building, with the prosecution and victims' representatives now to the judges' right and the defence to their left. The public gallery is built on a higher level. Visitors are now looking down into the courtroom, which is much bigger in size, making it

---

89   'A Threat to Justice,' Elizabeth Evenson, Justice in Conflict, 17 February 2016.

harder to see expressions on the faces of judges, prosecutors, lawyers and suspects. For today's hearing the staff has divided the public gallery. One block is largely reserved for the Kenyan delegation made up of politicians, senators and governors. In the middle block several seats are reserved for court officials and international diplomats. The block on the left is partly designated for the media. The separation creates an odd division between one African block near the suspects and two other very mixed blocks.

It is for the first time in the ICC's history that defence teams have submitted a 'no case to answer' motion. Presiding judge Eboe-Osuji notes the lawyers are also taking risks by not bringing their own evidence. But for now it is up to the prosecution to present its case. Trial lawyer Steynberg asks whether the hearing could be held behind closed doors. But the defence opposes a 'blanket' proposal because it would prevent the public from hearing what the state of affairs is. The judges indeed decline Steynberg's request.

The prosecution starts off with a legal matter claiming this hearing is about the 'quantity' and not about the 'quality' of the evidence. But judge Eboe-Osuji doesn't agree. He explains that the question before the court is whether on the basis of the evidence 'as it stands', the suspects can be convicted or not. Could a 'reasonable' trial chamber be satisfied 'beyond reasonable doubt' of the guilt of the accused.

'Shift-Control-5 and then you should get a split screen,' says Steynberg, helping out the judges struggling to keep up with his presentation via the new, sophisticated computersystem. 'Thank you for your guidance,' Eboe-Osuji responds. 'The mock trial was not wasted on me then,' Steynberg replies in his dry sense of humour, referring to earlier sessions where the officials could exercise with the new equipment. The new design of the courtroom has more drawbacks. The prosecutor warns the parties they will have to turn their screens so that the public looking down can't see the confidential documents being displayed. Although it would require exceptionally good eyes to be able to actually read the pieces of evidence.

Steynberg starts by explaining that the Rift Valley, with 64 percent of all killings, was at the epicentre of the post-election violence. Of a total of more than thousand people being murdered in Kenya during those violent months, 744 were killed in the Rift Valley. It explains why the prosecution mainly selected this region for its case. After this introduction Steynberg takes the court through the evidence. He focuses on the organisation behind the violence and recalls Ruto was allegedly involved in six meetings that were meant to prepare the mayhem. The first was on 20 October 2007, two months before the violence broke out, at Ruto's house in Sugoi, near Eldoret. Although Steynberg doesn't elaborate on the matter, this is a deviation from his opening statements back in 2013, when the prosecution claimed that preparations had started back in 2006, eighteen months before the bloodshed.

Steynberg tells that witnesses had testified that the network's goal was to prepare for war, to train Kalenjin youth and that weapons would be provided in order to evict ethnic Kikuyu. He explains that the network used coded language. For instance 'works' was a word for 'violence,' while 'tools' referred to 'weapons.' Witnesses had told the court that at the time, people had been 'waiting for the leader' to give instructions to attack. This person could be none other than Ruto.

The prosecution repeats its theory of the case, but it seems much weaker than during the opening of the trial. Meanwhile Khan is sending notes written on yellow post-its to his colleague David Hooper. Their client Ruto is sitting quietly in his chair. He writes and listens to what is being said, and looks quite uncomfortable.

Regularly judge Eboe-Osuji interrupts the prosecution to ask critical questions. He wants to know when exactly the network was formed, when the common plan to evict the Kikuyus was made and when ('if that's the case') Ruto had said that Kikuyu needed to be killed. While the deputy president is sitting with his hands folded and keeping his forefinger on his lips, Steynberg says there is 'no evidence' that Ruto literally said 'kill the Kikuyu and PNU.' Instead, the Kenyan leader is accused of actively calling to evict the Kikuyu and presenting them as 'grabbers' and 'parasites' that needed to be removed. Steynberg also reminds the court that Ruto's words carried more weight as he had been crowned in 2006 as the king of the Kalenjin and was thus in a position of authority.

The prosecution accuses the Kenyan politician of making an essential contribution to the plan, by organising the violence and paying for weapons in order to get rid of the Kikuyus. The operations were carried out by armed and often disguised youth. Their faces were covered with white clay to make it difficult for others to recognize the fighters – just like the first witness had told the court. They were transported to different places and provided with food, petrol and weapons, Steynberg explains.

So basically, judge Eboe-Osuji sums up, these are 'political thugs ready for action.'

Witnesses had also testified that after the violence a massive cleansing ceremony took place in the forest which was organised by the elders. Three thousand people attended the ritual, which was meant to clean the fighters from curses which could arise from killing people. One witness testified that Ruto's main assistant – Farouk Kibet – addressed the crowd, saying that Ruto was thanking the youth for their unity during the violence and for carrying out the plan.

Trial lawyer Steynberg is getting to the end of his presentation. But he has been concentrating so much on Ruto, that he almost seems to forget the second accused: Sang, who is hanging in his chair and is writing, just like his lawyers do. It is a bit of a hilarious moment that softens the heavy atmosphere during this crucial hearing which will define the fate of the two suspects and that of the increasingly shaky case of the prosecutor. Steynberg says that the Kenyan broadcaster attended a preparatory meeting, where the common plan was discussed. A witness had told the court that Sang had named the Kikuyu parasites and weed that needed to be destroyed. He had called people to attend meetings, broadcasted messages to communicate the common plan to evict Kikuyu to a wider audience and incited people to take part in the violence. The peace messages he had also broadcast, only served as a distraction from his calls for war, the prosecution states.

Steynberg has come to the end of his presentation. He is standing with his arms behind his back. For the first time he looks up to the public gallery and stares at the Kenyan block for a few moments.

Press freedom

The next morning the delegation from Kenya is positioned in the hall of the ICC. Some twenty politicians and officials are waiting for the deputy president to arrive. They quickly line up when Ruto enters the foyer, walks towards them and starts shaking hands, and taps the men on the shoulders. As if he is making an official visit to some institute or hospital in his capacity as government leader. The ICC allows this 'presidential' ceremony to take place by ignoring it. A couple of Kenyan journalists are taking pictures and film the scenes. With my amateur camera I join in to take some snapshots.

Suddenly I am approached by a Kenyan woman, which is a rare thing, because I am largely ignored by the delegation. She asks who I am and for whom I am working. So I tell her that I am a freelance journalist. 'You can't take pictures of this gathering,' she responds. Flabbergasted I point to the Kenyan journalists who are energetically filming away. 'But they are with us,' she responds, and briefly looks at the Kenyans who are allowed to work unhindered. Her remark makes me wonder how independent the media that are present, actually are. Then she adds: 'I assume you will be deleting your pictures.' When I respond that of course I won't destroy my photos, she walks away, frustrated and angry.

A few minutes later, still in the hall, Ruto and his entourage make a big circle. They join hands, bow their heads and for minutes go into prayer. Then they hurry to the courtroom and the public gallery.

Sang's lawyer, Kigen-Katwa, kicks off with the defence's part. His client's innocence is 'manifest,' the counsel says. The prosecution might claim there was a hierarchy organising the bloodshed, the defence argues that the violence was spontaneous. The network did not exist, thus Sang couldn't make a contribution to it. The broadcaster never incited nor used words such as weeds, enemies, parasites or thieves. And even if he had, it would not have been criminal behaviour.

Eboe-Osuji has been on the ball. He listens carefully with his head resting on his hand, and his thumb against his cheek. When he wants to put a legal matter to the lawyer, he moves his hand away. The judge asks whether there has to be a kind of organisation, such as a network, before violent acts can be characterised as crimes against humanity. Indeed, confirms Kigen-Katwa, legally this is a prerequisite.

Later that day the defence counsel explains there is a practical reason why his client couldn't have committed the alleged crime of incitement, calling people to participate in the attacks: the government had ordered a media ban on live programmes after the results were announced on 30 December 2007 and the mayhem started. It meant that Kass FM was in a 'complete freeze' and was just broadcasting music and prerecorded peace messages.

Ruto looks up to the public gallery. With an almost invisible faint smile he connects with a lady and three youngsters, dressed in fancy casual jeans, shirts, boots and sneakers, sitting on the first row of the Kenyan block. His wife and three of their children have joined him to the hearings. One of the youngsters is reading a book, while another sibling has opened a dictionary. With a blank look Ruto's eyes search the public gallery. He is forced to look up, while the visitors are looking down on him. Finding it difficult to continue his gazing from that disadvantaged position, he soon lowers his face and turns his head. A guard walks towards the family and tells Ruto's son to take his feet off the iron frame holding the bulletproof glass in front of him through which he sees his father sitting below.

After the lunch break Ruto's wife is waiting for the curtains blocking the view to the courtroom, to open again. She appears a quiet woman, often looking sadly, modestly dressed and with two golden rings on her fingers. When I approach her, to ask how the last few years have been, with her husband being prosecuted, she answers: 'He will be set free, because we know the truth. We are Christians and we believe in God. I trust he will set him free.' And there ends our short conversation.

Apart from the Kenyans there are hardly any visitors to the public gallery. Most chairs are empty. In the courtroom below, Caroline Buisman, one of the lawyers defending Sang, is giving an exposé about media freedom and protected speech. She argues that the law allows people to say things that shock or otherwise disturb. 'Offensive speeches are not criminal,' she says. It all depends on the context, the proximity to the violence and whether people have acted upon the words.

While below me the defence is explaining the concept of free speech and defending journalism, a person taps me on the shoulder. It is Sonia Robla, the head of the Information and Documentation section at the ICC.

'We have been receiving complaints about you,' she says, 'that you have been disturbing the family.' It takes me a few seconds to understand what she is telling me. When I explain that I was just asking Mrs Ruto a few questions, which is simply the job of a journalist, Robla says she doesn't want to hear my side of the story and won't go into the matter. 'You have to go and sit there,' she says, firmly pointing her finger to the next empty block which has several media reserved seats. She tells me I can stay on my seat for a few more minutes, until it is time for the break. After that I have to move.

The timing of her intervention, which was probably demanded by the Ruto camp, couldn't have been more striking. With the defence lawyers pleading for press freedom, a journalist is told off for putting some questions to the family of the accused. It surely was an interesting media day at the court.

A borderline case

A row of posh black cars transporting the Kenyan delegation arrive at the court, the following day. When Ruto enters the main public hall of the court, walking in a loose and relaxed manner, the morning ritual of shaking hands starts again. This time not only the Kenyans, but defence lawyer Karim Khan and his right hand Shyamala Alagendra join in the prayer as well. Whispers of 'In the name of the father' sound in the lobby. A few minutes later Khan will address the judges in the courtroom, telling them that the Ruto trial is a 'borderline case.' There is no proof 'by any stretch of imagination' of meetings where violence was planned. Take for example the 20 October meeting, that allegedly took place in Ruto's house. Well, at that time his client was in Nairobi. Along with these main planning meetings disappearing from the evidence, so has the network, says Khan. It is telling that the organogram of the network, on which the prosecutor relied in the opening statements back in September 2013, hasn't been referred to in the current presentation. The military component, which was 'the engine' of the organisation, has 'completely disintegrated,' the lawyer argues. The same goes for the political, financial, tribal and communication sections. There were no guns, no trainings, no organisation. What is left is a 'dismembered network,' the defence stresses. The prosecution is 'in dire straits,' says Khan. He points out that it is also strange that there are no public reports of the cleansing ritual. How could this huge event have gone unnoticed while no fewer than three thousand people were said to have been participating, and the Kenyan judge Waki was already investigating the violence? 'It's a fictitious event,' says the counsel. He concludes in a typical Khan metaphor: 'The vehicle of the case can't carry the evidence. The chassis is broken and the wheels have come off.' It is a comparison that spurs an outburst of laughter at the public gallery.

Again Eboe-Osuji asks whether organisation and intent are necessary before violence can legally be categorized as crimes against humanity. Khan refers to the Rome Statute and confirms that 'organisational policy' is needed.

During the break visitors, journalists and lawyers rush to the cafeteria in the main hall. In the queue a man who knows the Kenyan case inside out and who would love to see Ruto and Sang convicted, acknowledges the prosecution doesn't have a strong case. The question is though: is it so weak that the judges will declare the case over and acquit the suspects?

Back in the courtroom Khan points out that Ruto is not a 'king' of the Kalenjin, as is alleged by the prosecution. 'My dear friend Fadi el-Abdallah is spokesperson of the ICC, but not the king of the ICC,' he says. In other words, Ruto didn't have royal powers over the Kalenjin. While Khan talks, he is constantly moving his arms and hands, pointing his fingers. When his black robe glides up, his wrist with a colourful beaded bracelet becomes visible, adding an unexpected frivolity to the sombre courtroom.

Towards the end the defence lawyer shows a few clips featuring his client. The parties are looking at the screens on their desks, while the audience follows the images on the monitors at the public gallery. The visitors on the first rows are twisting their necks to be able to view the video. 'We want a peaceful election,' Ruto is saying while he is seen campaigning in Kenya. Although the deputy president can react with a certain insecurity when unexpectedly asked a question by media, he is an excellent speaker, with great charisma when he is on stage. Hundreds of people cheer, applaud and repeat his words. He talks of ending poverty, tribalism and criminal gangs. Khan has been tearing the prosecution's case apart, and now he is boosting the image of his client, who is 'a model of responsibility.'

When the hearing is over, one of Ruto's daughters, suffering from the Dutch winter cold, rushes out of the courtroom to the hall where she quickly puts on her coat and gloves. The politicians, the senators, the ambassador, the protocol lady, the family, Ruto and Sang gather in the foyer as well. Briefly they discuss the hearing. Then one by one the Kenyans leave through the slow-turning bomb-resistant revolving door. It is raining outside. A man holds up an umbrella for the deputy president, who calmly walks over the bridge towards the exit of the ICC.

A month later there is another setback for the prosecution. The appeals chamber unanimously decides that the judges handling the Ruto & Sang trial erred in allowing the prerecorded testimonies of five witnesses. The appeals judges conclude this 'negatively affected the overall position' of the two accused and was to their 'detriment' because the defence could not cross-examine the witnesses about these statements. They reverse the decision taken earlier by the trial judges, which means the prosecution can't use the original statements of these five witnesses as evidence.

What now? Originally started as the Ocampo Six, soon the case became – when the charges against two suspects weren't confirmed in 2012 – the

Ocampo Four. A year later the prosecutor withdrew the accusations against Francis Muthaura, so the case became the Bensouda Three. In December 2014 she had to let go her case against Uhuru Kenyatta leading to the Bensouda Two. The question is now whether the prosecutor has sufficient evidence against Ruto and Sang. Will it remain Bensouda Two? Or will the Kenyan cases end up as the Bensouda Zero?

Termination

As if a massive dam just has collapsed, the tweets start flooding the Internet. The ICC's website goes down. It says: 'ERROR. The server is busy now. Try later again.' It is late afternoon, 5 April 2016. The massive commotion is the signal that the decision of the judges has been published. Unfortunately the ICC doesn't manage to make the ruling generally available immediately. In the frenzy mistakes are made. A journalist tweets that the trial will continue. A lawyer who did get hold of the decision just adds to the confusion. He tweets a page claiming it is the conclusion of all three judges, while in fact it holds the opinion of only Eboe-Osuji.

In Kenya the twitter-sphere is alight. In a celebratory mood 'Mr. Sospeter' tweets: 'Our God is indeed a live #William_Ruto and Mr Sang are now free from #ICC.' Another tweeter says: 'This calls for some bottles, God has been faithful #ICC has been defeated I lack words to express how happy I am.' While Aubin Rukera tweets: '#ICC should just be dissolved! #Useless #Racist #Neocolonial tool used by The West against #African leaders.'

@fameafrica shows more restraint summarizing: 'BREAKING: #ICC judges throw out charges against #Kenya's Ruto.' While the tweets keep on racing, and the ICC server is still down, a colleague manages to email a prerecorded video clip with the spokesperson of the ICC to other journalists. In his quiet tone Fadi El Abdallah explains that the judges have decided – by majority – that the case against Ruto and Sang 'is to be terminated.' Judges Eboe-Osuji and Fremr concluded that the prosecution 'did not present sufficient evidence on which a reasonable trial chamber could convict the accused.' They agree that the charges will be vacated and the accused 'discharged.' Some figures are mentioned as well. Over a period of 157 trial days the judges heard thirty prosecution witnesses, including two experts. The evidence consisted further of photos, maps, videos and thousands of pages. But it was not enough.[90]

In his personal explanation judge Fremr stresses that the 'entire' case 'hinges' upon the question whether there is enough proof showing the existence of 'the network', which planned and organised to evict ethnic groups such as Kikuyu, Kisii and Kamba.[91] But he concludes that the prosecution 'hardly identified any concrete evidence showing the existence of either the network or the common plan.' There is also 'no evidence' that Ruto 'was behind any of the local activity' or ordered violence. 'To the contrary, the evidence shows that Mr Ruto called for an end to violence,' Fremr writes.

Reading the judges' analysis, it becomes clear how the case might have suffered from witnesses withdrawing and recanting their statements. Take a series of crucial preparatory meetings at the home of Ruto, where allegedly operations were discussed. Here the prosecution relied on prior recorded testimony of three witnesses, which however can't be used in the case. This means 'none of the alleged preparatory meetings is supported by evidence,' Fremr writes.

In a shocking account the judge details what happened with evidence about the training of Kalenjin youth. The only remaining evidence is from witness P-800, as the prior recorded statements of two other testimonies could not be relied on. Initially P-800 declared that he had seen youngsters leaving in lorries. Upon their return, around November 2007, these youths told him they had been at a training camp. But in court the witness said that this information about the training trip came from witness P-495, who had received the story from again another source.

In July 2013, just before the start of the trial and after meeting certain 'individuals', P-800 had apparently changed his initial account in return for a bribe. He signed 'a pre-written affidavit, in which he recanted his earlier statement, despite knowing most of its contents to be untrue,' Fremr states. At trial also P-495 recanted 'his entire prior recorded statement' and 'expressly denied knowledge of any training of Kalenjin

---

90   Ruto and Sang case: ICC Trial Chamber V(A) terminates the case without prejudice to re-prosecution in future, ICC press release, 5 April 2016.
91   Decision on Defence Applications for Judgments of Acquittal, ICC, 5 April 2016.

youths,' Fremr writes. Worse, P-800 also admitted being involved in witness interference himself. He arranged that P-495 would meet the 'individuals' as well, recant his story and approach yet another witness to change her testimony. (Paul Gicheru and Philip Kipkoech Bett, who are wanted by the ICC for witness tampering, have allegedly been involved in the bribing of these two witnesses.[92])

Presiding judge Eboe-Osuji agrees with his colleague there is a lack of evidence. But he goes one step further: 'The proceedings are declared a mistrial due to a troubling incidence of witness interference and intolerable political meddling that was reasonably likely to intimidate witnesses.' It is 'better', he says, to allow the prosecution to start a fresh case in the future, than 'rewarding' these practices 'with a verdict of acquittal.'

The judge admits though that he has been struggling with a difficult question: 'Was the prosecution's case weak because there really was no better evidence left to be obtained and tendered – without the factor of witness interference and political intimidation? Or was it weak because the prosecution did the best they could with the only evidence they could eke out amidst difficult circumstances of witness interference and political intimidation?' The judge concludes that 'because of the tainted process, I am unable to say. It is for that reason that I prefer declaration of a mistrial as the right result.'

Eboe-Osuji, who likes to use rich language, adds that the 'interference was bolstered and accentuated by an atmosphere of intimidation, fostered by the withering hostility directed against these proceedings by important voices that generated pressure within Kenya at the community or national levels or both. Prominent among those were voices from the executive and legislative branches of the government.' Although Fremr agrees there was a 'disturbing level' of witness intimidation and 'inappropriate attempts at the political level to meddle with the trial and to affect its outcome', contrary to Eboe-Osuji he doesn't 'consider the impact to have been of such a level so as to render the trial null and void.'

Fremr also stresses that it has 'not been shown' that the accused were involved in the witness interference, although they did 'profit' from the fact that 'several key witnesses' fell away. The muddiness of the whole

---

92 'Who are the witnesses in the second Kenya bribery case,' International Justice Monitor, 23 September 2015.

affair is the reason why the suspects are not acquitted, as Fremr normally would have preferred. 'The extent of the evidence of interference is enough to make acquittal of the accused grossly unjust,' Eboe-Osuji writes in his decision. The ICC – or a national judiciary – can reopen the case when the prosecution has sufficient evidence against the two Kenyans.

The chamber is however split. The third judge, Olga Herrera Carbuccia, has a different view altogether. She says that the prosecution's case has not 'broken down'. There is 'sufficient evidence', if accepted, on which a 'reasonable' chamber could convict the accused.[93] But being in the minority, the opinion of her two colleagues to terminate the case is decisive.

On twitter there is not only support for the accused, as many express their concerns and disappointment. Take Kenyan born law professor Makau Mutua who tweets from the USA: 'This is the darkest day for the victims of Kenya's 2008 post-election pogroms. Impunity has triumphed over justice at the ICC.'

Not done yet

'Hallelujah! God is great. Our God is Faithful,' tweets Ruto, celebrating that his prayers have been heard. He had been waiting, in the company of his wife, co-accused Sang and politicians, for the decision to be announced. The deputy president is seen 'hugging and shaking hands with those present,' the Daily Nation writes.[94] A picture of Ruto, broadly smiling, being on the phone, is circulating on the Internet. He doesn't however address the media immediately, but leaves that to his lawyer Khan, who is interviewed on CitizenTV by Jeff Koinange, slamming the prosecution for its lousy work.

President Uhuru Kenyatta issues a statement saying: 'I am delighted that Ruto and Sang's innocence has been vindicated by a decision of no-case-to answer at the ICC. This moment was long overdue but no less joyful.' The termination of the case 'brings to a close what has been a nightmare for my nation,' Kenyatta states.

---

93   Dissenting Opinion of Judge Herrera Carbuccia, ICC, 5 April 2016.
94   'DP William Ruto's reaction after ICC drops case,' Daily Nation, 6 April 2016.

The next day prosecutor Fatou Bensouda, looking defeated and her usual sparkle gone, sends out a video message. Seated against a blue background with the logo of the court she reads out her statement on autocue.[95] The prosecutor stresses that the judges 'declined to acquit the accused' because of the circumstances. Other evidence might have been available to the prosecution 'had it been able to prosecute the case in a different climate, less hostile to the prosecution, its witnesses and the court in general.' Bensouda stresses the importance of witnesses as cases 'stand or fall' on their willingness 'to come forward and tell their story in the courtroom.' But in this trial there was 'a relentless campaign' against prosecution witnesses subjecting them to 'intimidation, social isolation and threats.' Then she says something that makes the prayer sessions that had been allowed to take place in the main hall of the ICC in The Hague, less innocent as it seemed. Bensouda says that during public prayer rallies in Kenya, politicians and community leaders branded prosecution witnesses 'as liars who had all given false evidence.' In the end, a total of 17 prosecution witnesses withdrew. As the Kenyan government provided 'only selective assistance' to the court, her office didn't have full access to documents and records that might have 'shed light on the truth.' The prosecutor concludes: 'This case was ultimately eroded by a 'perfect storm' of witness interference and intense politicization of the court's legal mandate and work.' Due to 'the onslaught' against this case, the victims have been denied the 'justice they so rightly deserve.'

She takes the opportunity to thank 'all those, inside and outside of Kenya, who bravely and tirelessly facilitated and supported our work in Kenya because of their conviction and commitment to the cause of justice.' Bensouda adds that she has been 'deeply touched and humbled by the extraordinary courage, conviction and perseverance of so many Kenyans with whom we have interacted.' The judges have sent, by not acquitting the accused, 'a strong message: witness interference and perverting the cause of justice will not be tolerated at the ICC,' says Bensouda. 'Time is on the side of justice.'

But for now though, the cases against the Ocampo Six have crumbled to the Bensouda Zero.

---

95 Statement regarding Trial Chamber's decision to vacate charges against Messrs William Samoei Ruto and Joshua Arap Sang, OTP, 6 April 2016.

Defence calls for investigation

The defence slams back. On 2 May 2016 Khan, lead counsel for Ruto, calls for an independent investigation with regard to prosecution witnesses who have 'deliberately given false testimony' to the judges (such as P-800) and intermediaries who allegedly have been 'coaching' witnesses to give 'false evidence' to the prosecution investigators (including P-800 as well).[96]

If that's not enough, the lawyer also discloses suspicions that ICC staff members may have been 'engaged in sexual relations with witnesses and their families' in Kenya. Possibly they have also been 'bribed by witnesses,' Khan writes. 'These ICC staff members have fostered an environment in which defrauding and telling lies to the ICC was encouraged.' (Later he will explicitly state that his accusations are not directed at OTP staff.)

According to Khan these witnesses, intermediaries and 'possibly' ICC staff members may have committed offences against the administration of justice, listed under Article 70 in the Rome Statute. The defence lawyer explains that he informed deputy prosecutor James Stewart back in 2014 about this delicate matter, who rejected the proposal to investigate the allegations as they were in the middle of the trial. Stewart rather wanted to wait for the final decision. Now that the trial was over, Khan decided it was the right time to request the judges to order the OTP to appoint an independent prosecutor, from outside the institution. This person should only be reporting to Bensouda and her deputy, the lawyer stresses, and be separated by 'Chinese walls' from all staff members dealing with the Ruto trial.

But the prosecution responds on 24 May that it won't embark on such a mission.[97] The first argument is a formal one: Ruto and Sang are no longer accused persons as the charges are vacated. There are other reasons as well, such as the fact that the defence has not handed over all the information to the OTP, rendering it impossible to make an assessment of its value. So far the material is 'insufficient to warrant judicial intervention,' Bensouda says.

She calls the allegations that ICC staff might have had sexual relations with witnesses and could have been bribed by witnesses, 'unsubstantiated,

---

96   Public redacted version of Ruto defence request to appoint an amicus prosecutor, Defence William Ruto, 2 May 2016.

97   Public redacted version of Prosecution's response to the Defence requests to appoint an amicus prosecutor, OTP, 24 May 2016.

sensationalist and in some respects gratuitous, given their apparent irrelevance to any potential Article 70 investigation.' The defence's public accusations have clearly infuriated the prosecution, with Bensouda adding that it is 'nothing more than unsubstantiated hearsay or speculation, and patently an insufficient basis to level serious and public allegations of misconduct against ICC staff members.' Such accusations, based on 'patently flimsy grounds,' is contrary to counsel's duty, she says. 'It might be concluded that the sole purpose of their inclusion was to publicly embarrass the ICC and its staff members. At the very least it was reckless conduct that has brought the court and its officials into disrepute,' Bensouda writes. She asks the judges to 'consider' submitting to the registrar a potential breach of the code of professional conduct for counsel, or to 'issue an appropriate censure' to Karim Khan and his team. The judges agree with the prosecutor that the case is terminated. If the defence teams want to open a case against witnesses and intermediaries, they should bring their complaint before other judges of a pre-trial chamber.[98] And so these filings seem to portend a last phase in this messy process, that originally started as a quest for the truth.

Kenya and the ICC are, however, far from done. Three people are still wanted by the court. Walter Osapiri Barasa, Paul Gicheru and Philip Kipkoech Bett are accused of intimidating and bribing witnesses, such as P-800 whose situation has just been described by judge Fremr. Bensouda is calling on the Kenyan government to surrender the three men. But at a prayer rally following the collapse of the Ruto & Sang case, president Kenyatta said that the trio won't be handed over. A week later the Kenyan attorney general Muigai, who is responsible for the troubled relation with the ICC prosecution for not handing over materials that might have led to new evidence against the president, insists that the witness tampering cases are a matter for the Kenyan courts.[99] The suspects can be 'effectively prosecuted' at home, Muigai says. So far the three haven't been put on trial in Kenya, nor have they been transferred to The Hague.

98   Decision on the Ruto Counsel's Request to appoint an Amicus Prosecutor, ICC, 2 June 2016.
99   'ICC witness fixers should be tried in Kenya, AG Githu Muigai says,' Daily Nation, 21 April 2016.

4

DEMOCRATIC REPUBLIC OF CONGO
The first verdict

The public gallery is packed. High heels are clicking on the parquet. Diplomats, journalists, legal specialists and other ICC-watchers are noisily searching for a seat. A slim woman, dressed in a black jacket and trousers, enters the public gallery. Visitors whisper: 'What is she doing here?' – and cast curious glances at the first row. Movie star Angelina Jolie is being seated for this historic hearing, on 25 August 2011. She is a strong supporter of the court and has been financially supporting the Lubanga Chronicles, a project that distributed news, radio and video clips about today's case in the Democratic Republic of Congo (DRC).

The trial of Congolese rebel leader Thomas Lubanga Dyilo, which has dragged on for many years, has finally arrived at an end stage. All the witnesses have been heard. Evidence has been gathered and presented. The prosecutors, defence lawyers and the legal representatives of victims will now present closing statements in this landmark case, which was the very first before the court.

A guard orders silence on the public gallery, which is separated by sound- and bulletproof glass from the courtroom. Slowly the curtains go up and the visitors view the brownish setting, with furniture and panels on the walls all in light coloured wood, and the carpet striped in beige. In the moments of silence before the hearing begins, a solemn atmosphere comes over this high mass of international criminal law. 'All Rise', says the court officer, his voice audible through the headphones. In one wave the audience and parties get up when the three judges, dressed in dark blue robes, enter the courtroom. They make a small bow to the court officers, prosecutors, the defence lawyers and the victim's legal representatives, all in black robes, who answer with a little nod.

On the left sits the suspect, dressed in a smart suit, between two guards. A wedding ring shines on his left hand – a reminder of a family life with a wife and eight children.

Lubanga (born in 1960), who once studied psychology, was the leader of the Union des Patriotes Congolais (UPC) and its armed wing Forces Patriotiques pour la Libération du Congo (FPLC). He is being prosecuted as a co-perpetrator for the war crimes of enlisting and conscripting children under the age of fifteen into his UPC/FPLC and using them to fight in hostilities between 1 September 2002 and 13 August 2003. Critics say the charges are far too limited and fail to address the true magnitude of the tragedy. During the war in Ituri, a province in the east of the DRC, Lubanga's Hema fighters committed other horrific atrocities as well. They murdered, raped, tortured and looted other ethnic groups such as the rival Lendu, who are accused of similar crimes. When the war reached its peak, from 1999 to 2003, at least 50,000 people were killed. During this period the province was occupied by Uganda, that armed and trained several rebel groups, fuelling the Hema-Lendu conflict, while Rwanda and the DRC supported other armed factions in the region.[100] Today the team of the Office of the Prosecutor (OTP) will kick off. Fatou Bensouda, at the time still deputy prosecutor, is blessed with excellent presentation skills. She stands solid as a rock. Her voice sounds convincing when she starts her address. 'Today we stand before this chamber to submit that the evidence presented in this case has proved not just beyond a reasonable doubt, but beyond any possible doubt that Mr Thomas Lubanga is guilty of the war crimes charged against him, crimes that affected hundreds of children. Those children were trained in about 20 camps around Ituri, a territory bigger than the Netherlands. They were used to fight in conflicts. They were used to kill, rape, and pillage throughout the twelve–month period of these charges.'[101] While Bensouda is making her statements, prosecutor Luis Moreno-Ocampo is sitting behind her. With his fingers he smooths his three-day beard and subconsciously makes a V-sign.

Then the audience is offered a glimpse of the suspect's old life. Images from a video, shot in 2003 and dubbed as crucial evidence by the prosecution, are played and shown on the screens in the public gallery. The audience sees a tall and slim Lubanga, dressed in military fatigues and loosely swinging his arms, walking through his training camp

---

100   'Ituri: Bloodiest Corner of Congo,' Human Rights Watch, 8 July 2003.
101   Official transcript, ICC 25 August 2011.

Rwampara with the hills of Ituri in the background. He is surrounded by dozens of men and boys. Some are wearing a uniform, others a worn out t-shirt and trousers. The warlord rallies his men. 'The work you know, being enlisted in the army, trained, using weapons, is blessed,' Lubanga encourages them. Some boys look very young. And that is exactly why the prosecutors show the video. The evidence that the militia leader has used child soldiers seems, with these images, irrefutable.

From the dock Lubanga stares with an empty look in front of him. He bows his head. As if he realises that with the video and the other presented evidence, his fate is sealed.

The DRC government had referred the conflict in Ituri to the ICC in April 2004, and then the prosecution started investigations. On 16 March 2006, Lubanga was transferred by Kinshasa to the ICC, being the first suspect the court got hold of. After the prosecution's summation it seems unlikely his detention will soon come to an end.

Turbulent case

The presentation by the prosecutor goes smoothly. But the case itself was a turbulent one. Twice the judges halted the proceedings and both times they demanded the release of Lubanga. The first instance was in 2008, just before the start of the trial, as a reaction to the prosecutor's refusal to hand over possibly exonerating information. On a confidential basis the team of Moreno-Ocampo had received documents from sources, such as the United Nations. These sources objected to disclosing this information to the defence or even the judges. However, the chamber decided that this made a fair trial impossible. The second time the trial was halted was in 2010, following the prosecutor's refusal to comply with an order from the judges to disclose the identity of a dubious Congolese intermediary, who had been involved in the search for witnesses and had allegedly been preparing them to give statements against Lubanga.

In both cases the issue of release blew over. The prosecutor cooperated, the appeals chamber reversed the earlier decisions and the warlord remained in the detention centre, which was becoming more crowded. As main supplier, the DRC had extradited another two suspects: Germain Katanga and Mathieu Ngudjolo Chui, both arch-enemies of Lubanga during the war in Ituri. The former Congolese vice president, Jean-Pierre Bemba Gombo, had fled to Europe after losing a power struggle at home, and had been handed over to the court by Belgium. France transferred the Rwandan suspect Callixte Mbarushimana in January 2011. After a slow start, the ICC finally had gathered pace. Other African cases would follow.

To give the historic hearing in the Lubanga trial extra prestige, the prosecutors have invited a special guest, who personally gave an impulse to international justice. 'As an American soldier, I survived the indescribable horrors of World War II and served as a liberator of many concentration camps,' begins Benjamin Ferencz with a remarkably strong voice. He explains how he was appointed, shortly after the liberation, as prosecutor at the Nuremberg War Crimes Trials which 'mapped new rules for the protection of humanity' as it charged and punished Nazi leaders. 'I was 27 years old then. I am now in my 92nd year.'

With his impressive record Ferencz has a sacrosanct status which reflects on the ICC's prosecutors, putting them in a post-WWII tradition. But since this veteran has nothing to do with the Lubanga case and in that respect his words have no legal impact, his speech is also a bit of a show. Especially when Ferencz, after a short description of the development of international criminal law, makes a reflection on the heart of the case. A few hours earlier, behind the scenes, he had been engaged in a heated debate with a court official about the issue of child soldiers. That discussion was captured by a film crew and ended up in the documentary The Court. While the official pleaded that the child soldiers were forced to commit terrible crimes, Ferencz showed no sympathy for these minors, calling them murderers and perpetrators who had followed orders.

But apparently he had given in, had been convinced, or at least had accepted that inside the courtroom, he was invited to present the OTP's views. Now addressing the judges, he recalls that some of the UPC's training camps were holding 'between 8 and 1600 children under the age of fifteen.' However, 'words and figures cannot adequately portray the physical and psychological harm inflicted on vulnerable children who were brutalised and who lived in constant fear.' He explains how their childhood was stolen and how these 'young victims' were deprived of education and human rights. 'Imagine the pain of mothers crying and pleading at the door of the camps, still suffering and wondering what happened to their children.' It is a moving speech, which ends with a lofty call: 'Seizing and training young people to hate and kill presumed adversaries, undermines the legal and moral firmament of human society.

Let the voice and the verdict of this esteemed global court now speak for the awakened conscience of the world.'

Then the legal representatives of victims take the floor. For the first time in the history of international criminal courts and tribunals, victims have the possibility to present their views and observations before the court, though they are rarely present themselves. They are represented by legal counsel. Today, no less than six victims' lawyers address the court. When Lubanga hears about the terrible trauma his crimes have caused, the warlord shakes: no. The light of the fluorescent lamps is reflecting on his sweaty forehead.

The defence

Many seats in the public gallery are empty this second day of the closing statements, 26 August 2011, now that it is Lubanga's lawyers' turn to speak. Most visitors come just for the prosecution. Maître Catherine Mabille puts on her orange reading glasses. The respected defence lawyer from Paris appears not at all impressed by the presentation of the prosecution. She drives her attack to the core of the investigations: the child soldiers.

Mabille reminds the court that the prosecutors called nine former child soldiers as key witnesses during the trial. It was said these minors had been 'abducted forcibly at the ages of 10 to 14, at a time when they were still in school, and that they were subjected to military training of extreme cruelty and then sent to the frontlines,' the lawyer states.[102] However, their testimonies were rubbish. Eight of the children were never soldiers in Lubanga's rebel army, the defence counsel stresses. The ninth child was recruited in 2003, but continued to lie in court about the circumstances of his enlistment. 'All of them lied about their age,' states Mabille, a crucial element in a case concerning child soldiers said to be younger than fifteen.

With increasing astonishment, visitors listen to Mabille's words. Her team of lawyers discovered the lies by travelling to Ituri to investigate the case. They visited schools, went through the enrolment registers and results sheets. That's how they found out that the child soldiers had actually been going to school 'during the time when they claimed that they had been

---

102 Official transcript, ICC, 26 August 2011.

subjected to danger or to cruelty within the ranks of the FPLC.' Voting cards proved some were older than they had claimed. Family members testified in court, confirming some of these children had never been in the rebel army. Parents that supposedly had died or disappeared, were in fact alive. Mabille: 'The prosecutor claimed that he was going to present proof of massive enrolment of child soldiers in the DRC, but his evidence, rather, shows that there was a massive number of false witnesses called by the prosecution.'

The lawyer gains respect from the public gallery. Yesterday Lubanga seemed guilty as hell. Suddenly nothing is certain. How to read the words of Mabille? It is part of the usual strategy of defence lawyers to cast doubt on the prosecution's witnesses. But where are the boundaries between fact and manipulation? Why did those child soldiers lie? 'They lied before the court because they had been asked to lie,' says Mabille. Not by the prosecutors, but by Congolese intermediaries. The problem that had led to a stay of proceedings in 2010, the activities of an intermediary, continued to haunt the case.

Intermediaries

How had the OTP been handling this investigation? The prosecution had assigned this task to a small team of twelve investigators, who encountered many problems. In the early days the officials felt it was too unsafe to travel to Ituri, where militia were still active. When they established a base in the town of Bunia, which was under the protection of the UN, the circumstances remained very basic (often there was no shower) and difficult. The investigators would rotate every ten days, but weren't with enough staff to have a permanent person on the ground. It was hard to find public locations where 'they could safely meet potential witnesses without attracting attention' of the local community, writes lawyer Caroline Buisman, who has been defending ICC suspects and also writes academic articles.[103] Investigators feared that informers would be subjected to reprisals such as abductions if local people found out they were providing the ICC with incriminating information about rebel leaders. The protection of local sources was a serious concern. The

---

103 'Delegating Investigations: Lessons to be Learned from the Lubanga Judgment,' Caroline Buisman, Northwestern Journal of International Human Rights, 2013.

court's investigators decided to avoid contact with leaders of schools, churches and municipalities, and wouldn't visit schools to cross-check the statements of the child soldiers. Working in relative isolation, the team sought to subcontract part of its work to Congolese intermediaries.

It became customary for the ICC to involve local persons if the terrain was too risky for its staff or too dangerous for witnesses to be seen talking to foreigners. Often these local liaisons are employed by NGOs or government institutions. They can travel in the area without raising suspicion, to contact potential witnesses. But in the DRC, with a number of these intermediaries, the situation had spiralled out of control. According to Mabille some of these local liaisons had told the child soldiers who were testifying as witnesses, to take on false names and to present false information. They even produced false documents such as birth certificates.

Possible signs of deceit had surfaced during the trial's first testimony, on 28 January 2009. After the first questions about his recruitment by Lubanga's rebel army were put to him by Fatou Bensouda, this former child soldier started stuttering and backtracking. 'As I swore before God that I would tell the truth, the whole truth, your question puts me in a difficult position with regard to my truth, because I said that I must tell the truth,' he told the court. After Bensouda explained to him she just wanted to know whether he went with the UPC, he answered: 'No, I did not go with them.'[104]

When the prosecution reminded him that earlier he had stated that he was taken by Lubanga's rebels when he was on his way from school to home, he replied: 'No, that's not the case.' He explained that his previous statements about his abduction didn't come from himself. 'It came from someone else. They taught me that over three and a half years. I don't like it. I would like to speak my mind as I swore before God and before everyone.'

He explained he had been invited by an NGO which supported troubled children, and seemed to suggest it was at their request he decided to testify against Lubanga. Responding to the prosecution, who asked him whether he had been taken as a child to a training camp, he said: 'I didn't go. They taught me those things. They really deprived me. I couldn't

---

104 Official transcript, ICC, 28 January 2009.

follow my mind. I told myself that I would do what they wanted. But in coming here, I told myself that I would say what I know to be the truth.' Many observers at the time thought the witness withdrew his earlier incriminating statements because he couldn't face the confrontation with Lubanga, who was sitting in full view in the dock. When the child soldier testified again, two weeks later, on 10 February 2009, the ICC had installed a curtain between him and Lubanga. Under the name Dieumerci the young man told the court about his abduction by the rebel army when he was just eleven years old, his time in training camps where he endured severe beatings, lived in dire circumstances, and was forced to kill.[105]

Manipulation

Several months later however another former child soldier admitted he had lied. Mabille quotes witness P-15, when he explained in court: 'I met an intermediary of the prosecutor who told me the following: You have to change your name. You have to change your identity. Don't give the true story that took place.' The witness told the judges: 'I call them crooks because instead of letting me give the true account of things as they happened, instead of letting me tell my experience, these people invented statements that I had to repeat here in order to manipulate the situation.' How did this work? During the trial a defence witness had explained how a Congolese intermediary, known under the codename P-316, requested him to pretend he was a child soldier and to testify in the case against Lubanga so the warlord could be convicted. The witness had described how the relationship with this intermediary had developed: 'At that point in time, he had money, and he would buy drinks for me. He used to give me a little money, and so I accepted to lie.' The witness added: 'He told me that I was going to leave Bunia and that I was going to go to the white man's country.'

Such a promise must have been appealing to a witness living in poor conditions. In a cynical way, it was by no means without grounds. 'The witnesses, the alleged child soldiers, were all put into protection programmes, and they were relocated,' Mabille discloses. If witnesses are in danger they can be brought to safety through the protection

---

105   Lubanga trial, week 3, child soldier tells of killing, International Justice Monitor, 13 February 2009.

programme of the ICC. The court can move them to another country and give them an income, health care, education and housing. Often this applies to 'insiders', who are part of the criminal network of the suspect and willing to testify against their former partner in crime. But also victims are relocated. An attractive perspective, defence lawyers claim, that can also be an incentive for a lie.

While Mabille proceeds with her statement, her opponent, prosecutor Moreno-Ocampo is sprawled on his chair. The arm of his reading glasses in his mouth, swinging from one side to the other, between his lips. 'As the trial continued, the defence demonstrated that certain intermediaries of the office of the prosecutor had prepared witnesses to come and give false accounts before the court,' Mabille says. She holds several intermediaries – P-316, P-321 and P-143 – responsible for 'an operation of manipulation of evidence' as they allegedly asked their recruited witnesses to lie by pretending to be child soldiers.

No proper investigations

How is it possible that Moreno-Ocampo's team had not discovered the lies and false evidence themselves? 'Simply because the prosecutor did not carry out proper investigations,' Mabille stresses. While the defence team had been in Ituri to check the allegations against their client, the ICC investigators had neglected their task. Mabille quotes an unsuspected source: Bernard Lavigne, who was in charge of the Lubanga investigations. He was called by the judges in November 2010 to explain what was going on. Lavigne confirmed that with regard to the 'five or six' child soldiers, who as witnesses fell under his responsibility, 'we never went to families to identify ourselves as such with a view to interviewing these children or their relations.' He admitted that 'we never went to schools to ask the headmasters or directors […] to give us the various files on the children so that we could cross-check their ages,' Lavigne testified.[106]

The prosecution simply didn't verify itself the identities, says Mabille, but left this task to the intermediaries. It is sheer nonsense, the defence argues, that security issues blocked ICC officials from checking the statements and ages of the child soldiers, as the court had brought these young

---

106 Official transcript, ICC, 18 November 2011.

witnesses to safe areas. 'The very fact of putting witnesses in protection programmes should have enabled the prosecutor to carry out such investigations, it would seem to me, without putting them at risk,' the defence lawyer states.

She concludes that the 'entire evidence' is 'tainted' by the methods applied in these investigations. Mabille: 'It has been shown that most of the evidence has been falsified, that fraudulent agents have had an impact on the reliability of the statements made by the witnesses, witnesses who admitted having been manipulated, and therefore the entire evidence presented by the prosecution has been manipulated.'

What remains as proof against Lubanga? Just some images and impressions, says Mabille. But examining 'a video or photograph does not make it possible beyond any reasonable doubt to determine the age of an individual.' It is a valid argument which the defence, as part of their theory of deceptive appearances or optical illusion, will continue to repeat.

State intervention

While Mabille builds up her case, she tears the evidence of her opponent apart. She paints a disturbing image of the Congolese context in which the prosecution operated. 'The danger of false testimony is a danger in every single court around the world, and even though in this case the proportion of false testimony reaches an unequalled level, this is perhaps not the most serious danger to the International Criminal Court in this very case.' More serious issues are the 'threats' against the independence of the court, the lawyer claims, because there is the risk that the OTP is being used by certain states. 'We do not allege that the prosecutor intentionally served the interests of one of these powers. But it has been shown that the Congolese government in many ways intervened, directly or indirectly, in the investigations as well as in the judiciary process,' the defence lawyer claims.

Mabille returns to the matter of the 'fraudulent' intermediaries, whose identities all remain confidential. At least one of them, P-316, is a 'direct agent of the Congolese government,' she says, in a 'high level of authority in a governmental agency directly related to the central power, directly related to president Kabila.' To protect his identity, she can't be more specific. But other sources claim that P-316 works for the Congolese secret service. The influence of the national authorities on the trial goes even further, she says. A defence witness lost his job as a government official when the authorities heard he wanted to testify in The Hague. Two witnesses were arrested when they returned to the DRC and one of them was severely mistreated by the army.

After 45 minutes the lawyer has come to the end of her damning presentation. 'Quite remarkable accuracy in relation to timing, maître Mabille,' smiles presiding judge Adrian Fulford. With a touch of British wit, he compliments the lawyer for timing her presentation so well, while nicely ignoring its damning content, which is a serious attack on the prosecution's work.

Prosecutor Moreno-Ocampo keeps his head bowed. But after yesterday's panic, Lubanga has gathered courage. The Congolese warlord looks self-assured. And then it happens. Lubanga stares straight into one of the camera's that is installed in the courtroom to film the proceedings. The lens zooms in on his face. His imperative look comes closer. These are just camera images, but even in this very indirect way, his intense eyes manage to intimidate visitors at the public gallery. If this man is capable of that, simply by a stare caught by a camera and transmitted to a monitor in the public gallery, while he sits behind bulletproof glass in court with guards next to him, how powerful must his presence have been when he was a warlord on the battlefield?

His lawyer seems to have destroyed at least part of the evidence – the testimonies of nine child soldiers – used as evidence against her client. But Mabille said nothing about the other 27 witnesses who were called by the prosecutor. For outsiders who have not closely followed all two hundred hearings, with large parts of the trial taking place behind closed doors, it is difficult to see through the legal rhetoric. But it is clear that something went wrong in the approach of the prosecutor. Later, in October 2012, the War Crimes Research Office of the Washington College of Law of the American University, would publish a highly critical report about the ICC's criminal investigations. Regarding the Congolese liaisons in the Lubanga case, the report's authors conclude there was 'no formal process within the OTP for checking the background of individuals who presented themselves as willing to serve as intermediaries.'[107]

---

107 'Investigative management, strategies, and techniques of the International Criminal Court's office of the prosecutor,' War Crimes Research Office, American University, 2012.

Judge Fulford – bold face, rings on his left and right little fingers – addresses the suspect: 'Mr. Lubanga, we understand that you wish to make a short unsworn statement, and if that is correct, now is the opportunity for you to do so.'

The warlord gets up and starts his address in the solemn language of the court. 'Throughout the course of this trial before this august chamber, it has been impossible for me to recognise myself within the context of the actions ascribed to me and the intentions attributed to me,' Lubanga says. Indeed, he assumed 'certain responsibilities' and he did so 'with a view to combatting the inhumane treatment to which all Congolese citizens in Ituri were subjected. I did so only with a view to trying to save what is dearest to every man, to every human, namely life, and I did this within a spirit of reconciliation.'

Guided by the 'convictions' and 'noble values' which he had learned during his education, which 'fashioned my personality,' he actually had taken action 'against the recruitment of minors.' He appeals to the judges 'to understand that all through the terrible moments which we experienced in Ituri in 2002 and 2003, I never had the feeling that I failed or did not act consistently with the values I talked about.'

His words mark the end of the hearing. The judges withdraw to study the evidence. What follows is six months of silence. Until the public gallery is again flooded by visitors for the first verdict in the history of the ICC.

Verdict day

The decision is still secret. Today, 14 March 2012, it will become clear how the judges have evaluated the evidence presented by the prosecutor and the arguments of the defence.

Even seasoned experts have no idea what the outcome will be. Slowly the luxaflex curtain, blocking the view on the courtroom, goes up. Like a magnet, Lubanga attracts all attention. The warlord, sitting in the dock, shines like a diamond. Proudly he wears an impressive white African robe that falls loosely on his body. From top to toe, Lubanga has dressed himself especially for this day. On his head he has a white fez. In his dazzling outfit Lubanga distinguishes himself from the dark robes around him. The symbolism can't be missed. A white dove amidst the crows. Seemingly relaxed, Lubanga folds his hands under his chin while the magistrates have taken their seats.

Tension is rising when judge Fulford, known for his strict guiding of hearings, reads the verdict. There is the first sledgehammer blow. Not for the suspect, but for the prosecution, which 'should not have delegated its investigative responsibilities to the intermediaries,' the judges conclude, 'notwithstanding the extensive security difficulties that it faced.'[108] Fulford explains the judges have spent 'a considerable period of time investigating the circumstances of a substantial number of individuals whose evidence was, at least in part, inaccurate or dishonest. The prosecution's negligence in failing to verify and scrutinise this material sufficiently before it was introduced led to significant expenditure on the part of the court.' Because the OTP didn't keep proper oversight, intermediaries were 'potentially able to take advantage of the witnesses they contacted,' while alleged child soldiers, given the fact that they were young, were 'vulnerable to manipulation.'

These are serious accusations from the chamber. The judges decided that the testimonies of nine witnesses and victims are unreliable. Their statements are excluded from the deliberations on guilt. Fulford goes on to explain that there is a risk that the three main intermediaries P-143, P-316 and P-321 'persuaded, encouraged, or assisted witnesses to give false evidence.' Ominously he adds: 'These individuals may have committed crimes.' According to the rules, however, only the prosecutor can initiate an investigation into such malpractices.

Stoic, prosecutor Moreno-Ocampo listens to the criticism, which is tainting the reputation of his office. The question that now descends over the courtroom is how this reproof will affect the verdict.

With considerable speed, Fulford reads further. 'Multiple witnesses testified credibly and reliably' that child soldiers had been recruited, trained, abused, forced to fight and used as bodyguards. Video images of the training camp in Rwampara 'clearly' show recruits under the age of fifteen. Children were part of his army which Lubanga was building to control Ituri. The warlord himself had included minors in his presidential guard. Lubanga's face shows increasing concern while he starts to understand what is coming. With the tough wording of the decision read by Fulford, it is as if the prison door is being shut with a loud bang.

---

108   Official transcript, ICC, 14 March 2012.

The judges underline the warlord did not operate on his own. Fulford names a few co-perpetrators. One of them, commander Bosco Ntaganda, is well known to the court. Years ago the ICC filed an arrest warrant against him. The Terminator, as he is known, was still a fugitive at the time of the Lubanga verdict. Under the eye of international Blue Helmets, he lived a luxurious life in Kivu, an immense area south of Ituri. His name surfaced as one of the leaders of rebel movement M23, terrorising the east of the DRC – until his spectacular surrender to the ICC almost exactly one year later.

The judges don't agree on everything. But they decide that despite the serious mistakes and many problems, the prosecution has proved 'beyond reasonable doubt' that Lubanga committed the war crimes of conscripting and enlisting children under the age of fifteen years and using them to participate actively in hostilities.

Unanimous in their verdict they rule: guilty.

Suddenly the warlord is hopelessly overdressed in his white robe. His lawyers turn towards their client to support him. But the prosecutors are in the best of moods. Despite many blunders, their case is saved. The judges of the ICC have just convicted their first war criminal.

Deceptive appearances

An immense white and black insect is crawling over the shoulder of a boy. These bizarre images appear on the screens of the public gallery three months after the verdict. The defence is presenting this strange video during a special sentencing hearing on 13 June 2012. The session is to allow lawyers and prosecution to introduce arguments which the judges can consider when deciding on a punishment for Lubanga.

'There is someone with an insect on his shoulder and a cap on his head in that footage. Do you recognise that person?' defence counsel Marc Desalliers asks witness Augustin Mbogo Malobi (born in 1983), who is testifying through a skype connection from an ICC office, probably in Ituri.[109] The witness belonged to Lubanga's presidential guard. He has just said that his youngest colleagues were 17, 18, and 19 years of age at the time. So no child soldiers. When the video also shows a tattoo, he says: 'I am the one. In fact my name is written on my arm, Mbogo.' Desalliers

---

109   Official transcript, ICC, 13 June 2012.

asks the court officers to 'play this image in slow motion' to be able to see more clearly what is written on the arm of the witness.

But irritated, judge Fulford intervenes. 'Just pause for a moment, please, before that happens. What's the point of this, Mr Desalliers?' he asks. The defence lawyer explains that the judges have concluded that Lubanga had recruited and used child soldiers, 'solely' by estimating their ages from images, and based on these pictures had decided their client used minors in his army. A very problematic method, according to the defence, because people can appear much younger than they are in reality. They want to show that Mbogo looks like a little boy in the video, but in fact was much older.

But Fulford stops the lawyer's explanation. 'This is gravely in danger of amounting to an attack' on the verdict, he says. With his two colleagues he will withdraw for ten minutes to discuss the defence's strategy. While the judges leave the courtroom, the lawyers are standing with their heads down, like schoolchildren who have just been reprimanded by their teacher. The prosecutors can't control themselves. They laugh at their opponents' possible miscalculation. On their return the judges say they will not accept the defence's approach. Once more the lawyers try to explain the importance of their observations on 'deceptive appearances.' In vain.

A severe sentence

A better farewell gift for Moreno-Ocampo is hardly imaginable. It is his last day in court as prosecutor, a position the Argentinian lawyer has held for nine years. Next to him sits Fatou Bensouda, who already has been elected as his successor by the countries that are members of the ICC. For the last time Moreno-Ocampo will address the judges. He takes his place behind the transparent table lectern and states that Lubanga should get 'a very severe sentence.' The prosecution will request a punishment 'in the name of each child recruited' and 'in the name of the Ituri community.' And while he works towards a crescendo, Moreno-Ocampo demands a sentence in the name of the Hema and Lendu who suffered under Lubanga's militia, in the name of the citizens 'from all over' the world, and if that is not enough, in the name of states that signed up to the ICC to combat impunity of these crimes. 'Mr President, your Honours, the prosecution requests the chamber to impose a sentence of 30 years of prison to Mr Thomas Lubanga,' Ocampo states.

As top leader of his militia he deserves the second highest punishment (after life sentence) which the court can impose, he explains. 'In a domestic prosecution each separate act committed against a child will call for a serious punishment. The International Criminal Court should not be more lenient.' Being the top leader, nobody could refuse Lubanga's orders and so he was involved in every child recruitment, the prosecution underlines. One more time Moreno-Ocampo describes the cruel treatment to which the child soldiers were subjected. After being abducted and trained by terror, the 'children were launched into battle zones where they were instructed to kill everyone, regardless of whether they were men, women or children. All were the enemy. That was the education Mr Lubanga provided to the children recruited by the militia.' He recalls how girls were used as sex slaves. The children who survived 'have permanent physical effects or have ongoing psychological trauma.'

But as soon as Moreno-Ocampo explains that his 'crimes affected the education system in Ituri in its entirety,' the convicted war criminal can't hold his laughter. Scornful, Lubanga hides his grin behind his hand and challenges his opponent with a cynical stare.

'However,' stresses Moreno-Ocampo with his feel for theatre, 'the prosecution would like to offer Mr Lubanga a last chance to mitigate his guilt. Today, or maybe tomorrow, but in this courtroom Mr Lubanga can offer a genuine apology.'

From the dock the warlord smirks, while shaking his head: no. Undisturbed, Ocampo sums up the list with conditions, such as showing genuine remorse, before the prosecutors would 'recommend a reduced sentence of 20 years.'

When maître Mabille announces that her client will speak soon, two persons at the public gallery happily give each other a fist bump. In the meantime Lubanga searches the audience with his eyes, until he catches the look of a visitor, and compels it like a prey.

After his presentation Moreno-Ocampo is slumping in his chair. Bensouda next to him, sits upright, as always. Fulford seems to doze off a bit. The defence raises again the issue of 'optical illusion' that can occur when video and photos are used to establish the ages of the child soldiers, especially if they suffered malnutrition (or as the lawyers call it: 'dietary deficiencies') when growing up. Just by looking at footage the judges simply can't have assessed the number of children that allegedly were recruited. And if the fight against impunity is so important, why has only their client been selected? Although the presidents Museveni (Uganda), Kagame (Rwanda) and Kabila (DRC) should have been prosecuted as 'first-ranking accused,' the prosecution has chosen them as 'privileged partners' guaranteeing 'impunity to those most responsible for the massacres committed in Ituri,' the lawyers underline.

Exaggerations and lies

After a day full of twists and turns Lubanga gives his speech. 'I was deeply overwhelmed and saddened by it, appalled to note that after three years of trial we have not been able to unmask all the exaggerations, lies and masquerades. I have been portrayed as a warlord, pitilessly, taking hold of the children of the Ituri in order to feed his desire for power,' the convicted war criminal says. He points out, however, that while the UPC militia comprised about eight thousand men, the prosecutor did not manage to present one single child soldier in person to the court. Is this an indication, Lubanga wonders, that there was simply no child below fifteen in his army, or in such small numbers that 'it is today impossible to find even one?'

Some say, Lubanga goes on, that the children from his Hema group didn't want to testify against him out of loyalty. But other ethnic groups were also part of the UPC army. The prosecutor hadn't found child soldiers among these groups either to come and testify. He refers to the judgment where he read that a witness had seen him at the Mongbwalu road abducting a child to enlist it in his army. 'I would like to assert before this court that I never, I never could have stooped to such a low level to commit an act which is contrary to all values that are dear to me.' He sticks to his earlier statements that he is innocent. 'What is certain however is that I, Thomas Lubanga,' he says, with a slight hitch, 'I was always – I always stood in a position to any such enlisting – or was opposed to that.'

When he switches to his experiences in Ituri, the horrors of the war enter the courtroom. 'On several occasions, I saw hundreds of bodies savagely chopped up by machetes, bodies burnt alive in huts, villages completely destroyed, thousands of people fleeing in desperation, and sometimes I fled with them in circumstances where often what mattered was only one's life, and I have been deeply hurt by this situation.' Ituri changed into a 'vast cemetery,' says Lubanga. 'Yet unfortunately no political or military official genuinely undertook to attend to the security of the people. Their lone concern was money and power.' Instead he, Lubanga, would take responsibility. 'Not for money, not for power, but for peace.'

Lubanga presents himself as an honourable leader who is innocent and had fulfilled his duty, but unfortunately was wrongly convicted by judges as a war criminal. In these last moments of his address he takes the opportunity to bear 'homage to the memory of all the victims of the atrocities' in his homeland. 'I pray, or I hope, that the peace for which I worked so hard can return definitively to the Ituri. I thank you.'

The prosecutor remains silent. These are not the words which will change Moreno-Ocampo's mind to demand a lower sentence for the man sitting opposite, in the dock.

The sentence

Nervously Lubanga ticks with his fingers on the table in front of him. Over the years he has spent possibly more than a thousand hours in this chair. His lawyers are seated in front of him, as always, like a buffer. A photographer focuses a huge telescopic lens on the Congolese rebel leader. During special hearings the news agencies are permitted by turn to enter the courtroom for less than two minutes to take pictures which will then be distributed all over the world.

Today, 10 July 2012, Lubanga will hear his sentence. Fulford starts to speak. Although the judges haven't been able to establish exactly how many children were in Lubanga's army, it has become clear that 'the involvement of children was widespread.'[110] He explains that the chamber 'did not conclude that Mr Lubanga meant to conscript and enlist boys and girls,' but that he was 'aware that, in the ordinary course of events, this would occur.' The judges conclude that Lubanga is intelligent, well-educated and would understand the seriousness of the crime of recruiting and using child soldiers. It is this 'marked level of awareness,' which is a relevant factor for the judges in determining the 'appropriate sentence.' They note though, that 'nothing suggests' that Lubanga ordered the punishment of these child soldiers, or was aware of these abuses.

But first Fulford says that the judges 'strongly' deprecate the attitude of Moreno-Ocampo towards the issue of sexual violence.Not only did the prosecutor fail to include sexual abuse or sexual slavery in the charges,

---

110   Official transcript, ICC, 10 July 2012.

but he even 'actively opposed' such a step, while on the other hand he advocated that these crimes should be counted as an aggravating factor for the sentencing. Fulford explains that judge Elizabeth Odio Benito was of the opinion that the harm to children and families, especially as a result of cruel punishment and sexual violence, should be given attention when measuring the sentence for Lubanga, and would have condemned him to 15 years in prison. But Fulford and his colleague disagreed. The judges also reflected on the fact that the suspect was 'respectful and cooperative' during the trial.

There is the voice of Fulford: 'Mr Lubanga is sentenced to a total period of 14 years' imprisonment.'

In the public gallery, people start counting. With the deduction of his years in ICC detention, since 16 March 2006, Lubanga will have to serve another eight years. The lawyers turn to their client, shake his hand and talk to him. A few months later they appeal. Just like the legal representatives of victims do. The prosecutors demand a higher sentence for the convicted war criminal.

Early release

It will take the appeals chamber two and a half years to confirm, on 1 December 2014, by majority, the guilty verdict and the prison term. Thus Lubanga remains in the ICC detention centre. His direct victims are now entitled to reparations, but that is easier said than done. At the court a new set of judges, the prosecution, defence, victims representatives and Trust Fund for Victims are engaged in an endless legal battle to settle this matter (see chapter 10).

The following summer, in 2015, the ICC starts the procedure to determine whether his punishment could be reduced. It has become practice that convicts can be released after having served two-thirds of their sentence. Lubanga's lawyers have no faith in the panel's presiding judge, Silvia Fernández de Gurmendi, handling this procedure and ask for her disqualification. But their request is dismissed. All parties involved can make their arguments on the matter of early release.[111]

---

111 Decision on the review concerning reduction of sentence of Mr Thomas Lubanga Dyilo, ICC, 22 September 2015.

Hoping to be set free, Lubanga underlines that he is married, has eight children and is almost daily in contact with them. They also visit him regularly. In other words, he has a family to return to. If he would be released, he would like to resume a post-graduate study in psychology at the University of Kisangani, focusing on inter-ethnic conflicts. His goal is to look at 'stereotypes' and 'prejudices' with the aim of working towards a situation where 'tribal groups' can 'live together in harmony.'

On a positive note, the registrar notes that Lubanga follows the detention house rules and behaves well, especially to the other detainees and staff. But he hasn't shown 'regrets or other form of dissociation from his crime.' There are several other issues that might block his early release. It is not certain that he will be admitted at the university, and the prosecution suggests that studying in Kisangani is in fact an excuse for his real intention: returning to Ituri. A home-coming seems very problematic as the victims say he won't be able to come back to the community in 'a spirit of peace and reconciliation.' They note that Lubanga didn't respond to their email in which they asked him to think about actions promoting social stability and peace. The Congolese authorities fear that people in Ituri might be re-traumatized when Lubanga returns. Besides, there are elections planned in the DRC and his release could lead to all kinds of problems. Many in the UPC still see Lubanga as 'hero' and there could be disturbances if large crowds gather.

On top of this, the prosecution alleges that from the detention centre, Lubanga has contacted witnesses for his old buddy Bosco Ntaganda, who is also being prosecuted by the ICC, and possibly tried to influence these persons. The defence denies the allegations. But things don't look good. The judges acknowledge there is 'a prospect for the resocialization and successful resettlement of Mr Lubanga in the DRC,' but they don't see other factors in favour of early release. They decide, on 22 September 2015, that Lubanga will have to stay inside. The next review is in 2017. Lubanga won't await that analysis in ICC's detention centre. On 19 December 2015 he is flown back to the DRC, as Lubanga preferred to serve his sentence at home. He is staying in the Makala jail in Kinshasa. It was from this prison that he was taken in 2006 to The Hague, to be prosecuted, convicted and sentenced by the ICC.

5

CENTRAL AFRICAN REPUBLIC
Two trials against Jean-Pierre Bemba Gombo

Three female judges walk into the courtroom and take their places in
the comfortable chairs on the modest platform that gives them both
prominence and an overview. It is the first hearing after the winter recess
in the trial against the Congolese warlord Jean-Pierre Bemba Gombo.
On behalf of her two colleagues, presiding judge Sylvia Steiner wishes
everybody 'a very happy year.' And she adds: 'The chamber also wishes
to convey to Mr Gombo its condolences for his loss.' His stepmother,
who raised him from the age of twelve after he lost his biological mother,
has passed away. The Congolese suspect had requested provisional
release for four days to be able – 'as the head of the family, in accordance
with African traditions' – to attend her funeral in Belgium. This was
'an exceptional circumstance' the judges agreed. For 'humanitarian
reasons' they gave permission for the journey. But referring to security
arrangements between Belgium and The Netherlands, the judges only
partly granted the request, limiting the trip to one day.[112] There were
other restrictions as well. Bemba and his defence team were for instance
not allowed to 'reveal any information' about his presence in Belgium.
So yesterday, Monday 10 January 2011, Bemba was taken by Dutch
police to the border and handed over to Belgian colleagues. He was
allowed to see his stepmother's remains and to attend the requiem
mass in a church in Waterloo before he was taken back to the ICC
detention centre in The Hague. The judges had decided that Bemba
would be responsible for covering all the costs. Apparently the security
arrangements had worked out, the detainee now being present in the
courtroom.

---

112   Decision on the Defence Request for Mr Jean-Pierre Bemba to attend his Stepmother's Funeral, ICC,
      12 January 2011.

Together the three judges represent almost every continent. Steiner is Brazilian and partly from German descent. Joyce Aluoch is from Kenya. Kuniko Ozaki is Japanese. Three women – a symbol of the female emancipation that has rooted at the highest circles of international criminal law. A few minutes later Steiner gives instructions that the witness can be led in. The blinds go down. Nobody in the public gallery is allowed to know who that person is. A number is her pseudonym. When the blinds go up, the middle part stays down, protecting witness P-87 from the gallery's view. Two curtains on the sides give extra cover. The witness' face is unrecognizable, as it appears split into little moving cubes on the monitors for the visitors in the gallery and via the livestream for the public at large. Her voice sounds distorted. 'Madam witness,' is how she will be addressed during her testimony.

When the court officer reads the oath to her, the cubes on the screens move in rhythm as the witness repeats the words. In a friendly manner, judge Steiner will a few minutes later explain to her: 'If at any time you feel tired, or distressed, or in need of a break in the questioning, you should simply say so and the chamber will take a short break to give you some time.'[113] Invisible behind the blinds, a psychologist sits next to the witness to support her during her testimony.

On the left is the man who is at the centre of this trial: Jean-Pierre Bemba Gombo. The former militia leader and vice president of the Democratic Republic of the Congo (DRC) sits between two guards. Bemba is a big man with a considerable belly and a round face. He is wearing a nice suit. Watching him from the public gallery gives one the uneasy feeling of being a – caught – voyeur. Bemba looks back at you, straight in the eye. The Congolese leader used to be a powerful man with a varied career. He was born in a family that moved in high circles. His father was a wealthy Congolese businessman who was close to dictator Mobutu Sese Seko, when the DRC was still called Zaire. Jean-Pierre studied in Belgium and lived a life in luxury.

Being part of the establishment, the young Bemba met African leaders. Later he would own an impressive business empire and was reportedly among the richest in the country. The multimillionaire had enterprises,

113 Official transcript, 11 January 2011

such as the local branch 'Bralima' of Dutch beer company Heineken which he inherited from his father, and a TV station.[114]

But Bemba had other – political – aspirations as well. In 1998 he became a warlord when he set up the Mouvement de Libération du Congo (MLC) and its armed wing, that would control the entire Équateur province – an area in the north of the country larger than France.

In the words of the ICC's prosecution: 'Jean-Pierre Bemba's search for absolute power in the Democratic Republic of the Congo led him to establish a military force of more than 20,000 men. This gave rise to a movement that was controlled by Jean-Pierre Bemba, led by him, for him, by him. The movement belonged to him. Jean-Pierre Bemba used his army as a personal tool and as a bargaining card, a bargaining chip, so that he could become a major player within politics within the DRC.'[115]

That position of MLC commander-in-chief would become fatal to Bemba. Not because of the behaviour of his troops in their own country, but because of their crimes in the neighbouring nation. In 2002 then president Ange-Félix Patassé of the Central African Republic (CAR) requested that Bemba send troops to help in quelling a coup d'état. CAR's army general François Bozizé, who had been sacked two months earlier, had retreated to Chad. From there he had launched an attack on his own country with the aim to overthrow the sitting president Patassé.

The rebellious general had reached Bangui, the capital city of the CAR, by 25 October 2002, and was just one kilometre away from the presidential residence. At that moment Bemba's forces arrived to support the Patassé government. Just like they had done in 2001, when they were asked to crush a similar rebellion. During that first intervention, the ICC's prosecution alleges, there had already been 'cases of sexual violence, pillaging and murder.'

This second time, Bemba would send a brigade, consisting of two MLC battalions under the command of colonel Mustapha Mukiza to the CAR. In the beginning Bemba's troops totalled 500 men, but at its peak the brigade consisted of 1500 to 2000 men. Patassé would not only call in Bemba's men, but Libyan troops and Chadian militia as well. To no avail.

---

114 'Beer and Bemba: how ICC big fish links to Heineken,' International Justice Tribune, 13 April 2016
115 Official transcript, 12 November 2014.

The president would lose the violent struggle with his opponent Bozizé, who finally grabbed power in 2003. Bemba had bet on the wrong horse. At first the CAR started national investigations into war crimes, but then in 2004 the head of state, general Bozizé, asked the ICC to take over the job of prosecuting the persons most responsible for crimes committed in his country. He handed over the files, including those incriminating Bemba, to the ICC. Two years later the highest court of the CAR ruled that the country's justice system was unable to prosecute international crimes cases. It would take until 2007 before prosecutor Luis Moreno-Ocampo opened a full investigation. The national leadership cooperated and the ICC was allowed to conduct site visits. Moreno-Ocampo came to meet with the authorities. During her testimony P-87 will tell that he also met with victims and even had his photo taken with her.

Although the country is known for its history of violent chaos, coup attempts, revengeful leaders and the involvement of many militia, only one person, not even a national, but one of the 'neighbours', was prosecuted by the ICC: Bemba. The ICC would charge him with two counts of crimes against humanity (murder and rape) and three counts of war crimes (murder, rape and pillaging) allegedly committed by his men in the CAR. On 24 May 2008 the Congolese leader was arrested in Belgium. A few weeks later, on 3 July, he was transferred to The Hague. After delays and failed attempts by his lawyers to have him released, the trial started on 22 November 2010.[116]

The bad people

It is the prosecutor's task to present today, through witness P-87, part of the evidence that, as a commander, Bemba bears responsibility for the international crimes committed by his MLC militia. It is the first time the ICC is prosecuting a person in this specific capacity. The witness will be under great pressure. P-87 will have to talk, in public, about very painful experiences. The lawyers defending Bemba will point at inconsistencies in her story. A trial being a test of strength between parties, which involves strategic and legal thinking to serve tactical goals and higher ideals of justice.

---

116 Case Information Sheet 'The Prosecutor v Jean-Pierre Bemba Gombo,' ICC, 26 July 2016.

The game has started. The defence is asking whether one of the curtains can be pulled back a little because two lawyers who will do the cross-examination can't see the witness. With a polite smile Steiner says: 'I am informed by the court officer that it is not possible to get the curtain closer to the window because of the public gallery, so the curtain is in the very same position as always.' She suggests the lawyers could swap seats? But the defence gives it one more try. 'Last time it was dealt with, with a kind of a pin.' Steiner doesn't fall for that option. There is a good reason why the witness is shielded: she needs to be protected. Any risk that the public could view her has to be ruled out.

The defence doesn't give up that easily and argues that their client Bemba can't change positions, while he has 'the right' to see the witness. But the judge sticks to her point: 'The standard proceeding is that of course the accused has a view, can see the witness, but through the monitors, and not directly, because the curtains have been always there in the very same position.' And that's it. 'We shall follow your recommendation,' maître Nkwebe Liriss, Bemba's lead counsel, responds politely.

The judge asks the witness about the meaning of the oath. Steiner: 'Did you understand that you must give answers to questions asked that are true and accurate to the best of your knowledge and belief?' The witness: 'Yes, I have properly understood that.'

Prosecutor Petra Kneuer, a woman with a serious frown that seldom disappears from her face, will be the first to question witness P-87. Carefully she takes the woman back to that dreadful day in 2002 that would upset her life completely. 'Please,' underlines Kneuer, 'do not reveal your identity, or the location where you live, or for example names of family members or neighbours from which you could be identified.' If she needs to share such sensitive information, the judges can order to go in private session and then the public won't hear what she says. 'Do you understand that, madam witness?' The cubes on the monitor move as the witness answers: 'Yes, I understand.' Over the headphones the voices of the interpreters are heard translating the witness' language Sango, into French and English for the judges, the court officials, the parties and the public.

It is early in the morning, 30 October 2002, when the witness sees how young men in her neighbourhood in Bangui start running. 'They said that the men had come, that they were bad people, they were the Banyamulenge,' she tells the court. Many neighbours had not waited for the moment that Bemba's militia, locally referred to as 'Banyamulenge', would arrive. They had fled in fear. Witness P-87 though, had decided with a young brother and a third person to stay in a house of her extended family. Despite the threat she sold coffee, as she was used to. Until events would take a terrible turn.

The coffee-seller sees how MLC soldiers are returning from the market with pillaged goods. When evening falls, her family home is targeted. Three of Bemba's soldiers enter the house and steal valuable items such as the television, radio, chairs and mattresses. Robbed and frightened, witness P-87 and her family members are left with a looted house.

But while she is telling the judges about her ordeal, the woman makes a little mistake. By accident she gives away some names. Fortunately, the public gallery is almost empty. Just a few visitors heard the names. The proceedings in the courtroom are also web-streamed by the ICC, so everyone with a computer and Internet connection can follow the hearings. To be able to suppress and cut confidential information that is accidentally released by a witness, such as now happened, the video images are broadcast with a thirty-minute delay. Nevertheless, judge Steiner will keep on reminding the witness: be careful and avoid pronouncing names.

The pillaging is just the beginning. That same evening again three Banyamulenge enter the house. The leader of the group forces the coffee-seller to the veranda at the back of the house. He keeps his firearm in his right hand, puts down his torch and throws her on the ground. While the court's interpreters translate her words, the woman tells without pausing: 'He took off his belt and took off my underwear and he got out his penis. He penetrated me and he started to sleep with me and I had my hand on my head. When he finished he ejaculated, and he got up and he stood up before me and he closed his belt and he called one of his companions.' She would be gang-raped by three MLC militiamen. 'When I stood up the liquid was running out of my vagina.'

In a few sentences witness P-87 describes the terrible crime that must have devastated her. But she says nothing about the physical pain of the violent penetration, nothing about the emotional harm of the gang-rape, nothing about her trauma. 'I was angry,' she summarizes her feelings. When she enters the house, she sees that her attackers have stolen her family's savings from the safe. 'The money that I had from selling coffee, that money was taken as well.' Unmoved, Bemba listens to the testimony of witness P-87 about the crimes allegedly committed by his men and for which he as commander is being held responsible.

In an interview, much later, Steiner will explain that because of the nature of the crimes the ICC is dealing with, it is extra important to have female judges. 'The African women who come and testify about rape and other humiliations are so ashamed and traumatised that they usually only look at me. Or they look down. But never at a man,' Steiner explains. 'They pretend there's no one else in the courtroom. No prosecutor, no defence, no suspect.'

Heels are clicking on the parquet of the public gallery. A well-dressed woman, wearing a long skirt with matching jacket, waves at Bemba and takes her seat. A man sits down while giving a respectful nod to the accused. The supporters of Bemba have arrived. The Congolese are sitting as close as possible to the former politician/warlord/businessman, who, from behind the thick glass, exchanges knowing glances with them.

The family of P-87 still had one valuable object in the house. Bemba's men would return to get it. When the witness suddenly hears a loud noise in the home, she tries to find out what is happening. Through a 'little hole' in the door that was made of planks, she peeps into the bedroom where her brother is trying to protect a motorbike from a MLC soldier who is about to steal the vehicle. She can't see well. But she hears her brother saying: 'No, no.' And then it happened. 'I heard three shots,' she says. Her brother moans three times. Then there is silence.[117] He has perished, murdered for a scooter. When P-87 sees him covered in blood, she is 'completely staggered, taken aback.' In despair she runs to her neighbours. But it is too late, too dark and too dangerous to do anything. Only the next day the family is able to wash the body. That's when she sees her murdered brother has three bullet marks on his chest. Only with great effort and being harassed by Banyamulenge, the family manages to bury the body. The motorbike is still in the house. The militia did not manage to take the moped. The lock proved to be of excellent quality.

A cross for each bullet hole

At the end of the second day of the testimony, the defence starts its cross examination. When Bemba was arrested, his bank accounts in Portugal

---

117 Official transcript, ICC, 12 January 2011.

were frozen. The ICC was convinced the suspect was able to pay his own lawyers, but because of delays, the court decided in 2009 to advance the bill for his defence. The Congolese leader has, just like other suspects, an international team of lawyers. Several come from the DRC, others from the United Kingdom and Australia. Much later Bemba paid the court back – the costs for his defence had increased to some 2 million euros. Defence counsel Nicholas Kaufman, an Israeli born in the United Kingdom, is doing part of the cross-examination of witness P-87. He wants to know how the ICC investigators had interviewed her. What language were Bemba's men speaking? Why didn't she see a doctor after the brutal rape? 'In our country, in order to see a doctor, you have to have money. As all the money I had, had been stolen, I couldn't go to see a doctor,' the witness explains. Only years later, when she was in contact with the ICC investigators, she was medically examined.

On the public gallery people are laughing. 'The witness tells lies,' a Bemba supporter whispers. Another Congolese says: 'She is a whore.'

When it is time for the break, the visitors take the stairs down to the lobby. There the Bemba supporters assemble around the machines with coffee, soft drinks, chocolate bars and other snacks. Healthy food is not available for visitors. The court's restaurant is located in the office part of the building and only accessible for ICC officials and their guests. While taking a sip from his coffee, a Congolese journalist says he's angry with the ICC because it is biased against Africans. Why is Bemba prosecuted, he asks, while the former American president George W. Bush walks free despite his devastating invasion of Iraq?

Two ladies of a Congolese human rights organisation say they don't believe witness P-87. 'Indeed, something did happen to her. But it can't have been Bemba's men, because the witness was talking about Banyamulenge. This ethnic group lives in the east of Congo, while Bemba's men come from the north.' The ladies make a comparison: 'It is as if the witness says that the criminals were Dutch people, while calling them French. So not very logical.' Indeed, it is a fact that ethnic Tutsis in the east of the DRC are generally called Banyamulenge. But the ICC prosecutor alleges this is different for people in the CAR, who refer to Bemba's men as such.

On the last morning of the cross-examination, 14 January 2011, Kaufman asks the coffee-seller to point out on a diagram of the human body exactly where the bullets had hit her brother. The question leads to confusion. The witness is not able to put the marks on the design. She makes a big circle on the torso. But that is not what Kaufman wants. He insists she puts the exact marks.

The witness: 'I told you that all the wounds were found on this part that I have circled.'

Kaufman reacts: 'Madam witness, that I don't dispute, but did you see three holes? Three wounds?'

The witness: 'Yes, I saw three impacts of bullets on his chest that went out behind on his back and that frightened me.'

'So,' Kaufman goes on, 'please put a spot, or an X, or whatever you want, where you saw the hole – each hole – within that space. Draw the hole.' But the witness doesn't manage and so the issue continues for a while. She explains that much time has passed since the killing. 'I may have forgotten, but I said that there were three impacts of the bullets on his chest and the big wounds were on his back.' Kaufman reminds her that the team of the prosecution exhumed her brother's remains. 'And is this not the reason now why you don't want to draw on that diagram I gave you, the exact points of impact, because you're frightened of contradicting the prosecution's evidence?' Bemba's lawyer asks.

By then prosecutor Kneuer has had enough. 'Madam President, the defence counsel is arguing with the witness, not posing questions,' she says. 'Sustained,' Steiner decides.

One of the other lawyers, Aimé Kilolo Musamba, also has several questions. The young counsel has big eyes that reflect drive and ambition. He wants to know about the command structure of the militia that raided the witness' house and – again – the language issue. Many of Bemba's men are said to come from the Congolese region just below the Oubangui river that separates the CAR and the DRC, and they speak Lingala. 'Do you know, witness, the four African countries in which Lingala is spoken?' Kilolo asks.

'No, I do not know them,' the witness says.

Judge Steiner sees the prosecution is standing up: 'Madam Kneuer?'

'Madam President, I am doubting the relevance of this line of questioning,' the prosecutor says.

But Kilolo insists that language is a 'fundamental' matter in this case as it relates to the identification of the perpetrators. The witness said the attackers belonged to Bemba's militia because they spoke Lingala. But can a person who speaks Lingala only come from the DRC, or also from

Congo-Brazzaville, Angola or even the CAR where, as the lawyer claims, Lingala is spoken as well? In other words, were these attackers indeed Congolese militia or did they belong to another group for instance from the CAR itself?

Kneuer is irritated. 'Madam President, the witness answered this question already. I'm sorry, this is not a quiz. My colleague is harassing the witness and also, notwithstanding that he gave an argument for the relevance, the witness also said that the Banyamulenge, or the perpetrators, came from the other side of the river. Are we doing now geographics to define which other countries who are speaking Lingala, where they are located?'

Judge Steiner, who knows the topography by heart and would blindly know her way in the CAR, ends the dispute. 'Let's refer this issue to the expert on linguistics, please.' Two months later 85-year old William Samarin, retired professor from the University of Toronto, will declare that Lingala is one of the three major national languages of the DRC and spoken in the centre of the country, while 'less than 1 percent' of the people of the CAR would have proficiency in Lingala. But many Central Africans will be able to identify the language because 'a great deal of Congolese music, that is music in Lingala, is heard on the Central African radio,' the professor explained.[118]

After a few more questions the intense testimony is over. Steiner thanks the woman for 'the time and trouble' she has taken to come all the way to The Hague to give evidence. 'In order for the judges to find the truth, it is critical that witnesses like yourself are prepared to give evidence to assist us on the relevant issues in this case. We are aware that probably this has been inconvenient for you and possibly it may have involved some personal risk.' She refers to the Victims and Witnesses Unit (now: Victims and Witnesses Service), the special section of the ICC that takes care of the protection, well-being and logistics of victims and witnesses. The VWU will monitor her to see whether she has special needs upon returning home. 'So, once again, thank you very much,' Steiner says. The blinds go down so that the witness can leave the courtroom safely in anonymity. The coffee-seller finally can go home. Bemba is being taken back, in a van, to the international detention centre in Scheveningen – now a part of The Hague, but once a fishing village – where he has been

118 Official transcript, ICC, 25 March 2011.

detained since July 2008. For the court, the weekend starts. Judge Steiner told me in our interview that her social life in Brazil, where she first had been a lawyer, prosecutor and then judge, had been far more lively. After working hours, she would go out with colleagues and enjoy dinners and parties. In The Netherlands she is more on her own. 'Since I am in The Hague I am reading ten times more books. Usually two books at the same time. I love movies. So I have an awful lot of DVDs and I go to the cinema. I travel and go out for dinner,' Steiner said.

Le Pharaon and other supporters

'There is no justice in this world! Not at all!' In the lobby of ICC's public gallery, a man is loudly raising his voice. Such noise is quite unusual in this setting, where people mostly converse politely with each other. 'Our president Jean-Pierre Bemba is innocent. They have no proof that he has committed any crime. I call upon the prosecutor to release him,' rages Michel Bayela Nsimba, who out of loyalty tries to follow as many hearings as possible in the Bemba trial to support his leader. Overcome by emotion, he shouts: 'I am Congolese. My heart is bleeding for my president. Bemba has a wife. Bemba has children, who live without their father. They are traumatised.'

The taciturn colonel Liboto-Ngoy is sitting calmly in one of the red armchairs in the lobby. In the old days he served in Mobutu's army. His nickname: 'Le Pharaon' (The Pharaoh). For ten years he was Bemba's bodyguard. No, he grins, when I ask him whether he had been armed with, for instance, a pistol. Proudly he stretches his arm to show the length of the fire-arm he was carrying those days. 'We protected our leader with a Kalashnikov,' the bodyguard explains. They travelled together everywhere. But not to the Central African Republic, where his boss has never been, the bodyguard insists.

When Bemba transformed his MLC army into a political party, the political career of the Congolese millionaire seemed to go very well. After a peace agreement had entered into force in the war-ravaged DRC, Bemba would flourish as a popular vice president from 2003 until 2006. 'He is a real democrat,' Liboto-Ngoy says. The bodyguard also had protected his boss during the 2006 elections when Bemba however failed to win the top prize. The DRC presidency was again won by Joseph Kabila. The strained relations between the leaders worsened.

During a violent conflict in 2007, that started with a bloody row between Bemba's bodyguards and Kabila's forces, hundreds of people were killed in DRC's capital city Kinshasa.[119] Bemba fled to the South African embassy, then flew to Portugal and later arrived in Belgium. Kabila, the strategist, had managed to rid himself of a political rival, Bemba's supporters claim. And – via the ICC – so did Bozizé, the former coup plotter and then CAR head of state. They are convinced that the two presidents, Kabila and Bozizé, hatched up the plan to have the ICC go after the MLC leader. On 23 May 2008 the judges had confidentially ordered Bemba's arrest. The next day he was apprehended by the Belgian police. 'It was a trap. And very well prepared. A political arrest,' Liboto-Ngoy says. Just like other supporters, he wonders why the ICC had only arrested and prosecuted Bemba, but not his rival Kabila, or Bozizé or the Rwandan head of state Paul Kagame – presidents who are accused of being responsible for gross human rights violations during the wars that raged across central Africa.

Indeed, Bozizé benefitted from the ICC prosecution of Bemba in three ways, write the academics Courtney Hillebrecht (assistant professor of political science at the University of Nebraska-Lincoln) and Scott Straus (professor of political science and international studies at the University of Wisconsin-Madison).[120] In an article for the Washington Post, they explain that the CAR president's cooperation with the court was very profitable for him. First, it 'showed Western partners and donors that Bozizé was committed to accountability and the rule of law.' Second, it offered 'a mechanism' to get rid of one of his 'potential challengers.' And third, cooperating with the ICC 'helped Bozizé distract from and delay any possible investigation into his own troops' wrongdoing. International courts can take years – as with Bemba – to open, hear and adjudicate a case.'

Le Pharaon still feels he's responsible for the family of his boss. Years ago a demonstration was held in The Hague for the release of Bemba, he starts to tell. 'When the police tried to hit Bemba's wife with a stick, I protected her. They sent two police dogs to attack me,' says Liboto-Ngoy. Regularly he visits his boss in prison. 'He is doing well. Although he is always a bit

---

119 'ICC: Congo's Former Vice-President Arrested,' Human Rights Watch, 30 May 2008.
120 'Last week, the International Criminal Court convicted a war criminal,' Washington Post, 28 March 2016.

reserved,' says the bodyguard, whose tight face slowly relaxes a bit. An older, visually impaired Congolese woman, wearing big protective orange spectacles, participates in the discussion. With her hands on her walking-frame she comments that it is absolutely normal that Bemba keeps some distance from ordinary creatures. 'He is a chef, a leader. One can't expect from him to mingle with just anybody.'

Every day, Liboto-Ngoy says, he sends a report to Bemba's wife who lives in Belgium and follows the hearings mainly through the Internet. Bayela is looking very stressed and his face shines with perspiration. He tells that when he comes to the ICC, he prefers to sit in the first rows of the public gallery, as close as possible to Bemba. 'I want to be able to see his face, because he reminds me of Congo. I look at him. He looks at me. Sometimes I get tears in my eyes. Why don't they let him go?' he laments. There is only one hope, says the bodyguard, and that's judge Sylvia Steiner. 'She is presiding the trial in a balanced manner. We have faith in Sylvia.'

Defence in trouble

But Sylvia would not remain the friendly judge. On 27 June 2013 the court holds a special hearing to discuss the halting trial. The prosecution has finished the presentation of its witnesses long ago. But there are many hiccups with the schedule of Bemba's witnesses. It is regrettable and remarkable, says Steiner, that the defence is not warning on time about delays. But Kilolo ignores the irritation of the judge. After lead counsel Nkwebe Liriss died in February 2012, he is now the head of the defence team. Nick Kaufman, who questioned witness P-87, is off the case. Kilolo starts his exposé with a mathematical summary that won't improve the tense situation.

The lawyer reminds the judges that the defence were given 230 hours to present their case in court. Until now '92 hours and 7 minutes' have been used, Kilolo reminds the chamber. He also explains that the defence has decided to take thirteen of its original 63 witnesses off the list. It is not easy to organise everything on time, he says. Many witnesses stay in three unnamed countries, where authorities are rather uncooperative. There are also witnesses who cancel at the last moment, call sick or have a position in the Congolese army which makes it hard to get permission to testify in favour of Bemba.

The defence still has some two dozen people on its list. Most are not travelling to The Hague, such as the coffee-seller did when she testified for the prosecution, but stay in Africa and testify through video-link. They have to go to a secret location, usually a mission of the United Nations, where the ICC has arranged an office. With this measure the court bypasses the logistical hurdle of getting witnesses to The Hague. Possibly another reason the court choses for the testimony via video-link is that it will prevent situations such as in September 2012, when one of Bemba's witnesses who was brought to The Netherlands, while in the middle of his testimony, suddenly disappeared after the weekend.

Kilolo doesn't want to point fingers, he says, but the video-link is causing a lot of headaches. It is the responsibility of the court to make this approach work. Not only with regard to the technical part, but logistics as well. Witnesses don't always receive their passports and visas on time in order to get to the regional ICC office. It is not the defence's task, but that of the registry to take care of these matters, Kilolo adds.

The atmosphere in the courtroom is frosty. Steiner refers to the hours the defence was allotted by the court, but with a withering comeback. These 230 hours should not be spread out over ten years, she says. Kilolo, however, has more grievances to add. The prosecutors had much more time for their case. If the case was handled honestly, the defence would still be owed another eight months, he argues. But that goes beyond what Steiner deems acceptable. 'Before we speak of a fair trial and justice …' she says. The judge points out that the prosecutor has the 'burden of proof' and therefore is differently placed to the defence.

After a heated discussion, the chamber nevertheless gives in. The defence is given until 25 October 2013 to finish its presentation. The judges are openly disgruntled about the delays. A few months later however it will turn out that a very different matter might explain the irritations. There is a secret operation going on of which the outside world still has no idea.

Bemba is not responsible

After the summer holidays the remaining witnesses testify with considerable speed. Bemba is leaning in his chair. He looks tired. Several compatriots are sitting as usual in the public gallery. It is 11 September 2013 when one of his last witnesses is giving testimony. From a secret location, witness D-15 speaks through a video-link. His face and voice are distorted. An official of the registry is sitting next to him to support the witness. D-15 explains that Bemba's troops who were active in the neighbouring country fell under the command of the army of the CAR. His testimony supports the arguments of the defence: Bemba is not to blame and can't be held responsible for the MLC's actions in the CAR, simply because he had no power over them while they were abroad.

The video-link session with D-15 runs arduously. The connection is lost a few times, and sometimes the sound is too poor with the interpreters having a hard time following what D-15 says. There are moments the witness says he can't hear the start of questions, so maître Kilolo has to repeat them. At several occasions the lawyer decides to read documents put to the witness. One of the interpreters says there is a 'hum' on the line.[121]

Many other lawyers would not have accepted such problems during examination. It is surprising that Kilolo doesn't protest against the way things are going. But there have been other curious moments as well. A few weeks earlier a guard told me I was not allowed to take notes while sitting in the public gallery. It was a decision taken by the judges, he explained. I also notice that the transcripts of witness testimonies, like that of D-15, are no longer being published on the ICC website. (Now, after the trial, most transcripts are displayed.)

After one more time extension, the lawyers get to the finish. On Friday 22 November 2013, exactly three years after the trial started, almost all witnesses are heard. Kilolo argues for a few more weeks so that the last two witnesses can make their statements as well. But the judges refuse.[122] The defence has managed to present 34 witnesses, who have told the court what they knew, saw, did, experienced and heard. And so this major part of the trial is finished. The parties can start preparing their closing statements.

Deterrence

When I interviewed Steiner in 2011, she said that 'deterrence' was the main goal of the ICC. 'We send the message that the most serious crimes will not remain unpunished. I don't have the illusion that we can stop

---

121 Official transcript, 11 September 2015.
122 Corrigendum to Decision on issues related to the conclusion of the defence's presentation of oral evidence at trial and on the 'Defence Request for an Order for Cooperation,' ICC, 19 November 2013.

this violence completely. But possibly people will think twice before they participate in these crimes,' she said, as they might end up in The Hague to be prosecuted by the ICC. However, the reality was that her trial did not provoke such a change in the country where the alleged crimes took place: the Central African Republic. During Bozizé's presidency violent conflicts and skirmishes continued.

In 2012 the country becomes the scene of horrific atrocities again. The Séléka, a coalition of mainly Islamic militia including former military officials, grabs power the following year during a bloody civil war. Bozizé flees. The Christian majority in the CAR fights back and forms its own militia: the anti-Balaka. While both groups are killing, raping and burning, the Muslim minority is almost completely forced out. The g-word is mentioned: there is the threat of genocide. A million people are on the run, fleeing the violence. French and African peacekeepers are flown in, but hardly manage to stop the atrocities, with several of these troops committing crimes such as rapes themselves.

On 9 December 2013 prosecutor Fatou Bensouda says she is deeply worried about the 'deteriorating security situation' in the CAR which has contributed to 'the escalation of unlawful killings, sexual violence, recruitment of child soldiers and other grave crimes, across the country.' She appeals to the warring parties – including the Séléka and the anti-Balaka – 'to stop attacking civilians and committing crimes, or risk being investigated and prosecuted by my office.'[123]

Two months later she places the CAR on the list of 'preliminary examinations.' Meanwhile a partial peace is achieved, and an interim government is installed. In an official letter with the national logo 'Unité, Dignité, Travail' (Unity, Dignity, Work), the new president of the République Centre africaine writes a letter to the ICC referring on 30 May 2014 the latest outbreak of violence for investigation to the court. Just like the first referral, ten years earlier, the CAR authorities are not able to carry out national prosecutions into international crimes themselves. On 24 September 2014 ICC prosecutor Bensouda announces

---

123 Statement of the Prosecutor in relation to the escalating violence in the Central African Republic, OTP, 9 December 2013.

she is opening a formal investigation stating that 'the list of atrocities is endless. I cannot ignore these alleged crimes.'[124]

Many experts doubt whether international tribunals and courts have much of a deterrent effect: that people refrain from crimes as they are afraid of being charged and punished. But with the violence flaring up, it is clear that the Bemba case did not contribute to prevention of crimes. The chances of this trial having such an effect were probably very limited from the start: no national of the CAR, but one foreigner was prosecuted by the ICC for the 2002-2003 violence. As if Jean-Pierre Bemba Gombo was the only bad guy in town.

But how do you measure deterrence? In his feature for The New Yorker, journalist Jon Lee Anderson describes what happened at the catholic mission in the town of Bossemptele, in the west of the CAR, where more than a thousand Muslims, having survived a massacre, were protected by the priest and nuns.[125] Father Bernard Kinvi told Anderson that one day the Christian anti-Balaka abducted three refugees. One of the nuns of the mission however went to the group's leader, explained that the camp fell under the jurisdiction of the ICC and if anything would happen to the three Muslims, he himself could end up in The Hague. 'It was a lie,' a smiling father Bernard told the journalist. 'But when the anti-Balaka leader heard that, he agreed to let them go,' Anderson is quoting the priest. So it could well be that, against all odds, at least three people, and possibly the other thousand refugees at the mission as well, owed their lives to the deterrent threat of the ICC.

A second case against Bemba

It is a grey Sunday when on 24 November 2013 a startling press release comes in. The ICC is bringing incredible news. It is a message one has to read twice to fully grasp its content. Bemba's own lawyer, Aimé Kilolo Musamba, has been arrested. At the request of the ICC, several countries cooperated together in a large operation that was carried out in the weekend. While maître Kilolo was apprehended in Belgium, another member of Bemba's legal team, case manager Jean-Jacques Mangenda

---

124 Statement of the Prosecutor on opening a second investigation in the Central African Republic, OTP, 24 September 2014.

125 'The mission. A last defense against genocide,' Jon Lee Anderson, The New Yorker, 20 October 2014.

Kabongo, was arrested in The Netherlands. In the DRC, member of parliament and a prominent figure within Bemba's MLC party, Fidèle Babala Wandu, is handcuffed and sent off by plane to The Hague. The French police arrested a defence witness, Narcise Arido. Their bank accounts have immediately been blocked by the authorities. Bemba is also arrested, in his detention cell. He now has a second case going against him.

Later his wife, Lilianne Bemba, will tell me that she had been unaware of what was going on when she travelled that weekend to The Hague to visit her husband, as usual, on the Saturday. 'I arrived and waited for ten minutes. Then the guard was telling us that we would not have the rendezvous.' She was told that her husband was okay, but she wasn't allowed to see him. No reason was given. The guard insisted she shouldn't worry, but Mrs Bemba didn't understand what was going on. 'I tried to call Kilolo, but no answer. I tried to call Mangenda and other lawyers of the team, but nobody answered the phone. Also Kilolo's wife didn't pick up the phone. I was beside myself and thought he [Bemba] might be sick and that they were afraid to tell the truth. After 72 hours my husband called me. He had been set apart from the others, in isolation,' Bemba's wife explained.

The five men – Bemba and the four other suspects – are accused of working together to bribe their own defence witnesses so they would give false testimony in Bemba's benefit and to present forged documents. It is the second time the ICC is putting Article 70 of the Rome Statute, offences against the administration of justice, into play. A month earlier the Kenyan journalist Walter Barasa was indicted for similar offences, with the difference that he allegedly targeted prosecution witnesses. If found guilty, these men risk a sentence of five years' imprisonment, a fine, or both.

Upset and angry the group of Bemba supporters is standing in the lobby of the ICC. 'Why, why has the prosecutor done this?' sobs the elderly lady with the orange spectacles. Together with other Bemba loyalists she is getting ready to go up to the public gallery for the first appearance that takes place today, 27 November 2013. During this hearing the suspects are led before the judge for the first time in this new bribery case. 'He will be coming,' the lady says about Bemba's former bodyguard Liboto-Ngoy, alias Le Pharaon, who hasn't arrived yet.

Lawyers, diplomats, court officials, young interns and some journalists have taken a seat. Behind the thick bulletproof glass, three suspects are sitting in a row, each separated by a guard. Bemba looks exhausted while he checks out the visitors who have turned up for a new episode in this drama. Next to him is the Congolese politician Babala, who has been surrendered immediately by the DRC and is now detained in The Hague. The man who draws most attention is sitting furthest away from the public. Just a few days ago he was pleading in court, dressed in his solemn black lawyer's robe, for his client. Now maître Kilolo, in a dark blue suit, has to undergo the humiliation of appearing as an accused before the judges. Insecure, the counsel looks around him, but then casts a fierce look in the courtroom.

Cuno Tarfusser, an Italian judge with dark blond spiky hair and spectacles with red frames, opens the hearing. Slightly stuttering, he asks the teams of the prosecution, registry and defence, in this new case, to present themselves. Then the formal identification of the suspects takes place. With some difficulty Bemba gets up from his seat. His arm sweeps in a broad cutting move when he grabs the microphone to sum up his name and birth data. Maître Kilolo points out a mistake in the arrest warrant. Though he was born in Kinshasa on 1 January 1972, he isn't Congolese, but a Belgian citizen. Babala, born in 1956, is the oldest of the three. The two other suspects haven't been surrendered yet. The Netherlands is still keeping Mangenda, who as a case manager did the coordination of Bemba's defence. France is holding Arido. The reasons are unknown to the public, as there are still many riddles in this case.

'I am very surprised,' Bemba responds to the judge.[126] He admits there have been discussions in court about certain documents, and promises to 'provide the necessary evidence to show that, as far as I'm concerned, I have been acting in good faith regarding these documents.' But charges of corruption? 'I differ regarding this word, which is far too strong a word.' While restraining his anger, Kilolo starts to explain what happened last weekend. The lawyer was in Belgium when he was arrested. In fact, he was just leaving a meeting about an investigative mission 'to identify a number of criminal law experts who were actual specialists in handwriting and specialists in radio transmissions,' which was related to forged

---

126 Official transcript, ICC, 27 November 2013.

documents. The approach taken by the court, arresting him like that in Belgium, was unnecessary. 'I was surprised to be deprived of my freedom, given that I spent most of my time in The Hague within the very premises of the court where I have my offices.' He points out that if prosecutor Fatou Bensouda would had called upon him, he would have responded. 'I do deplore the way, the strong-arm tactics, the humiliating way in which use was made of an arrest warrant. A mere summons to appear would have sufficed. I would have appeared. I don't think anyone doubts that point,' says an irritated Kilolo.

'I didn't interrupt you because I understand your emotional moment,' Tarfusser responds. Opposite the suspects sits Bensouda, straight as a line and unmoved by the accusations launched at her for not calling for a prior hearing or meeting with the accused lawyers.

The Congolese politician Babala also narrates of his arrest, and complains that rules with regard to dignity were violated. 'At 2.00 a.m. in the morning with thirty policemen, my house was broken into, and my children traumatised,' he starts. But judge Tarfusser says the ICC can't help it, because the Congolese authorities are responsible for the way the arrest was carried out. Paul Djunga Mudimbi, Babala's lawyer and a member of the Paris bar, explains that the Congolese television 'has been broadcasting – until today – video images of the arrest of Mr Babala, his transfer, and he can be seen in a small cell. He is badly dressed and in humiliating circumstances, and he was handcuffed right up to the time he boarded the plane.' This is going against the interest of dignity and the presumption of innocence, he adds. 'Your court should request the DRC to stop immediately the broadcast of these pictures. We also wish that your court should demand that the DRC hand over the videotapes of those images,' says counsel Djunga.

While the pleas and complaints about events are expressed, Bemba is closing his eyes, folds his hands as if he is praying and keeps them to his face. It seems like an attempt to find some peace amidst the mess his case has turned into. In the ICC detention centre, the three suspects who are now being led before the judge, have not been allowed to communicate with others and are being questioned separately.

The hearing is nearing its end. Until one of the lawyers suddenly realises he forgot an important issue. Among maître Kilolo's belongings that have been confiscated are also his iPad and Blackberry. The whole strategy of the defence in the main case, dealing with international crimes in the

CAR, are on those devices. Obviously this information should not fall in the hands of the prosecution. 'The seized materials are in the possession of the registry,' Tarfusser explains. The judge is stammering a bit when he tells the parties that the court will take care of separating, in a 'very strict manner,' those materials, and see to it that the prosecution will not receive private or any privileged defence information that is related to the main case. 'The chamber is very much aware of it and handles it very carefully,' Tarfusser underlines, while closing the hearing. Because Bemba's lead counsel has been arrested, his main case will from now on be in the hands of Peter Haynes, a British lawyer in his team.

Colonel Liboto-Ngoy, alias Le Pharaon, walks downstairs. He is dressed in black trousers and shirt, topped with a white jacket. 'We still have faith in the justice system,' he says, 'but not in the prosecutors. This is not normal!' The face of Bemba's former bodyguard has some bruises around his cheekbones. 'It is the stress because of all this stuff,' he explains. Stress? 'Yes, I was hurried and bumped into something.' Le Pharaon sees the arrests as an attempt by the prosecution to save its main case. 'They have no evidence against Bemba. In fact, we have proof that the prosecution has presented false witnesses.'

He refers to a person such as witness P-73, who came to The Hague in February 2011 to testify against Bemba. In earlier statements the man had told investigators that his daughter had been raped by MLC militia. The rebels also had taken valuable items such as a motor-bike and a machine to make bricks. But in court he made a complete switch. He said that ICC officials had suggested him to make these accusations against Bemba's men. They had pointed to the advantages of cooperating with the prosecution and how the witness would receive more money from the court if he increased the estimated harm. The witness suggested this ICC official might have thought he could receive a percentage of the court-paid reparations. He also made another correction to his earlier statements: his youngest daughter was not raped by one of Bemba's men but might have consented to having sex, notwithstanding the girl being just ten years old at the time.[127] [128]

127 'Witness: court official advised me to make false claims,' International Justice Monitor, 28 February 2011.
128 Official transcript, ICC, 28 February 2011.

It was a confusing testimony, but Bemba's bodyguard sees it as a confirmation of his claim that 'most victims who testified are not real victims. The prosecutors have been giving them money in order to testify against Bemba.' While continuing to express his discontent, he is getting ready to join the other supporters and to leave the court. 'There is nothing we can do, but wait. Arresting a member of parliament at dawn by thirty policemen is a scandal. That is really too much.'

An anonymous tip-off

It will take months before there is more clarity about what had happened behind the scenes in this second Bemba case. On 12 February 2014 the prosecutor publishes a previously confidential document that she had sent to the judges many months ago. In this filing, Bensouda explains how her staff became aware of possible witness interference and what resulted from the consequent investigations.[129]

It was a tip-off that started the case. On 14 June 2012 the information desk of the prosecution receives an email from an informer. This person claims he can provide information about a bribery scandal: a range of witnesses is being paid by the defence to make false statements to Bemba's benefit. To check whether the informer is trustworthy and the story could be true, Bensouda's staff spends three months emailing with this person. They also look for evidence that could support the claims, such as information from the money transfer company Western Union. Indeed, sums of money, totalling some 100,000 American dollars, appear to have been transferred from individuals close to Bemba to a dozen witnesses. While the secret investigations begin, the OTP also tries to double-check facts in the courtroom with witnesses who are testifying. They think they have uncovered that the defence is presenting false documents.

The prosecution suspects Bemba, who would 'clearly benefit from coached testimony calculated to exonerate him,' of 'orchestrating the scheme' from his prison cell. How? The former vice president is probably using the telephone in the detention centre to manage the operation. One of the scenarios is that he pretends to be contacting Kilolo, so that the phone call would fall under the privileged – and thus private – communications

---

129 Public redacted version of the Request for Judicial Assistance to Obtain Evidence for Investigation under Article 70, OTP, 12 February 2014.

between client and lawyer, while in reality he is calling other people. One of those contacts would be the Congolese politician Babala, who was chef-de-cabinet during Bemba's tenure as vice president.

Instead of warning the defence that they are likely engaged in illicit practices, the prosecution keeps quiet, which means the interference doesn't stop, but continues.

On 20 March 2013 Bensouda sends an 'urgent request' to judge Steiner and her two colleagues leading the main case, asking them permission to expand the bribery investigation. But the judges say they should not be the ones dealing with this case. It is a matter for their colleagues from a pre-trial chamber.

In the meantime, the main trial against Bemba is continuing. Judge Steiner, who was so irritated when the defence asked more time for their witnesses, was fully aware of the ongoing secret investigation against the lawyers.

Bensouda addresses one of the pre-trial chambers on 3 May 2013. Five days later judge Tarfusser gives permission for further investigations.[130] He orders the registry to hand over to the prosecutor 'the complete log of all telephone calls placed or received' by Bemba during his stay at the detention centre, and 'any available recording of all non-privileged calls' either made or received by the suspect. After analysing these telephone data, the prosecution submits that the materials 'strongly support' the allegations of a scheme 'to bribe witnesses in exchange for false testimony and false documents' and that Kilolo, Mangenda and Babala are being employed by Bemba.

But the prosecution wants more. Bensouda's office would like to request the authorities of The Netherlands and Belgium to collect logs and recordings of telephone calls placed or received by Kilolo and Mangenda. The matter will be settled. On 29 July 2013 judge Tarfusser thinks such an operation is a good idea and gives his authorisation to go ahead. After having received the request from the prosecution, a Dutch investigative judge allows phone tapping from 1 October until 23 November 2013. Two of Bemba's lawyers are now being wiretapped.

---

130 Decision on the Prosecutor's Request for judicial order to obtain evidence for investigation under Article 70, ICC, 29 July 2013.

Action against the judge

The case is extremely delicate as the prosecutor is directly investigating her opponents in court. How can it be prevented, that while checking phone calls and other materials, the prosecution also collects confidential information from the defence that would disclose the lawyers' strategy in the main case and give the prosecution an unjust advantage against Bemba? If that would happen, it would lead to an unfair trial. The prosecutor finds a unique solution: an independent counsel. And so a new – anonymous – person enters the scene.

In the same decision permitting the phone taps, Tarfusser allows the hiring of the independent counsel. This professional, who is fluent in Lingala, is tasked with 'reviewing the logs of telephone calls,' listening to the recordings and transmitting only the relevant information to the prosecutor. The identity of the counsel is kept secret for the public, but a source says he is a member of the Brussels bar.

After one and a half year of investigations, Tarfusser starts writing his arrest warrant, which is confidentially issued on 20 November 2013.[131] The judge describes the collected evidence as: 'money transfers effected through international services, particularly Western Union and Express Union, telephone call records, transcripts, translations and summaries of recorded communications, text messages ('SMS'), witness statements and emails.' The work by the independent counsel, too, has resulted in a 'wealth of material to support the prosecutor's claims.' Tarfusser concludes: 'The record contains at this stage a considerable and indeed quite remarkable quantity of items of evidence which furnish objective and incriminating information and details pertaining directly and specifically to the prosecutor's factual allegations.'

The lawyers of the five suspects in the bribery case, however, have strong and deep criticism on the way things have been going. Jean Flamme, who at the time is the defence lawyer for case-manager Mangenda, says that with all this material the prosecution could dispose of 'the complete defence strategy' in the main case. During the initial appearance of his client, Flamme had explained to the court that Bemba's lawyers had discovered a letter from a prosecution witness who was asking the OTP

---

131 Warrant of arrest for Jean-Pierre Bemba Gombo, Aimé Kilolo Musamba, Jean-Jacques Mangenda Kabongo, Fidèle Babala Wandu and Narcisse Arido, ICC, 20 November 2013.

for money that was promised to him. Another 22 witnesses had similar complaints. They had even organised a meeting to discuss the problems. In other words: who was buying witnesses? Bemba's defence team had been ready to ask the court to call back these witnesses and to have them testify over this matter. The lawyers had phoned each other about the issue – conversations that had been tapped, Flamme argues.

These are serious allegations against the prosecution's handling of witnesses in the main case. Interestingly Flamme's poignant remarks are not in the court's transcript of the hearing published on its website, although they can be heard through the recordings of the session that are circulating on YouTube. It will take until 25 July 2014 before the defence makes any headway, and Tarfusser decides that the OTP also has to present information with regard to payments to all witnesses. The details will have to be filed to the chamber.[132]

This is such a sensitive case that it reverberates throughout the ICC legal establishment. Lawyers are shocked about the arrest of their colleagues. Some have a hard time believing Kilolo and Mangenda overstepping rules. They are also worried that their own phones and computers might have been tapped by authorities and the court, which is an unpleasant feeling, to say the least.

Judge Tarfusser had announced on 5 December 2013 that in the bribery case there wouldn't be a public confirmation of charges hearing, which is usually an open series of sessions during which the prosecution presents its first evidence. Lawyers are protesting. Nick Kaufman, who used to be one of Bemba's lawyers in the main trial and is now defending him again in the corruption case, says: 'This case is the first of its kind to be litigated at the ICC. And the extraordinary measure sought by the prosecution, namely the arrest of a lawyer and his client during his trial, deserves to be the subject of full public scrutiny.' Flamme is critical as well: 'To have no public hearing is unusual in a case of this importance: a case that harms the careers of these lawyers for the rest of their lives.'

The judicial fight is getting tougher. The defence teams in the bribery case resist the role of the 'independent counsel.' They doubt his independence and mandate, and criticize the fact that there is no legal basis for this

---

132 Decision on the "Request seeking the Prosecution to provide to the Kilolo Defence specific information relating to its reimbursement of Prosecution witnesses", ICC, 25 July 2014.

position, as the Rome Statute doesn't provide for it. Some lawyers have such serious doubts about Tarfusser, who acts like single judge in this phase of the case, that they take a significant step. The counsels of Kilolo, Mangenda and Babala want the judge to be disqualified and be taken off the case because he has become too much involved with the investigations. He hasn't shown 'impartiality', but rather has been acting as a 'second prosecutor' and 'greatly' prejudiced the 'fundamental rights of the suspects,' says Kilolo's defence lawyer.[133] But the court stands by Tarfusser. He stays on the case.

The network

There are serious delays in the processing of the vast amount of materials such as laptops, smartphones, computers, documents, emails and telephone taps that, for instance, the Dutch authorities have assembled at the request of the prosecutor. With a delay of three months, on 30 June 2014, Bensouda has the 'document containing the charges' ready.[134] In this 'DCC' the prosecution describes how the network allegedly has been operating. Bemba is accused of being in charge of the 'common plan' which he directed and carried out by using a phone line for privileged contacts with his lead counsel. The others all had their role as well. Kilolo bribed witnesses, scripted their evidence, rehearsed their false testimony with them, so they knew what to say in court. He also presented forged documents. Mangenda had a 'key role' in the planning, passing on necessary instructions and information and offering logistical support. Babala passed on information, bribed people and ensured that the money was made available. He would transfer sums to Kilolo, Mangenda and others so they could pay witnesses and their relatives. Arido is accused of providing forged documents, procuring false witnesses and influencing witnesses.

The DCC also mentions two of Bemba's sisters, Caroline Wale Bamanisa Bemba ('petite soeur') and Françoise Ndokwa Bemba, as being involved in the scheme. They provided Kilolo with money to pay witnesses. According to the prosecution all the persons involved had 'collectively transferred over USD 100,000 since January 2012,' which was around

---

133 Defence Request for the Disqualification of the Single Judge Cuno Tarfusser, 1 May 2014.
134 Public redacted version of "Document Containing the Charges", 30 June 2014.

the time that Kilolo took over the lead in Bemba's defence from maître Nkwebe Liriss who was terminally ill.[135] One of the witnesses implicated in the scheme is known as D-15, whose testimony went surprisingly messy. According to the prosecutor the following had happened. On 10 September 2013, one day before he enters the courtroom for his testimony, D-15 receives a phone call from Kilolo. The lawyer instructs him what to say and to lie about Bemba's 'command and control of MLC troops operating in the CAR,' the prosecution alleges. After the first day of his testimony, Kilolo again phones him to tell him what his questions the following day in court will be. The witness will for instance have to testify that he doesn't remember what language Bemba was speaking with his troops. They rehearse some false declarations.

In total, fourteen of the thirty defence witnesses are implicated in the scandal, the prosecution states. But what would they gain from these activities? According to the prosecution they were making money. The witnesses received amounts that could vary from one hundred euros to fifteen thousand euros. Several were told they would testify in The Hague, which would give them the possibility to stay in Europe after their testimony, for instance by requesting asylum.

Interim release

In the meantime, Tarfusser has rejected, in March 2014, the requests for interim release for Bemba (already six years in detention for his main case) and the four suspects who by then are several months behind bars. The judge wants to prevent the defendants from escaping justice, continuing to commit offenses and frustrating the bribery case. The appeals chamber is looking into the matter as well. In the middle of the summer, 11 July 2014, three of the five appeals judges agree with the decision of their colleague.[136] And so all suspects remain in the ICC detention centre. Three months later, however, Tarfusser changes his mind. On 21 October 2014 the ICC publishes his decision by which the judge orders the release of the suspects. Tarfusser argues that the length of detention before trial should be related to any potential punishment for this offence: a fine and/

---

135 Public redacted version of "Prosecution Submission on the Confirmation of Charges," OTP, 30 July 2014.
136 Judgment on the appeal of Mr Aimé Kilolo Musamba against the decision of Pre-Trial Chamber II of 14 March 2014, ICC, 11 July 2014.

or maximum five years' imprisonment. The prosecution objects, but the protest is rejected. Two days later Kilolo, Babala and Arido are set free in respectively Belgium, DRC and France. On the condition that they will respond when the ICC calls them.[137]

The interim release of Mangenda is however temporarily blocked. The United Kingdom, where his family is staying, suddenly withdraws his visa. The Netherlands, not only an ICC member, but also the host state where Mangenda has worked for eight years, refuses to allow him to stay. His counsel Flamme is furious and speaks of an 'illegal' detention. He hopes that Belgium, which has an agreement with the court to host persons on interim release, will take him in. The DRC, where Mangenda is from, is deemed too unsafe. In the end, The Netherlands allow him to stay and so the case-manager is released. Bemba remains detained for the main case. (Half a year later, on 29 May 2015, the appeals chamber decides that the four should not have been set free, but as they have been released such a long time ago, they won't have to be rearrested.)

On 11 November 2014 the judges of the pre-trial chamber decide there are 'substantial grounds to believe' that the prosecution's evidence against Bemba and his four co-accused is strong enough to commit the case to trial.[138] They confirm the charges – but only partly. The accusation that the group has forged and falsified documents and presented these materials as evidence, hasn't been proven though. These charges are taken off the list. The remaining accusations will have to be proven in court. Another set of judges will be handling the trial.

Listening to intercepts

With no fewer than five suspects in the dock, the courtroom is packed when the trial opens on 29 September 2015. A tired looking Bemba sits with his defence team in the back. In front of them are politician Babala and pointman Arido, while former lead counsel Kilolo and case manager Mangenda take the first rows. Each suspect has three lawyers with him. When the charges are read Bemba rubs his face with his hands, while Kilolo is sitting straight up, looking at the judges or taking notes. Babala

---

137 Aimé Kilolo Musamba, Narcisse Arido and Fidèle Babala Wandu released from ICC custody, ICC press release, 23 October 2014.

138 Decision pursuant to Article 61(7)(a) and (b) of the Rome Statute, ICC, 11 November 2014.

looks down when the accusations against him are pronounced. Arido, blinking with his eyes, seems the most nervous of all five. When the judge asks how they plead, Bemba gets up first. With his remarkable soft voice, he pleads not guilty. The others do as well.

On the first day of the trial it is prosecutor Bensouda who starts with an opening speech that seems less inspired than usual and is general in tone, explaining that 'this is a case about shielding the integrity of the court's proceedings from offences against the administration of justice.'[139] After a short introduction she gives the floor to senior trial lawyer Kweku Vanderpuye. He immediately starts telling in more detail what happened to D-15, whose testimony had shown hiccups, hums on the line and other sound problems. 'On the evening of 12 September 2013, at 20.59 hours, while defence witness D-15 was in the middle of his testimony, a sworn witness in the Bemba trial, Mr Kilolo called him,' Vanderpuye says. The call was clearly in violation of the rules that prescribe the defence is not allowed on its own to get in touch with witnesses when they testify, as it is the chamber that has to decide on such contacts. 'He called him to make sure the witness got his story straight,' Vanderpuye adds. In that conversation Kilolo explained to D-15 that he needed to reduce 'the knowledge' Bemba had about atrocities allegedly committed by his forces in the CAR. Then Vanderpuye plays an excerpt of the intercepted conversation, so the court and public can hear how Kilolo instructs the witness to downplay reports by Radio France International (RFI) about cruelties by MLC soldiers and to say that these crimes in fact only concerned pillaging, but not murder and rape.

While listening to the intercept, the audience hears that D-15 (whose recorded voice is distorted by the court in order to protect him) doesn't always fully understand what the lawyer wants from him. 'I couldn't follow the bit, I couldn't, I couldn't really follow that bit, counsel,' the witness is heard saying to Kilolo. Then the defence lawyer explains to D-15 what will happen the next day in court: 'I'm going to ask you: "The rumours in question, what type of crime did they concern? Did they concern the rape of women, or murders, or pillaging?" I would like that to be limited to the absolute minimum by speaking simply of stolen goods.'

139 Official transcript, ICC, 29 September 2015.

Witness D-15 gets it: 'Yes.'

Kilolo responds: 'Okay. So there we are. So, that was to mitigate the element of knowledge. That was my primary concern.'

Apparently the witness again doesn't fully grasp it, and so Kilolo, who indeed does use quite a bit of legal language, goes over the issue once more. 'I wanted to confine ourselves simply to the pillaging.'

Witness D-15 says: 'RFI spoke of pillaging? Mm-mm.' And Kilolo fills in, mouthing: 'That's right. But not of raping women or of murder.'

During his overview of the case Vanderpuye plays several intercepted calls and regularly refers to D-15. At one point Mangenda had sent Kilolo the confidential list with questions that the legal representative of victims was planning to put forward to this witness. One of the questions was: 'Who took the decision to withdraw MLC troops from the CAR? And why?' This is an important matter because Bemba is being charged on the basis of his command responsibility over his troops, but the defence's argument is that their client had no power over them. While the witness is in the middle of testifying, Kilolo rehearses this part as well with D-15. The lawyers want him to explain that 'Bemba took the political decision,' but the 'military order' came from the CAR authorities.

Kilolo also wants to make sure that the witness will give the right answer about his contact with the defence. When the intercepts are played, the visitors at the public gallery hear the lawyer suggesting to D-15: 'The last telephone contact, between us two, we can consider it goes back – no, we won't say last year, but this year, but at the start of the year. So since January.' That is exactly what would happen, explains Vanderpuye, when the witness testifies 'under solemn declaration' that the last time he had contact with the defence 'was in January 2013.' In reality Kilolo and D-15 spoke at least 37 times, totalling more than 6 hours, in the period between 11 July and 13 September 2013.

The suspects

Kilolo was not alone in this operation. The prosecution sticks to its first analysis. 'Bemba was the main beneficiary of the criminal plan. He was at its centre. He gave the key decisions,' Vanderpuye explains. Kilolo was 'the face' and 'the front man' of the plan. He dealt directly with the witnesses and made sure they got the script right. Mangenda was 'fully engaged' and 'often the go-between' between Kilolo and Bemba. 'He relayed instructions and he reported back as was necessary in order to carry out their criminal plan, particularly when Mr Kilolo was in the field with witnesses,' the prosecution lawyer says.

From his cell in the ICC detention centre Bemba instructed not only his lawyers, but also his 'long-time political ally' Babala. The member of the Congolese parliament, and also a lawyer, was 'in near daily contact' with his detained friend. The two not only talked politics. Babala was the 'treasurer' in these criminal operations. It was his responsibility to make sure the money was available for the payments authorised by Bemba, and to get the money to the right people at the right time. He would use his own driver to make payments himself.

Arido, a jurist by training and a former member of the Central African armed forces (FACA), was based in Cameroon. He recruited 'false' witnesses to testify for the defence in the Bemba trial, promised them money and relocation in Europe in return for their statements. He also 'scripted false information for the witnesses to testify about concerning their military service, their status, their rank and their training, in full knowledge that some of his recruits were never members of the FACA, let alone members of any militia during the conflict period,' Vanderpuye tells the court.

While the prosecution is presenting its case, for a while Bemba is closing his eyes. Kilolo is becoming increasingly uneasy as the public hears his voice in the audio-clips in which he is allegedly coaching witnesses such as D-15.

Even in this conspiracy though, things did not always work out the way they were planned. Arido had promised a group of witnesses 10 million francs CFA (15,000 euros) and that they would go to The Hague. But the plan changed. They were to testify from Cameroon. Witness D-2 was 'unhappy' about the location shift and refused to testify. But Kilolo told him to 'calm down.' The next day the lawyer gave the witness a sum of 500,000 francs CFA (750 euros) and said: 'This isn't ... a bribe but a gift from Jean-Pierre Bemba.'

'Faire la couleur'

According to the prosecution the suspects had developed a coded language which they used among themselves. 'Faire un whiskey' refers to a Western Union transaction, while 'café' refers to money and 'livre' to currency. 'Faire la couleur' meant coaching of witnesses. Babala introduced the term 'service après-vente' to ensure the loyalty of witnesses when things didn't go smoothly. Witness D-55 got irritated and worried, and refused to testify unless he could speak directly to Bemba. Indeed, Kilolo got Bemba on the line who thanked the witness personally, Vanderpuye explains, 'for agreeing to testify in his favour.'

Sometimes the lawyer got tired of it. Kilolo complained about Bemba being too demanding. The counsel was also irritated he had to start rehearsing the story from scratch with witness D-13, who had forgotten the script, because his testimony had been put off for such a long time. 'It completely wore me out,' Kilolo told Mangenda over the phone.

The prosecution only needs the morning to present its case. The painful hearing is done before the lunch break. 'The importance of this case for the office of the prosecution and the court is difficult to overestimate,' says Sergey Vasiliev, an international criminal law expert and assistant professor at Leiden University. 'It is a testing ground in terms of how such a case can be built evidentiary. It could provide a blueprint for the Article 70 cases in the future, a few of which are underway.' Vasiliev refers to the case against the Kenyan deputy president Ruto, in which three Kenyans have been charged with similar offences, although in that situation, prosecution witnesses were allegedly pressured.

Vanderpuye has one more allegation against Kilolo and Mangenda. Apparently they had used Bemba's 'panic' when he first heard about the Kenyan bribery case, to 'take advantage of that situation in order to benefit themselves.' The lawyers pretended that some of Bemba's witnesses needed to be given money so they would shut up. Babala understood the situation and made 2000 euros available, which allegedly disappeared in the pockets of the two lawyers.

First witness

Much is expected of the first witness, who appears in court the following day. But P-433, testifying with face and voice distortion, isn't speaking about the bribing as such. He is an analyst working at the OTP and his job was to study the telecommunications and to help the prosecution getting 'an understanding of what their evidence meant.' He explains that of 897 calls or text messages between Kilolo and defence witnesses, 110 occurred during a period when contact with witnesses was forbidden.[140]

---

140 Official transcript, ICC, 30 September 2015.

Although this first trial for offences against the administration of justice is an important testing ground for the ICC, it is quite hard to follow. To protect the identities of witnesses, there are a lot of closed sessions. These persons, who allegedly lied under oath and received money for that, are in a delicate situation, having evolved from defence witnesses in Bemba's main case, to prosecution witnesses in the Bemba bribery case. Vasiliev explains that corrupted witnesses are giving evidence which is self-incriminating, as it implicates them in the same alleged offences to which they are testifying. 'This potentially puts them at risk of being criminally prosecuted at the ICC or domestically, as well as the risk of reprisals,' says Vasiliev.

They are therefore given extra assurances. On 13 October, presiding judge Bertram Schmitt explains sessions can be closed because 'evidence which is self-incriminating to the witness must be kept confidential.' These witnesses are also provided with a duty counsel to assist them during the trial.

The testimony of P-260 reveals a glimpse of what happened during the alleged evidence fixing. The witness admits to the judges he had given false testimony in the main trial and that he formed part of a larger group of witnesses who also lied in court. It had been Arido who 'explained to me in great detail what I was supposed to say.' P-260, who never had been a soldier, was supposed to present himself as 'sub-lieutenant' to Kilolo. He adds that another person promised him he would 'change countries' of residence. Although Kilolo never made him a promise of relocation to Europe, he 'reassured us that following our testimony we will not be forgotten,' the witness said.

P-260 also talks about cash he received: 50 euros from Kilolo for transportation, 10,000 CFA (15 euros) for food from Arido, 250 euros via Western Union for travel costs, and 550.000 CFA (850 euros) as a 'small gift' from Bemba. When he couldn't reach the ICC staff to pay for his hotel bills and other expenses, he called Kilolo to resolve the matter. Apart from these expenditures, P-260 also asked the lead counsel for 550,000 CFA (850 euros) to enrol his kids in school.

Closing statements main case

Meanwhile, how were things going in the main case? On 12 and 13 November 2014 – one year after the arrests in the bribery case, and four years after the start of the CAR case – the parties are making their oral closing statements. The prosecutor, legal representatives of victims and the defence will give, each from their point of view, a summary of the international crimes case. From the dock Bemba looks through the bulletproof glass at the public gallery, which is not even full. Among the visitors are Kilolo, dressed in a beige suit that bears the marks of that morning's raindrops. Mangenda, wearing a dark blue suit, a big watch and snakeskin boots, is present too. They had been released from ICC detention a month earlier.

The defence is now in the hands of Peter Haynes and his crew. Surprisingly neither Fatou Bensouda nor her deputy James Kirkpatrick Stewart are present. Presiding judge Steiner speaks slowly and clearly as she opens the hearing. Her first words are dedicated to two persons who are dearly missed. Maître Zarambaud, the former legal representative of victims, who had passed away on 16 January 2014. He was 'an exceptional lawyer whose dedication to acting for the victims in this case was unwavering,' says Steiner.[141] Maître Nkwebe Liriss, Bemba's former lead counsel, had died on 26 February 2012. 'His legal insight is missed by the court,' she underlines.

Trial lawyer Jean-Jacques Badibanga is leading the OTP's team. He starts by explaining that 'all the evidence' points out that between 14 October 2002 and March 2003, the people of the Central African Republic were 'subjected to the worst possible barbaric acts' at the hands of Bemba's soldiers. The MLC leader 'knew from the very outset' that his men were committing these crimes and had 'the power, the authority and the means to prevent these crimes from occurring or at the very least to punish the perpetrators,' says Badibanga. But Bemba had other things on his mind. His ambition to become vice president in the transitional government of the DRC, was his 'top priority.' He didn't care about his 'undisciplined troops,' didn't pay them and didn't take his responsibility as a commander to stop the crimes. This historic case allows the ICC make it very clear, that 'each time that a military leader sends armed men, soldiers or militia into a military operation and civilians are targeted, that person must be held responsible,' says Badibanga.

---

141   Official transcript, ICC, 12 November 2014.

Sexual abuse

This is also the first case before the ICC in which the 'vast majority' of the crimes were sexual in nature. The young assistant trial lawyer, Horejah Bala-Gayes, will tell the court about the harrowing events in the CAR. She explains that in each area where MLC soldiers gained control, they organised themselves into small groups of three to four men. During house-to-house operations they raped and pillaged, exactly as had happened to the coffee-seller, witness P-87. They murdered civilians who resisted attacks or were suspected of supporting Bozizé's troops. Bala-Gayes explains that MLC troops not only raped women, but also children and men with authority. 'They raped whomever they wanted. They raped at night and in broad daylight. In homes, compounds and private spaces. They raped on the streets, in the fields and in public as civilians fled for their lives away from the violence and combat.' A school and an empty police station were used as rape theatre.

While Bala-Gayes is talking about these horrific crimes, behind me on the public gallery one of Bemba's supporters is protesting and commenting. 'Liar,' he says loudly. 'Liar.' The common pattern, the prosecution alleges, was that two or three perpetrators raped the same victim, as the coffee-seller had experienced. But there were also victims who were gang-raped by four or even twelve militia. Bemba's men raped with 'complete impunity,' Bala-Gayes says. 'MLC troops raped victims in front of their family members. They sometimes forced one family member to rape another. Sons were sometimes forced to rape their mothers in front of their fathers. MLC troops raped wives in front of their husbands. They raped children in front of their parents,' Bala-Gayes says.

While the prosecution details the individual histories of the victims, Bemba is often looking down. Take witness P-69, who was a man with authority within his neighbourhood. MLC militia entered his home, dragged his wife to a room where four soldiers raped her. Then two other militia turned to P-69 and raped him orally and anally. Bala-Gayes: 'Bemba's men did that to show him that he could not defend himself or his wife.'

It had been difficult for victims to tell in court what happened to them. Witness P-69 had explained how he was mocked and stigmatised by his community. Another male victim, P-23, was raped for hours in public, while his wife and children sexually abused as well. Victims felt they had lost their dignity and were ashamed. Couples divorced. Their lives were ruined. Several were infected with HIV, and some had died of the disease. Witness P-82 was the youngest rape victim to testify. At the time she was about twelve years old. She had tried to run away, but two of Bemba's men caught her. They had batons with them and injured her knees and legs. Then they violently raped her. 'They took me by force and they put my arms behind me. They bent me over and they did these horrific things to me,' she had testified. 'I am no longer able to associate with the other girls. Everybody makes fun of me.'

The sexual violence wasn't exactly a secret among Bemba's men. Soldiers talked openly about the rapes in the presence of their commanders. One MLC militiaman was 'notorious' for raping only children under the age of ten because he believed it would cure him of the HIV virus. At least one commander knew about it, but he didn't stop his subordinate.

Why did Bemba's troops carry out their rape campaign? An expert witness, psychiatrist André Tabo, had explained there were four main reasons. First, MLC soldiers saw defenceless victims as 'war booty.' Second, rape was a form of sexual release. Three, by raping, the militia punished victims who were suspected of supporting Bozizé's men 'simply because they lived in former rebel-held territories.' Four, Bemba's men sought to 'destabilize' their opponents by raping 'their loved ones and their neighbours,' the trial lawyer says. Rape was used as a weapon of war.

Looting and killing

After the coffee break the prosecution team shows their evidence of the other crimes: pillaging and murder. The MLC troops not only looted houses of ordinary people, but also the premises and belongings of the military, the government, companies and even churches. 'No person or entity was spared,' says Thomas Bifwoli, the next prosecution trial lawyer who speaks today. The looting was well organised and large-scale. After gaining control of an area, the militia soldiers searched houses and offices. They took what they wanted: vehicles, foam mattresses, utensils, mobile phones, radios, clothes, motorcycles, shoes, freezers. People who were resisting were beaten, raped and murdered.

The stolen goods were loaded on trucks, buses, vehicles and push carts, or even carried by the militiamen on their heads and shoulders. Civilians were often forced to help. The items were shared among the soldiers. Valuable goods such as vehicles went to top officers such as field commander Mustapha Mukiza, while other items were given to foot soldiers who sold these looted goods back to the local population. The prosecution argues that pillaged items were also transported to the Oubangui river, loaded on the ferry or boats and taken to the DRC. Sometimes even a plane or helicopter was used to transport motorcycles and generators. Witness P-33 testified that Bemba 'distributed these looted vehicles to some MLC officials' in his headquarters in the northern Congolese town of Gbadolite, which was, following the Oubangui river, some 200 kilometres east of Bangui. 'As a result of MLC pillaging, most CAR civilians were reduced to beggars and paupers as their properties and lifetime savings were taken away by MLC troops. Most testified that they could no longer provide for their basic needs such as food and medical care after the conflict,' says Bifwoli.

Murder was part of a policy to humiliate and punish civilians, and to instil fear, states the prosecution. The coffee-seller heard how her brother was shot, because he refused to give up the family's motorbike. 'The MLC troops boasted openly about killing civilians,' tells Bifwoli. One of colonel Mustapha's drivers, nicknamed Dragula, was known for openly murdering civilians. According to the prosecution a 'smiling' Mustapha told Dragula one day that he was killing too many people. During a visit to the CAR, Bemba saw with his own eyes the corpses of civilian victims murdered by his troops.

The prosecution also explains how citizens could identify Bemba's men. They were recognized because they spoke Lingala, had Congolese accents and by their attire – although these aspects were much contested by the defence. Other witnesses could identify the attackers simply because the militiamen would brag that they were MLC troops and that Jean-Pierre Bemba was their president. During the closing statements the prosecution explains why the people of the CAR called MLC troops 'Banyamulenge', which normally refers to an ethnic group in eastern Congo. It was because colonel Mustapha and most of his MLC officers leading the operation, came from that region and were of Banyamulenge ethnicity.

After the long and terrible list of atrocities, the prosecution underlines that the suspect sitting in the dock is responsible for this terror campaign waged by his MLC forces. For this part of the evidence, the prosecution not only called victims to testify, but is also relying on about eight witnesses who possibly were militia members themselves or at least had more inside knowledge of how things worked within the MLC (three were located in the CAR; five were based in Gbadolite). When it comes to formal authority, Bemba was the MLC president and as commander-in-chief he was the highest in military rank. 'The military wing was Bemba's fiefdom,' says trial lawyer Eric Iverson.

Bemba sits with his arms crossed, reading a document and every now and then putting aside a page. At other instances he is looking down, rocking slightly back and forth. On the public gallery his bodyguard and other MLC supporters are shaking their heads in anger and disbelief. A man in the public gallery has turned up the volume of his headset so loud that the French translations are audible for other visitors.

The difference between the detained Bemba sitting silently in the dock, and the powerful man who years ago was in control of a large militia army of thousands of men, is difficult to grasp. The prosecution recalls how witness P-36 said that 'not a single bullet could be taken out of the warehouse to any location without Bemba's authorisation.' Although he himself was in the DRC, Bemba was constantly informed of the operations in the CAR, 'down to the most minuscule details.' In his office he had a detailed map of the neighbouring country updated with the most recent intelligence from the field, which enabled him to direct operations, alleges the prosecution. When colonel Mustapha received an order from Bemba to attack the town of Damara, one hundred kilometres north of Bangui, he told his officers: 'The chairman just called. We have to attack.' Witness P-213 had testified that Mustapha could not even move one kilometre without Bemba's permission.

The MLC leader could order arrests and investigations, the prosecution explains. On 30 October 2002, when his troops had been in the CAR for just a few days, Bemba launched an investigation into reports of pillaging by his men. Seven suspects were charged with robbery and attempted extortion of goods including '10 litres of petrol, some aspirin, 60 euros, a bottle of perfume, three compact discs and two mobile phones,' the prosecution says. They were brought before a court martial in Gbadolite and convicted to sentences ranging from 3 to 24 months. 'But the only objective was to convict someone to please the international community and to permit Jean-Pierre Bemba to wash his hands of the matter,' insists prosecution lawyer Massimo Scaliotti.

A few weeks later, in December, a commission of inquiry is sent to Zongo, a Congolese town on the banks of the Oubangui river facing the CAR capital of Bangui, for a second investigation. The delegation found no evidence of looting or other crimes. 'This investigation was a clear attempt to whitewash the MLC crimes in the CAR,' alleges Scaliotti. In February 2003 Bemba launched a third investigation to address allegations broadcast via Radio France International (RFI). He dispatched some soldiers in his helicopter to Sibut, a town in the CAR, to film and question local residents. 'It was a piece of propaganda,' explains Iverson, concluding: 'So he had the power, but the shame of the matter is that he didn't effectively use that power to stop any of the serious crimes that were happening in the CAR.' After Bemba pulled his troops out of the CAR back to the DRC, March 2003, he personally pinned new ranks to the epaulettes of his officers.

Tsunami

It is the legal representative of victims' turn to speak. Legal assistant Célestin Nzala is the person who keeps in touch with the 5229 persons in the CAR who are registered as victims in this case. He provides them with information and takes their questions, comments and concerns back to The Hague. When Bemba's troops 'invaded' the CAR, Nzala explains, 'it was as if a tsunami had swept over the land causing desolation throughout the entire population.' Rape was 'by far' the most common crime, and that's why Nzala and the prosecution pay more attention to this crime than to other atrocities.

The lives of the victims 'have been utterly destroyed,' Nzala says. Rape causes devastating harm, but in the CAR the suffering is aggravated because sexual matters are taboo. Victims saw their marriages break down. They were rejected by their communities. There was the problem of diseases such as Aids. Some victims, who were pregnant when they were raped, lost unborn children. Or they became pregnant and gave birth to unwanted babies.

He tells that the Trust Fund for Victims (TFV), an agency created alongside the ICC, was ready to provide assistance to victims, but this project was not carried out because the latest civil war that had erupted in the CAR had made the situation too dangerous.

Nzala explains how killings by MLC troops robbed whole families and even entire communities of their breadwinner. Some families suffered doubly because they hadn't been able to locate the bodies of their loved ones. The looting caused deep misery, as it forced people to live in 'extreme utter poverty.'

Although the victims have put hope in the ICC, they also criticize the court for opportunities missed, because the trial takes so long and no verdict has been pronounced. 'If the decision had been handed down earlier,' Nzala says, 'this would have prevented the crisis that once again has cost them so much. If the decision had been handed down earlier, there would have been a deterrent effect.'

No payment

When the hearing opens the next day, 13 November 2014, Bemba seems slightly more at ease. He looks at the audience. When he sees Kilolo sitting on the first row, he holds up his thumb and greets his former lead counsel with a big smile, but then immediately goes back to a straight face. The public gallery is almost empty, and will only slowly fill up during the morning. The visitors are a mix of MLC supporters, Bemba's former lawyers, some experts and journalists. Among the audience are also Yannick-Jenny Fernhout-Kottaud and a friend, who live in The Netherlands but originate from the CAR. The two ladies feel they represent and honour the victims in their country.

Judge Steiner is putting her headphones on and a court officer helps her with her computer. The hearing continues with the presentation of the lawyers of the victims, who have their own independent position, but often follow the line of the prosecution and therefore are sometimes seen as 'the second prosecutor.' Maître Marie-Edith Douzima-Lawson, who has been representing the victims in this case during all these years, explains what Bemba's army actually looked like. It was composed 'mainly of young people,' she says.[142] Among them there were 'kadogos', child soldiers. The army also included women, sometimes even carrying babies, participating in violent acts. Bemba didn't pay his troops. 'No one within the MLC received any wages,' Douzima says.

The militia were dressed in a 'unique' way, the lawyer claims. But when she describes their clothes, a picture of a messy lot emerges. Some soldiers were wearing uniforms with sports shoes, while others were dressed in civilian clothes. Other troops wore a mix of military shirts with civilian trousers, and vice versa, or traditional clothes. Their berets had various

---

142 Official transcript, ICC, 13 November 2014.

colours: red, black, green. It can be hardly called an identifying feature, unless it was the variety in clothes that distinguished them.

Douzima stresses that the CAR military authorities had no power over the MLC. Authority is a key feature in this case because it defines whether Bemba was responsible for the behaviour of his troops. The two forces 'did not cooperate well at all,' the victim's lawyer says. Witness P-31, a colonel within the CAR army, had told the court that when the MLC arrived in the capital Bangui, they immediately started looting and even stole musical instruments from the national military orchestra. The witness also had seen how at one point 30 officers from the CAR army had been 'tied up, disarmed and stripped' down to their underwear. Douzima repeats that Bemba was aware of the violence and the abuse, through phone contacts and reports, but didn't take real measures to repress the crimes. The court martial he organised in Gbadolite was 'merely a sham.' A few low-ranking soldiers had been convicted to prison terms for theft and looting, but 'once the international press had gone, the soldiers were freed.'

She then turns to her clients. The victims have waited for justice for twelve years now. Time is precious. Some 'will not be alive the day that the decision finally is handed down.' The harm can't be undone, the lawyer insists. 'Nothing can give back the stolen childhood of the children, the quiet life of the families, the peace of the community.' The girls' virginity can't be restored. Broken marriages can't be repaired. It is impossible to bring back family members who died. But a verdict will tell the victims that 'their suffering has not been forgotten.' It will be essential 'for generations' who hopefully 'will see the days of impunity coming to an end in the Central African Republic.'

Towards the end she addresses the judges: 'Under these conditions, your Honours, Jean-Pierre Bemba must be found guilty and criminally responsible for crimes against humanity and war crimes.' In her last sentence she also refers to the deterrent effect that a conviction could have, as the victims will be able to say: 'No, this shall never occur again.'

Defence

The defence has the daunting task to counter these arguments. Lead counsel Peter Haynes speaks slowly and clearly. He has been on the team since the early days of the trial. When his colleagues were arrested for bribing witnesses, he took charge of the defence. Before today's final submissions, Haynes had discussed with his team what their attitude would be. He gave them instructions to keep 'poker faces', not to show any reaction, nor look at the public gallery. It might explain why the lawyers completely ignored their former colleagues Kilolo and Mangenda sitting in the audience.

It hasn't been much of an open trial, says Haynes. 'The majority of witnesses in this case were afforded almost complete protection of their identities with the result that huge swathes of the evidence in the case have been heard behind closed doors, or as we say euphemistically, in private or closed session.' He wonders: 'Why were we so protective?' Because just two witnesses – who were friends and in constant contact with each other – complained about being intimidated in this case. 'More worryingly,' Haynes says, a number of hearings took place under 'ex parte circumstances', which means that 'not everybody is present.' The lawyer will adjust the impression the court and public might have after having listened to the prosecution and the legal representatives of victims. Take the claim that the MLC committed a 'massive number of offences' all over the country during the five months the troops were in the CAR. 'In a particularly demonstrative expression, Mr Nzala yesterday referred to it as a tsunami of rape,' Haynes notes. 'Just stand back and think about this for a moment,' he says. If there was a tsunami, 'all over the country,' then why did the victims testifying only come from a limited area telling about rapes occurring in a limited timeframe, until mid-November 2002. The 'tsunami', he says, 'depends on the direct evidence of people from a tiny ring around Bangui over a period of 13 days.'

Moreover, there is 'insufficient' evidence to support the claim that MLC troops were responsible for any offences prior to 30 October 2002, says Haynes. This means that the testimony of at least four witnesses can't be counted on because the violence they suffered, happened before that date. He stresses that 'more than half' of the rapes experienced by victims in this case can't have been committed by the MLC and should be excluded from the trial which, in the view of the defence, basically is just about 15 incidents: nine of rape, five of pillaging and one murder.

Clothes and language

Haynes also tackles the impression that the MLC were the only troops in town. The forces loyal to Patassé comprised of 'no fewer than seven or eight militia components.' The MLC was just one of them, among troops from Sudan, Libya and Congo-Brazzaville. There were also the opponents: general Bozizé and his 'barely trained rebels' coming from the north. Towards the end of 2002 there were 'thousands of men, some wearing military uniforms, some not, but all armed and dangerously marauding around Bangui and its outskirts.' It has been impossible to identify these different forces by their dress or weaponry, because 'everybody in this conflict was wearing a FACA uniform or civilian dress or a combination of military and civilian clothes,' Haynes says. So there was no way MLC soldiers could be recognized from what they were wearing.

That leaves only language as way of identification. But the fact that a soldier 'spoke a few words of Lingala' doesn't prove he was a member of the MLC or came from the DRC, says Haynes. Lingala is spoken by 'a significant' part of people living in the CAR and by 'all factions' in the events. Within the forces of Bozizé there were 'elements' speaking Lingala 'quite deliberately to disorient their victims, to frighten them by using a language they didn't understand and, of course, to throw them off the scent as to who their attackers were,' Haynes argues.

The defence lawyer points out that Bozizé's troops, who were fighting to topple president Patassé, were no angels. When they entered Bangui on 25 October 'they immediately began looting and a day later killing,' says Haynes. Bemba's men, who were sent to crush the coup, came to the CAR calming things down. 'They were welcomed as the people who drove away Bozizé's rebels.'

Witnesses and victims

The lawyer says it is 'entirely understandable' that during their testimony, witnesses and victims tried to 'sanitise' the actions of Bozizé's forces. 'His men were guilty of many crimes,' Haynes explains. But it would be hard for people to criticise Bozizé as he had won the violent conflict, seized power and became president of a 'shocking' regime. He integrated his rebel forces, other militia and remnants of the defeated army into a national force. 'It would have been beyond brave to accuse anyone from amongst that number of any crime,' says Haynes. What's more, the national investigations into the crimes committed during the five-month conflict, from October 2002 until spring 2003, were conducted by the authorities under the Bozizé regime. It is no surprise, says Haynes, that the CAR investigators 'heard no complaints against Bozizé's men or members of the FACA' as they were now in power.

From the beginning the investigations have been biased, the defence alleges. An organisation called Ocodefad (Organisation pour la Compassion des Familles en Détresse) was 'the almost sole provider' of witnesses from the CAR and functioned as intermediary for the ICC's prosecution. Haynes says he doesn't want 'to pitch' this matter 'too high,' but notes that Ocodefad 'derived part of its funding from the Bozizé government.' The organisation was led by 'the dominant' Bernadette Sayo, who had resigned her position as a minister, but 'that's a subtlety that was probably lost on the membership of Ocodefad and it plainly didn't curb her involvement with victim-witnesses as the chamber knows well.' Haynes underlines that this organisation 'only promoted the interests' of people who said they were victims of Bemba. 'It simply wasn't possible to be a member and say you had been attacked by anybody else.' He also questions 'the industrial scale of the victim participation scheme.' Over five thousand persons have been registered as victims in this case: people who directly suffered from the charged crimes. 'One must just pause to think of that,' notes Haynes, because this implies that every MLC soldier who was deployed in the CAR committed 'three or more offences each, or a small group of them literally doing nothing but offending.'

Most of the victims' applications were approved 'way after the trial had commenced,' Haynes stresses. Intermediaries charged money from victims to fill in applications forms and 'advised people to make false claims of crimes and increase their claims of loss.' Many applications contain 'outrageous claims of compensation,' sometimes 'running to hundreds of thousands or millions of dollars per head,' the defence lawyer states. While Haynes is pleading, two women at the public gallery get up from their seats and leave. Yannick-Jenny Fernhout-Kottaud, who has been living in The Netherlands for 25 years and runs a foundation promoting African culture, will later explain that she and her friend couldn't bear to listen to the defence. The way Bemba's lawyers describe the fate of the victims was too painful and brutal for them to endure.

The defence points at other aspects with regard to the selection of witnesses. Why was former president Patassé, who had asked Bemba to send his men to the CAR, not been heard? 'I know he's dead, but he wasn't dead in 2009 or 2010 or 2011 and nobody went to speak to him or interview him so far as I'm aware.' Nor the prime minister, senior ministers or the general chief of staff of the CAR were called to testify. 'Wouldn't you want to hear from them to understand how this composite coalition force was commanded? Who gave the orders, who was responsible for discipline, who arrested the people who did wrong?' Haynes wonders. The prosecution chose not to call these officials. 'It leaves you with very poor quality evidence on an issue which could have been really clarified by those at the heart of the action.'

Instead, the evidence on the command issue is given by four witnesses, says Haynes. They weren't ministers, senior army officers or even soldiers on the ground. The lawyer describes them as a seller, a person who made clothes, a low-ranking official and an intelligence person for the Congolese government. 'Tinker, tailor, soldier, spy,' he summarizes. When Haynes is wrapping up his analysis, which he presented with great conviction, he looks briefly at Kilolo, who is sitting in front of me. During one of the breaks I would briefly meet the former lead counsel. Kilolo says he feels 'sad' he has been discharged of the task to defend Bemba. 'I gave six years of my life to this case. But I am satisfied, because I have done all the work on this case, up until the closing statements. And I have complete confidence in my colleagues,' Kilolo comments. He has no contact anymore with Haynes, but they occasionally meet when they visit Bemba at the detention centre. 'The fact that I have been released is a good sign that Bemba will be set free as well. The evidence will prove his innocence.'

Command responsibility

Co-counsel Kate Gibson will deconstruct the prosecution's accusation that Bemba was in charge of his troops and therefore is responsible for crimes they allegedly committed. In a lively and energetic way, the young Australian lawyer first looks back. Gibson reminds the court that the ICC's prosecution had initially concluded that the late president Ange-Félix Patassé coordinated and directed the MLC forces. 'There was no suggestion that Mr Bemba retained commanding control of the troops who crossed the Oubangui River into Bangui to fight alongside the FACA forces in October 2002,' she says. In the beginning her client was charged as a 'co-perpetrator' with Patassé. But as the ICC judges didn't confirm the 'co-perpetratorship,' Bemba was then being tried as a commander.

Gibson stresses however that her client was not in command, because his men were 'resubordinated to the hierarchy' of the Central African forces. She refers to the testimony of witness P-36, who told the judges that the procedure was to mix 150 MLC troops with some thirty FACA soldiers. 'And this is logical. Without the FACA troops by their side, the MLC would have been lost. They didn't know where they were going. It wasn't their country.' The military operations were coordinated through the command centre for operations of the CAR.

There's 'not a single documentary piece of evidence', Gibson argues, that shows any orders from Bemba to his troops in the CAR, nor is there proof that he used two phones to give orders. 'It's all just guesswork,' she says. Gibson sums up: 'The idea that Mr Bemba was sitting in his living room monitoring troops in a foreign state, in a conflict in which only a fraction of his soldiers were involved and sending command orders to them over an unreliable communication system when he didn't know the first thing about directing tactical operations, just isn't plausible.'

In international criminal law the concept of 'superior responsibility' requires that a person has knowledge that his troops were committing crimes. But Gibson argues that all Bemba heard at the time were mixed reports and rumours. When her client was informed about possible crimes, he did all he could to find out what was going on. Bemba wrote letters to the UN and to the human rights organisation FIDH. Moreover, he sent three commissions to check the rumours. 'All three reported that either the crimes hadn't occurred, or they had occurred but they'd been committed by the other side,' says Gibson. Senior MLC members went in a helicopter to Sibut, a city in the centre of the CAR, and invited national and international press, including Radio France International that had reported about crimes. A film was made of the mission. 'The population described being terrorised by Bozizé's rebels and saved by Bemba's men.' Gibson explains that Bemba didn't fail to take all necessary measures to prevent or repress the commission of crimes. He made sure his recruits were taught the code of conduct. Because many were illiterate, the soldiers 'would repeat the provisions and sing them.' The MLC leader instructed all brigade commanders back in 2000 that the death penalty would apply to troops convicted of murder, treason and rape. 'There are lists in evidence of MLC soldiers convicted and imprisoned for criminal conduct and those who were executed,' the lawyer stresses.

Bemba's force had a mobile martial court moving around the MLC territory. During the 'Gbadolite trials' seven MLC soldiers who'd been caught stealing in the CAR were convicted. 'There was no culture of impunity. There was no climate of toleration of crimes. Mr Bemba took necessary and reasonable measures to prevent their commission,' Gibson reiterates.

There is one last aspect the lawyer wants to address. 'Why would Mr Bemba have wanted to assume operational control over MLC troops fighting in a foreign war?' Commanding his troops from the DRC would be a full-time job. 'The prosecution told you yesterday that Mr Bemba was a man on a quest for ultimate power in the DRC. It gives no explanation as to why he would dedicate months of his time at such a critical juncture in the history of the DRC, to directing military operations involving less than 10 percent of his troops in a foreign state,' the lawyer underlines. 'It's not only implausible, it's not supported by the evidence.' Bemba wasn't in command of his troops in the CAR. Therefore, Gibson concludes, there is no other option than an acquittal.

Faith and hope

Judge Steiner thanks the lawyer and points to the time. It is almost one o'clock. 'We will now suspend for the lunch break,' the magistrate says. Everybody is getting up while the three judges leave the courtroom. The visitors go down to the lobby, where family, friends and political allies of Bemba are in an upbeat mood. 'As Congolese we have come with many to support him. I am very positive. The defence has shown Bemba's innocence. Ever since he was arrested in 2008, I remained confident,' says Jean-Jacques Mbungani, who is leading the MLC in Europe. 'The ICC has been used by the presidents Bozizé and Kabila to get rid of Bemba. But we have faith. Our hope for his release is the hope of an entire nation. When he returns, it will be a national celebration. He will play a major political role in our country.'

In one of the red chairs in the foyer sits Lilianne Bemba, modestly dressed in a white shirt and a black skirt and a small golden chain around her neck. She comes rarely to hearings, but today she is present. Her three daughters – modern and hip youngsters – have joined her. Her two sons stayed at home. It is now six years since their father is behind bars. 'It has been very difficult, but despite the problems we keep going,' Mrs Bemba sighs.

'No,' she answers shaking her head, her children are not bullied at school by other students for having their father detained. 'They are met with a lot of compassion. We get a lot of support from our family, friends and many Congolese people,' she says. Lilianne Bemba is relieved hearing the closing statements. 'I am satisfied that the truth, which has been hidden for so long, finally comes out. The prosecution wants a 'bête noire' and will do anything to have my husband convicted. Just think about all these closed hearings during the trial. But I can see the exit now, which will be good for us. I see light at the end of a very long and dark tunnel.'

Then it is time to return to the public gallery. 'Good afternoon and welcome back. Mr Haynes, you have the floor,' says Steiner. But the defence lawyer apologizes because he hasn't much more to say. 'It's a privilege to be the last person to address the chamber in this case, and I thought I ought to mark the particular odyssey we've been on these last four years,' he says. Haynes thanks his colleagues, the judges and the ICC staff helping the defence in forming an 'ad hoc legal team to get this case from the conclusion of the evidence to today.'

He briefly goes back to what Bemba's supporters also consider being the heart of the matter. Haynes says the case was 'shepherded' before the ICC by two men who had 'the most profound interest' in seeing Bemba's political career and life interrupted: Bozizé and Kabila. But it wasn't a strong case, he underlines. The prosecution's investigation has been 'selective, narrow and verging on unfair.' It has failed to prove the charges. 'We know that you have a difficult and brave decision to make,' he says to the judges, adding that 'the correct verdict upon this evidence and after this trial process would be the acquittal of Mr Jean-Pierre Bemba. Thank you.'

The last words are for presiding judge Steiner, who thanks all the parties and the court's staff for their cooperation and understanding. Now the judges will retire to come to a decision, which will be delivered in 'a reasonable' period of time. She adjourns the hearing. 'All Rise,' says the court usher and then the three judges leave the courtroom.

The visitors hand in their headphones, which they had needed to follow the hearing. The wife of Bemba reaches the elevator together with her daughters, her husband's former bodyguard and other supporters. They are pressed together in the small cabin, when Yannick-Jenny

Fernhout-Kottaud and her friend step in as well. 'That is a nice boubou you are wearing, where is it coming from?' Mrs Bemba asks Mrs Fernhout, possibly unaware that the lady in the African robe is particularly close to the victims of her husband's militia. 'It is from the CAR. We are the only ones from our country present today,' Mrs Fernhout answers. Then a Congolese women whispers to Mrs Bemba: 'She is not on your side.' The atmosphere in the small cabin turns tense. When the lift touches the ground floor, the CAR ladies, who are in the minority, leave the court as quickly as they can.

Across the street, in front of the ICC building, the Congolese are gathering in a celebratory mood. They are shaking hands, tapping on shoulders and hugging each other. Former counsel Kilolo is among the crowd. Kate Gibson is being kissed on the cheeks. Numerous selfies are made and immediately checked on the cell phones. Loud applause and cheering rises up when Haynes is leaving the court and crosses the street to join, just briefly, the supporters. With great enthusiasm the crowd hails him as their hero. Everybody positions for a large group photo. Smile! Then a blue van with dark windows is departing from the court building. The crowd starts waving, cheering and shouting: 'Libérez Bemba! Libérez Bemba!' When the car is passing, on its way to take the suspect to the detention centre, a woman shouts. 'He is our president. He is innocent!' Haynes doesn't stay long among the crowd. Soon he moves away and crosses the street to stand next to the ICC's fences, check his phone and watch the Congolese party. He is laughing. 'I usually don't get drawn into this kind of thing. I am a British lawyer. But it is lovely to be welcomed in this way,' he says, smiling, with slight unease and embarrassment. The most beautiful thing for him was to hear his team member Kate Gibson, who has been on the case since the beginning and today addressed the court for the first time. 'The judges probably never heard her voice before. I am sure they were impressed by her presentation.' Then he briefly sums up: 'It is a weak case. But if the judges find my client guilty, this will have a lot of consequences for governments who are sending their troops on peacekeeping missions.'

The verdict

It will take an awfully long time, almost one and a half year, before the judges reach their decision. On 21 March 2016 dozens of Congolese are waiting in front of the new court building located at the edge of the sand dunes near the Dutch coast, to get in. Unfortunately, most haven't registered and will not be allowed to enter, despite the fact that the ICC's permanent premises have huge public indoor spaces. Foreign diplomats have received tickets in advance and the international media have been given the chance to register as well. But most Congolese supporters will have to stay outside.

After two security checks visitors enter the public gallery. Just before the hearing is opened, the ICC's protocol officer stands in front of the visitors. The tall blonde man warns in French that it is forbidden to point at people in the courtroom. If visitors will make such moves or for instance will shout in reaction to what the judges say, the curtains will be drawn. This is clearly a message for the Congolese among the audience. On the first row, the family is being seated. Mrs Bemba, wearing a colourful red and blue dress with big flowers, is accompanied by her children, family members, Congolese politicians and other acquaintances. The former counsels Kilolo and Mangenda, and old time friend Babala are present as well. But relatively speaking there aren't many Congolese visitors among the public. Some friends of the judges also have managed to get a seat. Mrs Fernhout is there, but no official from the CAR has come to this crucial hearing.

The curtains are slowly opened. Bemba, in a dark blue suit, looks around. Despite the tensions and the fact that the courtroom is huge compared to the old one, there is something familiar about seeing the three judges, who have been handling this case for so long, taking their seats. When Steiner wants to start, she has difficulty opening the microphone. After some silence, the equipment is properly switched on and she welcomes everybody. In polite words Steiner warns the public in the gallery, assuming the visitors 'will be respectful towards the chamber throughout the reading of the present judgment, and I would just remind them to abstain from making any sort of manifestations during the hearing.'[143] Bemba is leaning forward and looks intensely at the judges, while Steiner starts to read the verdict. Strikingly her co-judges Aluoch and Ozaki keep their eyes fixed on the computer screens in front of them. There's no moment that they look into the courtroom. What message can be read from their attitude? Steiner says there have been 330 hearings in the case.

---

143 Official transcript, ICC, 21 March 2016.

The judges heard 77 witnesses: 40 for the prosecution, 34 for the defence, 2 for the legal representatives of victims, and one called by the chamber. An additional three victims gave their views as well. The judges issued 1,219 written decisions, notifications and cooperation requests as well as 277 oral decisions and orders. To get an idea of the magnitude of the case: the evidence totals 733 items, including 5,724 pages of documentary evidence. In total 5,229 persons are given the status of victims.[144]

When she gives a summary of the conflict, Steiner explains that after president Patassé called in Bemba's help, MLC troops and a limited number of FACA forces advanced, 'beginning on 26 October 2002' through various locations in the Central African Republic. By pointing to this date, the judges crush one of the arguments of the defence lawyers who claim that the Congolese fighters arrived five days later and could therefore never have been responsible for several of the charged crimes. While reading on, Steiner tells that Bemba would send a total of 1500 MLC soldiers. There is another blow to the defence when she says that the 'evidence demonstrated that in the course of the 2002-2003 operation MLC troops committed many acts of pillaging, rape, and murder against civilians, over a large geographical area.' These included Bangui, PK12, PK22, Bozoum, Damara, Sibut, Bossangoa, Bossembélé, Dékoa, Kaga Bandoro, Bossemptele, Boali, Yaloke, and Mongoumba.

Reviewing the witness testimonies, the judges found there was evidence of three people being killed by the MLC. No less than 28 people were raped. There was even a family where three generations were raped: P23, his wife, three daughters and his granddaughter. Some two dozen people and families were the victims of looting. The testimony of the coffee-seller has been accepted. The judges recognize the death of her brother, the fact that she was gang-raped and the looting of her house. Based on the clothes, the language, the way they identified themselves to the victims and the troop movements at the time, the judges conclude that MLC soldiers were the perpetrators of these crimes.

The chamber adds that the atrocities presented in court by the witnesses are 'only a portion' of all crimes by the MLC forces in the CAR, and were part of a widespread attack on the population. After the rebels of general Bozizé had departed an area, MLC soldiers would do house-to-house

---

144   Summary of Trial Chamber III's Judgment, ICC, 21 March 2016.

searches. They would target people to 'self-compensate for inadequate payment and rations' and to 'destabilise, humiliate or punish suspected rebels, rebel sympathisers, or those who resisted pillaging and rape.'

The judges also conclude that Bemba 'had effective authority and control over the MLC forces that committed the crimes.' He was the group's president and commander-in-chief of its military wing. He took 'the most important' decisions, had the powers of appointment, promotion and dismissal. Bemba had direct lines of communication to commanders in the field, via radios, satellite phones and mobile telephones. He used a well-established reporting system. As commander he could initiate inquiries and establish courts-martial. He also had the ability to send troops to the Central African Republic, or withdraw them. Although the MLC forces cooperated with the national authorities, they 'were not resubordinated' to the CAR military hierarchy.

On the first row of the public gallery, where Bemba's family is seated, a young man is sitting bent over, with his head down. He knows what is coming. Bemba himself is watching the judges, while the defence is sitting with straight backs. Judge Steiner continues to read the 21-page summary of the decision. Her two colleagues are still focusing on their computer screens on their desk.

'Bemba knew that the MLC forces were committing or about to commit the crimes,' the judges conclude. Not only did he receive intelligence about combat situations, but also about the crimes. He followed international media reporting allegations of rape, pillaging and murder by his soldiers. Bemba visited the CAR himself on a number of occasions. But he failed to take the 'necessary and reasonable measures' to prevent his men from committing crimes. He issued just general warnings to his troops not to mistreat the civilian population. His investigations into the crimes were very limited. These interventions were 'not properly and sincerely executed' and were 'a grossly inadequate response to the consistent information of widespread crimes.' He omitted to punish or replace commanders. His soldiers were not properly trained in the rules of international criminal law. If instead he would had taken the right measures, these 'would have deterred the commission of crimes and generally diminished, if not eliminated, the climate of acquiescence – which is inherent where troops have inadequate training, receive unclear orders, and/or observe their commanders committing or collaborating in crimes.'

There it is. The judges declare Bemba 'guilty' as a military commander of murder and rape as crimes against humanity, and also of murder, rape, and pillaging as war crimes committed by his MLC forces in the Central African Republic.

Triumph and shock

The verdict is a triumph for the prosecution. The chamber has completely followed its reasoning. The judgment also sets a new precedent, as it is the first time that the ICC convicts a military leader who has sent his troops to fight abroad, for his responsibility as a commander for the crimes his men committed. It is also the court's first conviction for sexual crimes, which is a victory for Bensouda, who has made prosecution of these atrocities one of her main goals.

But there is a serious downside as well. With Bemba being the only person charged and convicted, this is a one-sided case. Other alleged perpetrators in the CAR – for years the ICC has been dependent on the cooperation offered by president Bozizé, who is seen as a potential suspect as well – have not been punished. Despite the hopes of judge Steiner and the victims, this case did not have much of a deterrent effect in the CAR, which has gone through terrible episodes of violence in recent years. While the judges are leaving the scene, the convicted war criminal is taking in his defeat. Briefly Bemba touches his head with his hand. Then he gets up. With the guards accompanying him, Bemba strides, carrying a file under his arm, out of the courtroom.

The curtains are closing and the view into the courtroom disappears. With an empty look, Kilolo is staring in front of him. While the visitors are getting up, suddenly there are sounds of sobbing. Some members of Bemba's family are crying. Women are comforting them, by putting their arms around them and gently rubbing their backs. A white handkerchief is passed on. But then a guard tells me to go. The head of the ICC's information department is irritated when I refuse to leave as I want to wait to see how the supporters are coping. 'Show some respect to the family,' she snarls.

In the main hall I meet Bemba's bodyguard. 'We are in a complete shock. We didn't expect this at all,' says Ngoy-Liboto, smartly dressed in a black suit with a golden pen in his pocket. 'Absolutely, I thought he would be acquitted. I have constantly attended this trial. Many witnesses made mistakes. There were so many inconsistencies. We feel Bemba is sacrificed. This decision is so painful. It hurts.' The bodyguard is lost for words. While an MLC representative is being interviewed by a TV crew, Bemba's family has left the public gallery and has gone downstairs to the cloakroom, which is located in the basement of the building. They have retreated to the women's toilet. A couple of Congolese men have positioned themselves as informal security on the stairs. They refuse access to anybody who wants to go down to fetch a coat, or to visit the toilet. Two Congolese women are getting angry because they need to get their belongings as they have a car waiting outside. But the men don't give in. The ICC security guards, usually so strict and authoritarian, don't know what to do. They laugh clumsily and let the Congolese men have their way.

On her own, a tall woman in a bright long green dress with a scarf nicely wrapped over her grey hair, is observing the scene from a distance. She sees the bewilderment, confusion and sadness among the Bemba supporters whose hopes have been dashed. 'I feel for the family. I am really sorry for them,' says Yannick-Jenny Fernhout-Kottaud, who sympathises with the victims, but recognizes how hard it must be for Bemba's children who just heard their father is now a convicted war criminal. 'But I don't feel sorry for Bemba himself, because he never showed any empathy.' Fernhout-Kottaud is the only visitor originating from the CAR who came to listen to the verdict. 'I am proud to stand here, at this historic moment, to somehow represent my country,' she says. 'I am happy for the victims that Bemba is convicted. Although I realise that their lives are broken. Just think about a small girl, who was raped in front of her family, and then rejected by her community, now living in disgrace. The verdict today won't give her back her life.'

By then the defence lawyers and Bemba's family have retreated to a room for a short meeting. When Kate Gibson comes out of the briefing she says she can't understand that the judges came to this conclusion. 'Have we been sitting in the same courtroom for all these years?' Gibson wonders. Haynes says he is 'very, very disappointed. You expect to lose something, but not to lose everything in the case.' He spoke briefly to Bemba who is 'disappointed and angry with the judgment,' but in the 'measured way' of someone who realised long ago that he is a detainee. Bemba's life has been on hold for eight years, Haynes says. With the guilty verdict his hopes of rebuilding his family life are shattered. But being his lawyer, Haynes' mind is already with the next phase: the sentencing and the appeal.

New hearings

Two months later, mid-May, there are a few more hearings, which give the prosecution, defence and legal representatives of victims the chance to present their views on what an appropriate sentence would be for the convicted Bemba. The defence has found a witness, Fridolin Ambongo, who is prepared to come to The Hague and testify in favour of the MLC leader without protective measures.[145] He wears a white shirt and a suit jacket, but the white clerical collar and the necklace with a cross tell he is not an ordinary man. Ambongo is a Congolese bishop and president of the Justice and Peace Episcopal Committee covering the DRC, Rwanda and Burundi.

While answering questions by counsel Haynes, he tells about the time the MLC came to run the Congolese province of Équateur. For decades this large area in the northwest of the DRC had been neglected by the Mobutu regime, the bishop says. When in 1997 rebels led by Laurent Desiré Kabila advanced to conquer the DRC, the Mobutu soldiers decided to 'loot, destroy and rape' before they fled the region, he tells. The situation grew worse when Kabila's men took control of the province. They terrorized the area. So it was 'good news' when Bemba's forces arrived. Ambongo explains: 'The first feeling for the community was that finally we had peace again.' The MLC didn't loot and instead offered security. Hospitals started to work again. Schools were reopened. The rebels also gave permission for the export of coffee.

The bishop paints a very different picture of Bemba's men, than the image which has emerged from the criminal trial, where MLC soldiers have been condemned as killers, rapists and looters. Ambongo denies any wrongdoing by the troops in the Congolese Équateur.

The legal representative of victims, Douzima-Lawson, notes that the bishop should be quite familiar with the neighbouring CAR as he had been on missions to the country. 'Do you know whether the soldiers of the MLC were in the CAR between 2002 and 2003?' she asks. 'I think things have to be said quite carefully,' answers the bishop, pointing out

---

145   Official transcript, ICC, 16 May 2016.

that he heard Bemba's men were in the CAR, but that the fight was basically a power struggle between Patassé and his former defence chief Bozizé. 'I did hear that there was abuse committed in the area, there was violence committed, but whether it was done by MLC troops, we heard this a very long time afterwards.'

Whether a bishop, who insists he doesn't know much about the CAR, will be of any help to Bemba in mitigating his sentence, remains to be seen. Then it is time for the prosecution to call its expert witness. Daryn Scott Reicherter is a psychiatrist and associate professor at Stanford University, where he is the director of the programme for Human Rights in Trauma Mental Health. He is an expert in cross-cultural psychiatry and has been treating patients who have been severely abused, raped and tortured, coming from Asia, the Middle East, Africa, Central and South America. At the request of the prosecution he has written a report about the impact of rape by the MLC in the Central African Republic, titled: 'The Mental Health Outcomes of Rape, Mass Rape, and Other Forms of Sexual Violence.' Not only does he know the vast volume of international scientific literature on this subject, he also specifically looked at the testimonies of the witnesses in the Bemba case.

Reicherter formulates carefully. His main argument, that victims of rape are likely to have serious mental health problems, might not be surprising. It is his explanation of aggravating risk factors that is shocking, as it shows the layers of the harm. His testimony makes clear how deep and massive the scars of sexual violence in the CAR must be. How it totally destroyed the lives of victims.

While answering questions, he tells the court that the way the MLC forces committed rape, increased the risk of mental harm. Reicherter points to the fact that people were gang-raped, family members being forced to commit the rape, or to watch the crime after which husbands were sometimes even murdered. When rape occurs during conflict, victims lack the sanctuary of a safe environment where they might have a chance to recover to some extent. MLC soldiers considered their prey to be war booty and sought to destabilise and punish people suspected of being rebels or rebel sympathisers. Rape, an interpersonal crime, was used as a weapon of war. 'While increased prevalence rates are expected for a population of rape victims, the alarmingly high rates of post-traumatic distress in the current population in the Central African Republic underscore the heinous and pervasive nature of the crime,' the psychiatric report is quoted in the courtroom.

Mental harm can express itself in nightmares, poor memory, intrusive thoughts, memories of the rape, mood and other anxiety disorders and even cognitive problems. All such consequences might be long lasting. The psychiatrist explains that people with a post-traumatic stress disorder (PTSD) overproduce the stress hormone 'to the extent that it actually causes brain damage.' It also occurs that they are no longer able to properly regulate that stress hormone in the ordinary way, where it has normal peaks and valleys. To explain what this means, Reicherter takes himself as an example. For his testimony he travelled from the USA to The Hague. 'Being jet-lagged, being a little anxious before I came out here, I would have a normal movement of my stress hormone.' It will go up when he needs it, and it will go down when it is time to sleep. But people with PTSD tend to be unable to regulate this stress hormone. 'It sort of ends up being in this unmoving place, which is very pathological.' There are other serious consequences as well. The psychiatrist points out that women who have PTSD from rape are more frequently faced with violence in their life. The reason is that victims behave differently, he says. 'Their biological and psychological outcome has changed from the original insult and therefore they become at risk for re-victimisation.'

It would be wrong to think that young people might have a better chance of healing. Reicherter tells that the effect on them is worse. 'Children who are raped have astronomically high lifelong prevalences of mental health disorders.' The expert explains that they are vulnerable, as they are still developing their personalities. When below the age of twelve, they still learn 'how to trust other people, how to love other people, how to think about relationships.' Maybe they aren't even ready to think about sexuality. 'If that person is raped by a man, it can create pathology that's not a post-traumatic stress disorder, but I think it's more fundamental to their personality development. Therefore, I would be concerned that it could cause deeper and longer lasting pathology for children.'

The current insecurity in the CAR will make things only worse, because traumatised rape victims continue to be in an unsafe situation, without a chance of recovering. Instead, their situation will become 'more chronic.' If victims receive no mental health care, this will only add to the deep misery.

The damage will even expand beyond the harmed individual. Sexual violence is likely to affect families, future generations and communities. Traumatised mothers can lose interest in looking after their children. The fact that the harm resulted in 'potentially permanent changes in their brain and therefore their behaviour' will have an impact on how parents treat each other and their children. As the happiness is gone, Reicherter says, marriages break down. Women who are left to raise their children on their own, might not be able to feed their children. Especially when they lost everything due to pillaging. Often victims become a pariah in their community. In populations where the parents are survivors of traumatic experience, their children 'went on to have greatly exaggerated rates of mental health disorders,' and even their grandchildren would be affected. That's why his report states: 'The effects of rape of a single individual are felt across multiple generations.'

Victim 555

The psychiatrist speaks as an expert. After his testimony two women who were raped by the MLC, tell their harrowing story. They are called by the legal representative of victims. The women haven't travelled to The Hague, but are in the CAR and will be heard through video-link. Their stories will confirm the theoretical presentation by the psychiatrist.[146] But before that happens, the court has to solve some technical problems. Defence lawyer Haynes says he has no sound in his earphones (not just the visitors at the public gallery, but also everybody in the courtroom is wearing them to be able to listen to the translations between French, English and other languages such as Sango in this case), while the interpreters hear a 'humming sound on the line.'
Presiding judge Steiner: 'Testing, testing. I think we have the connection with Bangui open. Maybe this is the reason why. Mr Haynes, can you hear me now?'
The lawyer says he can hear her voice in the courtroom, as he is sitting just a few metres away from the judges. 'But your voice isn't coming through my headphones,' he says, adding with that typical British wit: 'I'm probably less important. But the interpreters aren't hearing you either.'

---

146 Official transcript, ICC, 17 May 2016.

The court officer asks the IT technician: 'Can you please mute the connection for a few minutes.'
Steiner: 'Now can you hear me? Not yet?'
Interpreter: 'Now the sound is perfect for the interpreters.'
Steiner: 'Yes, we cut the connection with Bangui while the technicians will see what is going on. So in the meantime I can continue reading.'
The judge recalls that the identities of the two victims are protected so the public will not know who they are. They won't give a testimony under oath, which means the parties won't question them as they would if it had been a sworn statement. Steiner points out that if the lawyers seek some clarification from the victims, they have to 'use short simple questions and language which is easy to understand, avoiding legal terms, long sentences and double negations.' The court has been advised by its psychologist that questions about sexual violence have to be formulated 'in the least embarrassing manner possible.' The victim has to be observed closely. 'In case of signs of nervousness, distraction or emotional reactions, a break is offered to the victim.'
When Steiner is done, she is informed that the connection is working, and the woman can start telling her story.
'Madam witness, good morning. Can you hear me?' asks Steiner.
'Thank you, madam President,' says the victim, who speaks Sango and is 'present' through video-link.
'Can you hear me? The sound is good?' Steiner checks.
'I can hear you correctly,' the victim answers.
Steiner: 'I need a test from the English interpretation booth, please.'
The interpreter: 'Testing 1, 2, testing 1, 2, can you hear me?'
Finally, everything seems to work. After some more instructions the woman can start telling the court what happened to her and her family in her hometown Bossangoa, 300 kilometre north of the capital Bangui. When the inhabitants heard that Bemba's soldiers were on their way, they fled into the bush fearing reprisals as the area was labelled as being in favour of putschist Bozizé. The MLC men arrived by firing their guns, killing old and handicapped persons who had been unable to flee. They pillaged the whole town. The victim's house was ransacked as well, with Bemba's soldiers stealing clothes, shoes, tools, utensils, bedding, mattresses, cassava mills and the ground nut mills.

When she was discovered hiding in the bush by the MLC soldiers, together with her aunt the victim ran deeper into the woods. But Bemba's men caught the women and took them to the place where their family was sheltering. 'They then asked my father and grandfather to give them money in exchange for our freedom,' victim 555 tells the court. But when her family responded they did not have that money, the soldiers threatened 'to kill me and my aunt.' The MLC rebels then took the two women. When her father fried to follow them, he was beaten with rifle butts. 'They said they were going to kill us.'

A commander took victim 555 into an abandoned house. 'He forced the door open and he raped me.' She was only fifteen or sixteen years old. 'I was still a virgin,' she tells the judges. For a week she was repeatedly raped. Then she was taken to Bossembélé, a town more south on the road to Bangui, where the rapes continued, an ordeal she shared with other young girls. One was about twelve, others were some fourteen years old. There was no way of escaping from the MLC soldiers. 'We were not free in our movements at all. We ate with them. We shared the same food. If we wanted to go and rest or to relieve ourselves, we had to ask for permission to go to the toilet. We were always followed and guarded by one of them.' When Chadian troops arrived in Bossembélé, the MLC troops fled back home, to the DRC. But they took victim 555 with them. An MLC soldier considered her to be his wife. 'We slept in the bush and once we were on the other side of the river, I didn't feel well. I had stomach pains. I went to the hospital. I was examined and I was told that I was pregnant.' She was forced to stay with her captor. 'But given that they were rebels, they weren't paid. It was his parents, his family who helped us to live. He didn't receive a salary.' So she and her captor lived with his parents in the Congolese town of Zongo, on the southern river bank right across the CAR capital Bangui.

She gave birth to a child, who died six months later. Then she had a second child, a girl. Four years she lived with her captor in several Congolese towns. She was forced to have sex with him. All that time she had no contact with her family. 'They thought that I was dead. A funeral had already taken place, and they did not expect to hear any news from me.' When the MLC was demobilised, her captor decided to stay in the army and went to Kinshasa, while she went to stay with his family in Zongo. That's when she finally managed to flee.

'When I arrived in Bossangoa, my family welcomed me. They were surprised to see that I was still alive and that I had a child with me.' But she was not welcomed by the rest of the community. 'I was stigmatised. They said: Oh, it's a wife of the Banyamulenge who is in town.' Upon her return victim 555 was confronted with a lot of sad news. During the conflict her father had been taken to an MLC base and beaten. He suffered 'tremendously from their actions,' the victim tells, without explaining further. She met her aunt, who had contracted HIV, and had since died. After the looting, her family had not been able to re-establish their lifestyle and lived in utter poverty. 'They were farming and involved in a little bit of trading in order to be able to afford something to eat, even clothing themselves was difficult.' She herself couldn't pick up her old life either and couldn't return to school. 'It's something I regret and it's something that really hurts me in fact,' she says.

The victim now has four children. She explains that her oldest daughter is the child of her captor. After that she had two children with a man in Bossangoa. But it was not a happy relationship as his family didn't accept her. 'My sisters-in-law branded me as being the wife of Banyamulenge. And they, given that my aunt died because she was HIV positive, in their eyes I too am HIV positive.' After her husband died, victim 555 decided to live with her own family. She would meet a married man, with whom she had her other child. But he abandoned her. 'So I now live in family, if you like, with my four children for whom I am responsible.'

Judge Steiner intervenes: 'Madam witness, I see that you are showing signs of distress. Would you like to have a break, a short break, or you prefer to continue?'

Victim 555: 'We can continue. We can continue the questioning.'

The woman tells the judges she earns a bit of money with buying vegetables and reselling them in small markets. 'It allows me to feed the children and to have a little bit of money to clothe them and to take care of them.' But it is not enough to send them to school. She lives with one of her aunts, who also has children. 'When the children fight, sometimes I say things that I don't mean to say. I would like to live in my own house with my children. You know yourself, living within a family is not always easy. If I were alone, it would be bearable, but that's not the case. That's how it is. This is the impact of what happened to me in my youth,' she says.

When she compares herself with others, she feels sad because of the 'huge difference' she sees. 'Some of my peers, some of those I studied with, today work and have a salary. Today I have none of that. I could have been married, married to one man. But I'm deeply depressed,' she says. 'I have had suicidal thoughts.'

Victim 555 worries about the daughter she had by her captor, as she doesn't know her father, nor where he is. 'I ask God, if I die, what will happen to that child? The three others which I had, I know that their father's families are there, and if something happened to me, those children could go and live with the family of their father. But when it comes to this child, what will her fate be if anything happens to me?'

When asked why she is taking part in the proceedings before the court, she says: 'I wanted to talk about it publicly, and I wanted to talk about the suffering that I'm going through. I wanted to testify to what the Banyamulenge had put me through and to the consequences which that has had on the life that I lead today.'

She wants justice to be done. When she heard Bemba was declared guilty, she was 'delighted.' She adds: 'I'm happy that somebody will pay for the abuses carried out', such as the many killings, but it 'changes nothing of my living conditions.'

When her testimony has come to an end, Steiner addresses her: 'Madam, I thank you very much for the time and trouble you've taken to come before this court to give your views, your concerns, your testimony about the facts you were subject to.'

'Merci,' says victim 555.

Steiner: 'Thank you again very much, madam. The representative of the Victims and Witnesses Unit will accompany you and give you all the necessary assistance after your appearance before the chamber.'

A destroyed life

Victim 480, who also testifies through video-link, has a similar account of a destroyed life. On 25 January 2003 the woman and her father were on the road when Bemba's troops intercepted them. They were beaten, tied up and abducted. The goods they had with them were stolen. In the police post in the town of Bossembélé victim 480 was gang-raped. When she was taken to a base behind a gas station, the raping continued, leaving her covered with wounds. 'I spent three days at this base without eating. I was not able to wash myself. Every morning there was a new team that arrived and every day they raped me. There were always three or four people who raped me and that for the three days I was there.' Her father, who was tied up and severely beaten because the MLC troops accused him of being the person who supplied the rebels, was forced to witness the raping of his daughter. Others had to watch the sexual violence as well. 'My father was powerless. He couldn't say anything. The men were armed. Nobody could do anything about it.'

When the woman was finally freed, she looked for her father, who was in his sixties. But she couldn't find him. With the help of the Red Cross, his body was discovered six months later in a mass grave in the town of Damara, some 100 kilometre southeast of Bossembélé. His disappearance caused great sadness in the family. 'He had four wives and he had 23 children. He was a big tree with many branches and in whose shadow we all felt safe,' she says poetically. The woman explains how his death blocked her from rebuilding her life. Her father would help her by giving money from his pension, which allowed her to become a trader. Now that support had stopped. She also found out she had Aids. After everything I've been through, I'm no longer the same person, not in the physical sense because I'm frequently ill.' Her health is very delicate. She has pains in her lower abdomen and her back, and frequently suffers from a fever. There are other consequences as well. 'I have to admit that I don't have a sentimental life, if you'd like, feelings. I'm HIV positive, and that is a determining factor.' She doesn't have money for medication, and is following some free therapy. Her children don't know that she is HIV positive. 'They're not very old, and children of that age, if they were to know that their mother was suffering in this way, then it's like having a death sentence hanging over you. So I thought it was better to not to tell them so as not to have them carry this burden.'

After the rape her children dropped out of school. Her daughter stopped attending class because she became pregnant. Her son passed his driving test and became a driver. 'I don't have the money to pay for their schooling.' All she can do is rely on a higher force. 'I believe in God. And I feel he will not abandon me.'

Being registered as an official victim in this ICC case, she will fall under a reparations scheme which will be determined by the judges after a suspect has been convicted. Victims will have to be extremely patient though, because this process can last for years, even after the appeals phase (see chapter 10). So far this lady didn't even receive proper medication to treat

Aids. 'Today I am nothing,' says victim 480. 'I hope that the court will be able to ensure some form of reparations so that I can continue to live properly during the time that remains for me on earth.'

She says that giving her statement before the ICC has been a positive experience. 'I feel good. I feel liberated. I feel relieved because I've been able to express what I've been feeling for years. And I think that having had the chance to let this out, I feel good, I feel better.'

No less than 25 years

The following day, 18 May 2016, Fatou Bensouda addresses the court about what the appropriate punishment for Bemba would be. The prosecutor argues that this case requires a 'serious and effective sentence' to reflect 'the gravity' of the crimes and Bemba's 'high degree of responsibility.'[147] The goal of a prison sentence is not only to publicly reprimand the convicted commander for his criminal conduct, but also to send a message that the ICC is committed 'to end impunity for such grave crimes that cause such mass suffering and violently tear the social fabric of society,' says the prosecutor. The sentence should serve as an 'acknowledgment of the harm done to the innocent victims.' It will also 'pursue the objective of deterring other military commanders from committing serious crimes.'

The prosecutor reiterates that Bemba failed as a top commander because he didn't prevent his troops from committing atrocities nor did he punish them when they offended. 'What he did was to release his armed men into the civilian population in the Central African Republic, where they engaged in an horrific campaign of pillage, rape and murder.' Ordinary men, women and children are still 'haunted by the horror of what happened to them and what they saw happen to other victims. Lives have been destroyed and emotional scars have been etched in the memory of countless victims,' says the prosecutor.

In this specific case the prosecution sees no mitigating circumstances. Instead, there are two aggravating circumstances: the victims were particularly defenceless and crimes were committed with particular cruelty.

---

147 Official transcript, ICC, 18 May 2016.

Taking all these factors into account, Bensouda recommends that the sentence 'should not be less than 25 years of imprisonment.'

Caricature

The defence doesn't agree. Lead counsel Haynes tells the judges that his client has been 'incorrectly and unfairly caricatured' during this trial. Very few of the witnesses who described Bemba actually ever met him. 'They knew little of his life, little of his work, little of his thoughts.' Bemba had become a sort of 'mythical figure to many, especially in the Central African Republic,' like 'a ghoul to be feared' or 'a bogeyman' – fictional characters. That's how Bemba has been presented by the prosecution, the legal representative of victims and some of the witnesses.

Haynes argues that in reality the MLC forces were 'disciplined and well trained.' In the Congolese province of Équateur, the forces were responsible for health care, education, transport, justice and defending the region from military attacks. The lawyer points out that Bemba brokered peace in the eastern Congolese district of Ituri, which was ravaged by war. He worked for multiparty democracy in DRC. The defence underlines that Bemba sent a 'relatively small military force' – less than 10 percent of the total of 20,000 MLC troops – to the CAR. 'They were sent to support a democratically-elected leader in a neighbouring state who was facing a violent military coup and who asked for that assistance.' So his support was 'not just legal but was probably well-intentioned.'

Haynes admits that the judges found that Bemba's decision to send his troops 'ultimately resulted in crimes being committed against innocent Central African civilians.' But the defence repeats that basically this case is about 3 murders, 28 rapes and pillaging. That makes the Bemba trial different from cases with regard to the former Yugoslavia and Rwanda, where 'commanders are implicated in the extermination of 7 to 8,000 Bosnian Muslim men and boys in Srebrenica, or where troops of Rwandan commanders contributed to the genocide of hundreds of thousands of Rwandan Tutsis and moderate Hutus.'

Besides, Bemba was far removed from the crime scene and not even in the country. He didn't participate in the crimes nor did he encourage or order his troops to commit these atrocities. 'He wasn't motivated by any particular ethnic or religious or racial hatred. He had no discriminatory motive. He didn't share the intent of the soldiers who committed the acts. Mr Bemba's culpability arises from his failure to control a small fraction of his soldiers who were thousands of miles away fighting in a foreign conflict and who committed crimes over a relatively limited temporal period.'

He hands over to his colleague Kate Gibson. She warns the court that there are conflicts, such as the recent violence in the CAR, which resulted in much higher numbers of killings. So if Bemba would receive 25 years in a case with less victims, how will the ICC then punish more severe cases? She takes the court through the mitigating factors, such as Bemba's commitment to peace. The lawyer also points out that his detention already lasts eight years, during which he has lost his lead counsel, his father, stepmother and grandmother 'whose graves in Kinshasa he has never visited.' His five children are adults, but they 'have been deprived of the emotional and pastoral and educational care of a father.' According to the detention unit his family is of the 'utmost importance' for him. Gibson stresses that prison officials stated Bemba behaved well in detention showing 'his respect, his warmth, his good humour, his compassion for the other detainees, sharing everything he has from clothing to food, his concern for the people around him.' (The argument of good behaviour might sound rather awkward, given the fact that Bemba is in the middle of a second trial for running a scheme from his detention cell to bribe his witnesses.) That the prosecution painted him as a person with no regard for human life is 'just propaganda,' says Gibson. This image doesn't fit with a person who authorised the death penalty for soldiers who committed rape. It doesn't fit with a person who worked for the development of the Équateur in the DRC. It doesn't fit with the picture painted by bishop Ambongo, who said that when the MLC arrived, it felt like 'life began again.'

When Haynes takes over from his colleague, he underlines 'how frustrating' it must be for Bemba to be detained all these years 'not being a businessman, not being a politician, not being a husband, not being a father.' His wealth 'has been almost entirely dissipated by freezing orders and legal fees.' Notwithstanding, Bemba 'fully' cooperated. 'He has been courteous and respectful to the court,' stresses Haynes. Bemba is 'the only accused' who worked with the registry 'to transfer his resources to the court to pay for his legal fees.' There is no risk he will reoffend because he will never command an army again. His conviction rules out a return to politics, says the defence.

Haynes warns the judges that a 'massive sentence' will be hailed as 'a victory for justice, a victory for victims, a victory for the fight against impunity. You'll get the headlines. But as we say in England, today's headlines are tomorrow's fish and chip paper.' In the long run a very harsh punishment though will be regarded as an 'aberration, a freak, and to cause jurists in the future to regard the ICC's jurisprudence, not as the centre of the solar system, but rather Pluto, seldom seen and never visited.'

He invites the judges to have a look at the defence's study which makes clear that commanders in similar circumstances received sentences at the lower end of the scale. The chamber can only come to the conclusion that Bemba 'has not just reached, but has long ago passed the point at which his detention should have been ended.' With these arguments the three days sentencing hearings are over. Now Bemba, the victims, the parties, the experts, the national authorities and the wider audience will wait for another month to hear what the punishment will be.

The sentence

At the entrance of the courtroom an official is handing out a leaflet called 'ICC Rules of Decorum.' Little pictograms on the handouts explain the main do's and don'ts. Everybody needs to remain silent. People under 16 years are not allowed to enter. Pointing at people, recording, bringing in telephones, camera's, drinks and food is forbidden. Most visitors though are regulars, who have been coming to ICC hearings for years and probably know that if they fail to adhere to the rules or otherwise engage in 'inappropriate conduct,' they may be 'immediately expelled from the premises' and thereafter denied access.

It is 21 June 2016, the beginning of the summer. Three months ago, at the start of spring, Bemba was found guilty. Today the judges will deliver their decision on the sentence. The first rows on the right of the public gallery, where usually the family and supporters of the defendants take place, is still empty. Only last minute they arrive, with Bemba's wife wearing a chic, nicely fitting red dress. His former bodyguard, Le Pharaon, is in charge of security. On top of his suit he wears a fluorescent jacket of the sort that people keep in their car boots for emergency situations, when they need to step out of the vehicle and be very visible on the road. At a measured distance from the Bemba block sits Yannick-Jenny Fernhout-Kottaud, wearing an elegant beige head scarf with some glitter. She feels she represents the victims, but still hopes the sentence will not be too severe. 'He has been convicted and that in itself is already very humiliating.'

From below in the courtroom Bemba, the convicted war criminal, looks up to the gallery, which is just half full. Then he slumps back in his chair almost disappearing behind the computer screen in front of him on the desk.

The judges have arrived. When Steiner starts to read the summary of their decision she explains that to determine the appropriate sentence the judges considered many aspects: the gravity of the crimes, the gravity of Bemba's culpable conduct, plus his individual situation. They studied the evidence and looked whether there were aggravating and mitigating circumstances.[148]

To create no misunderstanding about the scope of this case, the chamber reiterates that the specific crimes that were brought before the court, were only a portion of the total number of crimes committed by MLC forces during their operations in 2002-2003 in the CAR.

The murders in this case are of 'serious gravity,' says Steiner. The killings were committed when the victims were resisting pillaging, just like happened to the brother of the coffee-seller. Their deaths affected other persons who may be 'directly injured' both mentally as physically. Surviving relatives will have to live without the deceased and miss their financial, physical, emotional, psychological or moral support. The impact of the deaths 'rippled through the relevant communities.'

The judges found that the crime of rape in this case is of 'utmost serious gravity.' The judges list the many physical problems the victims have been facing: vaginal and anal illnesses, abdominal pains, skin disorders, pelvic pain, high blood pressure, gastric problems, hypertension, miscarriage, infertility and HIV. The chamber points out that the victims suffered psychological and psychiatric consequences, such as PTSD, depression, anxiety, guilt, nightmares and humiliation. The victims were rejected and stigmatised by their communities.

The fact that the rape victims were 'particularly defenceless' constitutes an aggravating circumstance. Armed MLC soldiers targeted unarmed victims in their homes or places where they had fled to. They were beaten,

---

148 Official transcript, ICC, 21 June 2016.

restrained, threatened and held under gunpoint. At least eight of the known rape victims were between 10 and 17 years old.

The judges decided that 'particular cruelty' constitutes a second aggravating circumstance for this crime. Rape was used as a weapon of war. MLC soldiers raped to punish civilians who were suspected rebels or rebel sympathisers. The rapes were committed in combination with killing and pillaging. Other people were forced to witness the sexual violence including children, parents, siblings, other family members and neighbours. The victims were physically and verbally abused and threatened to be killed. The vast majority were gang-raped, orally, vaginally and anally penetrated. Rapes were sometimes carried out in an 'especially sadistic' way with entire families – elderly, men, women and children – victimized.

Steiner gets to the crime of pillaging, which is of 'serious gravity.' The judges point to one aggravating circumstance: the particular cruelty. Armed MLC soldiers targeted unarmed victims in their homes and places of sanctuary. Because Bemba's troops weren't paid, 'they self-compensated' themselves through pillaging. The judges mention the ordeal of the coffee-seller, P-87, whose compound was looted on 'three different occasions in a single day,' while she was gang-raped, her brother was murdered and she had to endure other violence and abuse as well.

As a military commander Bemba knew his forces were committing these atrocities, the judges say. But he failed to 'exercise control properly' and to take measures to prevent the violence. In fact, it was even worse. 'He did more than tolerate the crimes as a commander,' the judges stress. Through his inaction he 'deliberately aimed at encouraging the attack directed against the civilian population.' Finally, Bemba's position as MLC leader, his education and experience, 'increased the gravity of his culpable conduct.' Although the defence had done its best to paint a different picture of their client, the judges didn't find mitigating circumstances.

Then the judges come to the sentence itself. While the prosecution called for a prison sentence of at least 25 years, the defence stressed that a sentence higher than 12 to 14 years would 'infringe' on Bemba's rights. After balancing all the factors, the judges come to the following conclusion. Murder – legally defined in this case as a war crime and a crime against humanity – carries a sentence of 16 years of imprisonment. Rape – both a war crime and crime against humanity – counts for 18 years. The pillaging, as a war crime, is punished with 16 years. Because the highest of these three sentences reflects the totality of his culpability, the judges sentence Bemba to a total of 18 years of imprisonment. The time he has spent in detention, since his arrest on 24 May 2008, will be deducted from this sentence.

In the dock Bemba briefly looks up, as if he hopes for some help from above. Bensouda is writing and finishes her last sentence. Then she closes the salmon pink folder, as if she closes the case. Although the prosecutor has won this trial, she doesn't show it. With a serious look she watches Steiner thanking the parties, court officials and visiting professors who assisted the bench through all these years.

Subdued, the supporters of Bemba, the convicted and sentenced war criminal, leave the courtroom. They had their biggest shock when the judges found him guilty. Former bodyguard Liboto-Ngoy is performing his duties and stands next to Bemba's wife. She embraces the older visually-impaired lady who has been a faithful supporter of her husband visiting many of the hearings in this trial. The bodyguard is too busy to give his opinion about the sentence. But another MLC member is willing to comment: 'I am unhappy with Steiner because she only listened to the arguments of the prosecution.' In the main hall defence lawyer Gibson is being interviewed by the press agency AFP. She just spoke to her client. 'He is extremely disappointed,' says Gibson.

But Mrs Fernhout-Kottaud is satisfied. 'It is a reasonable sentence. Personally I thought of a twenty years' prison term. But this is a good sentence. This is a big lesson for chief commanders who are sending their troops abroad. I hope the sentence will work as a deterrent so this will never happen again.' But what struck her again today was her impression of Bemba. 'I see no emotions. As if he couldn't care less about the victims. He seems like a cold person. I do try to imagine myself in the positions of all persons involved, and even that of Bemba. But I have to admit that my soul is with the victims who are so terribly harmed. Therefore, I am glad with this sentence. The judges have done well – from the beginning to the end.'

A new phase

The trial has lasted almost six years. Now a new phase has started. There is the matter of settling reparations for the thousands of registered victims, a lengthy process which can take years. In the meantime, the defence has filed an appeal against Bemba's conviction. The lawyers claim that judge Steiner and her colleagues erred 'in a number of ways' by adopting 'wholly inapposite procedures, misinterpreted and/or misapplied the law and took an unjustifiable approach to the evidence.' If the chamber had 'behaved in a proper judicial manner, the appellant submits it would inevitably have found him not guilty of those charges.'[149]

The lawyers claim there is 'a mistrial.' During the main case the defence hasn't referred much to the second case against Bemba, for his involvement in bribing his witnesses. But in their appeal the counsels underline that Steiner and her colleagues were confidentially informed back in March 2013 that the prosecution was investigating the defence. This meant that the judges were 'in possession of information that a defence intermediary was acting in a fraudulent manner, and that certain defence witnesses were imposters.' The chamber however never disclosed this important information to Bemba's lawyers.

Nothing was done 'to safeguard the rights and confidentiality of the defence.' In fact, the prosecution cross-examined defence witnesses in the main case 'with the benefit of undisclosed information that was obtained in violation of defence privileges and immunities' and other rules. 'This undermined the fair and adversarial conduct of the proceedings,' the lawyers write.

Bemba and the ICC are far from done. Whether the secret investigations influenced the outcome of the main case, is to be seen. In the meantime, significant progress has been made in the bribery trial, which began on 25 September 2015 and moved on with considerable speed. Within half a year the evidence against the five suspects is presented and contested in court, though largely behind closed doors. On 31 May 2016 both sides are ready to present their closing statements.

Closing statements

In the soft morning sunlight three men are walking towards the ICC building. The lawyers Kilolo and Mangenda are joined by the Congolese politician Babala. Together they proceed to the entrance. But the suspects in the bribery case don't form one tight group. Number four, Narcisse Arido, comes by himself. Bemba obviously doesn't walk free. He is

---

149   Filing in compliance with decision ICC-01/05-01/08-3370, Defence, 20 June 2016.

brought in from the detention unit, one kilometre down the road. In a few minutes' time all five defendants will be sitting in the dock. Inside the courtroom Kweku Vanderpuye, a man with a small grey goatee, is turning his chair to the left and then to the right, as he prepares himself for his presentation. After the prosecution has had its say, no less than eight lawyers and even two suspects will take the floor during these two-day hearings. When the judges indicate that Vanderpuye can start his statements, he gets up, arranges his documents and pushes on the button of the microphone in front of him in order to present the prosecution's evidence. 'Four years ago, the Office of the Prosecutor received an anonymous tip that the integrity of the Bemba trial was being compromised, that witnesses were being paid for false testimony,' Vanderpuye recalls the very start of all this. Now the five suspects are charged with no less than 180 counts of offences against the administration of justice for corruptly influencing witnesses, presenting false testimony and falsely testifying. 'As you know,' he says, 'this case has been heavily contested. There have been hundreds upon hundreds of filings by the defence and by the prosecution, over 370 written decisions have been issued by this court.'[150]

That's no surprise with such a heavy legal presence: five defence teams consisting of international top lawyers and four suspects being jurists themselves. Vanderpuye insists that 'the accused have had a fair trial.' One more time he summarises the roles in the organisation. Bemba 'directed' the operation. 'He okayed, he approved, he authorised and he instructed the acts of the other participants. Everything revolved around him, everything went through him and everything was for him, the chief beneficiary of that plan.' Defence lawyer Kilolo was 'the prime implementer, the planner, the scriptwriter, the one who auditioned the witnesses for their roles and their participation in the trial. He was the face of the organisation.' Mangenda was Kilolo's 'right hand.' He helped to plan the activities, carry out the scripts and relayed instructions and information back and forth. Babala was 'the treasurer' controlling the finances. As his 'confidant' he waited for Bemba's authorisation and approval. Then he 'dispensed the money needed for the overall strategy to

150 Official transcript, ICC, 31 May 2016.

function.' Arido was 'the man on the ground,' casting and 'lining up' false witnesses to testify in Bemba's favour.

With over one thousand pieces of incriminating evidence, the case 'could not be stronger,' says Vanderpuye. Nothing changes 'the hard facts proved by the evidence before you,' he tells the judges. Nothing changes 'the words of the accused' captured in intercepted conversations.

Indeed, where in other cases the OTP has a lot of trouble getting evidence because of security issues or countries not cooperating, here the alleged offences partly occurred right under its nose. Vanderpuye lists an abundance of materials: records of money transfer agencies, the material seized from the accused, SMSs, emails, documents, material provided through the cooperation of states, the call data records from telephone companies and the testimonies. The prosecution insists it bases itself on 'proof, not speculation. Reality, not fantasy. Common sense.' All this points in one direction, says Vanderpuye: the guilt of the defendants. During this trial the prosecution called 16 witnesses. Half of them are 'complicit' witnesses who allegedly had been bribed in exchange for exculpatory evidence for Bemba in the main case. 'All of them effectively admitted lying in their testimony,' says Vanderpuye. Although 'some were more evasive than others in regard to admitting those lies, their evidence before the court proving the accused's responsibility was crystal clear.' Nevertheless, he warns the judges they should look 'with caution' to the statements of compromised witnesses because 'they may try to minimise' their own conduct. But the prosecution is confident that the judges will be able to see at which points they 'were telling the truth.'

He gives an overview of the witnesses. Take D-15, who 'denied certain lies,' but also clearly told of 'the accused's corrupt acts to influence' him. D23 admitted he was a fake witness because he was never a soldier in the Central African army nor had he 'personally witnessed the events in the Central African Republic about which he testified in the main case.' He was given money and a laptop just before he was about to testify, but Kilolo allegedly told him he should never disclose having received those gifts to the court. This warning was suspicious, because 'if the payments were made and the laptop was a normal cultural gesture, there would have been no need to hide the fact of it,' says Vanderpuye. D23 was contacted 'at least' six times by Kilolo during the course of his testimony, which is against the rules. As a defence witness, he repeated what Kilolo told him to say about for instance the structure of the command of the CAR army.

Witnesses D2 and D3 feature quite a bit in Vanderpuye's account as well. They too admitted that they were 'never soldiers, that they were never trained as such' and recounted how they were approached by Arido, who made a deal with them. In return for their false testimony they were promised the possibility of 'relocating to Europe' and some 10 million CFA (15,000 euros). However, Arido would only be able to coach them well if he knew the 'theory' of the defence. The 'only way' to know, was 'through Bemba's lawyer,' says Vanderpuye.

In Yaoundé, the capital city of Cameroon where Arido resided, there was a meeting in May 2013 where Kilolo and Mangenda gave phones to several witnesses 'so they could remain in contact with them when testifying,' as the court's Victims and Witnesses Unit (VWU) takes away their regular phones once they are in the care of the unit, just before testifying. After that meeting, the witnesses were paid some 550,000 CFA each (about 850 euros). In the main case, however, D2 had lied saying he received nothing from the defence, no compensation for expenses or for his testimony.

While the prosecution had been investigating the bribery case in secret for more than a year, at one point Bemba's lead counsel and case manager had become aware that something was going on. On 11 October 2013 Mangenda tells Kilolo that he received information from a court staffer who disclosed to him that they were being investigated. (Two officials working on court management, had been dismissed by the ICC over this matter, a source had told.) Bemba panicked when a few days later he was informed by Kilolo. The two lawyers 'seized the opportunity to exploit' Bemba's fear 'to get a little money out of him,' says Vanderpuye. 'They agreed to tell Bemba that the leak to the prosecution emanated from defence witnesses in Cameroon and that they would need to be paid off, aiming to pocket the money.'

The prosecutor points out that Bemba had a lot to lose in his main trial. 'His stature, his standing, his political power, the possibility of a successful presidential election, his freedom. He had every reason, every motive to do exactly what the evidence shows that he did, attempt to guarantee the favourable outcome of his trial by any means necessary, including the offences charged in this case.'

Towards the end of his exposé, Vanderpuye responds to a question which was posed by the French ICC judge, Marc Perrin de Brichambaut, who wants to know where in the closing brief does the prosecution explain 'the common plan' between Bemba, Kilolo and Mangenda? 'We don't have a specific document that anybody subscribed to, saying that there was a plan. We don't have a specific meeting that occurred where anybody said: this is the plan,' Vanderpuye admits. It is a matter of 'circumstantial inference', he says. If a series of witnesses who don't know each other, all lie about the same thing, this means there must be a common plan set up by the main suspects.

Whether that explanation satisfies the judges, is to be seen.

Problematic recordings

The prosecution is sticking to its theory. But since the trial largely took place behind closed doors, it will even be more interesting to hear how the defence teams counter the allegations. The first to speak is Melinda Taylor, who is representing Bemba. The main courtroom of the new permanent premises is huge, but the lawyer is positioned right under the overarching part of the public gallery. Therefore, most visitors can't see her directly. They have to rely on the screens on which the court is directly broadcasting the proceedings. Taylor starts by saying she always feels 'proud,' 'privileged' and 'honoured' to defend clients and uphold their rights before a court. But this is 'particularly the case' with a person like Bemba 'who greatly cares for his family and for the future of the Democratic Republic of Congo,' she asserts. The defence lawyer adds: 'It is also a reflection of his liberal, modern and somewhat overly trusting personality that he selected me to be his only counsel in this case.'

Taylor speaks loud and clear. A detained suspect like Bemba, she says, has limited control over what his lawyers do. Indeed, he would decide on the 'objectives' of his defence, but his lawyers determine how to 'carry them out.'

Then she attacks a fundamental part of the prosecution's evidence. Taylor explains that her client's phone calls were recorded over two channels: one for Bemba and one for the person he was talking with. However, when combined, not all recordings were put together in the right way. It happened that the voices were 'misaligned.' This means that the mix doesn't reflect the real time sequence of the conversation. It is not what the speakers in reality said. 'Effectively if you say hello, I say goodbye. Person A is talking about the weather. Person B is responding about a funeral,' Taylor explains.

During the trial the defence had called expert witness Phillip Harrison, a forensic consultant specialised in analysing evidential recordings. He calculated 'the average misalignment' of the recordings that he analysed, as 27 percent. 'That means the odds of a particular section being reliable is even less than the odds associated with rolling a dice,' Taylor insists. But in a case where recordings are used to show illicit conduct, the 'proper sequence of speakers is of paramount importance.' As a result, 'the transcripts produced by the prosecution cannot be considered to be a reliable reflection of the actual conversation,' Taylor explains.

When she tries to play recorded conversations to show what she means, something goes wrong. Suddenly the recorded voice of Bemba is blasting loud through the headphones. Everybody is reaching for their ears, while a smiling presiding judge Bertram Schmitt sees the fun of it. He is a man who guides his cases with a combination of flexibility and firmness, appreciating such small distractions. After several attempts, Taylor finally manages to play a conversation dated 13 August 2013 between Bemba and Babala, where the prosecution alleges that Bemba is annoyed because 500 euros hadn't been paid to five witnesses. But the interesting thing is that while Babala is hanging up, Bemba continues speaking. 'That means the two channels are misaligned by 40 seconds at the end of the conversation,' says Taylor.

Furthermore, Bemba might have talked with Babala about payments of money, but as such 'there is nothing illegal or improper as concerns compensating witnesses,' the lawyer insists. Paying witnesses? The ICC's prosecution and VWU 'do it all the time.' Anyhow, the intercepts 'did not establish that he knew and intended for his defence to rely on false testimony,' nor that witnesses were 'to be paid' for this purpose.

The problem with the prosecution, says Taylor, is that the office has been looking with 'guilt tinted glasses' to the case. 'By constantly repeating the refrain the defendants were coaching or corrupting witnesses, the prosecution has sought to transform conversations on banal or legitimate topics into evidence of conspiracy. They have done it by inserting interpretations of codes into the text, bolding words, using subjective translations and randomly linking unrelated phrases.'

Taylor wonders: where is the proof that Bemba instructed Aimé Kilolo, Jean-Jacques Mangenda, Fidèle Babala or Narcisse Arido to bribe witnesses in exchange for false testimony? 'Well, wherever this mythical evidence is, it's certainly not in the prosecution's closing brief. Instead, the prosecution has asked the chamber to infer, to speculate.' She explains that the OTP had 'extensive, unparalleled access to defence records, documents, accounts, communications' but could not find evidence against her client. 'If the truth was out there, the prosecution had no excuse for not finding it.'

She stresses that as a detained person, Bemba was unaware of many things that happened. 'When you are in jail, your life is defined by the four walls surrounding you. It doesn't matter how big those four walls are or how modern. A cage is a cage, even if it's gilded. And a person in a cage is not free as long as the door is shut.' Taylor says there are 'multiple conversations' where Bemba is frustrated because he couldn't contact people, was being told 'incorrect information' and didn't know what his lawyers were working on. People were able to lie to Bemba and hide information from him because he had 'no way to check, he had no way to verify what was said to him.' She adds: 'He didn't meet witnesses. He didn't pay witnesses. He didn't coach witnesses.'

The judges, prosecutors and lawyers of the other defence teams are looking at Taylor, while she is pleading to prove her client's innocence. Bemba was 'a passive victim, not a perpetrator,' she says. Not her client, but Kilolo and Mangenda 'concocted this plan.' Not for the benefit of Bemba, 'but for themselves,' alleges Taylor, who for the first time seems to point an accusing finger at the other main suspects.

She underlines that Bemba's defence team 'was not a criminal organisation.' The group included people like Peter Haynes, Nicholas Kaufman, Kate Gibson plus a variety of legal interns and assistants who haven't been charged. Taylor points out that they had a difficult task because it was not easy to defend a former vice president of the DRC. 'Witnesses had every reason to be scared to testify for the defence' because they were 'interrogated' by the Congolese authorities before their testimony. 'Defence team members, including Kate Gibson, were detained by national authorities, subjected to illegal searches.'

There were many other problems. The reviewing of the applications of the more than five thousand persons who applied to be registered as official victims was a 'constant source of work and distraction.' Bemba's funds were frozen. There was no investigations budget. If, during the defence of Bemba 'someone clearly crossed the line, then of course the chamber should enter a conviction. But there cannot be one line for the prosecution and one line for the defence. The line also cannot be set so low that the defence counsel or assistants trip over it,' she says. 'Please do not criminalise the work the defence has to do, in order to defend their clients vigorously, independently and effectively.'

Taylor is finishing her presentation. Her client 'was a defendant in the main case, but he should never have become a defendant in this case.' She then addresses the judges one more time, calling on them to acquit Bemba.

'All of that noise for this?'

After the lunch break it is the turn of the Kilolo defence. First the lawyers will make their submissions, but the highlight will be towards the end of the day, when the accused counsel himself will address the court. 'This case is an illustration of the excessive zeal exercised by the all-powerful prosecutor against the defence,' says maître Paul Djunga Mudimbi, a member of the Paris bar.

After his opening remarks the counsel says that the evidence adds up to nothing. 'All of that noise for this?' The lawyer then refers to an element the prosecution has omitted from its oral statements today: the amounts of money that were paid to the witnesses. When it comes to Kilolo, he personally gave cash or transferred funds totalling 3,649 euros, which was divided over ten witnesses. For instance D2 received 1,069 euros, while D3 got 1,130 euros and D64 had 75 euros. Djunga also gives an overview of what five other persons – including Arido, Babala and one of Bemba's sisters – have been paying. In the prosecution's 'document containing the charges' together these persons transferred a total amount of 2,506 euros. Interestingly, D15, whose recorded voice when speaking to Kilolo featured so much in the prosecution's statements at the opening of the trial, can be excluded from this discussion since there is no evidence that any money has been sent to him. The same goes for two other witnesses who received nothing. In summary, the alleged corruption in this trial is related to a total of 6,155 euros divided between ten witnesses. This is very much below the amount of 100,000 US dollar the prosecutor 'so pompously' talked about at the start the trial, underlines Djunga.

He also points out that 'none' of the complicit witnesses called during the bribery trial said that Kilolo 'had given them money and told them that it was a kind of corruption or retribution for the false testimony they were expected to give.' Moreover, Simo Väätäinen, an expert on witness protection, told the court there is 'no prohibition' for defence teams 'to cover witness costs during investigations' for accommodation, transport, meals, medical attention or travel for young children in order to bring families together.

Djunga makes an interesting comparison. The prosecution says that D2 received some 550,000 CFA (850 euros) from Kilolo. 'That very witness received, when testifying as a prosecution witness, P-260, the amount of 573,000 francs CFA, that is about 874 euros, and additionally 7,176.84 euros. He also received 1,248,000 francs CFA per month for hotel and food allowances.' Or take witness D3, who allegedly received 600,000 CFA (900 euros) from Kilolo. 'That very witness received, when appearing as a prosecution witness P-0245 in this case, the amount of 1,844,400 francs CFA. The witness requested money to furnish his house and the reason being that his furniture was old and rudimentary. To that effect he was given the amount of 286,000 francs CFA to buy new furniture.'

Briefly Djunga wants to tell something about his client. Many esteemed colleagues, such as chairmen of the Brussels bar, have confirmed 'the honourableness, the probity and the dedication' of Aimé Kilolo 'to the service of justice.'

According to the lawyers three witnesses claimed that Kilolo 'allegedly gave instructions on the content of their testimony.' But the defence wonders how trustworthy they are. Besides, expert Väätäinen, who was called in to testify, had explained it is a general practice for all parties to meet 'potential witnesses' before they appear in court to review their testimony with them. There is no rule 'which prohibits a calling party from putting his theory in the case, or even some evidence to the witness in order to elicit their comments.' He also explained that it is not prohibited for the calling party to give the witness a phone.

Then Djunga gives the floor to his colleague Stephen Powles, who right away argues that 'so much of what the prosecution say is based on speculation and not proof. Fantasy, and not reality.' He stresses 'it is pure speculation and perhaps even double standards for the prosecution to assert that assistance given to witnesses by the defence is somehow criminal, while monies given to them by the prosecution is legitimate.' Powles underlines that the interpretation of the use of 'code words' is also speculative. 'The language could mean anything and the prosecution simply chose to interpret it in line with their theory of guilt of the accused.'

After all these hundreds of filings, written submissions, witnesses, documents and transcripts, says Powles, 'we will wait patiently for just two words from your Honours: not guilty.'

'I am an innocent man'

Presiding judge Schmitt looks at Kilolo. 'I give you the floor now.'
The lawyer gets up from his chair and clears his throat. He is standing upright and looking his confident self. Not dressed in his lawyerly black robes anymore, but wearing a grey suit, a light blue shirt and deep red tie. He will explain to the judges how his defence team in the main Bemba-case worked. It was made up of four counsels, two assistants and a case manager. 'A grand total of seven people,' Kilolo says. They worked closely together in all aspects. While a hundred potential witnesses were identified, a theory in the main case was drawn up with the help of two experts, based on a 'careful analysis of the evidence.' The lawyers spoke to former fighters, people who saw the atrocities that affected entire villages in the CAR. These testimonies were 'quite emotional' at times. Some witnesses 'even broke down and cried.' But Kilolo insists that 'no objective consideration allowed us to presume at the time that those witnesses might have been lying.'

The defence was supported by a certain Kokate, a former captain within the CAR armed forces. He became the official intermediary for the defence and identified a number of soldiers and civilians as witnesses. 'I had nothing, nothing, no item of information that would lead me to believe that Mr Kokate would have brought false witnesses,' says Kilolo. Haynes and Gibson went on a number of field missions to meet and question potential witnesses. 'I really must stress this particular point: all the members of the team, all the counsels, all the legal assistants in the main case were convinced that these witnesses were clearly credible, clearly relevant and this conviction was based on the initial questioning of witnesses.' When the team selected the witnesses who would come to testify, they were explicitly asked whether they had been 'threatened, intimidated, promised inducements, anything like that in exchange for the statement given,' says Kilolo. They all said they had 'freely responded to the questions and not been subjected to any pressure or intimidation whatsoever.'

The defence began its investigations in 2011 and continued until November 2013. There were fact-finding missions to Cameroon, the

CAR, Congo-Brazzaville, France, Belgium, Sweden and the Ukraine. This required a lot of money for expenses such as travel, communications, housing and meals for the defence team, consultants, experts and dozens of potential witnesses. The total of costs for this was approximately 100,000 US dollars.

However, the ICC had determined that multimillionaire Bemba was not indigent. So he could not request free legal assistance from the court as did the suspects in other trials. Although the defence asked the court 100,000 US dollars for its investigations, according to Kilolo, 'we were never provided with such funding.' Thus, Bemba 'himself was to manage in some way or another to compensate his defence team and provide them with the resources necessary before any fact-finding mission,' explains his former lead counsel.

Kilolo stresses that 'all' within the defence team knew and agreed to this 'alternative source of funding' for the investigations 'because there was nothing illicit about any of this.' He adds: 'All of this explains the various flows of monies that have been mentioned by the prosecution.'

Coming to the end of his unsworn statement, Kilolo says: 'Your Honours, this trial has led me to question many things at a very deep level.' As it is necessary to reflect on one's actions and rules of conduct one must live by. 'A person must consider imperfections, and say: did I do something, did I fail to do something within the professional sphere and outside of that sphere?' Without answering that question Kilolo rounds up: 'I have learnt a great deal from this trial and today I turn to you, I am an innocent man. And if I look beyond the suffering I have already endured, I must say thank you.'

Presiding judge Schmitt responds: 'Thank you very much.'

The hearing for the day is done. The protagonist and main antagonists have addressed the court. The next day the teams for the other three suspects will address the judges.

Dodgy witnesses

'Your Honours, notwithstanding the prosecution's self-confidence, it's a good thing there was a trial,' kicks off Christopher Gosnell, lead counsel for Mangenda.[151] Because during the trial new things surfaced, which

---

151 Official transcript, ICC, 1 June 2016.

will work positively for his client. Witnesses D2 and D3, for example, confirmed that Mangenda did not participate in any discussions with them during the meeting in Yaoundé about their testimony, nor was he present during 'any undocumented payments to witnesses on that occasion.' He wasn't there when 'any improper, let alone criminal, purpose' was explained to the witnesses about why they were getting telephones from the defence. Despite all these facts, the prosecution sticks to its allegations against his client. Gosnell: 'More spaghetti into the pot. Throw it against the wall and hopes that something sticks.'

It is Gosnell who gives an explanation of what might have happened with the famous tip-off in 2012 which led to this trial. Every counsel who has worked on an international case, and especially the defence, has experienced meetings with witnesses 'that have left the lawyer extremely uncomfortable.' It happens. It is part of the job. But lawyers sometimes need to work with these persons. 'You can't just reject a witness that you sense is dodgy because, for example, you're worried that they might later make false allegations against you, false allegations in order to get benefit for themselves,' says Gosnell, hinting that an angry or calculating witness might have sent that first email to the prosecution, which eventually led to the bribery trial.

Towards the end, the counsel thanks his client Mangenda. 'He has suffered a great deal from these charges, including having been in prison at the time of the birth of his third child.' The evidence shows that Mangenda is 'not guilty of all charges against him.' Whether the former case manager will 'receive some vindication,' that is a matter which is now 'exclusively in your capable hands,' he says, addressing the judges. 'I thank you for your time.'

'What am I doing here?'

Maître Kilenda Kakengi Basila is ready for the final statements in the defence of his client, the Congolese MLC politician Fidèle Babala Wandu. 'A lie always takes the lift and gets there first, whereas, even when it takes the stairs, truth will always get there,' says the lawyer quoting the Congolese musician, Antoine Agbepa, from his album called 'Loi.' In other words: 'Truth will always triumph ultimately.'

The lawyer doesn't wait until the end of his presentation, but immediately asks the judges to acquit Babala. He points out that his client 'was very much outside any alleged plan to sabotage the judicial process in the main case. He is not complicit of any charge against him. His involvement in this case is the consequence of massive untruths,' Kilenda says.

The prosecutor investigated this case inadequately, which led to a misunderstanding of the exact relations between the five accused. Indeed, Bemba and Babala know each other very well. They 'have had friendly relations' since they studied at university in Belgium. Both were members of the MLC when it had become a political party. When Bemba was prosecuted by the ICC for the crimes his soldiers had committed in the CAR, Babala 'remained in solidarity with him, respecting the law and public order,' says Kilenda.

The lawyer picks up the point that was made yesterday by the accused Kilolo. Slowly a theory of the combined defence teams seems to emerge, that the issue in this case emanates from the fact that Bemba's defence team 'never had free legal aid provided by the court' in the main case. As his funds were frozen, money for financing investigations became a problem, explains Kilenda. The ICC's registry decided to pay for the defence team itself in the form of a 'sort of loan' that Bemba would reimburse later. 'This financing which just covered the fees of members of the team, was insufficient to cover the needs for investigations in the field, hindered by his deprivation of liberty,' stresses Kilenda. So Bemba 'called upon those close to him, to help him meet his needs,' the lawyer continues his explanation.

What happened next, is explained when Babala himself addresses the court telling his side of the story. At the time the Congolese politician responded to 'a call of distress' by Bemba. 'Along with his family, friends and co-workers, a chain of solidarity was set up with an aim to finding resources' so Bemba could pay his investigations and 'live decently' in the detention centre. 'That was the sole objective that I had in mind at the time,' says Babala. 'Coming to the aid of somebody one respects is a humanistic value, not a form of dishonesty.'

These efforts explain the regular contact between himself and Bemba's defence team. There was 'never any question' among these persons 'of corrupting witnesses or sabotaging the judicial process.' In fact, Babala would not have recognized his friend if Bemba, for whom he expresses 'great respect,' would have proposed such a thing. As vice president of the DRC, being in charge of economic and financial affairs, Bemba was involved in the fight against 'corruption, misappropriation of public funds and other such practises,' insists Babala. His friend 'did not hesitate to punish even his closest co-workers who were involved in such practises.' Babala gives an insight in what, in his view, further happened. Once Bemba was detained at the ICC, the two Congolese politicians kept in contact. Their telephone conversations were 'essentially political and private in nature.' The 'only times' they spoke about the ICC case 'was quite simply to ask how the last hearing went.'

But before Babala can continue, there is the voice of the court's interpreter: 'Could he please be requested to slow down.' Judge Schmitt addresses Babala: 'I understand, of course, that this is a very special situation for you. But if you also could please try to slow down a little bit. Thank you very much.'

Babala explains that they were simply used to speak in coded language during their phone conversations. 'This type of language could protect me because I was living in a dangerous country, and 99 of our telephone calls were political in nature.'

The Congolese politician underlines he is not a member of Bemba's defence team. 'I am not the manager of his possessions, and I was never aware of any alleged plan to corruptly influence witnesses and sabotage the judicial process or any intention of taking part in it. The prosecution has not brought and will never bring any probative evidence to contradict my statements. Quite simply because these elements do not exist.'

In fact, the accusations make no sense. 'If the funds sent to the defence team were unlawful, would it not have been more intelligent to hand them over mano a mano rather than send them via Western Union?' Babala wonders. 'I am not an imbecile.'

Then the politician grabs the opportunity to explain what happened during his arrest. Cynically he refers to judge Tarfusser, who handled the pre-trial phase of this case. 'I was very impressed by his capacity to read 1,550 pages of the prosecution's request for a warrant of arrest between 11.35 hours on 19 November 2013 and 11.48 hours the next day, which is an average of 193 pages per hour for a normal working day comprising eight legal hours of work.'

After the judge saw there was enough ground to have Babala – and the four others – apprehended, the arrest warrant was sent to the DRC. Then in the middle of the night, from 23 to 24 November 2013, the politician was woken around 2.40 a.m. by the barking of his dogs. 'I glanced out of my window,' he tells. From there he saw in his garden approximately thirty individuals 'wearing balaclavas and armed with Kalashnikovs, tear gas and grenade launchers.' Quickly Babala brought his wife and children into safety in their rooms. 'Out of modesty, I shall not mention the trauma they experienced.' Then he tried to call the president of the national assembly and the town governor. 'To no avail.'

When he opened the door, at least six persons pointed a gun at him. 'The thought that went through my mind at that moment was that I was close to death.' About a hundred policemen were guarding the area. He was placed in a jeep and driven to the intelligence services offices. Over the police radio Babala heard that a colleague had been assassinated. 'You can imagine my terror at that moment because I did not know that a warrant of arrest had been issued against me and the prisons of the intelligence services are close to the Congo river, a favourite spot for extrajudicial executions.'

The following afternoon he was brought to the Congolese prosecutor general, who informed him about the arrest warrant. 'I was then taken to the air force base at Kinshasa airport where I was presented to the officers of the ICC, who then handcuffed me, gave me a bulletproof vest and loaded me onto a Falcon jet bound for The Hague.' Babala stresses that the ICC chartered 'an entire plane for me alone', even though he doesn't face charges of genocide, war crimes or crimes against humanity. 'I do not believe that this is the best way to use taxpayers' money.' He recalls that he 'had not either slept or eaten nor had I been able to drink any water for two days. And also you should know throughout the flight I was handcuffed the entire time.'

The whole arrest was filmed and broadcast continuously in the DRC 'with nothing but contempt for my human dignity.' He felt like being condemned by the media. The broadcasting went on for a week until the pre-trial chamber of the ICC ordered it to be stopped 'because of the presumption of innocence.' In the meantime, the Congolese minister of information and the national prosecutor had claimed in press briefings 'that I was guilty of the charges.' So why, Babala asks, 'did the ICC never note that any of my rights had been violated whilst my counsel and I have constantly talked of this?'

When the issue of interim release came up, the Congolese authorities impeded his return to the DRC 'presenting me as a danger to public peace,' says Babala, 'while I was elected to universal suffrage on two occasions. I never broke the laws of my country.' Judge Tarfusser and the prosecution didn't counter but repeated the Congolese arguments. In fact the ICC 'requested that I chose a host country in case the Congolese authorities continued to oppose my return to the DRC, forgetting that for one, my arrest took place in Kinshasa and, two, I am a Congolese national and not a stateless individual.'

Wondering whether he is 'the victim' of an 'agreement' between the ICC and the DRC, Babala argues: 'Do human rights not exist before the ICC or do they simply not exist when opponents to the current regime face prosecution? Your Honours, would an American, would a Frenchman or would a German have been arrested under similar conditions? Is one still in the 21st century damned because one is born in Africa or more particularly born in the DRC?'

He reminds the judges that as an MP he had voted in favour of ratifying the Rome Statute, leading to the start of the ICC. But in his case the court didn't take its responsibility. 'I think that the acquiescence of the ICC with regard to the violation of my fundamental rights is a tacit form of agreement with countries like mine, who indulge lightly in the corruption of this practise, whereas to my mind the ICC should incite or even have a didactic role towards other, less advanced legal systems.'

He sums up that his arrest was a violation of the Congolese law, the Universal Declaration of Human Rights, the African Charter on Human and People's Rights, the International Covenant on Civil and Political Rights and the Rome Statute. 'Your Honours, in addition to these violations of the conditions of my arrest, transfer and detention, which harmed me deeply and profoundly and affected me in an indelible manner, I returned to the main question: What precisely am I doing here?' With these words Babala finishes his statement: 'I lay my full trust in justice and I thank you.'

Presiding judge Schmitt: 'Thank you very much.'

Another personal drama

The last to speak is the defence team of Arido, who is the only suspect coming from the Central African Republic. The closing statements of his lawyers are not the clearest presentation, but they underline there is no evidence against their client. The accusations make no sense. Arido couldn't influence the four witnesses as he didn't know what the strategy of the Bemba defence was. Their client was asked by Bemba's lawyers to write an expert report. For this work he apparently received 8,451

US dollars. But now the prosecution wrongly accuses him of using this money to corrupt witnesses.

As a suspect in this case, Arido became involved in more personal drama. His counsel Charles Achaleke Taku doesn't elaborate too much on the matter, but in his own country Arido is falsely labelled as a 'génocidaire,' a person who committed genocide. This all started when the prosecution allegedly made a mistake when it was trying to access the financial records of Arido and his family with Western Union in Vienna, Austria. The ICC request to the authorities wrongly stated: 'Against Arido, Subject Matter – Genocide.' That's how the misrepresentation started, the lawyers say, as Arido is not accused of genocide, but offences against the administration of justice.[152] The defence explains that Arido wasn't even in the CAR when the violence erupted in 2002, because he had already fled the country a year before.

The ICC didn't address the matter in time, and now Arido and his family are being threatened. 'The issue before all of us is why the silence from the OTP, particularly why the silence from this institution,' says co-counsel Beth Lyons. She adds: 'He is marked as a génocidaire in his own country, on the continent, throughout the international community. And this is not a mark that can simply be erased. You can't put whiteout on it. You can't blank it out. It can't be stamped out.'

Briefly the lawyers touch upon the fact that Arido was originally on the list of defence witnesses in the main case against Bemba. Despite tickets being bought and arrangements being made, he didn't come to The Hague to testify, but stayed in France. Lyons says this 'had to do with a situation that was apprised by Cameroonian authorities at a particular time in 2012, where he felt threatened based on his role and work in the Bemba case and felt exposed as a witness, received no response from the authorities at the ICC, even to this date on this matter and ended up in France.' Returning to the issue of the bribery trial, the defence asks the judges to acquit their client.

The verdict

The ball now lies in the judges' court. They will decide on the fate of the five suspects. With the help of their staff, they are studying the vast

---

152   Official transcript, ICC, 1 March 2016.

amount of evidence. The transcripts of the closing statements alone consist of some 230 pages. But it takes the judges less than five months to come up with the verdict.

The public gallery is only half full this afternoon, 19 October 2016, while the court is getting ready for its first judgment in an Article 70 case. Bemba's wife hasn't come, as she did with the verdict in the main case against her husband. His former bodyguard, Le Pharaon, has been busy escorting the Congolese supporters through the building. When everybody is seated a court official stands before the visitors and explains, as if the public were children not knowing how to behave, the rules of decorum. The visitors are told it is forbidden to speak loudly at the public gallery or to point at people in the courtroom. They are requested that when they leave, 'please do that in an orderly manner, without making noise.'

The huge grey-greenish curtains that block the view into the courtroom, are automatically opened. The five suspects and their defence teams have taken their seats, with the prosecution sitting opposite them. The judges have arrived, taken their seats and are ready to read the verdict. Often they wait with their pronouncements on guilt or innocence until the end of their presentation, but presiding judge Schmitt says it right at the beginning: 'The chamber is satisfied beyond reasonable doubt that the accused committed offences against the administration of justice in this case. Mr Bemba, Mr Kilolo and Mr Mangenda jointly agreed to illicitly interfere with defence witnesses in order to ensure that they would provide evidence in favour of Mr Bemba.'[153] He confirms that the three suspects designed the common plan and tried to conceal their 'illicit actions' through using the privileged telephone line, payments through third persons, secretly handing over hand phones to defence witnesses and using coded language.

Kilolo sits most in the public's view. Just like Mangenda and Arido, he looks at the judge reading the verdict. Babala seems to be writing, while Bemba is invisible for the public, as his seat is positioned largely under the public gallery. Then judge Schmitt gives an evaluation of their personal involvement. He says that Bemba approved and authorised the

---

153   Official transcript, ICC, 19 October 2016.

plan to coach fourteen witnesses. The former warlord also gave 'precise instructions' and authorised the payments to witnesses.

When Schmitt comes to the role of Kilolo, the lawyer bows his head and looks down. According to the judges the counsel 'scripted, dictated and corrected' the testimonies, and told the witnesses 'to lie' about matters such as payments, promises and prior contacts with the defence. Kilolo was also involved in giving them money (amounts varied between 6 and 800 euros) and goods (such as a laptop). He violated the rules when he contacted witnesses shortly before and during their testimony, when they were handed over to the VWU. What he did was basically trying 'to obscure' the impressions the judges had of the witnesses. 'It may have been Mr Kilolo who spoke through the witnesses in the end,' says Schmitt.

Mangenda was fully implicated as liaison. He conveyed Bemba's instructions and assisted Kilolo in the illicit operations. When they went on field trips, he knew that his colleague coached the witnesses. Mangenda also helped in distributing cell phones to the witnesses. When the judges come to describe Babala's activities as 'financier' of the operations, they conclude that he transferred money to two witnesses. His role is more limited than the prosecution alleged. Arido recruited four witnesses, promised them 10 million CFA and relocation to Europe. He told them they had to give evidence as soldiers, although he knew these persons hadn't been in the army. 'He assigned the witnesses their alleged military ranks and handed out military insignia,' the judges say. Arido also helped them with their story about their 'purported military background, experience and training.' But the judges were unable to establish that Arido was further involved in the illicit coaching.

Then Schmitt asks the suspects, who have transformed into convicts, to get up.

'First please, Mr Bemba, rise,' says the judge.

The Congolese suspect gets up from his chair. The monitors at the public gallery show a defeated man. While he blinks his eyes, with a big frown on his face, he looks at the judges. Then, for the second time this year, he hears the feared words. 'Mr Jean-Pierre Bemba Gombo, the chamber finds you guilty,' says Schmitt, convicting him of corruptly influencing fourteen witnesses, presenting their false evidence, and having solicited the giving of false testimony. 'Mr Bemba, you may be seated.'

Then Kilolo, looking overwhelmed, has to rise. His usual bravado has disappeared, while the judges say they find him guilty. When he is permitted to take his seat again, he sits down and stares in front of him. While the convicts are one by one requested to stand up, prosecutor Bensouda is making notes. Mangenda is also found guilty of having fully participated in the coaching scheme, while Babala is guilty of 'corruptly influencing' two witnesses, but acquitted for bribing others.

'Mr Arido, please rise,' thus Schmitt instructs the last convict in a row, finding him guilty of corruptly influencing four witnesses, but acquitting him of having presented false testimony.

In just thirty minutes the judges are making an end to a long and embarrassing process, that started four years earlier, with an anonymous tip-off. At the end of the guilty verdict, the chamber has several closing remarks to make. This case was not 'about a grey area in law pertaining to defence behaviour,' but about 'clear and downright criminal behaviour of the five accused,' Schmitt says. 'No legal system in the world can accept the bribing of witnesses, the inducement of witnesses to lie, or the illicit coaching of witnesses.' With the verdict the judges want to send 'a clear message that the court is not willing to allow its proceedings to be hampered or destroyed.' Such behaviour will be punished.

A confidential application

Then Schmitt surprisingly turns to the prosecution, which apparently had sent a confidential communication to the judges with a specific request. Not disclosing its content, the judge asks: 'Just a yes or no answer for the moment, please.' A broad smiling Bensouda answers: 'Yes, Mr President.' This is an unexpected and dramatic moment. When the judges withdraw for a few minutes, visitors at the public gallery start speculating about what is going on, while Kilolo is sitting in the dock with his head down. This mysterious exchange though, could mean only one thing.

After fifteen minutes the judges are back in the courtroom. They give lead counsel Vanderpuye a chance to explain what this is all about. The prosecution has requested the judges, that in case of a conviction, 'the accused to be remanded to the custody of the detention centre pending sentencing in this case.'[154] Detention is an appropriate measure, finds

154 Official transcript, 19 October 2016.

Vanderpuye, in the light of the seriousness of the offences and the number of counts on which the suspects have been convicted. The prosecution thinks there are no reasons that justify the four on interim release to remain at liberty.

Obviously the defence teams don't agree. The sharp-edged lawyer Kilenda is given the floor. He points out that the prosecutor had 'a lot of time to prepare its motion' and asks twenty minutes for the defence teams to prepare their responses. 'That is a reasonable proposal and is conceded, so we have a break of 20 minutes,' agrees judge Schmitt. There is the call of the court usher: 'All Rise!'

Exactly twenty minutes later, the defence teams give their opinion. One by one the lawyers oppose the prosecution's plans. They point out that their clients are convicted, but the sentence is going to be determined later. It is by no means clear what the punishment will be. 'Therefore, we consider that the application of the prosecutor has no grounds. It has no factual basis or legal basis,' says Kilenda.

The lawyers underline that their clients already spent eleven months in detention, and while on interim release always obeyed orders from the court. There is no risk they will flee to avoid a possible detention. Referring to the prosecutor, maître Djunga comments: 'He cannot just stand up here, Mr President, and claim that you should detain him or them, simply because there is a flight risk. What is the risk, Mr President? How do you assess that risk?'

While slouching in his chair, Kilolo seems to take in the enormous blow he has just suffered. But slowly he is recovering and starts to sit up straight and to look around him.

A law firm

After the judges have retired once more for deliberations, presiding judge Schmitt says that first of all, the convicts always attended hearings and cooperated with the court. Second, most of them 'currently live with their families and have established a life in their current locations. They are integrated in their places of residency, all of which militates against them suddenly fleeing.' Third, the maximum sentence is a term of imprisonment of five years or a fine or both. Combining all these factors, the judges don't consider it necessary 'to issue an order of detention.' The prosecution's request is denied and the four convicts on interim release, continue to be at liberty. Bemba will remain in the detention centre, as he is serving an eighteen years' prison sentence for international crimes. This heavy session is over. 'Thank you very much to everybody,' says Schmitt. The curtains close. Slowly the visitors leave the public gallery. Soon the four convicts join friends, supporters and lawyers in the court's large main hall. Their lawyers are looking worried. 'It is a very serious judgment,' says maître Djunga. But his client Kilolo has recomposed himself and is beaming with confidence. He starts to say that 'disgraceful' interpretations were made by the prosecutor, but then stops, explaining he can't comment on his case, because one of the preconditions for his interim release is that he doesn't talk to the media about his trial.

The case hasn't prevented him from being an active lawyer. Kilolo has notified the court that in a few days he will go on another business trip to the DRC. 'I have a law firm, with one office in Lubumbashi and the other in Kinshasa,' says the convicted counsel.

The sentence

Calmly Kilolo is walking to the entrance of the court. Nothing is certain at this moment. Will he leave as a free man after the hearing, or will he immediately be arrested? Although he must have prepared himself for the worst scenario, he doesn't carry a bag with items he needs in case he might be imprisoned. The lawyer shakes his head. He doesn't want to comment to journalists. Five months ago Kilolo and the other four suspects in the bribery case were convicted. This morning, 22 March 2017, they will hear their sentence.

In the courtroom the parties are waiting for the judges to start. Prosecutor Fatou Bensouda has a salmon pink folder in front of her, while trial lawyer Vanderpuye brought a binder that carries the logo of the ICC. On the defence's side Kilolo, wearing a bright blue suit, is sitting in full view. He pulls the keyboard of the computer towards him and starts typing. Every now and then he looks at the screen. As if this is a normal day at work. Arido and Mangenda are sitting in between their lawyers. But Babala and Bemba are out of view, being seated below the overarching part of the public gallery.

Then the hearing begins. Presiding judge Schmitt explains that the chamber looked at the possibility of suspended sentences.[155] The Rome

---

155   Official transcript, ICC, 22 March 2017

Statute and the court's legal rules are silent about it. But that doesn't mean this 'intermediate' measure – between a sentence and no sentence - is impossible. These words sound like a prelude. After a deep sigh Kilolo, still looking worried, briefly casts an eye at the public gallery. Then, ignoring the judges, he concentrates on the keyboard and continues typing.

The judges deal with Babala first. They found one aggravating circumstance: his attempt to obstruct the investigations. On the other hand Babala's participation in the scam was limited. He illegally transferred money to only two witnesses. Besides he showed good behaviour throughout the trial and has no prior convictions. 'Mr Babala, please stand up,' says the presiding judge. The chamber sentences him to six months' imprisonment. But with the eleven months he spent in pre-trial detention deducted, 'the chamber considers the sentence of imprisonment as served. Mr Babala, you may be seated.'

Arido has been convicted for his involvement with four witnesses. The judges found no mitigating or aggravating circumstances, but they note his good behaviour and 'his peace, justice and reconciliation advocacy in Central African Republic and his generosity towards compatriots and persons in need.' He is asked to stand up. 'The chamber sentences you to eleven months' imprisonment.' This is exactly the time Arido spent in pre-trial detention, which will be deducted. This means he will walk free. Then the judges come to Mangenda, whose role was much larger. The case-manager has been involved in corruptly influencing fourteen witnesses, presenting false evidence and assisting in giving false testimony. The chamber found two aggravating circumstances: his abuse of trust vis-à-vis the court and his attempt to obstruct the investigations. When Mangenda is asked to stand up, judge Schmitt tells him that he is sentenced to two years in prison. But the chamber also considered his good behaviour, the consequences of incarceration for his family and the prohibition from working in his country of residence. The eleven months he already spent in detention are deducted and the remaining term of imprisonment is suspended, on the condition that he doesn't offend the coming three years.

An additional punishment

'I now turn to Mr Kilolo,' says the presiding judge. The former lead counsel is found guilty of the same offences as Mangenda. But judge

Schmitt explains that the chamber sees a third aggravating circumstance: Kilolo's abuse of the lawyer-client privilege. The chamber also looked at positive factors: his promotion of the legal profession in Belgium and the DRC, his involvement in an NGO, his 'constructive attitude' during trial, absence of a criminal record and disciplinary record with the Brussels bar. 'Mr Kilolo, please stand up.' The chamber sentences him to two years and six months' imprisonment. Also his time served is deducted and the remainder is suspended. But to 'discourage this type of behaviour by counsel,' Kilolo is punished with an additional fine of 30,000 euros, which will be transferred to the Trust Fund for Victims.

When Kilolo takes his seat, once more he deeply sighs and starts to make notes on a piece of paper. Then he puts down his pen and continues typing on the keyboard. For a few moments he exchanges looks with his lawyer Powles, who kindly smiles at him. Then Kilolo concentrates again on his typing before he takes a sip of water, while the judges turn to Bemba.

Bemba has been found guilty of bribing fourteen witnesses, presenting false evidence and soliciting the giving of false testimony. The judges cite the same aggravating circumstances as in Kilolo's case and add that Bemba 'took advantage of his long-standing and current position' as MLC president. But the chamber also notes that his 'actual contributions' when it comes to the 'implementation and concealment of the common plan were of a somewhat restricted nature' and points at his family situation. 'Mr Bemba, please stand up.' He is given a sentence of 12 months imprisonment, on top of the 18 years he is already serving for the international crimes his men committed in the CAR. As the judges want to 'discourage this type of behaviour and to dissuade the repetition of such conduct' Bemba has to pay a fine of 300,000 euros, which will be transferred to the TFV as well.

The department of tourism

Within half an hour the session is over. Clearly things could have been worse for the suspects. Arido, Kilolo and Mangenda are seen shaking hands with their lawyers. When a few minutes later they arrive in the main hall of the court, the news still needs to sink in. A young woman, wearing a cheerful dress with flowers and yellow sleeves, puts her arms around Kilolo's neck. The lawyer and his wife kiss. For a moment Kilolo, holding her waist, rests in her embrace. Then the couple is privately discussing some matters.

He gives in. For a few moments Kilolo is prepared to talk to journalists who are waiting for his first reaction on the punishment. He had been ready for anything to happen, he says. The counsel won't discuss the sentence in detail, but he will be able to continue his life. Although he lives in Belgium, his main job is now in his home country, where he not only owns a law firm. 'Since January I am the director of the department of tourism in the DRC. It is the most important position after that of the minister and the deputy minister. I am guiding a whole ministry,' he says, before excusing himself.

The bodyguard of Bemba, who just heard that one year has been added to his prison term, is disappointed. 'As such I wasn't surprised. I felt it coming,' says Le Pharaon, getting more emotional now that the first words are out. 'But Bemba should have been acquitted. This punishment is way too heavy.'

6

DETENTION
A new family

It was an ordinary Monday morning when officials of the American
embassy in the Rwandan capital Kigali saw an uninvited guest on their
doorstep. He had arrived before dawn and had been waiting nearby
in a car until the diplomatic mission would open that day, 18 March
2013. When he presented himself, the flabbergasted officials understood
they were dealing with the feared warlord Bosco Ntaganda. Nickname:
The Terminator. The rebel leader had a surprising request. Could the
Americans make arrangements to take him to the International Criminal
Court (ICC), that wanted him since 2006? Ntaganda had just lost a
power struggle within the Congolese militia group M23. He was in
danger. There were no powerful friends anymore who wanted to protect
him. He had crossed the border from the Democratic Republic of Congo
(DRC) to Rwanda, to discuss the options with his family. But his choice
had become limited: death or the ICC.

The diplomatic machinery cranked into gear right away. Rwanda, accused
of having supported Ntaganda and his militia groups for years, said it
would not block his surrender. Washington agreed to give a helping hand.
The smoothness of the operation was quite striking, as these two countries
are not members of the court. In The Netherlands a plane was arranged
to pick up Ntaganda within just five days. Overnight, between 22 and 23
March, he arrived at the international prison in Scheveningen, which is
part of The Hague, where a special block is designated for ICC detainees.
It is always a 'totally shocking' experience to be put on a plane in an
African country and to land a few thousand kilometres north, in The
Netherlands, explained Marc Dubuisson, director of the ICC's division
of court services. He is the person usually awaiting new arrivals at the
prison gate. 'To be in a totally different environment. Where people don't
speak the same language as you do. And where you realize, when you are

allowed to take some fresh air, that there is no sun in this country during six months of the year.'

Two suits

Immediately after their arrival new detainees, like Ntaganda, are checked medically and psychologically. At first they are kept isolated from the other inmates and put in a special cell where they can't harm themselves. Dennis Abels, a lecturer at the University of Amsterdam (UvA) who wrote his dissertation on detention at international courts and tribunals, however criticizes this policy. 'Such a decision needs to be based on the assessment by a doctor, because there are also prisoners who become more at ease if they have contact with other detainees.'

While being transferred to the ICC it happens that suspects travel without a suitcase and are dressed in light and airy clothes suitable for the climates of many African countries. That was the case with the former president of Ivory Coast, Laurent Gbagbo, who was taken to The Hague just wearing trousers and a shirt. As a service, a new detainee who doesn't have proper clothes, is given two suits by the ICC, so that the suspect will appear decently in court. 'It is about their dignity,' Dubuisson said. Suspects are presumed innocent until proven guilty. 'We shouldn't forget that these people could be acquitted and, so to speak, released tomorrow.' Within a few days after their arrival, suspects have to appear before a judge. Some are so confused about the extreme transition from African detention or battlefields to a safe but completely strange environment, that their feeling of alienation is visible when they appear in court. When Ntaganda made his initial appearance, 26 March 2013, he seemed utterly helpless. He sat huddled like a frightened and nervous bird between two ICC guards. His army fatigues were exchanged for an ill-fitting suit that increased the distressed impression he made.

Where had it all gone wrong? Ntaganda (born in 1973) was just a teenager when Tutsis in Rwanda were attacked. He fled to the DRC.[156] At the age of seventeen he joined the Rwandan Tutsi rebel army RPF, that would be operating from Uganda for many years. When extremist Hutus started the genocide against Tutsis and moderate Hutus in 1994, Ntaganda belonged to the RPF troops that entered Rwanda and ended

---

156 ICC: Trial of Bosco Ntaganda for alleged crimes in the Democratic Republic of Congo, HRW, 27 August 2015.

the extermination. He continued the battle hunting down génocidaires who had participated in the massacres, and other supporters of the former Kigali regime who had escaped with many thousands of Hutus to neighbouring DRC. Possibly he got there involved in mass killings, that might be seen genocidal in nature as well, according to the United Nations.[157]

From then on Ntaganda would be joining rebel movements in eastern DRC. When rebels were being integrated into the Congolese army, he would make it to the position of general.

Somewhere during those long years of conflict and fighting he must have derailed. The warlord is prosecuted by the court as commander of the military wing of the rebel movement Union des Patriotes Congolais (UPC) which fought an ethnic war against other groups in Ituri, in the eastern part of the DRC. Ntaganda is charged with five counts of crimes against humanity and thirteen counts of war crimes. He is accused of a long list of atrocities: murder, attacking civilians, rape, sexual slavery, persecution, forcible transfer of civilians, attacking protected objects, pillaging, destroying the enemy's property, enlistment and conscription of child soldiers under the age of fifteen years and using them to participate actively in hostilities.

A small African community

Ntaganda stays in the ICC detention unit among a small African community of suspects that regularly changes composition. There can be quite a bit of coming and going. Some detainees know each other from the battlefields. Ntaganda's alleged partner in crime was UPC president Thomas Lubanga Dyilo, who has been convicted and sentenced by the court in 2012 to fourteen years imprisonment. After having spent almost a decade in ICC detention, Lubanga was transferred to a Congolese prison on 19 December 2015 (see chapter 4). With the same plane Germain Katanga, who had been an enemy of Lubanga and Ntaganda during the war in Ituri, was also moved back to the DRC to serve his ICC sentence – and to face a new, Congolese trial.

When Ntaganda arrived in the Scheveningen prison there were three other militia leaders from Ituri as well. These Congolese however formed

---

157 DR Congo: Q & A on the United Nations Human Rights Mapping Report, HRW, 1 October 2010.

an unusual group. They weren't ICC suspects, but had been detained in the DRC. The Congolese government had agreed to send these prisoners to The Hague to testify as defence witnesses. After their testimony the three requested asylum in The Netherlands and stayed for more than three years in ICC detention (see chapter 11).

Another long-time detainee is Jean-Pierre Bemba Gombo. In the ICC detention centre the former Congolese vice president and warlord benefited for one year from the company of two of his lawyers, a befriended politician and an acquaintance, all convicted of bribing and coaching defence witnesses in Bemba's main case. The last four are on interim release since October 2014 (see chapter 5).

Ivory Coast surrendered in November 2011 its former head of state Gbagbo to the ICC, followed by his compatriot and cheerleader, Charles Blé Goudé in March 2014 (see chapter 7). In January 2015 Dominic Ongwen, a commander with the Ugandan Lord's Resistance Army, surrendered himself to US forces and was transferred to the court. A few months later, in September 2015, Niger extradited the Malian jihadi Ahmad Al Faqi Al Mahdi, who has been convicted by the ICC.

Two suspects have left the detention centre because the prosecution failed in their cases. Callixte Mbarushimana, the secretary of the Forces Démocratiques pour la Libération du Rwanda (FDLR), set up by Rwandans who partly had joined the genocide and then continued fighting in the DRC, was released from custody in 2011. After his trial Mathieu Ngudjolo Chui, a Congolese rebel leader from Ituri, was acquitted in 2012 (see chapter 11). Apart from these ICC detainees, there was a unique guest: Charles Taylor, the former president of Liberia, who was prosecuted by the Special Court for Sierra Leone. When for security reasons his trial was transferred to a special branch of the SCSL located in The Netherlands, he was detained in the ICC unit. In the meantime Taylor has been convicted to a fifty-year prison term, which he is serving in the United Kingdom.

So currently the ICC unit in Scheveningen holds six Africans: Ntaganda, Bemba, Gbagbo, Blé Goudé, Ongwen and Al Mahdi.

Painting and music

The regime in the court's detention facility is quite flexible. Only in the evenings are the suspects locked up in their cells. During the day they can move around inside the unit. 'We do all we can to make sure they have a life as close to normal as possible,' Dubuisson explained. The detainees can do sports and fitness, practice religion and make some money by working. They are also offered language courses and creative lessons such as in music. Bemba likes to paint, plays his electronic piano and is mindful of his health, so he exercises. Blé Goudé reportedly plays football with ICC detainees and the neighbouring inmates of the International Criminal Tribunal for the former Yugoslavia (ICTY). At least two, Gbagbo and Blé Goudé, have written their memoirs in their cells.

The French speaking detainees all learn English, Dubuisson told. This also enables them to communicate easier with the Dutch guards of the detention centre who are more likely to be speaking English. Because of the background of the detainees, the ICC asks the Dutch ministry of Security and Justice, that is employing the guards, for security officers who not only speak foreign languages such as French and English, but have an affinity with other cultures as well.

The detention centre is rented from the Dutch State. The court has a 'product & price agreement' with The Netherlands. The ICC can choose between three options: a unit of six, twelve or twenty cells against respectively a high, medium and low tariff. The prices are annually indexed. For a full year in 2014, the court paid 1.63 million euros for the twelve cell option. But the following year the number of custodial staff increased, which led to a higher price. In 2016 the court paid a total of 1.64 million euros for the six cell option.

For everything that falls outside the basic agreement, The Netherlands charges the court extra. 'Each time we request something which upgrades the levels towards a more international standard, we have to pay,' Dubuisson noted. Take family visits, to which the court was strongly committed. For the wife and children of Bemba, who are living in Belgium, it isn't very difficult to travel to Scheveningen. His spouse tries to see him every Saturday. But how to manage for a Congolese family member from a small village in the east of the DRC? Just getting a passport can be hard, let alone a visa for The Netherlands, which can be extremely difficult to arrange. Besides these hurdles, the costs for these expensive trips are so high that many families can't afford them. 'The kids don't have to pay for a mistake their father maybe has made,' Dubuisson underlined.

Family Visits

In 2010 the Assembly of States Parties created the Trust Fund for Family
Visits (TFFV), which pays for a 10-day visit for the family of an indigent
detainee. Initially the ICC managed to get Germany on board to finance
such trips. But as it received little financial support during the last few
years, the balance of the TFFV fell to just 9,372,55 euros in 2016.
The availability of funds has reached 'a critically low level,' the ICC's
presidency wrote on 11 August 2016, deciding in a matter raised by a
detainee.[158] The suspect's request to the court to pay for flight tickets
and hotel costs so his wife and children could come over to see him, was
denied by the chief custody officer, because 'for the moment the court
doesn't have the necessary funds to be able to respond positively to your
demand for a visit.' The detainee managed to find a solution as a friend
was willing to step in and pay for the family's travel and accommodation,
but that raised new questions with the registry about his family being
incapable to finance the trip. The president of the court, Silvia Fernández
de Gurmendi, however rejected the way the registry handled the matter,
and also decided there needs to be a more clear policy 'to avoid any
uncertainty for indigent detainees applying for supported family visits.'
She also ordered the registrar to actively seek donations for the TFFV.
Family visits have been hampered by other reasons as well. Take for
instance Ntaganda, whose wife had the opportunity to visit him
in The Hague. However, in an interview in August 2016, his lead
counsel Stéphane Bourgon said his seven children hadn't seen him
since his voluntary surrender in 2013. One of the main obstacles was
that they didn't have passports.[159] 'Since August 2014, we have been
trying to obtain passports for his children. Very recently, we made new
arrangements with staff members in the registry who are helping us in this
regard. This is a priority for us,' Bourgon said.
The detention centre has accommodated itself to family visits as it has a
special room for intimate encounters, where a detained husband can meet
his wife privately. 'The bare minimum for such a facility is a toilet and a
shower. The Dutch authorities made us pay for this as well,' Dubuisson

---

158 'Public redacted version of Decision on the Application to review the 'Decision on Complaint to the Registrar
  by [...] concerning Supported Family Visit,' ICC presidency, 11 August 2016.
159 'Q&A with Stéphane Bourgon, lawyer representing Bosco Ntaganda, part II,' International Justice Monitor,
  23 August 2013.

noted. It is generally known that Charles Taylor and his wife had a baby while he was detained. Also the spouse of Germain Katanga got pregnant in the ICC detention centre. They named their baby daughter Carolina, after his Dutch defence lawyer Caroline Buisman.

Baking cake

In the early years, the menu in the detention centre was a big problem. The suspects complained about the Dutch sandwiches, dishes, cheese and milk that were served, while they weren't able to get African food such as specific fish and other products. 'We fought for this for more than six years,' Dubuisson underlined. Finally ingredients for meals the detainees were used to have at home, appeared on the ordering list with goods they can buy. 'Yes, they cook themselves,' the court services director explained. Some suspects even develop quite some culinary expertise. One of them loved to bake, so often it would smell of fresh cake in the detention centre. They have other homely activities as well. The detainees do their laundry. They can send their suits to the dry-cleaner twice a month.
A computer is an important item. 'We are an e-court,' Dubuisson tells. The documents that are used in cases are all in electronic form. As computers however haven't reached to all corners of the African countryside, there have been detainees who first needed to do a course. Surfing freely on the Internet is not on the agenda. The computer a detainee has in his cell, has only one connection: with the court. If suspects want to communicate with their family, they have to write a letter by hand. Academic Abels, who never had direct access to the detention centre, finds it exaggerated that 'all mail is automatically checked.' But his overall assessment of the ICC unit is quite positive. 'It belongs to the best detention centres in the world, although in some aspects it could do better.'
Regularly Dubuisson visits the detainees. 'They all try to improve the quality of the food or to get more hours on the phone. They are all worried about their family. Maybe a child has had a car accident. Your wife is alone, so you could be a bit worried about that too.'
As director of the division of court services Dubuisson needs to stay neutral. It is up to the judges to decide about guilt and innocence of suspects. 'Maybe there are people who think they are killers. But they are individuals who behave normally. They are very intelligent and all have charisma. It is for a reason that they were leaders. You can have a nice

conversation with them.' It is known that Laurent Gbagbo is reading a lot – history, philosophy. His cell is stuffed with books.

The detainees are keen to watch television programmes about Africa. Just like any 'real men,' as Dubuisson puts it, they follow sports as much as they can. By watching the BBC and other international networks former top leaders keep themselves informed about world affairs, as they did when they were in power. Bemba lived quite a few years in Belgium, the country where Dubuisson originates from, and closely follows the developments there. 'He knows in great detail about what is happening in Belgium and is often better informed than I am.'

Hunger strike

Dubuisson's biggest concern is the possibility of death, naturally or by suicide. Depression often looms. 'You see that detainees feel better when they have a good result in court, or if there is a chance they might be released. But when the decision in appeal is negative and they remain detained, of course they feel terribly down. If there are objective signs there is something wrong, because a person doesn't want to talk or isolates himself in his cell, we immediately inform the medical unit. If there is a reasonable ground to believe something can happen, we move a person to a cell with infrared camera and will continue monitoring him.'

No doubt the detention authorities were on high alert when former rebel leader Ntaganda went on hunger strike on 7 September 2016. His lawyer Stéphane Bourgon told the judges that his client 'does not intend to resume eating normally in the near future.'[160] Ntaganda also refused to take the medicine prescribed to him. After having visited him on the second day of the hunger strike, Bourgon said that his client was in 'a very bad psychological situation' and that a psychologist needed to see him. A few days later, on 13 September 2016, the lawyer read out in court a twenty-minute statement written by his client. 'Even if I had wanted to be with you today, it is not possible. I feel too ill to come to the court, I am too weak to come to the court,' Ntaganda said, addressing the judges through his lawyer.[161] 'It matters not what I do, I cannot overcome this ill feeling. Reading, religion, sport, work do help to relieve me in short

160 'Ntaganda on hungerstrike, refuses to attend court hearing,' International Justice Monitor, 8 September 2016.
161 Official transcript, ICC, 13 September 2016.

moments, but the ill feeling nevertheless comes back. There is no way out.' While the lawyer was reading the dramatic statement, his client was not physically present in the courtroom, but participated through a video-link from the detention centre and could follow what was being said. According to a medical report Ntaganda was too weak to be transported to the court.

'I'm a revolutionary,' the former rebel leader explained through his counsel. 'I have fought in the most difficult situations. I have survived extremely dangerous events that very few people can even imagine. Many times I've almost died. I'm not afraid of dying. However, despite the acceptable detention conditions in prison, I have never been mistreated at a psychological level in the way that I have been since I have been in The Hague. For me, it's worse than harassment. That's the reason why I prefer, rather, to die than to suffer such treatment.'

According to Ntaganda he has been treated unfairly for more than two years. His separation from his family felt like a punishment. 'I no longer have any hope of seeing my wife and children again under normal conditions,' the Congolese suspect said through his lawyer. With his drastic actions Ntaganda was protesting against an order by the judges imposing restrictions on his communications and contacts with his family, after the chamber had been convinced by the prosecution that the former warlord was personally coaching witnesses and directing others to do so. 'I've been accused, tried and convicted for having intimidated witnesses without investigation, without trial, and without being able to defend myself. I am no longer capable of continuing,' Ntaganda argued. The defendant was allowed to telephone with just two persons: his wife and his mother, twice a week, for a maximum duration of one hour per week, with restrictions on the conversations. During the calls 'I can't speak about my trial or what I have experienced in The Hague. That's notwithstanding the fact that the conversations are listened into by an interpreter. There are three of us on the line,' Ntaganda said. The calls were supervised by the court and checked on the use of coded language. 'And if ever I have the misfortune of saying a word that the interpreter does not understand, then the conversation is cut.' Ntaganda could only speak to his children through his wife, or he records messages that are played to his children after the registry had reviewed them. When he receives a visitor, the meetings are monitored as well.

Ntaganda protested also against the circumstances that were likely to affect a possible visit by several of his children in December 2016. 'Only three of my seven children could come, for budgetary reasons, if I have understood well. Secondly, an interpreter and a security guard would be present during the entire visit and he would have a device in order to record everything that's said. All this in front of my children. Visits would be limited to four hours a day. And this for just a few days. And what is even worse is that once the short visit is finished, I can't even speak to my children while they're at the hotel, which is a few hundred metres away from me. My children have never come to Europe, they don't speak the languages they speak here, they don't have family in The Hague or in the surrounding area. There can be no doubt that a visit under such conditions would traumatise my children.'

The limitations were unbearable to Ntaganda. 'And there's my wife who I can't see privately. We are husband and wife, but I am forbidden from looking for support and comfort in the arms of my wife in private.' Ntaganda pointed at the logistical problems of such encounters. If he was with his wife, the children would be by themselves. But if the children would travel with their mother, he couldn't be alone with his wife. 'Clearly there is a wish to separate me from my family,' he complained. 'When I decided to surrender voluntarily over three years ago, I thought I could defend myself, but I now know it's not the case,' Ntaganda wrote. He pointed out that he had 'lost all hope,' as he couldn't see his wife and children under normal conditions. 'That is why I am ready to die.'

But Ntaganda would not starve himself to death in ICC detention. He stopped his hunger strike within two weeks, when the court quickly organised a visit by his wife, who came over for eight days. In the meantime his trial continued, and so have the investigations into the accusations that Ntaganda coached witnesses.

'It's like a family'

As they are far away from family and friends, the suspects depend a lot on each other, Dubuisson explained. The detainees usually get on with each other. 'It's like a family,' the court official noted. Although a defence lawyer pointed out that a new arrival with serious mental and behavioural problems had created tensions and even fear among the other defendants in the ICC detention block.

Caroline Buisman remembers how hard it was in the beginning for her client, Germain Katanga. She fought to get his conditions improved, a campaign that wasn't always appreciated by court officials. Only after a certain time Katanga began to feel more at ease. 'Especially when they started, as a group, cooking African meals. That helps. He managed to get on better with the guards as well. In the end Katanga was like the small brother of Lubanga, and also Charles Taylor looked after him,' Buisman tells. The men who had fought a bloody war against each other in Ituri – Katanga and Lubanga – were able to become friends in Scheveningen. Buisman: 'Reconciliation begins in the prison.'

7

IVORY COAST
One side on trial

11 December 2012. There is no visitor to be seen at the entrance of the International Criminal Court. Emptiness prevails. That's strange. Just like the other journalists and media that are following the ICC, I had received an email with an urgent request to arrive at least one and a half hours early. The reason: the expected high attendance for the hearing. But the only persons in the hall are two guards. They are standing next to the x-ray machine and don't have much to do. The security officers are instructed to check all media in order to fish out unregistered persons. It takes the guards some time to find me on the media list. When they finally tick off my name, I am allowed to enter.

'You are pretty strict today,' I tell the person at the desk in the lobby who hands over my media pass. 'It is because of the demonstrators,' the official explains. During the last hearing in the case against Laurent Gbagbo, his supporters were passionately protesting outside, in front of the ICC building. The Ivorians demanded the release of the former head of state of Ivory Coast, who is detained by the court on charges of crimes against humanity that were committed when he had lost the presidential elections in 2010. Within a few days the country became the scene of bloody violence that would rage for five months. Former president Gbagbo is accused of playing a crucial role in the mayhem.

His supporters are the main reason that the media are requested to come early. Apparently the court wants to make sure the press is inside before the Gbagbo fans arrive to prevent any trouble. But this Tuesday afternoon there are no masses to be seen. The sky above The Hague is grey. It is freezing cold.

Some twenty persons are sitting in the public gallery. Half of them are journalists from Ivory Coast. They are invited by the ICC to receive information about the court's work and to attend a hearing. The view of the courtroom is still blocked by the light green blinds covering the bulletproof glass. When the blinds go up, the dock appears to be empty. The accused is not present for this session about procedural matters, such as fixing a new date for the confirmation of charges hearing, during which the prosecutors present their first evidence, on the basis of which the judges will decide whether there are sufficient reasons to start a trial. These hearings were planned for 18 June 2012, but have been postponed several times. One of the reasons is that Gbagbo's lawyers claim he is not fit for trial and should be released.

Formally the investigations into what happened in the Ivory Coast were started 'proprio motu,' at the initiative of prosecutor Luis Moreno-Ocampo. Ironically, when he was still president, in 2003 Gbagbo's own government had said it accepted the jurisdiction of the court and promised to cooperate. Later the new leaders of Ivory Coast also urged the ICC to research the post-election violence. The judges decided that the court did indeed had a mandate. On 3 October 2011 they gave prosecutor Moreno-Ocampo the green light to open an investigation.

Three medical experts, three opinions

It is no big surprise that Gbagbo is not present for the hearing. If his health situation doesn't permit him to take part in a trial, as his lawyers state, it is only logical to stay away from a status conference. Since a few weeks there is more clarity about Gbagbo's physical and mental state. Three experts had been asked by the judges to check the suspect's health: doctor An Chuc; psychologist Bruno Daunizeau and psychiatrist Pierre Lamothe. On 2 November 2012 the court published the findings of the medical experts.[162]

Their observations are revealing. All three confirm that Gbagbo, who himself had witnessed serious crimes during the fall of his regime, is suffering from post-traumatic stress disorder (PTSD) and is 'hospitalised'; a state of mind where people have adapted to a forced stay in an institution to such an extent that they cannot take initiatives by themselves anymore. But that's where their agreement ends.

Doctor Chuc concludes that Gbagbo not only suffered 'physical pathologies' – it is painful for him to walk – but lacks the mental

---

162 'Decision on the fitness of Laurent Gbagbo to take part in the proceedings before this Court,' ICC, 2 November 2012.

capacities as well to 'understand and assimilate in detail the nature, causes and content of the charges against him.' According to the doctor, the suspect is unable to 'instruct a lawyer in a regular, sustained, relevant and consistent manner.' Physically he might be able to participate in the hearings 'if he takes breaks,' but mentally not.

The second expert, psychologist Daunizeau, says the suspect is suffering from a major depressive syndrome and concentration difficulties. He 'does not seem to have grasped the full extent of the proceedings against him,' and 'has no real capacity to issue to counsel clear, precise and strategically-meaningful instructions.' The psychologist also doubts whether he's capable of making a statement. Gbagbo's health situation 'does not correspond to his age, nor does it correspond to his level of culture, nor to what one would expect from someone in his professional situation.' He concludes that Gbagbo 'is the mere shadow of his former self' and 'unfit to prepare his defence.'

The third expert however comes to a very different conclusion. According to psychiatrist Lamothe, the accused 'remains easily fatigued' but he is capable 'of performing complex intellectual reasoning and of expressing himself at a scholarly level.' His observations also permit an insight into Gbagbo's personality. Lamothe says that the ex-president is 'far more concerned with salvaging his image,' how he will be 'judged by history' and 'conveying his political message' than with setting up his defence in this criminal case. Mr Gbagbo 'totally ignored' the charges, but was willing to go through the proceedings and hoped to be acquitted in the long run.

Such a diagnosis, from an expert who does not doubt Gbagbo's mental capacities, would usually be a great relief to the persons concerned. But for his lawyers this was not good news. The judges decided to follow Lamothe's line and concluded that Gbagbo 'is fit to take part in the proceedings before this court.' The chamber suggested adjustments such as shorter court sessions, facilities to rest during breaks, the possibility to excuse himself from all or part of the proceedings and to follow sessions via video-link.

The fate of the ex-president

There were similarities between the image of the former head of state painted by the three experts and the impression Gbagbo made during his initial appearance a year earlier, on 5 December 2011. He had just been transferred from Ivory Coast to the ICC detention unit in The Hague and was summoned to appear before the judges. He sat in the dock as a defeated man, attempting to understand his new situation.

When judge Silvia Fernández de Gurmendi offered him the opportunity to speak, Gbagbo got up from his chair. 'Your Honour, the conditions of my detention at the court here at The Hague are fine.'[163] In a way, Gbagbo almost seemed relieved to be in his current whereabouts. 'It is my arrest conditions that are not so correct,' he said. Gbagbo wanted to reflect on those days and began to explain how on 11 April 2011 he was arrested by troops of his political rival, the current president Alassane Ouattara – scenes that were broadcast worldwide by international media. He had experienced dreadful moments. 'I observed my minister of the interior killed right in front of me.' He saw his eldest son, who was arrested and detained, being hit. Gbagbo witnessed how his personal physician was beaten as well. 'I thought he was going to die, but fortunately he survived,' the former president said.

Remarkably though he didn't say a word about his wife, Madam Gbagbo, who in the Ivory Coast was suspected of having been implicated in setting up death squads. The marriage with Simone Gbagbo was said to have been an arrangement. But it was striking that he was silent about her fate because he had been captured by Ivorian troops together with la Première Dame. While Gbagbo remained physically more or less unharmed, the photos taken of his wife, surrounded by revengeful militia, suggested something else. Simone Gbagbo looked like a poor and battered woman. The straps of her torn dress hung on her arms. The shock could be read in her eyes. Although Gbagbo supporters could not confirm it, there were rumours she had been abused. Nevertheless, the former president didn't even utter her name during his first address to the judges.

Instead he talked extensively about himself. How he had been taken to Hotel du Golf where his opponent Ouattara had set up his headquarters. Two days after his arrest Gbagbo and his physician were taken to Korhogo, six hundred kilometres north of Abidjan. 'I was lodged in a house. There was a bed, a mosquito net, a shower, and at my request I was

163 Transcript not available anymore on ICC website, possibly lost when the design of the website was changed and documents disappeared or were archived under the wrong date.

offered two meals a day. I had been offered three meals a day, but I had decided to take only two.' Indeed, Gbagbo seemed to have lost weight. He had a hard time while detained in Ivory Coast. 'I knew what was happening outside only when it was raining on the roof. I was unable to see the sun, and the very few times that I was able to see the sun was when with difficulty, my lawyers arrived.' Only after considerable efforts was his counsel maître Emmanuel Altit given access to his client.

While Gbagbo was talking about himself in the ICC courtroom, suddenly he realised what impression he made. 'This is not an appeal for people to take pity on me. I am simply trying to describe the imprisonment that I was subject to. I was not able to take a walk. I was not able to go out and to see the sun. I had several other health conditions, in addition to those I already had, and I am no longer a young person. As you can realise, your Honour, I am not 20 or 30 years old. I am 66 years old today. My shoulder hurts, my wrists hurt. And when I arrived here, fortunately I was X-rayed, I was provided with medication.'

He continued his speech and explained how one day he was driven to the court of Korhogo. There an Ivorian judge gave him an envelope and said: 'Look, this is the warrant of arrest.' He did not immediately grasp the message. When he was led to a car, the former president thought he was taken back to the house where he had been detained, but instead he was driven straight to the airport. 'Where am I going by plane?' Gbagbo asked one of the guards. 'You are going to Abidjan,' was the answer. 'He did not even have the courage to tell me: "You are going to The Hague".' Gbagbo was in no way prepared for the trip. 'That is how I travelled without anything, except my pair of trousers and my shirt. I did not have anything else at all.' This approach hadn't been necessary, the accused said. ' If I'm told that, "Mr Gbagbo, you are going to The Hague," I will board the plane and I go to The Hague. But once again we were deceived.'

The judges had issued a secret arrest warrant against Gbagbo on 23 November 2011, to which the new Ivorian government had reacted immediately (as had been arranged at a meeting in Paris between prosecutor Luis Moreno-Ocampo and president Ouattara). The warrant was made public on 30 November, seven months after Gbagbo had lost power, when the former leader arrived in The Netherlands.

It was not out of self-interest, the suspect said, that he elaborated on the events. He was hoping that by telling the public about his ordeal, he could contribute to the prevention of similar situations. Gbagbo reiterated to the judge he would never have ignored a summons to appear: 'I will challenge that evidence and then you hand down your judgment.' With those words he ended his declaration. 'As for the detention here, the conditions are normal. I do not have any problem at all. Thank you, your Honour. Thank you.'

While he was telling the court about his fate, Gbagbo seemed to relive that joy of being at the centre of attention and addressing people who hung on his words. But it was also slightly awkward to hear a man who had been leading a country for a decade, just talking about himself. His speech lacked any broader reference to Ivory Coast, where the population had terribly suffered under the post-election violence. In a few months, more than three thousand people had been killed and hundreds of thousands had to flee their homes. But for the ex-leader nobody outside the small presidential group seemed to matter. I could not suppress the thought that Gbagbo was suffering from some sort of 'VIP-itis.' Very Important Persons, who have been in power for a long time, get used to the fact that everything turns around them and lose contact with daily reality.

It was not clear whether it was intentionally or subconsciously that Gbagbo presented himself as a sad old man. A tragic figure who had suddenly been put on a plane. In a throwaway line, he had referred to the accusations against him. The ICC's prosecutor had charged him with four counts of crimes against humanity – murder, rape, persecution and other inhumane acts causing great suffering/attempted murder – which were part of a criminal plan allegedly drawn up by Gbagbo and his inner circle to stay in power. The suspect hardly seemed to realise the weight of these charges. Would there be any truth to the rumours that not so much the president himself, but rather his wife had been the evil genius? On 22 November 2012 the ICC judges decided to lift the confidentiality of another arrest warrant. Simone Gbagbo was charged with the same crimes as her husband.

What was lacking though at the ICC were cases against persons from the entourage of president Ouattara, despite the fact that human rights groups had accused his rebels of committing bloodbaths and other crimes during the fight for power in the country. Unless the judges had issued other confidential arrest warrants, the prosecution seemed to be targeting the losing party only, and leaving the winners untouched. It would not be the first time the ICC was accused of victor's justice.

Demonstrating in the cold

It has been more than a year since Gbagbo made his initial appearance before the judges, when the confirmation of charges hearings start, on 19 February 2013. This time his fans have turned up. Hundreds of Ivorians, wearing caps and orange hats, are walking on the road along the ICC building. Some are dressed in the national colours – orange, white and green. A few carry placards. Most are Ivorian immigrants living in Europe. Policemen on bikes are lined up in front of the court to prevent the demonstrators from getting too near. Other officers are riding impressive horses, which make human beings look so futile and flimsy. With soft coercion the police is pulling the protestors together onto a small field opposite the court.

The Gbagbo fans watch with some distrust the journalists and media who are reporting on their demonstration. But when I ask a woman for comments, she immediately relaxes. 'We are from France, Italy, Belgium and Sweden. We want Gbagbo to be released,' she says. The woman is from Paris. But, out of fear, the Ivorian Parisienne doesn't want to give her name. 'I am afraid my family in Côte d'Ivoire will face the consequences of what I say and will be killed.' The woman sounds sincere in her concern. In Ivory Coast, she says, there is no place for Gbagbo supporters. 'No, we can't go back to our country. It would mean our death,' she says, just as the Dutch police has managed to push the Ivorians into a tight and easy to control group.

While his supporters are protesting in the cold outside, Gbagbo is appearing in the courtroom. He wears a dark blue suit and a light blue shirt with a tie. The former president looks to the public gallery and greets some of his fans with a mild superior smile. He looks well. It seems he has gained some weight since his first appearance fourteen months ago. The suspect is seated in the dock, between two guards. Next to him there are plastic cups. Defendants don't seem to get glasses to drink from. While the court officer reads out the charges, Gbagbo quickly exchanges knowing glances with his militants, who make up a large portion of the visitors in the public gallery.

The hearings have been adjusted to Gbagbo's condition and are spread out over shorter sitting days. The sessions take place in the afternoon, in blocks of one hour, presiding judge Silvia Fernández de Gurmendi explains. She underlines that the confirmation of charges hearings are not a mini-trial. After the sessions, taking place from 19 until 28 February 2013, the chamber will decide whether the case is solid enough to start a full trial. A few days earlier, on 15 February, Ivory Coast ratified the Rome Statute and became a full member of the court.

The judge gives the lawyers of Gbagbo the opportunity to speak first. They have launched an admissibility challenge arguing that this is not a case for the ICC. Dov Jacobs, a French legal expert teaching international law at the University of Leiden, stands up to start to explain that national authorities are always the first in line to prosecute international crimes. The Rome Statute says that only if a state is not willing or able, the ICC can take such a case. But Ivory Coast can do this one itself. The defence urges the judges 'to declare this case inadmissible' before the ICC 'more so because Côte d'Ivoire is neither unable or unwilling to prosecute president Gbagbo.'[164] In fact, the lawyers argue, the national authorities are busy with proceedings against their client, Simone Gbagbo and his ex-minister/militia leader Charles Blé Goudé. But it remains a curious argument. Does the defence really think Gbagbo would be better off being prosecuted in his home country? Judge Hans-Peter Kaul sighs deeply. His two female colleagues, Fernández and Christine Van den Wyngaert, follow the defence attentively. While Jacobs is pleading, Gbagbo raises his arm like a schoolboy, points his finger in the air and waits until presiding judge Fernández sees it. When she nods, with some difficulty he gets up from his chair and shuffles with stiffly legs to the door. The guards escort him. Within a few minutes Gbagbo is back from his sanitary trip and takes his place in the dock. After an hour the judge calls for the break.

Back in court, when the hearing is about to resume, Gbagbo waves at two young women on the first row in the public gallery. Happily surprised the Ivorian ladies look at the former leader, who responds with a broad smile but then quickly composes his face again.

Bensouda's message

After the defence's submissions, prosecutor Fatou Bensouda starts her plea, in French for the Ivorian audience to be able to understand her

---

164 Official transcript, ICC, 19 February 2013.

directly. 'Madam President, your Honours, the matter before you today concerns Mr Laurent Gbagbo, a president who sacrificed the political electoral democratic processes and preferred to resort to violence and crime in a bid to stay in power,' she says, with her deep voice. The people of Ivory Coast had voted peacefully in two rounds, the prosecutor explains. The first, on 31 October, was won by Gbagbo with 38 percent of the votes, followed by Ouattara with 32 percent. The second round took place between 28 November and 1 December. The following day, on 2 December 2010, the chair of the Independent Electoral Commission announced the provisional results, declaring victory for Ouattara, with 54 percent of the votes. The chair of the Constitutional Council though overturned that decision, claiming that Gbagbo was the winner of the elections. The two candidates simultaneously declared themselves president of the country.

What should have been the first presidential elections since the year 2000, turned into a bloody power struggle. Violence, hatred and division engulfed the country. During her statement Bensouda would lift her argument to a level that goes beyond the specific situation in Ivory Coast. 'We are here, Madam President, to send out a strong message to those who intend to attempt to get to power, or to remain in power, by use of force and brutality, to tell them that they shall henceforth be answerable for their actions.'

The following days the prosecution will argue that the suspect and members of his inner circle 'adopted a policy' and 'a common plan' to keep Gbagbo in power as president of Côte d'Ivoire 'by any means, including by lethal force.' Bensouda says her office will show that the pro-Gbagbo-forces are responsible for the deaths, rapes, serious injuries and arbitrary detention of countless law-abiding citizens. While she is speaking even Gbagbo seems to be impressed. With a sad look he is staring in front of him. His face is shining with perspiration. On the first row of the public gallery his supporters shake their dispirited heads.

'The prosecution is here to give a voice to these victims, to all the victims who suffered and those who continue to suffer,' Bensouda continues. 'The International Criminal Court cannot bring back the family members they have lost, or make them even forget the pain that they have suffered. But by charging Mr Gbagbo for the crimes committed, we aim at bringing justice to these victims.'

After her introduction her colleague takes over. Trial lawyer Eric MacDonald experienced a tremendous setback two months earlier, December 2012, when the judges concluded there was insufficient evidence to convict Mathieu Ngudjolo Chui. After a full trial the Congolese warlord was acquitted. Now MacDonald is handling the Gbagbo case. The trial lawyer tells the court that despite losing the elections the Ivorian suspect stayed on as president and commander-in-chief of the armed forces. While supporters of his opponent Ouattara took to the streets to protest, Gbagbo forbade demonstrations and 'deployed heavily armed soldiers who used lethal force against unarmed demonstrators in the streets,' underlines MacDonald.

According to the prosecution, the suspect was at 'the very centre of the decisions that led to the criminal activities of his forces against civilians.' He frequently held meetings with army commanders and his political allies. The former president nominated persons 'loyal to him, to key positions' in government, defence and security forces. He also reinforced the army by 'systematically recruiting young militia and mercenaries and placing them within the command chain in order to be able to control them.' He 'personally made sure that forces loyal to him received proper training, funding and weapons,' MacDonald explains.

His forces and militia were fully equipped and tasked to not only carry out attacks on Ouattara supporters, but also on religious and ethnic groups. They set up roadblocks where people were checked and assaulted. Neighbourhoods and institutions considered to be opposition bastions where targeted. Gbagbo and his inner circle 'turned a blind eye' to the crimes committed by forces loyal to him. 'No one was accountable,' MacDonald says.

'A press review'

Gbagbo's lawyers are not impressed by the arguments. Self-assured maître Altit looks straight at the prosecutors, when the following day it is his turn to present his defence. His team is grinning and laughing a lot and takes a casual attitude. In the first row of the public gallery mainly Ivorians are seated. Somebody points out the ambassador of Ivory Coast for me, who chose to sit as close as possible to the prosecutors and as far as possible from the suspect and his lawyers. Meanwhile the Ivorian woman, to whom Gbagbo had smiled, continues to flirt with the accused through the thick glass. Next to me sits a train conductor originally from Ivory Coast, but now living in Paris. He has taken a day off to be present at the case against 'his' president.

Maître Altit sweeps aside the evidence. According to the lawyer the charges are based on articles in anti-Gbagbo media and the 'partial use' of reports by human rights organisations.[165] The defence alleges that the 'Document Containing the Charges', which presents the prosecution's theory of the case, the charges and the evidence, is 'only a reflection of the accusations made by the rebel leaders and the pro-Ouattara press at the time of the crisis.' In other words, it is just a review of the anti-Gbagbo media and groups. With visible pleasure he points to a major blunder by his opponents. If the prosecution had done proper investigations, the counsel argues, they 'would not have presented to the defence images of violence which occurred in Kenya.' In short, the defence says that the Office of the Prosecutor (OTP) doesn't know what it is doing, is biased and hasn't done its job. 'There is no indication of any properly conducted investigation, let alone an investigation of both incriminating and exculpatory elements,' Altit argues. The prosecution 'relies on materials' communicated by the current Ivorian authorities. More importantly, the defence lawyer says, to be able to 'place the responsibility for the conflict firmly and exclusively on the doorstep of president Gbagbo,' the prosecution has to 'stick to the narrative' which was 'constructed' by his Ivorian opponents during the crisis.

This is serious criticism. If this is true, this means that Bensouda and her team weren't able to conduct their own investigations, but were possibly kept on a leash by the Ouattara government having a lot of influence on the case. 'Madam President, your Honours, it is a dangerous game that the prosecutor is playing by using a construction that has been put together by others,' says Altit.

'We believe he will be set free'

On the eighth and last day of this series of hearings, Thursday 28 February, Gbagbo himself gets the opportunity to address the court. The lawyers move the transparent table lectern to their client. The former head of state though speaks without looking at notes. 'On occasion I find

---

165 Official transcript, ICC, 20 February 2013.

myself back in the Ivory Coast, but on other occasions I find myself very far afield, sometimes extremely far afield,' Gbagbo starts his speech that meanders quite a bit, touching on several points he deems important.[166] 'Why is it, that in modern justice there are opposing camps?' he wonders. If the judges, prosecutors and legal representatives of victims would have asked him, he would have provided them all information, for instance about the decree he signed to deploy the army. Last week he told his lawyers he wanted to send the court the books he had written, but they said it was too late to introduce these materials. Addressing the judges he says: 'I will send a batch of books written by Gbagbo to the office of the prosecution, and I will send you also a batch of my books, because, well, that is the man who I am.'

He also wants to make clear that 'I was not governing hand in hand with the members of my family. Maybe it is done elsewhere in Africa, but not in Côte d'Ivoire under Gbagbo.' His lawyers listen, with poker faces, to their client, who continues his speech. 'I have been fighting for democracy and this was at a time when we didn't even know whether the Berlin Wall would crumble,' says Gbagbo. But the wall did come down and that helped Ivory Coast to introduce a multiparty system. He describes the civil war that erupted in 2002 in his country, how he led the negotiations and worked on dialogue, embracing democracy.

His lawyers glissade a little note to their client. Gbagbo looks at it briefly, casts an eye on the public gallery and the judges, and goes on. 'I am counting on you because I want all Africans who are supporting here, who are constantly present here before the court, outside of the prison, who are demonstrating back in their countries, taking part in marches ....' By then an Ivorian woman on the first row is leaning against her husband, who has put his arm around her. The speech moves her so much that she bends forward. But one of the guards approaches her and gestures her to sit up again, while Gbagbo finishes his address: '....I want them all to understand that the salvation of all African States is the respect of the constitution.' At that point the couple in front of me throws their fists in the air. The arm of the flirting woman, who has been staring at Gbagbo continuously to see whether she could catch his eye, goes up as well.

---

166 Official transcript, ICC, 28 February 2013.

When I ask her whether she knows the former president personally, she refers vaguely to 'family.'

Presiding judge Fernández closes the hearing. While the visitors leave the public gallery and take the stairs down to the lobby, a woman starts to sing. Her voice resounds in the staircase. 'We really believe he will be set free!' she jubilates. Downstairs supporters, shedding tears and with red eyes from crying, are discussing the case against the man they consider their president. Some are elated because they are sure that the presented evidence is worthless. They are convinced that this case will collapse and their leader will be released.

'A second chance'

The supporters might be right. Three months later, on 3 June 2013, the court publishes the decision by the judges. The chamber concludes, by majority, that the prosecution has presented insufficient evidence to give the green light for a trial. The magistrates note 'with serious concern that in this case the prosecutor relied heavily on NGO reports and press articles with regard to key elements of the case.'[167] The problem with these reports is that they contain 'anonymous hearsay evidence,' which is difficult to check and corroborate with other evidence. This must be a blow to Bensouda and her team, because the judges confirm the criticism of the defence. But acknowledging the 'seriousness of the charges' and the 'complexity of the case which involves a myriad of incidents allegedly committed by a multitude of perpetrators over several months,' the judges give the prosecutor time to investigate further and provide real evidence. A second chance for Bensouda's team to come up with better results.

That summer the prosecutor goes on a 'fact-finding' visit to Ivory Coast. On the last day of her stay, on 20 July 2013, she speaks to the media in Abidjan. She expresses her 'gratitude' for the 'warm welcome' the Ivorians have shown.[168] While thanking the government for its 'first-rate cooperation,' especially in coordinating logistics and security, she reminds the authorities this also includes an obligation to fulfil 'arrest warrants and requests for surrender.' Her speech is carefully formulated. Again she stresses that her investigations 'are being undertaken completely

---

167 Decision adjourning the hearing on the confirmation of charges, ICC, 3 June 2013.
168 Statement to the Press by the Prosecutor of the International Criminal Court, OTP, 20 July 2013.

objectively, impartially, independently, and in strict accordance with the law.'

'I am a communication consultant'

His name had been mentioned previously in the courtroom, but then the public didn't know that he was wanted by the ICC. On 30 September 2013 the court publishes an arrest warrant against Charles Blé Goudé, former minister for sports and youth – the third suspect in the Ivorian cases. He is accused of having directly instructed young people during the violence, who were recruited, trained, armed and included in the command structure of the Ivorian army. In a confidential arrest warrant dated 21 December 2011 the judges had decided that the Ivorian politician, dubbed 'a firebrand' by media, had to be captured and surrendered. But the militiaman had escaped the country and was held in Ghana, which only extradited him to Ivory Coast on 18 January 2013. Blé Goudé is charged with the same four counts of crimes against humanity – murder, rape, persecution, other inhumane acts/attempted murder – as the Gbagbo couple. When Bensouda visited Ivory Coast, the youth leader was already in a prison cell in his native country. But he wasn't given to her then. It would take until 22 March 2014 before he was handed over to the ICC.

In a seemingly vivacious mood Blé Goudé steps into the courtroom for his initial appearance. Broadly smiling he holds his fist in the air. While he keeps on waving to his supporters in the public gallery, he takes his seat in the dock, only to get up immediately again and throw hand kisses to his followers. He is the star, radiating with energy. His intense eyes are beaming with combativeness. 'I am a consultant in political communication,' he answers when judge Fernández asks him about his profession.[169] Blé Goudé, who was born on 1 January 1972 in the village of Niagbrahio, takes a sip of water from his plastic cup. The judge wants to know in what language he would like to communicate. In French, he says. She suggests he also speaks English and refers to the University of Manchester, where he studied conflict management. 'I come from a country which was colonised by the French. Therefore I speak French,'

---

169 Official transcript, ICC, 27 March 2014.

Blé Goudé answers. And no, the arrest warrant doesn't have to be read out. He has been informed about the accusations.

Then a long list with his rights are read to him: free assistance from an interpreter, time and facilities to prepare his defence, free communication in a confidential manner with the counsel of his choice, to remain silent, free of force to testify against himself or plead guilty, free to make statements without having to swear the oath, to receive communication of exonerating evidence, to challenge charges and evidence, present his own evidence, to be (not) present at the confirmation hearing or to participate in a status conference, to question prosecution witnesses, to have defence witnesses testify, and to recall certain decisions by the court.

'I will go back home'

'I'm wrongly accused of being the base of everything that is wrong,' says Blé Goudé, when he is given the opportunity to address the court. Despite the charges against him, he is convinced that his journey to the ICC hasn't been a one-way trip. 'What I do know is that I will go back to my home,' he says, adding that the conditions of his detention in Ivory Coast were terrible. 'I spent ten months locked up, naked. I wasn't well fed. Each evening, your Honour, I had to find a small bit of meat by myself and in a pot abusively called soup.' He was blindfolded when he was transported to different detention places.

Suddenly he was woken in the middle of the night, again blindfolded and put in a vehicle. He was seated in a chair with a hood on until the morning, when he was taken to the Ivorian prosecutor and informed about the arrest warrant. The next day Blé Goudé was flown to The Netherlands. 'I can tell you in this court that I'm in at the moment, if I am recognised guilty, may the law be applied with all its vigour. But if I am judged for what I have done and not for what I am, then I should be recognised innocent and should be allowed to go home.' And, he adds, 'I consider myself to be here to show the truth and I'm proud of that.'

The judge wants to know whether he has complaints about his detention at the ICC. But just like Gbagbo he says 'I have been well treated here.' However he does have 'a double feeling.' On one hand 'a lot of people cried' when he was taken to The Hague. But on the other hand, it didn't feel safe to stay in Ivory Coast. 'I was always afraid. Every day was a fight. I was like an object that people did what they wanted with, political

blackmail. I was ashamed for my country and my continent. And it was only when I came here that I saw that an individual could have rights.'
The public part of the hearing is finished. Blé Goudé and his lawyer Nick Kaufman would like to discuss certain issues with the judge, but prefer to do that behind closed doors. Again the suspect looks at his fellow Ivorians. The woman who previously was constantly seeking Gbagbo's attention is present as well. She turns out to be Blé Goudé's oldest sister, who lives in Sweden where she works as a nurse at the emergency unit of a hospital. A group of his fans walk to the bulletproof glass to be as close as they can to the accused. A man holds his thumbs up, another takes off his cap and a third gives a little nod as a sign of respect. The charismatic Blé Goudé smiles, grins and shows his clenched fist.
Outside a cold wind is blowing. Some women are weeping about their 'chouchou' being detained. 'Blé Goudé and Gbagbo have always been democrats. Ouattara has started this uprising. The real culprits are still out there and free. They have committed mass killings and have burned down houses in the west of the country. Our families are being threatened. This way there will never be reconciliation. Our country is a time bomb,' an older lady is sobbing. 'The ICC is not the end of the world,' says a real estate agent from Paris, 'but it is not fair that just one side is being prosecuted.'

A majority decision

Meanwhile the judges are still studying the case against Gbagbo. They are examining statements of 108 witnesses, more than 22.000 pages of other documentary evidence, and a large amount of audio and video material which are filed by the parties. When they finally reach a conclusion, on 12 June 2014, it is two against one. The majority decides there is 'sufficient evidence' that Gbagbo is responsible for the charged crimes and that the trial should start.[170] Judge Christine Van den Wyngaert however doesn't agree with her colleagues. Although the prosecution has submitted more evidence, 'the previously identified problem regarding reliance upon anonymous hearsay remains,' she points out.[171] 'I do not deny that horrendous crimes were committed against civilians by forces loyal to

---

170 Decision on the confirmation of charges against Laurent Gbagbo, ICC, 12 June 2014.
171 Dissenting Opinion of Judge Christine Van den Wyngaert, ICC, 12 June 2014.

Laurent Gbagbo,' the judge writes in her dissenting opinion. But she sees 'no convincing evidence' that Gbagbo 'at any point agreed with his alleged inner circle to commit crimes against innocent civilians.' In other words, there was terrible violence, but the judge sees no proof that Gbagbo and his inner circle formed a group with a common plan to intentionally target ordinary people to keep the president in power, nor that they prepared their supporters to do so. She points out that for instance many weapons purchases had no relation with crimes against civilians, but were 'likely' linked to the fact that Gbagbo's regime was facing 'a potent militarised opponent in several parts of the country, including Abidjan.' With that sentence she refers to the threats and violence by Ouattara's forces. But being in the minority, Van den Wyngaert's opinion doesn't prevail. In due course the court will determine a date on which the trial will finally start.

Half a year later, 11 December 2014, the judges unanimously confirm the charges against Blé Goudé. Although Van den Wyngaert partly dissents, again. She agrees that he is 'criminally responsible' for the charged crimes by the groups he was leading: the youth, mercenaries and militias.[172] But she sees no proof that the minister was part of the 'inner circle,' had any influence over the 'common plan' (if that ever existed) or had authority over the Forces de Défense et de Sécurité (FDS – the combined security forces of the army, gendarmerie, republican guard and police). He can't be responsible for the crimes allegedly committed by these official forces, while evidence for his role in other incidents carried out by his groups is 'rather thin,' Van den Wyngaert says. This doesn't sound like a rock solid case.

Although both men allegedly played different roles in the violence, there is a large overlap in the two cases. On 11 March 2015, the judges grant the prosecution's request to join the cases against Gbagbo and Blé Goudé into one. The chamber hopes to save time and money as two separate trials 'are likely to require more court hours and resources' and to prevent witnesses from going through the hardship of testifying twice.[173] Two months later the chamber sets the date for the joint trial: 10 November 2015.

---

172   Partly Dissenting Opinion of Judge Christine Van den Wyngaert, ICC, 11 December 2014.
173   Trial Chamber joins cases Laurent Gbagbo and Charles Blé Goudé, ICC press release, 11 March 2015.

Exhaustion and breakdown

New delays arise when the defence of Gbagbo announces that their client is not able to participate in a trial. The proceedings would lead to 'physical' and 'nervous exhaustion' or even 'a breakdown.' The lawyers claim the ex-president is unable to concentrate or to take part in 'any kind of activity.' At the request of the prosecution the judges order another medical examination by three experts. One of them is psychiatrist Lamothe, who evaluated Gbagbo's health back in 2012 as well.

After studying their reports the chamber finds that the experts 'unanimously' conclude that Gbagbo is 'physically and mentally able to attend and follow the trial proceedings.' He understands the charges, the details of the evidence and is able to instruct his counsel. In fact, compared to earlier checks Gbagbo's 'state of health has significantly improved,' the judges write on 27 November. He no longer suffers from post-traumatic stress or hospitalisation syndrome. Gbagbo is fit to stand trial.[174]

Wouldn't it be a good idea to hold parts of the trial in Ivory Coast or otherwise in Tanzania? The sudden request comes from Gbagbo's lawyers, filed on 25 September 2015. The reasons: it would be in the interest of justice and contribute to the ICC's goal of raising public awareness and outreach to affected communities. But none of the other parties agrees with the plan. The prosecution says that any possible benefit of bringing the trial closer to victims is overshadowed by security concerns. The hearings could lead to violent demonstrations and unrest. The legal representative of victims says the request 'aims mostly at providing a political tribune to the accused under the guise of opening statements.'[175] Last but not least, the government of Ivory Coast argues the move would put an unfair burden on the country, noting that the request was made just seven weeks before the start of the trial, and could lead to public unrest.

The judges explain they especially looked at 'security risks and logistical implications,' and decide to reject the possibility of holding part of the trial in Ivory Coast. And how about Arusha, the city in the north of Tanzania where the International Criminal Tribunal for Rwanda (ICTR)

---

174 Decision on the fitness of Laurent Gbagbo to stand trial, ICC, 27 November 2015.
175 Decision on Gbagbo Defence Request to hold opening statements in Abidjan or Arusha, 26 October 2015.

is located? There is no point, the judges reason, because that doesn't bring the trial 'closer to affected communities.' The Hague it will be.

One ICC suspect, however, will be prosecuted in Ivory Coast. The national authorities are not prepared to surrender Simone Gbagbo to The Hague. Instead they bring her, on different charges, before a local court. Three months after the opening of the trial against her, in March 2015, Ivorian judges find her guilty of undermining state security. Simone Gbagbo – nicknamed The Iron Lady, The Blood Lady or more favourably the Hillary Clinton of the Tropics – is sentenced to a twenty year prison term.

Start of the trial

They have come in their hundreds. Men and women, with their origins in Ivory Coast, travelled from countries such as France, Sweden and Italy and even as far as the United States of America to support their 'president' Laurent Gbagbo and his co-accused Charles Blé Goudé. It is a chilly Thursday morning, 28 January 2016. The trial which is about to begin, is the first to open in the ICC's permanent premises. Next to the court most of the Ivorian visitors are taking part in a demonstration against the trial. The mood is calm. Cyclists pass by on their bikes.

Some supporters have wrapped the Ivorian national flag like a cloak around their winter coats, others have caps on their head in the national colours orange, green and white. One guy is wearing a yellow fluorescent coat with, on the back, a large print of a picture of both suspects and the slogan 'proces de la honte' (trial of shame). Another supporter, who lives in Paris and travelled overnight to be present, is quietly holding his placard with the text 'Libérez Moi!!' under a photo of Gbagbo dating from the years the suspect was a handsome young man, incarcerated from 1971 until 1973, for opposing the one-party regime of former president Félix Houphouët-Boigny. 'He is a true democrat. He always fought for multiparty democracy,' his supporters cheer.

His imprisonment hadn't stopped Gbagbo, who was a history teacher and became director of the Institute of History, Art and African Archaeology at the University of Abidjan. In 1982 he joined a major teachers' strike and founded a party that would become the Front Populaire Ivorien (FPI). But soon he was forced into exile. He came back in 1988, managed to get a seat in the national assembly, but was again imprisoned for a short while in 1992. Many protesters in The Hague are too young to have personal memories of those days, but there are also a few old ladies among the crowd. One is pulling her shopping bag on wheels. Another carries a foldable chair to take a rest from time to time, while the crowd is shouting: 'Free Gbagbo, Free Blé Goudé!'

The ICC proudly states the new court complex is provided with a special designated area for demonstrations, but it is unclear where that location is. This protest takes pace peacefully on the pavement and the bicycle lane. Suddenly the mood changes when two dozen Dutch policemen armed with batons start pushing the protesters back. Some young protesters resist. On the spot they decide to have a sit-in. When agitated policemen start wielding their batons, a woman sitting on the pavement fears she will be run over and starts screaming.

It is an incomprehensible police action. There seems no reason for it. It lasts just a few minutes and it results in nothing as the crowd has hardly moved. When I leave the demonstration to make my way to the entrance of the court, a policeman who had been threatening to hit protesters with his baton and whom I photographed, follows me and orders me to identify myself. When I respond that I am a journalist and that I have to hurry because the trial is almost starting, he insists I identify myself. 'It is the law!' he says angrily. When I get my passport out, he refuses. It is my media pass he wants to see. Reluctantly I hand over the requested pass. The show of force puzzles me.

I follow the long queue at the entrance of the court. The extra checking and registering of the passports of visitors and media, is a new procedure for the court. Because of increased security measures, entering the building for 'special' hearings like the opening of a trial, which attracts lots of visitors, takes much more time than in the old court. Finally at the counter I receive an electronic day-pass and a red ticket which gives me access to the hearings. Without pre-registering it is impossible to get a seat. After two X-ray security checks, I finally reach my destiny – the public gallery.

The Ivorian ambassador and his assistant have taken their seats. On the right side I notice Pierrette Blé Hammar, the sister of Blé Goudé who lives in Sweden. When the curtains open her brother can be seen taking notes, while seated below in the courtroom. Dutch lawyer Geert-Jan Knoops, who only became his counsel in January 2015 and is still doing investigations, is looking up to the public gallery. During a press conference the day before, Knoops told the media that his client had 'faced difficult times' in ICC detention. Blé Goudé had been depressed in the early days. 'It is not easy for a man who calls for peace and reconciliation to be behind bars. But he believes in God and he believes he will return to his country as a free man who can contribute to peace,' Knoops said.

Gbagbo, dressed in a blue suit, a light blue shirt and wearing spectacles, briefly checks the visitors up at the public gallery and then puts on his headphones. He has been in ICC detention for more than four years now. His special advisor, the French businessman Bernard Houdin, told me during a break in the court's proceedings that Gbagbo spends his days reading about history, Africa, Plato, Virgil and numerous other subjects. His cell in the detention centre is filled with books. Houdin visits Gbagbo regularly. 'At one point the guards asked me: why is he in detention here, because he is such a gentleman,' the advisor says.

The astonishing thing is that half of the public gallery is empty. With so many people outside who would like to follow the trial in the comfort of a warm court building, the ICC's access management still has improvements to make.

This is a criminal trial

When the judges are seated, presiding judge Cuno Tarfusser starts with a personal statement. 'It is a shame,' the Italian magistrate says, 'that I am not in a position to conduct the trial in the French language. I understand French to some extent. I can read French somewhat, well enough. But to actually conduct a full trial and have a full mastery of legal French is quite another matter.'[176] He explains that his colleague Olga Herrera Carbuccia does speak French. But the third judge, Geoffrey Henderson, 'finds himself in the same situation' as Tarfusser. So the trial will be conducted in English.

The presiding judge has a second statement to make, which is directed at the Ivorian public. 'This is a criminal trial. This is not a political demonstration. This is not a game in which one side wants to win, and the other side shall be defeated. The people of Côte d'Ivoire are not on

---

176 Official transcript, ICC, 28 January 2016.

trial. Rather, this is a trial dealing with two individuals who have been charged by the office of the prosecutor with a number of crimes.'

Then he asks the court officer to read the charges. Gbagbo is taking off his glasses and listens with attention to the accusations made against him. The charges haven't changed much since the beginning of the proceedings. The former president is held criminally responsible for crimes against humanity committed by the pro-Gbagbo forces during four incidents – all in Abidjan. Count one: the murder of at least 160 people. Count two: the rape of at least 38 women and girls. Count three: other inhumane acts, causing great suffering and serious injuries, or attempted murder, involving at least 118 persons. Count four: persecution on political, national, ethnic and religious grounds against at least 316 persons.

Gbagbo raises his thumb, silently requesting the judges whether he can be excused. While the guards sitting next to him start discussing, the suspect doesn't want to waste more time and simply gets up to go to the sanitary facilities. Surprisingly, he walks much better than he used to.

The judges have also decided there is 'sufficient evidence to establish substantial grounds to believe,' as it is officially formulated, that Charles Blé Goudé is 'individually criminally responsible' for the following crimes against humanity committed by pro-Gbagbo forces: murder of at least 184 persons, the rape of 38 persons, other inhumane acts which caused great suffering and serious injury to 126 persons, and persecution of 348 persons. As Blé Goudé is charged for an extra incident, the number of victims in his case is higher.

Then Tarfusser asks: 'Mr Gbagbo, do you plead guilty or not guilty?'

The former president gets up and says in French: 'I plead not guilty.'

With the same question the judge turns to the co-accused. 'Thank you, your Honour. I do not recognize these charges and, therefore, I plead not guilty,' says Blé Goudé.

Tarfusser replies: 'Thank you very much.'

Before the prosecutor can start with her presentation, Gbagbo's defence team first raises several matters such as their objections against the role and position of the legal representative of victims, the huge volume of evidence amounting to 70,000 pages of documents and several hundred hours of footage and the high number of witnesses: 138. (This is equal to the total sum of witnesses in the trials against Thomas Lubanga, Germain Katanga, Mathieu Ngudjolo Chui, Jean-Pierre Bemba Gombo, Joshua

Sang and William Ruto). The discussion takes considerable time. When the hearing is briefly suspended for the coffee break, Blé Goudé is smiling to his supporters on the public gallery, while Gbagbo sends them an elegant hand kiss.

Forbidden dialogue

It is past noon when Bensouda is given the floor for her opening statement. Again she choses to begin in French, so her message can be directly understood in Ivory Coast: 'Let me be very clear right from the start, the purpose of this case is not to determine who won the elections in 2010, nor who should have won the elections.' She lectures that the 'purpose' of the trial is to establish 'individual criminal responsibility' of the two people accused, for atrocities committed by the pro-Gbagbo forces that included: the army, gendarmerie, police, republican guard, young patriots, militia and mercenaries. Their goal: 'to maintain Laurent Gbagbo in power no matter what.'

On the public gallery the visitors sigh loudly, while the court's security officers are on alert. One of the guards is standing with a stern face, his hands on his belt like a cowboy, next to the Ivorians. It is forbidden for the public to make noise, to talk loudly, to wave or point at people. Bensouda traces the conflict back to 2000 when Gbagbo won the elections and became president. From that moment he 'intended to stay in power by all means,' she says, using a phrase the prosecution will keep on repeating. This included resorting to violence. 'He relied on discriminatory laws to prevent his political opponents from standing in elections. He signed peace treaties, but obstructed their implementation.' As president and commander-in-chief Gbagbo had control over the FDS security forces. When it was clear he was going to lose the presidency during the 2010 elections, he launched a 'campaign of orchestrated attacks' against those whom he framed as his opponents: supporters of presidential candidate Alassane Ouattara and people who were perceived as belonging to the opposition because of their ethnic origin, religion and nationality – the Dioula, Muslims and persons originating from countries like Mali and Burkina Faso.

On the public gallery Ivorians start jeering. A spontaneous unpermitted dialogue develops between the prosecutor and the visitors, who are separated by the bulletproof glass. 'Ssssshhhh,' somebody is warning the others to be silent.

As usual during high profile hearings, Bensouda makes a more general statement: 'We are here today to send a very strong message to all those who plot to take power and to maintain themselves in power through the use of force and brutality' because 'they must and will be held to account for their acts' in accordance with the Rome Statute.

Then she switches to English and touches upon a sensitive issue: 'why the prosecution has charged these two men and not others, yet.' Not all the victims during the post-election violence were harmed by the pro-Gbagbo camp. The forces fighting for Ouattara are accused of massive atrocities as well. The prosecutor doesn't say it explicitly, but the reality is that because they emerged from the power struggle as the winners and now govern the country, the ICC apparently hasn't been able to charge anyone from that side. However, Bensouda reassures: 'My office is investigating both sides of the conflict. And this is what the office's legal mandate requires, this is what the victims deserve, and that is what the prosecution is committed to and is working to achieve.'

During the press conference a day earlier the prosecutor said that 'only last year I was able to intensify' the investigations in the pro-Ouattara camp. 'I can tell you it's ongoing and it has been intensified,' she added. Now addressing the court, she explains such efforts take time. 'I encourage the people of Côte d'Ivoire to be patient, and I urge the national authorities to continue to cooperate with my office in its activities. My office will seek to ensure justice and accountability on all sides.' But the visitors in the public gallery don't buy her promise and express their disbelief with a loud 'Non!'

Spin doctor

She turns to Blé Goudé. He was Gbagbo's 'mouthpiece, his spin doctor' proud to 'spin' the president's messages to 'mobilise the masses and to issue *mot d'ordres* or instructions.' Blé Goudé was the leader of the 'Jeunes Patriotes' and proclaimed himself as the 'général de la rue.' When used by a charismatic person, words can have tremendous power. 'He manipulated the youth with hateful rhetoric, identifying Ouattara supporters as the enemy and the legitimate targets for attack, claiming a version of patriotism that was a cover for persecution. He spread the belief that Mr Gbagbo's supporters were the true patriots, the real Ivorians. Everyone else was an enemy of the republic, a message that was repeated over and over through the state-controlled and other pro-Gbagbo media.' When Blé Goudé called upon the youth, they acted.

Bensouda confirms that her team will call 138 witnesses. Contrary to rumour, no witness had withdrawn from her list, the prosecutor had said earlier during the press conference. Her office will call victims, researchers and filmmakers to testify, but also insider witnesses who were close to the accused, such as politicians, FDS officers, militia, youth and mercenaries. Investigators and other ICC staff will describe the crime scenes they examined and photographed. The prosecution will also rely on official documents from the FDS and government, footage from the state-owned Radio Télévision Ivoirienne (RTI), videos taken by witnesses during the violence and documents found in Gbagbo's presidential palace. Experts will testify on issues such as ballistics, digital forensics, DNA analysis and forensic pathology.

To give the court and the audience an idea of what happened during those dreadful days, she describes the story of P-350, who was a supporter of Ouattara's political party, the Rassemblement des Républicains (RDR). On 16 December 2010 the witness joined the famous march towards the headquarters of the RTI. 'Because of her political affiliation, she was arrested by the gendarmerie,' Bensouda tells. For three days she was held separately with other women. 'During those three dark days, she was gang-raped at the prefecture of the police by armed gendarmes, whose very job it was to protect civilians from violence. The other women detained with her were also repeatedly gang-raped.'

The rapes and the many other atrocity crimes were never investigated by the Gbagbo regime, says Bensouda. The former president never ordered a stop to the murder, sexual violence, shelling and persecution of civilians 'carried out in his name.' This trial, Bensouda says, is about 'obtaining justice for the many hundreds of victims' of the post-election violence and to ensure there is 'no impunity for those responsible for such crimes, regardless of their power or position.'

It is the 'first case to reach trial' with regard to Ivory Coast. 'There will be others,' Bensouda reiterates her office's commitment to prosecute those most responsible for the post-election violence, no matter what 'political affiliation or side.' She concludes: 'We will not falter, Mr President, until this work is done.'

Technological hiccups

Her colleague, trial lawyer Eric MacDonald, a man with fairly long hair, a grey beard and dark brown moustache, will take care of the more detailed outline of the evidence. But the brand new technology fails when he tries to show a video clip. The prosecution had tested the system beforehand to prevent such problems, but at the *moment suprême* the equipment doesn't work. 'It's too new for our age,' Tarfusser jokes.

When it is clear the problem can't be fixed quickly, the judge suspends the hearing so that everybody can take a lunch break. When back in the courtroom, the problems are still not resolved. 'It worked five minutes ago, before entering now, so I don't understand,' MacDonald laughs away his irritation and embarrassment. 'The images move, but the sound is not on.' The technician who arrives to help the prosecution out, bows politely to the judges before he walks to the computer. When he is checking and pushing buttons, Bensouda looks on with great attention. 'Probably it's us,' says Tarfusser, trying to kill the time with another joke, 'who have the negative impact on the technology.'

Suddenly a loud '*VOUS AVEZ*!' bangs through the headphones, followed by silence. While hanging over the table lectern MacDonald says: 'It seems now the computer is frozen.' But a second later the situation has changed. 'Oh, it's unfrozen?' he says. 'We're playing the video.'

With a strong voice a confident president Gbagbo is addressing a large crowd of dignitaries and security forces in Ivory Coast, during one of the days he was still in power. The difference between the energetic man on the screen and the silent man in the dock is quite amazing. Gbagbo is heard saying: 'You are fighters for republican legality, as simple as that. When you are told that the republic is under threat, that's your cue to come forward and restore order in the republic. If there are any damages, the judges will put things right afterwards.' For people who aren't experts in Ivorian matters it is not immediately clear what makes these statements so dangerous. But MacDonald explains that this clip shows that 'Gbagbo was telling his subordinates to defend the republic, and that his political opponents are the enemies.' The security forces didn't need to worry about repercussions for their violent acts against their opponents, because in case of 'transgressions' the Ivorian courts would deal with it. With this speech, the prosecutor alleges, 'Gbagbo was giving, in effect, carte blanche to the FDS to commit crimes.'

Rise to power

In the biography that follows, MacDonald underlines that because it had taken Gbagbo 'so many years to reach the presidency,' he did not want to let go when he finally was in power. After the trial lawyer has given a lengthy explanation of how the pro-Gbagbo forces operated, he digs into history to give more context to the violence. The public will be getting a lecture about the power struggle among the big men of Ivory Coast. MacDonald traces the discriminatory poison that pitted ethnic groups against each other back to the nineties. It was the then president Henri Konan Bédié who introduced the concept of 'Ivoirité', which 'distinguishes between those considered to be native or pure Ivorians, predominantly southern and Christian, and those who were described as non-native, usually of northern origin and of Muslim faith.' Interestingly, Bédié partly developed the concept to undermine his political rival: Mr Ouattara, who was labelled a foreigner.

At the time Gbagbo and Ouattara were 'temporarily in alliance' against Bédié. Indeed, in 1995 Gbagbo 'spoke out against ethnically divisive policies such as Ivoirité.' Bédié was overthrown in 1999 by a coup led by general Robert Guëï, who organised elections the following year. During the 2000 polls, from which Ouattara was 'excluded from standing on the grounds of ethnicity,' Gbagbo emerged the winner. However his direct predecessor, general Guëï, refused to go. Then Gbagbo 'used the power of street protests' and called on 'Ivorian patriots from all cities and neighbourhoods' to continue their protest until his victory was recognized, lectures MacDonald.

Gbagbo became president. But when the opposition continued protesting, he accused them of trying to topple him. The new president took measures, announced a curfew and said that 'police, gendarmes and soldiers from all branches of the armed forces are ordered to use all means throughout the country to oppose troublemakers,' the prosecution tells. While part of the population felt sidelined, in September 2002 rebels from within the armed forces attempted a coup d'état against the Gbagbo government. They succeeded in the city of Bouaké in the north of Côte d'Ivoire, but failed in Abidjan. The conflict divided the country. The north was held by the rebels and the south by Gbagbo's forces. The French intervened. By 2004 a UN-peacekeeping force was deployed in the middle of the country. 'During this conflict, both sides committed crimes against civilians,' says MacDonald in a rare admission that the northern forces were no saints either. As the trial is focused on the two suspects, the prosecution's address is only about the atrocities by Gbagbo's forces, who back in those days allegedly paid militia to kill and rape civilians, while death squads carried out political assassinations. Peace agreements were undermined.

While the two suspects are listening concentrated to this history lesson, the Ivorian visitors at the public gallery become increasingly irritated. '*Ils sont fous* – they are crazy,' grumbles a man. While the guard is standing with his arms crossed, watching the Ivorians, another Gbagbo supporter says: 'They are not honest.'

What MacDonald basically says is that Gbagbo and his inner circle had ten years of experience in suppressing, attacking, killing and retaliating when they were preparing themselves for the elections. Early August 2010 Gbagbo promotes senior FDS commanders to the highest military rank. Two days later Ivory Coast is celebrating its 50th anniversary of the independence. During a speech before foreign and national dignitaries, Gbagbo calls on the army's loyalty saying: 'If I fall, you fall too.' According to MacDonald the true meaning of that phrase is: 'If Gbagbo lost the elections, the generals would lose their positions. Why? Because the rebel forces would take over positions within the FDS.'

Gbagbo's logbook

One of the trophies of the prosecution is the visitors logbook fom the presidential residence. This register holds the names of Gbagbo's guests and the length of their visit. It helps the OTP to establish what happened during the crucial period when the crimes this trial deals with, were planned and committed. 'The logbook indicates which inner circle members met with Mr Gbagbo when and for how long,' says MacDonald. He takes the audience through the appointments. On 29 November 2010, during the second election round, Blé Goudé visits Gbagbo. The following evening the youth leader returns, but this time his visit coincides with that of general Dogbo Blé. The two stay from seven until midnight. Other key members of the inner circle, such as chief of staff Mangou, come to see Gbagbo as well.

The president of the Constitutional Council visits him on 3 December 2010 in the morning and four hours later declares Gbagbo the winner of the elections. According to the logbook the head of state then meets with the FDS high command who 'confirmed their allegiance.' The next day Gbagbo is sworn in as president by the chair of the Conseil Constitutionnel. MacDonald: 'The ceremony took place at the presidential palace before ministers, dignitaries, and the high command of the FDS, among others.' When Gbagbo appoints his new cabinet, Blé Goudé becomes minister of youth, vocational training and employment – despite the fact that the youth leader was on the UN sanctions list for 'inciting the youth to violence and hatred.' His appointment 'conveyed a message of impunity' says MacDonald, 'to the youth galvanized to action by his rhetoric and *mots d'ordre*.'

By then it is four o'clock in the afternoon. 'We should close now for today, adjourn the hearing to tomorrow morning at 9.30,' says Tarfusser. It has been a long and intense day. The supporters at the public gallery get up, walk to the huge bulletproof window and start waving to the two suspects. '*Courage! Courage!*' they shout in French. Gbagbo laughs and waves back. His compatriots react with applauding for him. They throw their arms in the air and loudly encourage their man in the dock: '*Gbagbo, Président!*' Others shout accusations against the prosecution: 'They are liars! It is a corrupted lot!' Down in the courtroom, just before the curtain is closed, a broad smiling Blé Goudé is seen holding up his fist and then bringing his hand to his heart.

The first incident

The next morning MacDonald continues his dark tale of Ivory Coast, which by then had two rival governments. He will go through five incidents that the prosecution has selected to focus its case on. The Radio Télévision Ivoirienne (RTI) was of 'crucial strategic importance' for the Gbagbo regime, which had always used the station for broadcasting its messages, MacDonald explains.[177] Control was vital. But Guillaume Soro, the prime minister of the new internationally recognized Ouattara government, announces on 13 December 2010 he will install a new RTI director. He calls on his supporters 'to march peacefully' to the media organisation, located in the Cocody neighbourhood, on 16 December. The Gbagbo regime however was not going to have its major media outlet taken away. MacDonald tells how FDS units surround and blockade the Hotel du Golf where Ouattara's government was based. This is where

---

177 Official transcript, ICC, 29 January 2016.

allegedly Blé Goudé's responsibility comes in as he mobilized his 'Jeunes Patriotes' to help the military blocking the march. The youth minister appears on RTI television issuing a rather disguised warning, which the prosecution deems important for its case. Blé Goudé says: 'I would like to reassure the young people of Côte d'Ivoire, you have not lost your general. I am a 100 percent general and 1 percent minister. That clearly means I'm working to provide employment to young people. But at the same time, if I sense that my country has come under threat, that someone is trying to destabilize my country, I take off my suit, I put on my black hat, and I get things under control. I take charge. That needs to be clear in everybody's mind.'

During a rally in those frantic days Blé Goudé stirs up emotions. He accuses the UN-peacekeeping force and France of preparing a 'genocide' and organising the rebellion against Gbagbo. He tells a crowd he would 'dislodge' Soro and Ouattara '*à mains nues*' (with bare hands), without the use of weapons.

A climate of fear is installed, while the security forces prepare themselves. On the news the military spokesperson says the pro-Ouattara demonstrations are 'serious disturbances of the public order.' He warns that the march to the RTI is a trap, designed so that the security forces will end up clashing with the people of Côte d'Ivoire. Gbagbo meets the chiefs of the army, gendarmerie and police. All forces are getting ready. 'Your Honours, these coordinated efforts by Mr Gbagbo, Blé Goudé and the inner circle led to the commission of the crimes as charged in relation to the first incident of 16 December,' says MacDonald.

That morning demonstrators gather across Abidjan and begin their march. Gbagbo's forces are in key positions. They have set up 'checkpoints at roadblocks on the major access leading to the RTI' and are patrolling many areas in the city, says the prosecution. When the civilians start marching they are arrested, beaten, shot and detained. MacDonald plays a video showing people marching when heavy gun shooting is heard. 'Pro-Gbagbo forces opened fire on crowds of demonstrators in numerous locations in Abidjan,' the trial lawyer says, 'causing death and grave bodily injuries.' The images are followed by terrible scenes of protesters desperately shouting that people have been killed. A wounded person is taken in a car. A dead man lies on the street.

On the public gallery, the images stir commotion. Some Ivorians even start clapping, while below in the courtroom MacDonald tells that many women were raped. 'The violent crackdown of Mr Ouattara's supporters carried on in the following days,' he says. While the international community and human rights organisations protested against the violence, Gbagbo's inner circle insisted that their man was the legitimate president and 'that the sovereignty of the Republic of Côte d'Ivoire was at risk, that Gbagbo's supporters suffered an existential threat – meaning they were facing genocide – that they had to protect themselves and the country,' MacDonald tells.

After the incident there are daily rallies where Gbagbo, youth leaders and others address large crowds of youngsters to mobilise them. Security forces and government spokespersons go on radio and television to legitimise their actions while denying responsibility for any crimes, the prosecution alleges. Blé Goudé accuses the French president and the UN of supporting the rebels and blames them for the violence during the demonstration. When the human rights division of the UN's peacekeeping mission reports on the many human rights abuses since the RTI march, including 173 summary executions, there is a flat-out denial from Gbagbo's minister of interior.

Five years later however, Gbagbo and Blé Goudé find themselves as suspects facing trial in the ICC courtroom. For this first incident both men are charged with crimes against humanity. They are held responsible for the killing by pro-Gbagbo forces of at least 45 people in Abidjan, the rape of 16 women and girls, and wounding 54 people. These crimes occurred during and after the march to the RTI headquarters, between 16 and 19 December 2010.

The second incident

Only Blé Goudé is charged for the second incident. On 24 February 2011 the youth minister is on the RTI's evening news urging young people to stop the UN from driving and moving through Abidjan. He also calls on his followers to take part, the following evening, in a mass meeting at bar 'Le Baron' in the suburb Yopougon. After that Blé Goudé visits Gbagbo in his presidential residence, where he briefly meets the chief of staff of the army as well. On 25 February it is crowded in Le Baron as lots of young people gather. Blé Goudé is holding a speech ordering the youngsters to 'check the comings and goings in their neighbourhood and to report any stranger or foreigner entering their neighbourhoods,' says

MacDonald. The youth minister then moves to a next meeting where he repeats his calls. His orders are followed up, says the prosecution. Immediately pro-Gbagbo youth begin throwing stones at other youngsters in Doukouré, a neighbourhood of Yopougon. Units from the police, FDS and militia members join firing grenades. At least 13 members of the local community are killed. Half of them are burned to death. Roadblocks are set up, houses searched and the violence continues. Blé Goudé was 'never far from events,' says MacDonald. While his supporters are burning a youngster from Doukouré just outside the police station, the suspect drives by and stops for a few moments. Upon seeing the motorcade of four-wheel drive vehicles, his youth chant his nickname: '*Géneral, Géneral, Géneral.*' Some even run after the motorcade when it starts leaving the scene.

Later the Ivorian police would write a report about the searches by Blé Goudé's Jeunes Patriotes, stating: 'While they were looking for weapons and rebels, as soon as any individual seemed to them to be suspicious, he was automatically lynched and set alight.' MacDonald: 'Your Honours, the evidence will show that this initiator was no other than the accused Blé Goudé.' During speeches he would congratulate the youth for their work. 'He encouraged them to continue fighting and manning the roadblocks because they were, effectively, discouraging the rebels,' the trial lawyer states.

With regard to the incidents between 25-28 February, the prosecution holds Blé Goudé responsible for the killing of at least 24 persons and the wounding of at least seven persons, who primarily came from northern Côte d'Ivoire and neighbouring West African countries and were staying in Yopougon.

The third incident

While the violence at the roadblocks is continuing, the third incident takes place for which both Gbagbo and Blé Goudé are charged. On 3 March 2011 more than three thousand women gather for a peaceful demonstration in Abobo, the northern suburb of Abidjan. They call for Gbagbo to step down and to end the atrocities. MacDonald shows a video clip of women singing, blowing whistles and carrying twigs with leaves and placards calling Gbagbo a thief and murderer. The crowd has an enormous energy. But then an FDS convoy of five vehicles passes by.

There is a loud sound. People are running away in panic. Chaotic images show clothes left on the street.

The trial lawyer warns that the next video contains images that might shock. The clip shows dead bodies on the street and women with gaping wounds. The twigs with green leaves are covered in blood. When a women is lifted, and then put down again, visitors at the public gallery start laughing, because they hear that she is told to lie down. It reinforces their conviction that the images are fabricated.

MacDonald explains that the sound came from a vehicle which is seen in the video. Showing a picture of four screenshots he points to the smoke from a cannon after it fired. 'Seven women were killed as a result of this brutal shooting by the FDS units in the convoy. Several others were injured,' he alleges. There is however 'complete denial' in response to 'this horrific crime,' says the trial lawyer. The following day the RTI denounced 'the incident as a set-up, a montage, even claiming that these images were fake,' MacDonald explains. He adds: 'What did the commander-in-chief of the army, Mr Gbagbo, say or do in the face of such violence? Nothing.' He quotes Blé Goudé, who would later say that the FDS 'could not be responsible' because Abobo 'was in rebel hands at the time.'

The prosecution holds both Gbagbo and Blé Goudé responsible for the death of seven women and the wounding of at least three persons who had participated in the women's demonstration in Abobo, on 3 March 2011.

The fourth incident

Abobo would be targeted again, two weeks later, on 17 March. According to the prosecutor the FDS launched mortar shells onto the heart of the neighbourhood. MacDonald sounds increasingly outraged as he tells how a young mother and her five-year-old son were walking down the street when a shell landed right in front of them. 'Her body was riddled with shrapnel, but she survived,' he says. The trial lawyer intends to show a picture of the child, but requests a break 'because we have a technical problem.'

Back in court MacDonald explains that he had discussed the matter with his colleagues and they decided to show the picture later during the trial, but not now. Instead he tells how the mother saw injured and dead people everywhere, while she looked for her son. 'When I saw him, I saw that his nose had been blown off and a bullet had hit his head. Some of his brains were coming out. He was in the middle of the bodies of other people. He had just time to say 'Momma' and then he died,' MacDonald quotes her testimony. The victims were just ordinary civilians. 'They were targeted because they lived in Abobo and were therefore identified by Mr Gbagbo and his inner circle as the enemy, as perceived supporters of Mr Ouattara,' he says.

The prosecution is holding both suspects responsible for the killing of at least forty people and wounding at least sixty persons in or near the Abobo market, caused by the shelling of that busy area.

Fifth Incident

The end was near. From the north the 'Forces Nouvelles,' supporting Ouattara, had made their way to the south. By 31 March they marched into the country's main city. What followed became known as 'the battle of Abidjan.' Gbagbo had taken shelter in his residence, while there were rumours that Blé Goudé had fled to Ghana. It was a confusing time. Early April the RTI had been broadcasting at least three videos and messages with the youth minister claiming he had not left the country, and encouraging his followers 'to reinforce the roadblocks and continue fighting alongside the FDS.'

Members of the inner circle and the pro-Gbagbo forces continued to use the RTI to spread their message. 'They even asked civilians to go to Mr Gbagbo's residence to serve as a human shield,' says MacDonald. On 9 April 2011 there is a communiqué from the presidential residence saying that Gbagbo 'sympathized with the suffering' caused by Ouattara and his 'terrorists', encouraging people to keep up the fight. Two days later, after the bombardment of the residence, the Forces Nouvelles arrest the former president and members of his inner circle, who had been hiding in an underground bunker.

The crimes did not stop though. 'The common plan continued to be implemented,' says MacDonald. The forces loyal to Gbagbo were attacking neighbourhoods in Yopougon. The youth, militia and mercenaries forced their way into homes and assaulted civilians in the streets. Armed with Kalashnikovs and machetes they killed men identified as enemies. Women and girls were raped. Some mothers were violated in front of their children.

Witness P-185 was still a minor when she was raped by two Gbagbo supporters in her house. The fighters then abducted her father and two other men, threatening to kill them. 'P-185 never saw her father again,' says MacDonald. Then he plays a video which shows 34 bodies, which were found in a mass grave, now lying in a row covered by sheets and clothing.

Although Gbagbo had been arrested the day before and Blé Goudé had indeed fled the country, both suspects are charged with crimes against humanity committed in Yopougon on 12 April. They are held responsible for the rape of at least 22 women, the wounding of at least two persons and the killing of at least 68 people who primarily hailed from northern Côte d'Ivoire and neighbouring West African countries.

MacDonald is almost done with his opening statement, which is 80 pages long. Fitting the legal definition of crimes against humanity, the trial lawyer describes these last atrocities as a continuation of the 'common plan' to commit 'a widespread or systematic attack against perceived Ouattara supporters,' developed by the two accused which by 27 November 2010 had become a 'state policy.'

Breaking the silence

During one of the breaks I briefly meet Fanta Doumbia, a human rights activist from Ivory Coast. It is 'a relief' for victims that the trial has finally started, she says. But Doumbia underlines that with Gbagbo and Blé Goudé on trial the job is only half done. 'The court is about finding the truth. But if only one side is prosecuted, we will not know the whole truth. The two sides of the conflict will have to be prosecuted so that all victims get justice.' She also believes that when both sides are put on trial, the people might change their opinion about the court. 'Many see these trials as victor's justice. Therefore opinions are very polarised in Côte d'Ivoire.'

She has been following the hearing from the public gallery. At times it has been a painful experience seeing fellow Ivorians laughing about rape testimonies and gruesome videos of attacks and killings shown by the prosecutor. 'It is disturbing to see people reacting in such manner to victims who were hurt and even lost their lives.' She wants the trial to continue and hopes the court will expand the case with charges against the pro-Ouattara forces. 'Even an arrest warrant against a suspect from the other camp would be of great help to calm things down,' says Doumbia.

In the courtroom Paolina Massidda explains she is the legal representative of 726 women, men and children who have been registered as victims. The real number of victims in Ivory Coast is far greater, but to be able to be represented before the ICC, their suffering must be directly connected to the charges. People who were harmed during the many other violent incidents can't be registered for the trial, let alone the people who are victims of pro-Ouattara forces.

Massidda recalls that her clients suffered immensely. 'Sometimes they were kidnapped, tortured, detained without any reason for weeks in police stations and detention centres. Others saw their sons, daughters, mother, father, uncle, aunt, neighbour, brother or sister shot in cold blood. Sometimes right in front of them before their very eyes during attacks that took place in public places, in places of worship, in their homes or on their own property.' People were targeted because they were Muslim, or belonged to ethnic groups such as Dioula, Mossi, Senoufo and Baoulé, or were migrants from countries such as Mali, Burkina Faso and Niger. Entire communities had to go in hiding.

When she gives a historical overview of the country, Gbagbo leaves the courtroom for his sanitary break. This time he will stay away for quite a while. What most victims hope is to 'break 'the silence' about the horrible events they experienced. It is silence that prevents the acknowledgement of their suffering. 'Speaking out is the first step to establishing truth and providing access to justice,' the victim's lawyer says.

It has been very difficult for people to rebuild their lives. 'They have been traumatised by what they have experienced, and that still makes up a large part of their daily lives. It means that they are lifelong victims,' the lawyer says. Despite their continuing suffering they haven't had any 'real assistance' from the authorities. They still live in the areas where they were attacked. In the mixed neighbourhoods of Abidjan, victims are 'cohabiting with their tormentors.' Not only do they suffer 'constant re-victimisation' but also their safety and security is 'highly precarious.' Her clients are also disappointed in the Commission for Dialogue, Truth and Reconciliation (CDVR) that was set up by the current government of Ivory Coast. Reparations remain a 'pipe dream,' says Massidda. 'Because of the failures at the national level, the victims place all of their hopes in the ICC so that at last the truth will be out.'

'Heartfelt tribute'

A very pleased Tarfusser reflects on the last two days during which the prosecutor 'had about six hours' while the lawyer representing 'more than 700 victims did everything in 50 minutes.' He compliments Massidda for being 'to the point' expressing the views and concerns of her clients, without acting as 'a second prosecution position.' It is Friday, lunch time and almost weekend. The judge adjourns the hearing to Monday when the defence will start its opening statements.

But just before the curtains close, the Ivorians hurry to the huge window that separates them from the courtroom, to start the ritual of raising their hands and fists. Others make the V-sign for victory and peace. Then suddenly they loudly start singing a tribute to their two leaders now at trial.

Fiers Ivoiriens, le pays nous appelle
Si nous avons, dans la paix, ramené la liberté
Notre devoir sera d'être un modèle
De l'espérance promise à l'humanité
En forgeant, unis dans la foi nouvelle
La patrie de la vraie fraternité.

When the crowd gets to the end of the national anthem, two women start cheering: '*Libérez Gbagbo! Libérez Gbagbo!*' Below in the courtroom the former president is happily waving, while Blé Goudé looks up and smiles. A few minutes later in the main hall, a defence lawyer will say it was a 'heartfelt' tribute after 'all the accusations' they had to listen to during the last two days. Pierrette Blé Hammar firmly believes in the innocence of her brother and her president. 'They haven't done anything wrong. When your country is attacked, you have to defend it. They are in favour of peace, so why are they treated liked criminals,' she says. In her opinion 'the prosecution has no proof. We are sure they will be released,' she says before embracing another supporter. The atmosphere among the Ivorians is one of relaxation. People are discussing, hugging and taking selfies before they put on their winter-coats to brave the cold outside.

Gbagbo is a true democrat

Immediately after the hearing is opened on Monday morning, maître Altit is standing behind the lectern for his opening statements. The

French lawyer starts with the description of the last dramatic days in April 2011 when his client, former president Laurent Gbagbo, is still hiding in the presidential residence in Abidjan. For days French helicopters have been flying over, launching grenades, until that morning, at 11 hours, the 'entire residence is hit.' The gateways are broken down. French snipers are firing from nearby. The people in the residence, including families with women and children, 'are terrorized,' says Altit. 'They flee to the basement and await the final assault.'[178]

With a touch of cynicism the counsel explains that when French commandos storm the building, it will take them 'a good two hours' to 'fetch the first soldiers from the pro-Ouattara army who had been so busy looting the neighbourhoods in the north of Abidjan.' When the rebel forces finally enter the residence and seize Gbagbo, it is complete mayhem. Inside, many people are beaten or injured. 'Some were murdered by pro-Ouattara mercenaries and soldiers. Others were saved at the very last minute by French soldiers,' the lawyer tells. Initially supporters of Gbagbo frowned when they heard maître Altit would be the lead counsel, because he is French and might still not be free of colonial thinking. He was also seen of being too close to former president Nicolas Sarkozy, who is said to be good friends with Ouattara. The fans doubted whether he would be able to put up a good defence for Gbagbo which should include fierce criticism of the French authorities and their Ivorian ally. But their distrust vanished when they saw that Altit's team is committed to this case.

The defence team will show how wrong and untrue the prosecution has been in its claims that Gbagbo is a power thirsty despot and in its accusations that his forces attacked, terrorized, raped and killed innocent civilians. The reality is completely the opposite. Four defence lawyers will present their case with a massive load of history and video montage. It is a presentation that doesn't have a very clear structure, involving a lot of repetition and going back and forth in time. But the heart of the matter is the claim: Gbagbo's security forces were protecting the people, while the pro-Ouattara rebels were committing the violence. 'Rewriting history the way the prosecution has, is not only an attack upon the truth, it is an

---

178 Official transcript, ICC, 1 February 2016.

attack upon the people of Côte d'Ivoire, what they have suffered, what they experienced,' lead counsel Altit argues.

What happened is that 'spin doctors' working for Ouattara had conducted a 'smear campaign' against Gbagbo to make 'him out to be some kind of demon,' while Ouattara himself was presented as the 'good guy' and 'the legitimate leader of the country.' This was just a 'storyline' to make 'the new government seem legitimate', but legally it made no sense, says Altit. The reality is that Gbagbo is a 'true democrat' who 'struggled all his life' for a multiparty system in Côte d'Ivoire, Altit argues. He is a man who stuck to his principles and sacrificed himself as he went to prison and into exile. A man who knows that 'to build a country, you have to find a way to allow people to live together.' He did 'all he could to reunify the country, to restore the rule of law in the north and ensure national reconciliation,' Altit explains. While his lead counsel is telling his side of history, Gbagbo listens with great interest.

Interestingly, the defence strategy is largely focused on criticizing Ouattara and his forces, emphasizing the part that is missing from the prosecution's theory of the case. The presentation is a lot about the past as well. When legal assistant Jennifer Naouri describes Ouattara's curriculum vitae, she says he had been 'a Burkinabé citizen,' a very sensitive issue which had previously been used to bar him from participating in elections in Ivory Coast. But mostly she portrays him as an ally of France, the former colonial power that tried to keep Ivory Coast on a leash. With the help of the French he became prime minister in Ivory Coast in the nineties. He introduced privatisations from which multinationals and French business benefitted. While in office Ouattara suppressed the democratic opposition. Naouri recalls that in 1992 he had some 400 people arrested, including all opposition leaders and thus Gbagbo as well. After his attempt to take the presidency in 1993 failed, he fled the country. With the support of the French authorities he became deputy director general of the International Monetary Fund (IMF). Ouattara would come back though.

Armed rebel forces

The defence recalls that in December 2002, while Gbagbo is on a state visit in Italy, there is a putsch. The rebels take the north and 'ravage' the region. 'The main activity of these people was to engage in extortion, kill, rape people, and maintain terror amongst the population. Why? So as to line their own pockets,' Altit narrates. Despite their reputation, Ouattara would align himself with these northern rebels, who are 'the very same warlords who were involved in various attempts ever since the year 1999, to have Mr Ouattara come to power,' the lawyer underlines.

Just before the 2010 elections, with the backing of France, the Ouattara camp, which included warlords and 'hundreds of heavily armed mercenaries,' is allowed to set up its headquarter in Hotel du Golf in Abidjan. The campaign has France all written over it, the lawyers explain to the court. Ouattara has French bodyguards. The French ambassador visits him all the time. There are French logistical and financial resources. He has the support of French civilian and military advisors, spin doctors, while French friends fund the new pro-Ouattara TV station. 'The purpose of that television station was to call for civil disobedience and rioting,' Naouri says.

In the public gallery everybody is closely following the presentation. '*C'est la vérité*,' a visitor comments. It's the truth. The supporters of the two accused feel more at ease now that the defence is speaking. This is their storyline. 'It is going much better,' one man agrees. Blé Goudé listens with his hand under his chin and a finger before his lips. Gbagbo looks at the judges, and every now and then casts a look at his visitors. Prosecutor Bensouda is sitting undisturbed. Absorbing attacks on her investigations for being one-sided is part of the job. She takes notes, and every now and then she yawns. MacDonald is stroking his beard. Judge Henderson gently rubs his eyes, then puts his glasses back on and takes a sip of water. The Ivorian ambassador, a tall man sitting on the front row of the public gallery, constantly writes, just like his assistant.

One of the members of the defence is maître Agathe Bahi Baroan, a former member of the Constitutional Committee in Ivory Coast during the Gbagbo era. Being a lawyer from the country itself, she speaks with a different kind of authority. 'Your Honour, with all due respect I wish to pay my tribute to all the victims of the various armed crisis that have shattered Côte d'Ivoire since 1999,' she starts her part of the presentation. Maître Baroan explains that the people in her country 'are astonished' by the way the prosecution is handling the case. Although Bensouda's team has the task to investigate 'as completely and as impartially as possible,' it made a distinction between victims and has 'forgotten' about the people who suffered from the rebels.

Baroan refers to the massacres allegedly committed by pro-Ouattara forces in villages. She reminds the court of 'the hundreds of men, women and children' of Duékoué who 'were murdered most horribly.' Baroan tells how mercenary soldiers arrived in Abidjan, killing 'countless people' and engaging 'in a campaign of systematic rape.' Civilians were tortured and arrested. She blames Ouattara's warlords for the atrocities. Bensouda's team simply got it all wrong. 'You can see that the reality is the complete opposite of what the prosecution has said,' she states. While Ouattara's rebels were committing these atrocities, Gbagbo's forces of security 'were defending the local people.'

A second prosecutor

Detailing the crimes committed by the rebel forces, the defence starts to sound like a second prosecutor, but investigating the opposite camp. The lawyers describe several prominent rebels and warlords. Take Chérif Ousmane, who was called 'The Cleaner' by his soldiers. 'He's facing grave accusations because of his involvement in a number of massacres,' says Naouri. He took part in the final assault against Abidjan in March-April 2011, and his men are suspected of carrying out summary executions. Despite his ruthless reputation, on 3 August 2011 Ouattara promoted him to second in command of the security unit of the president of the republic.

The current situation is far from good. Baroan summarizes: 'More than 60,000 refugees live outside the country, and more than 20,000 people are displaced internally. There are hundreds of political opponents in prison, and when president Gbagbo was in power, there were no political opponents in prison. The people of Côte d'Ivoire are terrorized. The violence and the abuse continue. The rule of law is swept aside.'

The ambassador has stopped taking notes. Gbagbo's supporters have calmed down. Some of them live as refugees in Europe. Others have migrated long ago, but out of fear don't dare to visit family back home. One woman, who is from the north of the country, has just come out of prison in Ivory Coast – sentenced for political reasons, she says.

Lawyer Baroan says it is an 'incorrect and dangerous vision' to label the violence as an ethnic conflict, because it divides where there are no strict divisions and pits 'the south against the north, Christians against Muslims, Bété people against the Dioula.' This is not what Ivory Coast is about, she says, because people interact, mix and marry outside their group 'which provides for a very rich form of humanity.' Baroan takes her own family as an example. It includes Burkinabé, Wé, Malinké, Bété, Malians and people from Guinea, Cameroon, Germany and Belgium. 'We even have a Chinese person in our family,' she says. 'Myself, I see myself as Malinké and Bété. I consider myself to be a Christian, although my father was Muslim.' In other words: 'Ethnicity is not the key to understanding my country.'

'An insurrection'

When the defence evaluates the four incidents selected by the prosecutor in the case against Gbagbo, it's the 16 December march that receives most attention. This was 'not a peaceful' demonstration at all, says maître Altit. It was an attack that had been planned by Ouattara and his warlords. To back up this allegation, the defence team presents a video clip showing Guillaume Soro, prime minister at the time. The images will throw a different light on the organisers of the demonstration. Soro is supported by heavily armed rebel soldiers while he announces that the next day he will go to the RTI to appoint a new director general, snatching that important outlet from Gbagbo's regime. Then he orders the men: 'You have to prepare yourselves. You must mobilise on Thursday. We will be going to the television building. I am counting on you.' After that, rebel commander Wattao addresses his troops, who are standing in a tropical garden, with palm trees and a lagoon in the back. 'Morale, morale,' he shouts. When he is not satisfied with the reply by his men, he repeats his words. 'There you have it. The boss has spoken. For the moment we have nothing to say. We'll be ready for Thursday,' Wattao says. Another commander orders the men: 'Everyone is to be at the swimming pool in eight hours with all the military equipment. The fun is over.'

It puzzles the defence how the prosecution can maintain its theory that the Ouattara camp asked its supporters to 'demonstrate peacefully,' while these heavily armed rebels are getting ready for it. 'How can the prosecution claim that these images, this video footage of Guillaume Soro, providing instructions to the soldiers with their RPGs and Kalashnikovs didn't exist?' insists Naouri. The march was 'an insurrection' whereby rebel forces pulled up from the Hotel du Golf and other places in the city, opening the way for the protesters. 'The mercenaries, wearing civilian clothing, hid behind the demonstrators who were being used as a tool. They had actually been turned into human shields,' Altit explains.

The demonstrators weren't peace-loving either. 'They were bearing arms,' Naouri discloses. Defence witness D-30 told the lawyers he had seen 'many young people with machetes and sticks' marching along the road on their way to the RTI, calling slogans like 'the little Gbagbo followers will die.' The gathering of thousands of demonstrators was nothing more than a 'diversion.' The real purpose was 'to drive president Gbagbo out of power' at 'any price'. The rebel army launched 'a prepared, premeditated attack upon the forces of law and order,' Naouri adds. The fighting was violent. With a dozen deaths among their men, the national security forces paid a heavy price.

'Much remains vague'

Equally problematic is the prosecution's version of the women's march on 3 March, calling for Gbagbo to step down. Much remains vague about the demonstration, the lawyers claim. If you look at the footage this 'really doesn't seem to be a march with three thousand women.' But there is 'one particular anomaly,' says Naouri, referring to images showing a seemingly dead woman who tries to get up. Then another person gets up but a voice tells: 'Lie down. It's not over yet.' The defence finds it all very strange. If the woman 'was so badly injured, why wouldn't the person have tried to help her? She was clearly conscious. These various sequences seem to point towards a set-up, so to speak, something has been concocted.'

The defence also finds it 'difficult to understand' how the prosecution, with regard to the incident on 17 March 2011, accuses pro-Gbagbo soldiers of firing on 'a densely populated area in Abobo with a local market, a mosque, a hospital and private residences.' The lawyers need 'more information about the chronology' and the exact locations of the attack. Moreover, the shelling of Abobo has been dealt with by the Abidjan military tribunal, which acquitted the soldiers who were the alleged perpetrators because of lack of evidence. Naouri: 'How can one continue with charges here before the International Criminal Court when the direct perpetrators have already been acquitted?'

The prosecution's account about the attack on Yopougon, when Gbagbo was already captured in the presidential residence, is also 'quite vague.' It isn't even clear when and where exactly the attacks occurred, while 1,3 million people of mixed ethnic background are living in this suburb. In fact, the real story is very different from what the prosecution alleges, says Naouri. 'The people who committed the crimes in Yopougon after the fall of president Gbagbo, were the rebel forces who were wanting to install their leaders from the north in their new stronghold, and we shall demonstrate this.'

'A skewed version'

Naouri has presented most of the Gbagbo defence's case. Her French colleague, Dov Jacobs, will deal with the final matters. The true perspective on the whole affair is that Gbagbo was facing 'a rebellion and a foreign invasion,' he says. The Ivorian security forces and the civilian population were attacked by Ouattara's rebels from the north, and the authorities responded with 'legitimate legal constitutional means and resources.' The prosecution however sells a 'black and white version', a 'skewed version' of the post-electoral violence and the role played by Gbagbo.

Earlier the defence had quoted ICC pre-trial judge Christine van den Wyngaert who in June 2014 warned: 'In my opinion, there are no convincing items of proof showing that at any particular point in time Laurent Gbagbo decided, with his inner circle, to commit crimes against innocent civilians.' Coincidence or not, but a few moments later judge Van den Wyngaert was sitting in the last row of the public gallery, briefly listening to the trial.

Jacobs says there are also doubts about records that were seized from the presidential residence, such as the logbook. 'The prosecution has not demonstrated the authenticity of the documents and, as such, they must be set aside.' Equally 'groundless' and twisted are the allegations that Gbagbo made 'xenophobic speeches and incited people to violence.' The prosecution simply misquoted him. The story of the case 'is a semantic smoke screen serving to conceal the truth, the starting point of which is a hypothetical common plan, which has been constructed on the basis of thin air,' Jacobs argues.

It is half past three in the afternoon when the Gbagbo defence is wrapping up. The lawyers blame the violence on the Ouattara camp. They have described the other side of the conflict, which the prosecution left out from its account. It somehow highlights the problem with criminal proceedings, that create two opposing parties each giving their versions of what happened. If both accounts were put together, possibly one might get a more complete version of the modern history of Ivory Coast.

Judge Tarfusser announces that the next day the lawyers of Blé Goudé will present their case. 'Let me guess that probably you don't need the whole day because a lot has already been said.' Counsel Geert-Jan Alexander Knoops is already on his feet and switches on his microphone: 'Indeed, we will not repeat the arguments of the defence team of Mr Gbagbo, but still we estimate that we will probably need the full day.'

Bensouda excuses herself. The prosecutor tells the judges she won't be able to be present in court tomorrow. 'It is as a result of a prior commitment, which I have tried to change but could not.' At the public gallery the Ivorian visitors are jeering. 'She is ashamed because there are too many lies,' says someone. Another Gbagbo fan sneers: 'She is fleeing.'

'Thank you very much, Madame prosecutor,' says Tarfusser politely, unaware of the comments at the public gallery. When the judges have left the courtroom the discussion among the Ivorians continues. The sister of Blé Goudé repeats: 'Her case won't hold.'

'A man of peace'

Will he speak? Will the oratory talent from Ivory Coast, now sitting in the dock, address the court? Relief and pride are felt at the public gallery when defence counsel Knoops announces that his client Blé Goudé has indeed prepared a speech. But first his lawyers will explain what is wrong with the prosecution's case. The Dutch lawyer takes the court back to March 2011 and he quotes: 'To those who want to transform Ivory Coast into Rwanda, I say: "I don't want a civil war in this country".' These words were spoken by his client. He wanted the political stakeholders – Gbagbo, Ouattara – to sit together to solve the crisis.[179]

Knoops employs a strategy very different from that of the Gbagbo defence, who sought to attack the Ouattara camp. Instead, he has chosen to show that his client is a good man. When Knoops plays a TV interview, an energetic Blé Goudé appears on the screens. He is wearing a black cap and explains that an army can't give weapons to civilians when defending a country. Anyone who wants to pick up weapons has to join the army, which is the legitimate institution to use force. It brings Knoops to his point: is this the man who never instructed young people to stop committing violence, as the prosecution alleges? Why weren't

179 Transcript not available on ICC website.

these important words picked up by Bensouda's team? 'Because it did not fit their so-called common plan,' Knoops stresses. The prosecution has the facts 'wrong' and its case theory is 'not to be trusted' by the chamber. The truth is that Blé Goudé never instructed people to use violence, the defence lawyer says. What a difference with Guillaume Soro, who is seen addressing armed rebels 'to be ready' for the bloody march of 16 December 2010.

Knoops will prove his client is a man of peace and dialogue. He recalls that in 2009 – before the elections – the youth leader invited the American reverend and peace activist Jesse Jackson to Ivory Coast. Blé Goudé asked him to come and pray with all ethnic groups. He had one goal in mind: reconciliation. His intention was to reunite Ivorians and to overcome the political and ethnic differences that had split the country at the time, Knoops explains.

Defence witness D-9 will testify that Blé Goudé was perceived 'as too peaceful.' Rival organisations therefore refused to accept him as leader. Also prosecution witness P-156 recognises that he was 'never implicated in any violence.' Instead, Blé Goudé 'moved people with bare hands.' Knoops underlines he was 'a man of justice before the crisis, during the crisis and after the crisis.'

Neither is there a relation between his client and violence committed at the barricades. These were set up by civilians, who were so frightened when the rebels arrived in Abidjan, that they went into a 'psychoses of fear' and started to erect checkpoints. Blé Goudé however was not in a position to issue orders to youth organizations nor had he power over the checkpoints, the lawyer argues.

While Knoops is beefing up the image of his client, Blé Goudé sits calmly behind his lawyers, with the attitude of a statesman. Instead of inciting, the youth leader went to barricades to calm young people down, the lawyer tells. He even managed to organise from ICC detention peace meetings in June 2015 in Abidjan, in which all parts of Ivorian society and the international community participated.

His client was friends with Muslims and people from the north. For years he sheltered a woman from Burkina Faso. To support his claims Knoops presents a clip, where his client is seen visiting a community. While people are sipping coffee in an open-air venue, Blé Goudé addresses the audience with a fierce voice insisting that Muslims form part of the nation. 'It is with you that we defend Côte d'Ivoire,' the suspect is heard saying. In a following clip he is donating cement to a mosque.

Knoops says that his client's quest for reconciliation contrasts so strongly with the alleged common plan to keep Gbagbo in power, as developed by the prosecution, that it is simply impossible for Blé Goudé to have been part of it. 'The evidence will show there was no common plan. If there was a plan, we will show it was made by the Ouattara forces.'

Naked and beaten up

A shocking picture of Blé Goudé with a naked torso in a dark prison cell appears on the screens. His face looks swollen and beaten up. When the youth leader was imprisoned by Ivory Coast in January 2013, he was held in 'inhumane and degrading' circumstances before he was taken to the ICC, Knoops tells the court. A witness confirmed he had been 'tortured.' The abuse has wide implications. Any evidence from Ivory Coast should be treated 'with great circumspection,' the lawyer says, as it is likely to be biased.

He also criticizes the way the prosecutor has used the presidential visitors logbook as evidence. It just shows that the two suspects were in contact during the crisis. But not even that often. Over a period of 106 days

– from November 2010 until April 2011 – the name of Blé Goudé turns up only 18 times. 'It does not sustain the deduction that Blé Goudé was a prominent member of Gbagbo's inner circle,' Knoops stresses. Look at the registrations of 1 December. That day Guillaume Soro, the French ambassador and the representative of the Vatican are visiting Gbagbo. This refutes the 'thesis' that the logbook entries relate to an inner circle, 'unless these three people are part of this entourage,' mocks Knoops. 'No evidentiary conclusion can be drawn,' says the defence lawyer.

When Gbagbo gets up for his sanitary break, he taps Blé Goudé in a fatherly manner on the shoulder. As if he wants to say: no worries son, you will be fine. Altit looks confident when he casts an eye up to the public gallery. At the opposite side prosecutor MacDonald starts typing a message on his computer, while Knoops concludes: 'You saw Blé Goudé how he is. Not as the general de la rue in clownish clothes. But as the man who he is. The man who wants dialogue. It was his mission to turn the military page.'

I am Charles Blé Goudé

Finally the moment is there. 'You have authorisation, but I want to be clear, we are an international criminal court,' Tarfusser warns the next speaker. The lawyers quickly rearrange their desks and put the plexiglas table lectern in front of their client. Blé Goudé switches on his microphone. He adjusts his papers. He is smartly dressed, wearing a suit. Rimless reading glasses are resting on his nose. 'Mr President, your Honours, thank you for this opportunity,' he starts his address.

'I am Charles Blé Goudé,' says the man who doesn't need an introduction, introducing himself. Speaking calmly he takes the court on a trip through his country and his life. As a small boy he grew up with Muslims. He played with Muslim children. A woman who adopted him was Muslim, says Blé Goudé, while looking around. He is completely at ease addressing the judges and parties in the courtroom, deliberately inserting moments of silence to give his words more weight. For several minutes at a time he can speak by heart, before going back to his speech on paper. Showing the palms of his hands he says: 'I have no drop of blood on my hands.' While flexing his arms down, indicating there is a solid base, he adds: 'That's why I am in front of you with certainty and confidence.'

The suspect refers to the many critics in Africa who say that the ICC is 'a political court' condemning Africans before they are even judged. But Blé Goudé wants to make the judges a compliment. 'You have done quite well,' he says, 'from the start of this trial you indicated the impartiality of the court. That will reassure many people.'

But, he explains, because the prosecution is following the wrong storyline, a question came to haunt him during the night. 'I want to share it with you,' says Blé Goudé. Does the prosecutor look for the truth, or is it just about stigmatising and condemning a person at any price? Stressing that facts are sacred in the law, he says: 'We are not playing the lottery here.' Blé Goudé promises the prosecution it 'will learn a lot' during the proceedings. 'The truth will emerge from the ruins.'

He looks over his reading glasses and crosses his hands over his chest. Responding to the accusations that he incited people to hunt down pro-Ouattara supporters and kill them, he challenges his opponents: 'Let them show when I said it, what day and at which occasion.' The allegations simply can't be true, because in the middle of the crisis he had maintained that Côte d'Ivoire would always be a country with a mixed population. 'For me, the search for peace is not a seasonal thing. It is sincere.' The prosecution might call him 'an extremist' but the opposite is true. 'Yes, I say it without shame. I am afraid of the war,' states Blé Goudé, casting an eye at the public gallery where his supporters are listening in admiration.

A magnet

It is impossible to deny his power. Blé Goudé is a handsome man and a gifted speaker, blessed with a nice voice and enormous charisma. Self-confident, he looks the judges and prosecutors in the eye. There's not a moment of insecurity while he's pleading for himself in the official setting of the court. He is a magnet that attracts all attention. The prosecution's case is that he used these qualities for the wrong cause.

To back up his plea, Blé Goudé plays a clip of the 'Caravane de la Paix' which he organised in Côte d'Ivoire to promote peace. On the screens old images appear of the youth leader going around the country and speaking to people at gatherings. The voiceover is done by Blé Goudé himself, sounding a bit like a rapper. One of the persons in the video is a girl Prisca, who had been raped and was treated in hospital for months. It was her wish to have a house and a little shop. Blé Goudé helped her to make her dream come true. In the clip he is seen doing the official opening ceremony of the shop. 'These are the fruits of peace,' he is heard saying. Back addressing the court he points at his adversary, trial lawyer MacDonald. Although the prosecution might call him 'a criminal,' the reality is that he had helped Prisca and other victims. 'Between taking up arms or to do politics, I freely chose the second option,' he tells the court. 'For me democracy and weapons mix as badly as water and oil.' While throwing his arms in the air, he tells that when the country was in danger, he took the road of the 'bare hands.'

Briefly he describes his relationship with Gbagbo, who sits two metres away, watching the speech of his co-accused on the screen in front of him. He did not join the president because they are of the same ethnic group or religion, but because of his moral authority. 'Does the prosecution know that this sir has sacrificed his life for multipartyism and democracy?' Blé Goudé insists that Gbagbo never sent him to incite people or to commit crimes. Many Ivorians have 'respect and affection' for him, and they 'suffer' to see him here in the dock. 'Gbagbo doesn't have his place in prison.'

With interest, Tarfusser looks at Blé Goudé performing his speech. His lawyers follow his talk on the screens. Claver N'dry is visibly impressed. Knoops looks, pursing his lips in a little round, with great concentration, at his client. Blé Goudé goes on to explain that he invited rebel leaders to come to his village. The following video clip shows how a delegation of the Forces Nouvelles, dressed in dark suits, is received by singing villagers. Suddenly Tarfusser interrupts the suspect and asks him to end his presentation because there is not much time left. Blé Goudé understands. While wrapping up he directly addresses the judges. 'I count on you that the truth will be said. I count on you that I will be judged based on what I did and not based on some comments. I count on you that I will be judged on my actions as individual, and not on the basis of what they would have liked that I would have been.' He continues to look at Tarfusser and his two colleagues. 'I hope to be allowed to go back home, to continue my reconciliation work,' he says, while folding his hands together. 'But that is up to you. I thank you.'

On the public gallery people are sighing in adoration and even a suppressed cry is heard. Down in the courtroom Tarfusser dryly says: 'We learned a lot about the history and politics of Ivory Coast.' He promises that the chamber will study the charges and evidence presented by all parties in the 'most independent' way. After some discussion about the witnesses who come to testify, the session is adjourned. Blé Goudé looks up at his supporters and points to his heart. They reply with waving, in silence. Nobody is shouting. After a final warning from the guards that they will be expelled if they make noise, the Ivorians keep silent so that they will be allowed in the following day.

The supporters then rush to the entrance hall to welcome the defence teams. When a smiling maître Altit and his colleagues step into the foyer, they are stormed by enthusiastic fans who want to take selfies with the lawyer. He is their hero. An Ivorian man is hanging around the neck of one of his assistants. The Dutch lawyer Knoops looks on from a distance before he turns to Blé Goudé's sister to discuss some urgent matters.

The first witness

Almost a week after the start of the trial, the first witness is scheduled to testify. The fact that the court doesn't provide beforehand details about witnesses, makes it impossible for the public to be sure who will be giving testimony and makes it difficult to know how the cases are built up. Before the witness is led in, presiding judge Tarfusser lays down some rules. The most controversial decision is that the chamber won't permit 'leading questions.' The matter leads to hours of discussion with the defence lawyers, who argue this will hinder them during their cross-examinations. The debate takes all morning, until the hearing is adjourned at noon.[180]

Most Ivorians have returned to their homes and jobs. Just a dozen supporters are following the trial from the public gallery. The Ivorian ambassador and his assistant are, as always, present. In the old building the blinds had to be lowered before a protected witness could be brought into the courtroom. But in the new setting all witnesses are seated under the overarching part of the public gallery, which keeps them out of the view of visitors at all times. When protected witness P-547 has taken his seat, judge Tarfusser addresses him. In the new layout there is a considerable distance between the judges' bench and the witness box, a matter that will later be the subject of a remarkable discussion.

The judge explains to P-547 that 'nobody,' except the people in the courtroom, knows his name, and that he will be addressed as 'Mr Witness.' His pixelated face appears on the screens on the public gallery. His voice is distorted as well and sounds like that of a robot. Tarfusser warns the witness not to mention 'anything' that could disclose his identity. 'If you want to say something which could identify you, just tell me so that we can go in closed or private session.' But in the heat of the moment, this kind of self-control will prove to be difficult.

When Tarfusser says that the witness might need help with reading articles, it becomes clear that he is an illiterate person. The fact that extra breaks could be necessary, means he is probably vulnerable. The judge explains that everybody will have to speak slowly because the words are translated from Dioula into French and then English. 'It is your obligation, I repeat, your obligation to tell the truth,' Tarfusser tells the witness. 'Therefore, I would ask you to repeat with me the following words: I solemnly declare that I will speak the truth.'[181]

'I solemnly swear that I shall tell the truth,' says the witness.

---

180 Official transcript, ICC, 4 February 2016.
181 Transcript no longer available on ICC website.

Tarfusser adds: 'The whole truth and nothing but the truth.'

'All the truth and nothing but the truth,' the witness repeats.

'Thank you, Mr witness,' says Tarfusser. 'I have also to inform you that giving false testimony or, in other words, not saying the truth is an offence before the court and, as such, punishable. Do you understand this?'

'I understand,' says the witness.

Trial lawyer MacDonald will take the man through his testimony. While listening to his answers the public learns that he is an Ivorian citizen, a Muslim and belonging to the ethnic group Tagwana. He never went to school and used to be a truck driver transporting petrol and oil in a tanker, loading in Abidjan and delivering in several places. During the crisis he lived in the Yopougon neighbourhood 'Port-Bouët II.' He owned two houses, two plots of bare land and a car. The witness was a member of Ouattara's RDR. 'I was not a militant,' he explains to the court. He just organised meetings and called people to vote for the party.

The march

While testifying he is talking so fast, that the judge and prosecutor repeatedly have to ask him to slow down. P-547 is called to talk about his experiences relating to the first of the prosecutor's selected incidents. He explains how he heard prime minister Guillaume Soro on the UN radio calling people to gather on 16 December 2010 for the march to the RTI. The witness remembers they were instructed to show their 'bare hands', indicating they had 'no violent intentions' and were not carrying weapons. The march would be a message to Laurent Gbagbo that it was time to leave office because Ivorians had chosen Ouattara as the new president. That morning the witness took a shower, had breakfast, left home, drank a coffee in a small café, got in a 'gbaka' – a collective taxi – and then continued on foot. On his way he heard loud bangs and saw uniformed officers. 'Then I started to become scared. And I was saying to myself, what is the Republican Guard doing here?' But it didn't stop him from joining the march.

But then Andreas O'Shea, one of Gbagbo's defence lawyers, interrupts. 'Mr President, your Honours, my learned friend, Mr MacDonald, is a very experienced counsel before this court, and I've seen him on many occasions before. But this is not the way I'm used to him examining a witness. With respect, it is important that he exercises a little bit more control over his witness and takes the witness stage by stage through his evidence.' The defence counsel has a point. P-547 is going fast and his story is sometimes difficult to follow.

But Tarfusser says: 'May I disagree with you. I think that the witness is here to say the truth, his truth, and I think that he should not be guided.' For the moment the issue will end there. But the matter will come back later in an upsetting way.

P-547 picks up the story and tells how he and the other demonstrators got to a one-way street where special police forces had set up guns on sandbags. Soon his account becomes confusing, as he rushes through his most traumatic experiences. There were other security forces as well, holding clubs, shields and tear gas rifles. Again he saw officers of the Republican Guard. 'We put our hands up in the air,' the witness tells, 'but they used tear gas on us. The crowd panicked.' People tried to find a way out, but many couldn't draw back because of the chaos, the teargas and the large number of demonstrators. 'I ran a bit. I fell. I heard a gun-shot, I fell down, and I saw that my leg had been hit, broken.' His bone was sticking out. While the shooting continued, many people fell to the ground.

When the shots ended, he managed to sit up. A cargo truck with soldiers arrived. A man, wearing the uniform of the Republican Guard with a radio in his hand, ordered the men to take all the people who were on the ground. 'They gathered them up and threw them in the cargo truck,' says the witness without explaining what condition the people were in. Then the soldiers came to P-547. The leader of the unit ordered: 'You have to search him. And if you find a gris-gris or a knife on him, you'll have to kill him.'

The soldiers frisked him to see whether P-547 had an amulet that many Ivorians carry with them, believing it makes them invulnerable. At the time, the prosecution argues, it was seen as a sign the person was a rebel. 'They took my wallet and they did not find anything else. They gave that to their leader.' Although he lost his money, his life was spared. 'So I fell to the ground, and God saved me. Only the Lord knew,' the witness tells. But his ordeal was not over yet. The soldiers asked his name.

A mistake

Then it happens. The witness is so involved in telling about these dramatic moments in his life, that by accident he repeats his full name in court. P-547 is a protected witness, but everybody present, including the supporters of the suspects at the public gallery, hears his name loud and clear. The mistake sends a shock wave through the courtroom.

'You have said your name,' Tarfusser tells the witness in a reaction to the disastrous moment. Then MacDonald points at the public gallery. The judge looks up as well: 'I see people writing.' While improvising, Tarfusser orders that the names of the journalists have to be taken. He will cancel the transmission of the part of the hearing where the witness' name is disclosed. It is for these situations that hearings are broadcast through the ICC's website with a thirty minute delay, to give the judges the possibility to cut sensitive episodes. But in the chaos, Tarfusser forgets to mention whether there is a sentence for people if they disclose the name of a protected witness.

In the courtroom O'Shea requests the judges again to invite the witness to pause from time to time. 'It's probably also his passion that brings him to speak not too slow,' Tarfusser answers.

Continuing his testimony the witness explains that the Ivorian soldiers asked him why he was joining the march. He answered to the military: 'We voted, and we want justice.' That was not the answer the soldiers wanted. 'They hit me, I fell down,' the witness says. The leader told his men to beat P-547 to death. 'At one point, I heard a gun-shot.' Suddenly the soldiers were ordered to pursue two civilians who were running for their life. One officer who was still with the witness, asked his superior: 'Should I kill him, finish him off?' But then the witness heard him saying: 'This guy's nearly dead. He won't last.'

Another truck arrived and soon four gendarmes surrounded the witness. 'What is Ouattara giving you that you would sacrifice yourselves for him?' he was asked. 'It's not about him. This is about the country,' P-547 said. Again an answer that was not appreciated. 'They hit my left ear, and I still can't hear out of there, that ear.' He was severely beaten up. 'When I tell people what they did to me, nobody believes me. It was extremely painful. They stood on my leg to beat me. That was what hurt most. It was worse than being trampled by a crowd. The scars are still visible and my ribs hurt to this very day.' A rifle was pointed at him. But then the officers received a message on their radio and had to leave. 'Before they left, they told me they would be back to finish me off.'

MacDonald: 'And what happened? Did they come back to you?'

'No, they didn't come back,' the witness explains.

The next vehicle that arrived, would save his life. It was the Red Cross. The staff looked at his leg and tore off part of his trouser to use it to stop the bleeding. He was put in the ambulance. But when the vehicle left to take him to hospital, they were stopped at a civilian roadblock.

Listing names

Before the witness can continue this part of his testimony, Tarfusser has a look at the clock. 'We have now worked one hour and a half. We have come to the break,' he says. 'During this break ICC security will enforce the order to take the names of the journalists and the media.' The protocol officer is already standing next to the exit with pen and paper. He understands the situation better than the judge, because it is unlikely that professional media would disclose the witness' identity. Not only does he take the names of journalists, but those of the other visitors at the public gallery as well. In the main hall of the court some Ivorians are laughing because one of them, a representative of Gbagbo's political party, has the same name as the witness. He points out that even without the mistake, with all the details P-547 had already given about his life, it would have been easy to find out who he is. 'The identity of the witness will be known all over Ivory Coast within half an hour,' he tells.

Back in court Tarfusser addresses the audience: 'I want just to first apologise to the public for this little bit draconian measures we ordered, but I think it is necessary for the well-being and the security of the witness.' Again he forgets to explain what would happen if someone discloses the name of P-547.

The witness picks up his testimony where it had been left off. The Red Cross ambulance that carried him, ran into a roadblock manned by young people, armed with machetes and guns. Some were wearing a singlet, others were in army fatigue trousers. They threatened the Red Cross staff that if the vehicle carried people from the ethnic group Dioula, these patients would be killed. But the medical officers stood firm. After an intense debate, the ambulance could continue its way to a hospital in Yopougon.

Lots of injured people were being brought in. The doctors made two X-rays of P-547's leg. 'Then I was put into a bed, put on a drip.' He started to feel better physically, though around him it was hell. 'The wounded continued to arrive. And some of them were seriously injured. They were crying out,' the witness tells. 'Doctors were saying that they were going to save them. But some of them died because they'd lost too much blood. At least four people close to me died.'

As the security forces had stolen his phone too, the witness only managed to call his wife the next morning. 'I was able to tell her that I was still alive, even though she had been led to believe that I was dead.' P-547 was taken to another hospital in Cocody, but he was warned that 'anyone who had been wounded during the march' would not be treated there and be left to die. When he saw that the warning was true, he left for the Sainte Jane Leora clinic, where he was properly examined. His thigh had been fractured by a bullet. A metal connection had to be put in to keep the shattered bone together.

No treatment

Up until now P-547 is in constant pain. He hasn't been able to work since the attack, despite the fact that he has to take care of a family of eight, he tells Paolina Massidda, when the legal representative of victims puts questions to him. He manages to survive because he is renting out a house. His wife has a little shop. But there is no money for treatment. Although he needs surgery, his leg will never be the same.

Then Massidda asks him what 'would be of the greatest assistance to you today in your daily life?' He answers: 'I've spent my whole life as a driver. Even if I had a car and I had a driver to drive it, that could be useful.' He might even want to open a shop himself to feed his family.

'How do you feel today?' Massidda wants to know. His answer comes as a surprise. 'Personally today I'm happy,' he says. The fact that his name was disclosed, apparently didn't ruin it for him. 'I'm here in the courtroom for a trial and I'm happy because we place a lot of hopes in the court. Poor people have to be helped when certain acts are committed by the rich, by the leaders. Today I have nothing, that's true, but here I am addressing the presiding judge in the court and I thank the Lord and I'd like to thank you for giving me this opportunity. This sort of thing could perhaps contribute to reducing evil on earth.'

When Andreas O'Shea starts his cross-examination, he touches upon a painful matter. Who promised him that he might have an operation? 'Well, actually it's people from the court,' says P-547. The witness explains that his leg was examined but it wasn't possible to operate immediately because there was still pus coming out. That was, however, not the only reason why the court could not arrange an operation. 'I had to wait until I came here to give my testimony,' he says. The rules prescribe furthermore that the court only allows reparations after a guilty verdict. The witness is aware of that limitation. 'I was told that, God willing, at the end of the trial, the judgment, I would be given help to get treatment. But I have to say I no longer trust anything or anyone. I don't believe in promises, so I'll believe it when something has been done for me.' Nevertheless, the trial does have great significance for him. 'It's a very important case for me,' the witness says.

Much of the defence's cross-examination, however, makes P-547 irritated. When O'Shea asks him a not well-formulated question in French spiced with a heavy English accent, the witness answers: 'I don't understand what you are saying. You are changing my words, and that's not what I said.'

Suddenly prosecutor MacDonald gets up to intervene: 'Just one question, your Honour, just one note. I'll do this once, and I'm doing it now. The accused are laughing. This is a serious matter. There is a witness on the stand. Nothing is funny in this courtroom.' Tarfusser didn't see it, but he tells the suspects not to show 'their disagreement.' O'Shea has something to say about the matter as well. 'The witness was also laughing in response to my questions.' But Tarfusser shrugs it off: 'He is under much more stress in this moment.'

Small incidents continue to happen. At one point the witness tells O'Shea off: 'If you wrote that down, you have to erase it.' But then it is Tarfusser who intervenes. 'If the question is posed in a way which is deemed not to be pertinent or respectful, then it's the bench, the judge who will decide on that. But you have to just be calm and answer the questions, okay?'

An incident of utmost gravity

By now it is Friday. P-547 has been on the witness stand for three days. But that afternoon he is excused. The prosecutor has an urgent and strictly confidential matter that needs to be discussed behind closed doors. Sound and vision are cut. That day I have been watching the hearing from home, through the web streaming. Thinking that the public session is over, I am about to make some coffee, when to my surprise I hear sounds coming from my laptop and headphones. Immediately I put them on and I can't believe what I hear. It is MacDonald's voice. He is telling the judges that his office is monitoring social media. His colleagues have noted a 'disturbing' matter. Bloggers and journalists are trying to find out the identities of protected witnesses P-9, P-10, P-11 and P-44.

MacDonald, thinking the public can't hear him as it's closed session, goes on. Then disaster strikes. Unaware that the sound is left on and that the public can hear every word, the prosecutor says the names of the four witnesses. Suddenly the sound is switched off. But the harm is done. Two fatal minutes and the identities of crucial high level insider witnesses are known to the public. Soon their names, including their previous and current positions, are all over the Internet.

One can only imagine the scenes at the court that Friday afternoon and weekend. When the trial is continued on Monday morning, Tarfusser calls the incident of the 'utmost and inexcusable gravity' for which 'the whole ICC apologises' to the affected persons. The chamber has ordered an internal investigation to find out how this could have happened. 'We don't know yet if the reason for this is recklessness, superficiality, stupidity, and I don't even want to speculate about something else,' says Tarfusser.[182] He warns that 'any revelation of the identity' of a protected witness is an offence. 'Everyone inside the courtroom, in the public gallery, in Côte d'Ivoire and anywhere else' is to refrain from disclosing the names. It is an embarrassing scene. Tarfusser warns again journalists to 'balance' their right to inform, with the responsibility to not endanger witnesses. 'I really ask all the people to calm down. We don't want to ignite anything. We just want to do the best possible job, all of us, sitting here in the courtroom.'

For now it is back to business. The witness is asked in. O'Shea takes P-547 again through that terrible day in 2010. The question about the distance between the security forces throwing teargas and the witness, leads to a hilarious conversation. 'I am not an investigator. How could I have calculated that distance?' the witness responds. Judge Tarfusser tries to help out: 'There is no need to be an investigator, but just make an estimation. If they were just in front of you, like me and you, we are 30 metres apart.' But O'Shea doesn't agree with the judge's estimation of the distance between the witness box and the bench. 'I suppose it looks like about 12, 14 metres,' the lawyer says.

---

182 Official transcript, ICC, 8 February 2016.

'I would say more, I would say 20,' Tarfusser insists.

O'Shea: 'I'm just giving the estimation for the record.'

Tarfusser gives in, slightly: 'Before I said 30, maybe it's a little bit less, but I don't know.'

The debate shows exactly why it is so hard to testify. While even a judge and a lawyer can't agree on a proper assessment of the distance right in front of them, witnesses are in a much more difficult position, having to rely on their memory, talking about traumatic events in their lives, answering questions about details such as the colours and designs of uniforms, times, dates and indeed, distances.

The following day the defence of Blé Goudé is cross-examining the witness about other parts of his testimony. Then it is over. P-547 has been in court for almost one week. 'Thank you for your patience,' says Tarfusser. 'You are released, you can leave the courtroom.'

The trial against Gbagbo and Blé Goudé has started. Doubts have arisen about the possibility of more ICC trials against persons suspected of being responsible for the post-election violence in Côte d'Ivoire. A few days after prosecutor Bensouda said she had intensified investigations against the Ouattara camp, the Ivorian president announces he will not send any more Ivorians to the ICC. The national courts are ready to deal with these prosecutions, he says. Three months later, May 2016, the former first lady is put on trial in Ivory Coast for crimes against humanity. The case against Simone Gbagbo, still wanted by the ICC, sounds very familiar. When it comes to the main allegations, Human Rights Watch[183] writes that the Ivorian prosecutor accuses her of participating in a 'crisis committee' consisting of 'leaders from her husband's political party and key government ministers that planned and organized abuses against Ouattara supporters to maintain her husband in power at all costs.'

One year later, on 29 March 2017, Simone Gbagbo is acquitted. The charges for crimes against humanity aren't proved. The process was marred by a lack of evidence and fair trial concerns, states HRW.[183] The organisation stresses that the 'poor quality' of the investigations and trial only 'underscore the importance' of the outstanding case at the ICC.

183 Côte d'Ivoire: Simone Gbagbo trial begins, Human Rights Watch, 30 May 2016.
183 'Côte d'Ivoire: Simone Gbagbo acquitted after flawed war crimes trial,' Human Rights Watch, 29 March 2017.

8

THE DELICATE POSITION OF WITNESSES

No more daily broadcasts of the testimonies of protected witnesses through the website of the court. No immediate transcripts either. When it comes to the visitors to the public gallery, their names and nationalities will be noted by court officials. Judge Cuno Tarfusser reads the decision on these new and drastic measures that the chamber has reached, 16 June 2016. These steps are intended to provide more security for witnesses, in the trial against former president of Ivory Coast, Laurent Gbagbo, and his co-accused Charles Blé Goudé. There have been so many attempts, especially by social media, to find out the identities of witnesses at risk and blow their cover, that the usual protection of using a pseudonym, voice and facial distortion and many closed sessions is not sufficient, the judges say. When such witnesses have completed their testimony, the court will look carefully at what parts can be disclosed. Only then will some video clips and redacted transcripts be published on the ICC website.

The measures this specific chamber has taken, reflect the delicate position of witnesses and the duty of the court to take care of them. The ICC depends extensively on witnesses. Without persons who want to tell what they saw, heard, experienced or analysed, basically there would be no trials. Up until March 2013 a total of 199 persons had testified in the ICC's courtroom, according to a report 'Witnesses before the International Criminal Court.'[184] Since this study by the International Bar Association (IBA) was published, many more witnesses have given evidence before the judges. By January 2017 a total of 365 witnesses had testified, according to the ICC.

It requires courage, patience, a certain psychological stability and a good memory to testify. Many years can pass between the time the crimes

---

184 'Witnesses before the International Criminal Court,' International Bar Association, July 2013.

were committed, the first contact with investigators of the Office of the Prosecutor (OTP), local intermediaries or the lawyers of the suspect, and the moment a witness appears in court. During that period, lots of things can go wrong. The history of the ICC has shown that many witnesses have been facing enormous challenges and risks. By definition they are part of a case against powerful persons who are accused of having ruthlessly sacrificed other people. The stakes are high. If these leaders are found guilty, they can get long prison sentences. Pressure can come from suspects and their entourage, national authorities, but even from prosecution intermediaries and from the defence. Sources like social media have disclosed names of witnesses, persons have intimidated them and offered bribes, in order to force witnesses to testify in a certain way, to withdraw or recant their statements. Although the cases against the Kenyan suspects and the Congolese warlord Jean-Pierre Bemba Gombo in particular have become synonymous with witness interference, there have been incidents in most other cases as well, with serious consequences.

Different witnesses

How does the court protect witnesses? 'Don't tell anyone that you are going to testify in The Hague. If nobody knows, you run the least risk.' This advice is generally given as first protection against a hostile environment, officials of the Victims and Witnesses Unit said in an interview in 2011. This special section, now called Victims and Witnesses Service (VWS) is tasked with the support, accompaniment and protection of witnesses and victims. It falls under the registry and works for the whole court. The unit deals with the judges, prosecution, as well as defence and legal representatives of victims, and has contact with states and organisations outside the court. Taking care of witnesses and victims comes at a 'massive cost,' the IBA wrote. In 2013 for instance 6 million euro (or 5 percent of the then total ICC budget) was allocated to the VWS.

Obviously, just keeping silent is often not sufficient. It is always possible that over time suspicion arises that someone is a witness. Most importantly, a suspect has the right to know the identity of a witness. The parties will have to disclose the witnesses' identities to their adversaries in court in order for them to be able to build their strategy, run their own investigations and prepare cross-examinations.

The ICC has a set of measures – from simple to far-reaching – that can be applied to different levels of risk. The selection of security measures depends on the assessment of the danger a witness is facing. One of the factors is the background and position of that person. A very vulnerable group of witnesses are the victims who personally experienced atrocities such as rape, sexual slavery, torture, persecution, deportation, a murder attempt or pillaging, or who directly witnessed violent acts. These crime-based witnesses testify about horrific incidents which they survived but that deeply affected and hurt them. Not only their physical safety can be at stake, but also their social and mental well-being. They run the risk that giving testimony will traumatise them even further.

Insider witnesses are in an especially delicate situation. They have been part of the criminal network of the suspect. These insiders, or 'dirty-hand' witnesses, might know the accused. They have joined in setting up criminal plans, worked within command structures, received or distributed money, participated in violence and know from first-hand experience the suspect's record. These witnesses might have blood on their own hands. The fact that they turn against their former comrade, commander or leader, will be seen as treason.

Apart from these witnesses, international and local experts can also be called to give evidence: forensic analysts, language specialists, psychiatrists, doctors, historians, journalists, professors, ICT-specialists, human rights activists, officials and researchers. Usually they face lesser or no risks. They also need less support from the ICC as they are often more used to settings like a courtroom.

A range of security measures

What are the measures that the court can take, to try to keep witnesses safe? When people who are waiting to testify feel unsafe in their own environment in countries such as the Democratic Republic of Congo (DRC), Ivory Coast or the Central African Republic (CAR), sometimes the problem can be solved by something as simple as giving them a phone with the number of a special ICC official, whom the witness can call in case of peril and to discuss the situation. If a witness thinks that his or her environment is not safe, the court has the possibility to send personnel to check the place and take decisions to upgrade the physical security, by for instance installing better locks on doors or building a higher fence around the house.

There are situations where these measures provide enough safety. Because in some instances fear is based on emotions and less on actual danger, is the experience of the VWS. 'These measures have the advantage that they don't completely upset the life of a witness and don't attract much attention,' explained a lawyer working with the VWS who needed to stay anonymous.

The court can also ask the police to do extra patrols in the neighbourhood of the person who feels threatened. In most countries where the ICC is actively investigating however, the police has a bad reputation. The court therefore tries to sign an agreement with the authorities of these states to make sure there is a special unit available that can be trusted and is permanently on standby to protect witnesses. Such a police unit can undertake the special patrols in the area around the house of the witness, VWS officials noted.

If the court assesses that the situation for a witness in her or his environment is not secure, the VWS can decide to do an assisted move. At that point, the witness is included in the official ICC Protection Programme. The witness is brought to another village, town or city, where it is safe for him or her. If that's not sufficient because a person is in danger in her or his home country, the court will move the witness – with the family – to another country, which can be anywhere in the world. The VWS takes care of these persons by offering housing, income, medical care, education and schools for the children. This is almost standard procedure when it comes to insider witnesses, who have been part of the criminal network of the suspect. But it is often also offered to victims.

Different opinions

However, the prosecution and VWS often differed about their tasks, risk levels and measures, the IBA notes. The report says that 'early tensions concerning the precise division of responsibilities' between the two became 'a significant issue in the initial stages' of the cases against the Congolese warlords Thomas Lubanga, Germain Katanga and Mathieu Ngudjolo Chui. 'The two were unable to agree on the appropriate risk assessment for the admittance of witnesses into the ICC's Protection Programme (ICCPP), which led to litigation over the risk thresholds of witnesses and the need for protection.' The conflict resulted in the Joint Protocol on the Mandate, Standards and Procedure for Protection in March 2011 which, according to the IBA, 'significantly clarified the respective responsibilities and coordination mechanisms of both organs.' Still, prosecutors often push for maximum protection to secure as many potential witnesses as possible for their cases, while the VWS finds such a costly and radical measure not always necessary. The IBA quotes the registry saying that the prosecution 'is extremely demanding and does not accept easily refusals even when we strongly believe that a request for protection must not be accepted.'

But within the section itself things didn't always go smoothly either. 'Internal issues' saw the VWS 'losing qualified staff with experience in witness related matters. It also appeared to lack clear leadership at the management level,' the IBA writes.

State cooperation

With regard to witness matters, the ICC depends on good relations with national authorities on many levels: to get permission for court officials to question witnesses, to give them passports, to allow them to go to The Hague for testimony and to protect them. Obviously things get even more complicated when a witness needs to be relocated to another country. This is a pressing issue, as some witnesses will only be prepared to testify if such relocation is arranged. The ICC will then have to find another state, which accepts this witness.

On 21 November 2016, Argentina became the eighteenth country to sign a cooperation agreement related to witness protection with the ICC. 'When, in exceptional cases, the lives of witnesses are in danger, the court needs the cooperation of states to ensure that they do not suffer any harm because of their testimony,' said judge Silvia Fernández de Gurmendi, the president of the court, when she thanked the Argentine government.[185] However, the ICC added it needs more governments to sign such agreements promising to take witnesses in, if necessary together with their families.

Usually it takes at least six months between the initial contact with a host country and actual relocation, the IBA-report says. Some states haven't signed an agreement with the court, but work on an ad hoc

---

185 Argentina and International Criminal Court sign an agreement on Witnesses' protection, ICC press release, 22 November 2016.

basis, although in those cases it takes much more time (at least a year) to complete the relocation. There are also 'platform states' that are prepared to issue emergency visas and accept witnesses 'on a temporary basis, to facilitate immediate extraction (for example if they are needed urgently in court),' writes the IBA.

There is an obvious reluctance to sign relocation agreements with the court. One reason is that the work of the ICC can clash with interests of governments. 'Some states highlight the need to safeguard good relations between themselves and the originating state, particularly where there are close political ties,' the IBA report states. Others underline they don't have a national protection programme nor the legal framework to facilitate these arrangements. Especially European countries express concerns about the possibility of witnesses applying for asylum (see chapter11). Cultural issues come into play as well. Some African witnesses have several wives. How to accept polygamous families in countries where such marriages are forbidden by law?

Besides, hosting witnesses not only means protecting vulnerable victims. Insider witnesses, who almost by definition need relocation, are a whole different category. They have been active in serious organised crime, might know how to handle weapons and have harmed people. Not all governments are keen to allow potential war criminals onto their territory. The low number of official relocation countries constitutes an 'alarming shortfall' in the court's ability 'to protect victims and witnesses at risk,' the IBA quotes its sources. At the time the report was published twelve countries had signed a witness relocation agreement, compared to eighteen now. Meanwhile the court already felt the consequences, as the collapse of the Kenyan cases has been partly linked to the failure to protect (potential) witnesses.

It might be difficult to find countries that want to take prosecution witnesses, but the defence faces bigger problems. The lawyers of a suspect don't have the formal relations with countries which the ICC's prosecution and registry have. For the defence it can already be difficult to secure passports and visas from national authorities for its witnesses. 'The political reality of the cases is that some governments may have a vested interest in seeing certain ICC defendants convicted,' which explains their reluctance to support the defence, according to the IBA report. Notably, military who wanted to testify in support of a suspect, encountered problems. 'At times these individuals may agree to testify but do not want the court to make a formal cooperation request, for fear of repercussions if their government discover they are testifying,' the IBA states. It adds: 'Some defence witnesses have needed to flee from state parties to seek refuge in non-state parties, where they have no papers or status.'

How many witnesses are actually fully protected by the ICC? For a long time, the court refused to disclose these numbers, claiming it didn't happen a lot. 'A dozen,' said a top official at the launch of the IBA report. But the study itself mentioned a very different number. According to the IBA there were 'more than 300 witnesses admitted in the ICCPP' in 2013, adding 'there have been reports of extensive relocation in the two Kenyan cases.' In a footnote the IBA refers to media reports stating that some 80 Kenyan witnesses had been relocated to Europe. Then in January 2015, when the ICC sent out a press release about the violent death of a Kenyan defence witness, Meshack Yebei (who was provided 'a safe residency in a new location' but had returned home), the court disclosed that 'more than 650 witnesses, victims and families' members are provided with protective measures by the court.'[186]

Protection is needed, but there is also another side to it. Defence lawyers often point out that it can influence the quality of witnesses. The opportunity to live in another country, with the help of the ICC, can be a trigger for persons in dire circumstances to wrongly present themselves as a prosecution witness. How common this is, is unclear. But, for instance, in the Kenyan cases, defence lawyers have accused persons of offering themselves to the prosecutor in return for a better life abroad, although their evidence proved to be false.

But relocation might sound better than it is. In reality it is extremely difficult to live abroad as a protected witness. To be safe, these witnesses and their families have to cut ties with many of their former friends, acquaintances and family, and have to restart a new life. It is extremely hard to meet the conditions of living under protection.

Cases of witness interference

Notwithstanding the measures to safeguard witnesses, many ICC cases have been affected by witness problems, as is shown in the following brief overview.

---

186 ICC deeply concerned with reported death of Mr Meshack Yebei, ICC press release, 6 January 2015.

In the case against the Congolese warlord Thomas Lubanga Dyilo, local intermediaries who were working for the ICC's prosecution have been accused of pushing witnesses into telling lies in order to have the suspect convicted – in exchange for money or even relocation. The judges said that three intermediaries might have been involved in criminal acts. When it comes to witness issues, the Kenyan cases have been disastrous on many levels. ICC prosecutor Fatou Bensouda has been pointing out that in the case against the Kenyan president Uhuru Kenyatta and top government official Francis Muthaura potential witnesses have been killed, while others were too scared to talk to her team. She accused the Kenyan government of failing to facilitate the prosecution's access to critical witnesses. Ultimately, these two cases collapsed, which was partly attributed to the fact that key witnesses proved to be lying. This also raised serious questions about the prosecution's investigative qualities. The defence has been criticizing the prosecution for believing false witnesses. In the trial against the Kenyan deputy president William Ruto and broadcaster Joshua Sang, there have been constant witness incidents. Kenyan journalist Walter Barasa was apparently an intermediary, contacting witnesses on behalf of ICC's prosecution, before he allegedly moved to the other side. Barasa started to pressure several witnesses and offered them money so they would recant their incriminating statements against the defendants. Barasa is being charged by the ICC, but so far Kenya hasn't surrendered him to the court in The Hague. Two more persons, including a Kenyan lawyer, have been indicted by the ICC for intimidating witnesses in his case.

Even after relocation, Kenyan witnesses were not safe. They were allegedly harassed while staying in their host countries. Media reported in April 2015 how a Kenyan intelligence officer landed at Schiphol, the national airport of The Netherlands, where he was arrested and sent back to Kenya. The agent had been allegedly trying to meet a witness who had been relocated to The Netherlands for his safety.[187]

In January 2015 the court sent out a press release about the murder of Meshack Yebei. A few days later the defence in the Ruto & Sang case disclosed that the Kenyan man was their witness and that he had been threatened by a prosecution witness. However, the mutilated body that

---

187 'State: Why Dutch kicked out our man,' Daily Nation, 21 April 2015.

had been found and was thought to be that of Yebei, turned out to be that of another person. It would take weeks before Yebei's remains were found. There hasn't been a proper investigation into his death and how he died never became clear.

In the Ruto & Sang trial no fewer than seventeen prosecution witnesses withdrew their cooperation with the court. When the proceedings against the two suspects were terminated by the chamber because of a lack of evidence, presiding judge Chile Eboe-Osuji concluded the case was a 'mistrial' due to 'a troubling incidence of witness interference and intolerable political meddling.'[188] His colleague, judge Robert Fremr, wrote that 'other evidence may have been available to the prosecution' if the Ruto & Sang case had taken place 'in a different climate, less hostile to the prosecution, its witnesses, and the court in general.' Although there is no proof of personal involvement of the Kenyan suspects in any witness-tampering, the judges underlined that they did benefit from the interference. That's why Ruto and Sang weren't acquitted. If the prosecution has new evidence, including the testimony of witnesses, the case might be reopened.

In their turn, the lawyers of the Kenyan deputy president William Ruto wrote a filing in May 2016 accusing local intermediaries of 'coaching' witnesses to give 'false evidence' to the prosecution in support of the OTP case. Lead counsel Karim Khan disclosed suspicions that ICC staff members may have been 'engaged in sexual relations with witnesses and their families' in Kenya and possibly are 'bribed' by witnesses. 'These ICC staff members have fostered an environment in which defrauding and telling lies to the ICC was encouraged,' Khan wrote.[189]

In the trial against Jean-Pierre Bemba Gombo no fewer than five persons have been charged with bribing defence witnesses, so they would give a favourable, exonerating statement for the Congolese warlord in exchange for money and the promise of relocation. Among the suspects are Bemba himself and two of his lawyers. On 19 October 2016 the judges decided that all five suspects are guilty of witness tampering.

---

188 Decision on Defence Applications for Judgments of Acquittal, ICC, 5 April 2016.
189 Public redacted version of Ruto defence request to appoint an amicus prosecutor, Defence William Ruto, 2 May 2016.

The detained Congolese warlord Bosco Ntaganda has been accused that from his ICC cell, he personally coached witnesses and directed others to do so. The court then imposed restrictions on his contacts with the outside world. In protest against these measures Ntaganda went on hunger strike in September 2016, which he ended within two weeks. In fact, while still detained at the ICC, Lubanga was also accused by the prosecution of interfering with witnesses in the Ntaganda case.

In 2015 the prosecution accused Dominic Ongwen, a former commander of the Lord's Resistance Army, who is facing 70 charges of crimes against humanity and war crimes committed in northern Uganda, of having contacted several witnesses. The judges therefore imposed restrictions on his contacts with the outside world. The registry has to monitor his phone calls (except those with his lawyers). There is also a restricted list with persons he is allowed to call.

However, in 2016 a new issue arose, as Ongwen allegedly ordered people to pay money to eight potential prosecution and defence witnesses.

By working in detention, the suspect earned 25 euros per week, which allowed him to save one thousand euros. Ongwen handed over the money to his lawyers, telling them they had to transfer the euros to be distributed to his children and family, who are living in poverty in Uganda. The single judge ordered the lawyers to present an overview of payments made on behalf of Ongwen to potential witnesses. The problem here is that several of the women he forced into marriage with him, are the mothers of his children but also made a statement against him. The prosecution might actually consider a new case against Ongwen, for bribing and influencing witnesses.[190]

The security of witnesses is a constant concern for the judges handling the trial against Gbagbo and Blé Goudé. It forced them to stop the web-streaming of testimonies of protected witnesses, and to register the visitors present at the public gallery. Unfortunately, there was also the tragic disclosure by a prosecutor of the names of four (insider) witnesses in this case. It happened during closed session and the trial lawyer thought the sound was off, but in reality it was still on. The bitter irony was that the prosecution was just complaining how bloggers and journalists were

---

190 Decision on Prosecution 'Request for an order that Mr Ongwen cease and disclose payments to witnesses and that the Registry disclose certain calls made by Mr Ongwen,' ICC, 10 August 2016.

trying to get the names of these protected witnesses, and wanted to discuss how the court should deal with it. Such a disclosure is not only a huge embarrassment, but could have dramatic consequences as well.

Sexual abuse of witnesses

At the centre of the biggest scandal with regard to the safety of witnesses, was however the VWS itself. An official of the section sexually abused four persons in the DRC, who all had the double status of victim and witness, and were under the protection of the court. A number of other staff members were accused of 'inappropriate conduct.' The main perpetrator was fired. The court's registry commissioned an independent panel to do an external review, which was published in 2013. In their report the experts confirmed the crimes.[191]

The panel concluded that although the officer was responsible for his criminal conduct, the 'chronic and pervasive structural and functional shortcomings' of the VWS 'contributed significantly' to his ability to commit the sexual assaults over 'a prolonged period of time.' Once the local staff understood what was going on, they immediately informed the VWS headquarters in The Hague, which, however, mismanaged this case. Top officials 'did not seem to comport with the seriousness of these allegations of sexual assault committed' by a VWS staff member – 'the most serious type of allegation such an organisation could face,' the experts underlined. The field staff was left alone to deal with the matter for a long time. The panel stated that the shortcomings 'encompass the whole of the structure and functioning' of the VWS, which was described as 'dysfunctional' and a 'stovepipe' organisation, where people were hired on the basis of 'friendship,' staff was not adequately trained, information not shared and the dynamics of the local situations were not understood. The ICC underlined that 'disciplinary measures, including dismissal, had been taken in respect of certain staff involved.' The registrar reacted by saying he 'was analysing the content of the full report in order to assess whether further disciplinary action is required.' But after that press release not much has been heard about the scandal, nor whether the perpetrator

---

191 The external independent review submits its report on alleged sexual abuses in DRC, ICC press release, 20 December 2013. With a link to the report: 'Post incident review of allegations of sexual assault of four victims,' Independent Review Team.

was formally charged, as would have happened in many national systems around the globe.

Assisting witnesses to testify

With a growing number of incidents where witnesses are harassed and harmed, it might even be surprising that people still want to testify. But despite the pressure exerted by several intermediaries, suspects, defence lawyers and others, there are still people willing to come forward and tell the court what happened.

When witnesses who are called to testify need the court's assistance, staff members of the VWS travel to the country where they are staying in order to fetch them. 'For people who have never left their village in Africa and now have to give evidence in The Netherlands, the transition is huge,' explained a VWS psychologist who has to remain anonymous. Therefore the section works intensively on their preparation. 'We describe how The Netherlands looks like and show them a film about the court. We also explain the roles of the judges, prosecution and defence,' the woman said. The VWS staff tells them that the suspect is present in the courtroom, but that they don't need to be afraid of him because special measures are taken for their safety and that there are always security officers present in the courtroom as well.

The VWS can also help people to make up a cover story that explains their absence in the village when they have to testify. The unit can support them when a babysitter for the children is needed or workers that replace the witness at the farm, for instance.

Then it is time for shopping. Quite a number of witnesses are poor people, who have no money to buy clothes suitable for a cold and rainy climate like that of The Netherlands. 'It is very important for them to have nice clothes,' the psychologist explained. 'Some choose a traditional outfit, others go for western clothes. We do our best to buy suitable shoes as well. These small steps give people the feeling they are treated with respect.'

Taking the aeroplane can be an adventure as well. When the witness arrives, the support team is waiting at the airport, if necessary with items such as a proper coat. Officials that speak the language of the witness, bring the new arrival to a safe place in The Hague. For some persons again surprises await, if they have never used electricity, a toilet, running water or central heating. To make sure witnesses are at ease, they can get meals just like at home. The ICC also gives them some pocket money for their time in The Netherlands.

Getting used to the court

Before witnesses testify, the VWS helps them to familiarise themselves with the court and what to expect. This familiarisation period usually takes one or two weeks. The witness gets a tour through the court building and a demonstration in an empty courtroom, where the proceedings during a trial and the use of computers and microphone are explained. The ICC also does a last short psychological-social check to see whether the witness is able to give evidence or might need extra support such as more breaks during the hearing. Part of the preparations are the meetings with the prosecution, the defence lawyers and the legal representatives of victims. Witnesses also read their own statements, which they made earlier, often many years before. If they are illiterate, a court official will read the transcripts to them in their own language. Sometimes the party that calls the witness to testify – the prosecution or defence – gets the chance to undertake 'witness proofing' or 'witness preparation.' This term refers to a meeting shortly before the witness gives evidence in order to discuss matters related to their statements, 'which ideally facilitates a more accurate, complete and efficient testimony,' says the IBA report. Different sets of ICC judges have developed different approaches. In the Lubanga, Katanga, Ngudjolo and Bemba cases, witness proofing was not allowed. The judges in the Kenyan cases have given the prosecution permission to prepare witnesses on the subjects that will be dealt with in court, on the condition that these sessions needed to be video-recorded.

The aim of these preparations is to make sure people are as much at ease as possible, and to testify as well and accurate as they can. In the meantime, the psychologist discusses with the witness and judges the necessity of extra measures. This includes protective measures such as anonymity, facial and voice distortion so the public can't recognize a witness. The court can also order separate special measures for children, elderly persons, victims of sexual violence and traumatized persons. The judges can allow a psychologist or family member to be present during testimony, or the use of a curtain (as was done in the old courtroom) to shield the witness from direct eye contact with the suspect.

It is stressful for people to tell their story in court. Their memory will be tested to the maximum. The events they testify about often took place many years ago, while the circumstances at the time were often extremely violent, chaotic and traumatising which can make it extra difficult for witnesses to remember exact times, days, numbers, names of persons, colours, positions. They get questions such as: which date was it exactly, how many attackers did you see, can you point out where the body was penetrated by bullets? Questions that are not always easy to answer. Even experts sometimes can be seen struggling when trying to formulate their statements as accurate as possible.

Often it is also difficult, painful or dangerous to talk in public about the violent events that witnesses experienced. Insiders have to testify against former comrades or bosses, and might have to speak about atrocities they committed themselves.

Victims tell about humiliating incidents such as rape that not only involve pain and shame, but can also lead to rejection by society. Sometimes witnesses find it so hard to relive these experiences, that they start crying. Protective measures therefore also need to make sure that the public and the community back home don't know who the witnesses are, so they won't be recognized after having given their testimony, and can continue their lives in the best manner possible. As the anonymous VWS official said: 'We try to do all we can, so that they leave the court with a good feeling.'

9

LIBYA
Fighting for the Gaddafis

'Good afternoon everyone, you have no idea how wonderful it is to be here today to speak to you all,' begins Melinda Taylor, slightly nervous but with a broad smile and twinkling eyes, her press conference in a meeting room in the Mövenpick Hotel, located near the International Criminal Court. Immediately after these words of welcome however, the face of the Australian woman turns tense. Taylor is speaking as one of the lawyers of Saif Al-Islam Gaddafi, the son of the murdered Libyan leader. Both Gaddafis have been indicted by the ICC. But the counsel's recent visit to her client, who is being held in Libya, resulted in an outright drama. Together with three ICC colleagues she was arrested and detained. The group was held in Libya for 26 days: from 7 June until 2 July 2012. They have just been released.[192]

The international press agencies have positioned their cameras on high tripods at the back of the room. Chairs have been arranged in rows, where journalists have taken their seats. With laptops and note blocks on their laps, they are writing down Taylor's words. Whereas the ICC had chosen to communicate summarily via official communiqués about the detention of the team, after the release the defence decided to go public. In fact, there had been a big row between the lawyers and the court's registrar, who was against the press conference. So the defence had to organise the meeting with the media themselves.

Next to Taylor sits Xavier-Jean Keïta, who is the head of the Office of Public Counsel for the Defence (OPCD), an independent section of the ICC that supports all defence teams. In this case he is also the lead counsel for Gaddafi. Keïta had not joined Taylor and the others to Libya. Following their release after four agonizing weeks, campaigning night and

---

192 The four ICC staff members released in Libya, ICC press release, 2 July 2012.

day for his detained colleagues, he had booked, on his own account, the Mövenpick room for the meet up with the media, so Taylor could clear her name, explain who is responsible for the arrest and illegal confinement and convey the defence's concerns about the situation in which their client finds himself.

Libya wants to prosecute Gaddafi itself, but Taylor excludes the possibility of a fair trial. The recent events have 'completely underscored' that it is 'impossible' that her client will be tried in an 'independent and impartial manner in Libyan courts,' she tells the media.

The visit

The smile and twinkle in her eyes are gone. 'We had concerns about security before we left,' the lawyer explains to the journalists, but nothing pointed to the possibility that things would get so terribly out of hand. After Taylor and her ICC colleagues had arrived in Libya, they went to Zintan, some 150 kilometres southwest of the capital Tripoli, where her client Saif Al-Islam Gaddafi is held by militia. The Zintan Brigade had refused to hand him over to the national authorities, let alone to the ICC in The Hague, possibly because the militia wanted to use him as a medium of exchange to force concessions from the Libyan government. Although the visit had been officially arranged, Taylor managed to talk only 45 minutes with her client. 'Against all rules, the conversation was recorded,' she says. One of the matters they managed to discuss in that limited time was the question of who should represent him in his case before the ICC. 'I handed over other CVs but he said I should be his lawyer,' Taylor tells the media.

After that short conversation things went very wrong. Although as representatives of the ICC and defence they enjoy full immunity against arrest and detention, the four – Taylor, Helene Assaf (translator), Alexander Khodakov (senior advisor external relations and cooperation at the registry) and Esteban Peralta Losilla (chief of the counsel support section) – suddenly were incarcerated themselves. The arrests would constitute one of the major crises in the short history of the court, which is much concerned about the physical safety of its officials. Never before had ICC staff been detained.

At first there was confusion about who exactly was responsible for the arrests in Libya, a country haunted by armed groups and chaos. Several media had been reporting that the militia of the Zintan Brigade were behind the hostage-taking. But Taylor tells another story. During the press conference she explains that the detention was ordered by the Libyan prosecutor-general and was confirmed by the chairperson of the National Transitional Council, Mustafa Abdul Jalil. It looked like the two entities – the authorities in Tripoli and the Zintan rebels – were actually working together.

The official Libyan explanation for the detention was that the ICC delegation had endangered state security. Taylor was accused of secretly attempting to smuggle in documents, a secret and coded letter, a pen with a miniature video camera and a watch with a similar recorder into the room where she met her client.[193] The Libyan authorities described her as a spy, charged her and were arranging a trial against her. But being the lawyer she is, Taylor tells the media at the press conference that Libya never provided an 'order or decision concerning the legal basis for our arrest and detention. Or for the search and seizure of privileged and confidential ICC documents, or for the breach of Libya's promise to the ICC to implement a privileged visit with Mr Saif Al-Islam Gaddafi.' The lawyer stresses that she had done nothing wrong, and points out that as ICC officials, they were granted immunity. By detaining the team, Tripoli had violated international law. The ICC had reacted by saying that it would conduct an investigation itself with regard to allegations by the Libyan authorities against Melinda Taylor (she was cleared and would continue to defend suspects at the court in The Hague.)

In detention

The lawyer tells that the team was first held in a room in a house in Zintan and then transferred to the prison, which had military tanks in front of the building. Robbed of their freedom and in the hands of the Libyans, the four had no idea what would happen to them for weeks. Direct contact with the outside world was out of the question. Except for a 'monitored' visit on 12 June by an ICC delegation and the ambassadors of Australia, Lebanon, Russia and Spain. The detainees were allowed just a '5 minute' telephone conversation with their families, during which Taylor briefly spoke to her toddler at home. 'As you can imagine speaking

---

193   'Libya accuses Australian ICC official of passing secret letter to Gaddafi's son,' The Guardian, 25 June 2012.

to my two-year old daughter under such circumstances is both an emotional lifeline and heartbreaking.'

It was 'immensely difficult to be detained under such circumstances,' she continues, but she was 'incredibly lucky' to have the 'emotional support' and 'good humour' of her fellow detained colleagues. There were some other bright sides as well. The Libyans treated the four with 'respect and dignity.' They were served great food. The wife of the army commander appeared to be an excellent cook. Her couscous was fantastic. They were allowed to watch some television.

While the four were held in isolation, a massive international campaign was set up to get them out. ICC judges, staff, governments, lawyers, diplomats and NGOs were all committed to the quartet. Especially Australia, the country from where Taylor originates, moved heaven and earth to get them released. It worked. After a month, the president of the ICC, Korean judge Sang-Hyun Song, got the green light to travel to Libya to pick them up. It meant a great deal to Taylor that the judge came personally to Zintan to welcome the team and to take them to The Hague. Diplomats of Australia, Lebanon, Russia and Spain also travelled to Zintan to receive them.[194] The four were finally released. On pictures taken by media, Taylor and her interpreter are seen wearing black abayas and headscarves. On 2 July 2012 they entered the Italian aeroplane that would fly them to freedom.

UN referral

The detention took place against the background of a conflict between Libya and the ICC about who would prosecute Gaddafi. It was the United Nations Security Council that unanimously decided on 26 February 2011 to refer the Libyan situation to the court in The Hague. Following on from Tunisia and Egypt, the Arab Spring had awoken in Libya. In cities such as Benghazi civilians had started demonstrations in the streets. They demanded democracy and the end of the dictatorship under colonel Gaddafi, who had been in power for 42 years. But the regime responded with force, trying to crush the uprising. The Libyan protest degenerated in a bloody war between security forces and groups

---

194   The four ICC staff members released in Libya, ICC press release, 2 July 2016.

that remained loyal to the regime, and the opposition, civilians and armed militia.

The UN Security Council had decided to give the ICC jurisdiction over crimes on the territory of Libya, or by its nationals, from 15 February 2011 onwards. Almost immediately, on 3 March 2011, prosecutor Luis Moreno-Ocampo opened an investigation. Meanwhile the regime became more isolated. On 17 March 2011 the UN Security Council gave permission to enforce a no-fly zone above Libya to protect citizens. NATO would take over command. The United States, France, the United Kingdom and Italy were in the lead bombing Libyan army installations. While the court received the Libyan leaders of the revolt, the eccentric and ruthless ruler Muammar Gaddafi had never been a friend of the ICC. In an interview I had with Moreno-Ocampo, he told me about an annual meeting of the African Union, which had taken place in 2009 in Gaddafi's birthplace Sirte. When the conference was almost finished, the Libyan leader wanted to add something. He had decided on his own that the AU would no longer cooperate with the ICC. There was no need to discuss the matter. 'Be quiet. Proposal accepted,' Moreno-Ocampo quoted him saying at that meeting. In those days the Libyan leader was still one of the richest persons in the world and a significant power factor in Africa. Gaddafi had previously been accused of fuelling conflict and destabilising the region, but escaped prosecution by the Special Court for Sierra Leone that had looked at his role.[195] However, now his days were numbered. On 16 May 2011 Moreno-Ocampo requested that the ICC judges issue arrest warrants. A month later, on 27 June 2011, the court demanded the arrest and surrender of the Libyan leader Muammar Mohammed Abu Minyar Gaddafi, his son Saif Al-Islam Gaddafi and the chief of the military intelligence Abdullah Al-Senussi, for crimes against humanity. 'Bam. On the run for justice,' that's how Moreno-Ocampo, with a look of intense delight, summarized during the interview the impossible position the Libyan leader found himself in.

The three were charged with murder and persecution allegedly committed across Libya, specifically in the cities of Tripoli, Benghazi and Misrata, by using the security apparatus.[196] The judges were convinced by the

195 'Libya blamed for W Africa wars,' BBC, 9 March 2004.
196 Case Information Sheet, ICC, 13 June 2016.

prosecution's arguments that there was evidence of an official policy 'designed at the highest level of the state machinery, aimed at deterring and quelling the February 2011 demonstrations by any means, including by the use of lethal force.'[197] The Libyan leader, who had called his opponents 'rats', was quoted in the arrest warrant as having said: 'We shall move the millions to sanitize Libya an inch at a time, a home at a time, a house at a time, an alley at a time, one by one until the country is rid of the filth and the uncleanliness.'[198] Gaddafi's orders were obeyed. Security forces attacked civilians who took part in demonstrations or were perceived as belonging to the opposition. Houses were searched and protestors were shot at. Hundreds of civilians were arrested, injured and killed.

Saif Al-Islam Gaddafi, a man who had been studying in the United Kingdom and had travelled the world, had no official position back home. But the judges described him as the 'unspoken successor' and the 'most influential person' within the inner circle of the Libyan leader. He 'exercised control over crucial parts of the state apparatus, including finances and logistics.' The playboy son had 'the powers of a de facto prime minister.' Later, prosecutor Moreno-Ocampo would tell the media that he had been informed by the new Libyan authorities that Saif Al-Islam 'was involved in' the violence 'with his own hands, as he executed people.'[199]

Although the regime was teetering, the Gaddafis eluded the ICC. Strangely enough on 22 August 2011 Moreno-Ocampo wrongly claimed to the media that son Saif Al-Islam Gaddafi had been arrested.[200] When the Libyan 'heir' triumphantly allowed international media to film him outside a hotel in Tripoli as a free man, he made the ICC prosecutor look like a fool. The outside world didn't understand why Moreno-Ocampo had made this false claim. But during the interview I had with him a few months later, he explained it had been a strategic choice. He had made the bogus information public on purpose, to show the rebels that the ICC had a claim on him. 'I wanted to make clear that if Saif would be arrested,

---

197   Warrant of Arrest for Saif Al-Islam Gaddafi, ICC, 27 June 2011.
198   Decision on the Prosecutor's Application Pursuant to Article 58 as to Muammar Mohammed Abu Minyar Gaddafi, Saif Al-Islam Gaddafi and Abdullah Al-Senussi, ICC, 27 June 2011.
199   'Libya has evidence of killing by Gaddafi's son Saif – ICC', Malta Independent, 22 April 2012.
200   'Gaddafi's son Saif al-Islam is free,' The Guardian, 23 August 2011.

he should be surrendered. I tried to prevent them from killing him,' the prosecutor explained.

It was an awkward manoeuvre, but indeed the Gaddafis were in danger. The Libyan leader tried to flee, but was caught on 20 October 2011 by rebels in his hometown Sirte in a drainage pipe, tortured and savagely killed. The two other ICC suspects were on the run as well. International media reported that negotiations were held through intermediaries with Saif Al-Islam, now known as the 'prime minister' at large, and with the indicted former head of military intelligence, to surrender themselves to the ICC. To no avail. The two Libyans gambled, but lost. The Zintan Brigade caught Saif Al-Islam on 19 November 2011 at some distance of the desert town of Obar. Pictures show a frightened young Gaddafi with a light brown scarf draped around his head like a desert turban, in a plane to Zintan.

At first Al-Senussi, who was also the brother-in-law of the murdered leader Gaddafi, seemed to have escaped. But he was arrested in March 2012 in Mauritania when he tried to enter the country under a false name.[201] The former military man, nicknamed 'the butcher', was accused of having personally abused Libyans during his long career in the army. He has been blamed for the bloodbath in 1996 in the prison of Abu Salim in Tripoli, where twelve hundred prisoners were killed. He is also suspected of being implicated in acts of terror, bomb attacks, kidnapping and murdering dissidents abroad: cases over which the ICC has no jurisdiction, as these crimes happened before the UN Security Council's referral. After long negotiations Libya was rumoured to have transferred a large sum of money to the Mauritanian government – possibly two hundred million dollars – after which Al-Senussi was extradited to Tripoli in September 2012.

During the revolution the Libyan opposition had been at the side of the ICC, once in power the national transitional council made a turn around and rejected the idea of trials in The Hague. Libya wanted to prosecute the men at home, and prosecutor Moreno-Ocampo agreed that this actually might not be such a bad idea. On 1 May 2012 the Libyan authorities filed an admissibility challenge saying that the ICC didn't have jurisdiction to handle the trial against Saif Al-Islam Gaddafi. Tripoli

---

201 'Muammar Gaddafi's spy chief Senussi arrested in Mauritania,' The Telegraph, 17 March 2012.

pointed to the principle of complementarity, which means the ICC can only do cases if a country is unable or unwilling to do prosecutions itself. The Libyans argued they would very much like to take up this case. But defence lawyer Taylor said during her press conference that her client Gaddafi preferred to be tried by the ICC, and rejected the idea of a Libyan trial.

A new seating arrangement

'Did you have a good holiday?' Journalists are greeting each other on this autumn day, 9 October 2012, in the sombre media centre of the old court building. It had been a rather quiet period for the public. During the summer there had been no press conferences or special hearings, which usually are attended by the small group of journalists following the ICC and other justice institutions in The Hague. Today the reporters have turned up for a status conference. When the blinds go up, the seating arrangement appears different from usual.

Next to the prosecution team sit the representatives of the new Libyan government who will be pleading for Saif Al-Islam Gaddafi to be tried at home. The judges are not in yet and the prosecutors are chatting with the Libyan delegation. They are smiling, talking and appear to get on very well. The Office of the Prosecutor (OTP) agrees to a large extent that the case could be left to Libya, although it still has some questions.[202] Opposite sit Melinda Taylor and Xavier-Jean Keïta, OPCD-head and lead counsel in this case, representing their absent client. In the seats next to them are the legal representatives of the victims. Usually these parties have opposite views. But now they share the same goal: prosecuting Gaddafi in The Hague. Although their agreement ends there, as the defence will usually plead not guilty, while the lawyers for the victims will go for a conviction.

When the status conference is officially opened, the head of the Libyan delegation, Ahmed El-Gehani, is allowed to speak first. He presents himself as professor of law at Benghazi University and Rome University. He is the Libyan representative and national co-ordinator with the ICC. El-Gehani is a man with white-grey hair and bags under the eyes. The

---

202 Prosecution response to Application on behalf of the Government of Libya pursuant to Article 19 of the ICC Statute, OTP, 5 June 2012.

Libyan legal expert will explain how important national prosecutions are. 'Presiding judge, ladies and gentlemen, you know that Libyans can have freedom today for the first time since 42 years, but they are still affected by fear as a result of the Gaddafi government. They still have painful memories of the past,' El-Gehani starts his statement in Arabic.[203] During that 'murderous regime, thousands of Libyan citizens were victims of murder, torture, rape, enforced disappearances, persecution and other serious human rights abuses.' The crimes 'were a national tragedy that scarred the lives of virtually every Libyan citizen also outside the territory,' says El-Gehani. 'The reach of Gaddafi was total.'

But things are going much better now, the professor explains. The National Transitional Council has organised free elections. There is a new parliament, though it has proven difficult to form a new government and indeed there is not yet a new prosecutor-general. El-Gehani acknowledges there are still problems with armed militia that carry out attacks on towns and cities. But these groups will be disarmed. Briefly he mentions the act of terror, a month earlier on 11 September 2012, when the diplomatic mission of the United States in Benghazi was attacked. Four people were killed, including US ambassador Christopher Stevens.

The three judges listen carefully to the lecture of the Libyan representative, who explains that the authorities are not only 'committed' to carry out a 'fair trial' for officials of the former Gaddafi regime, but have an even larger aim. Libya also wants to 'create a judicial system which is fair,' showing its 'commitment to rule of law for all Libyans and in Libya as a whole.' The prosecution of Gaddafi officials will not only offer 'a unique opportunity for national reconciliation by a community that wishes to have justice done at home in Libya.' It will also help to rebuild the country as it would 'empower' and 'strengthen' the 'capacity of our judicial, prosecutorial and investigative organs, and this will lead to the setting up of a new Libya, the Libya that we are struggling to build.' But this takes time. El-Gehani explains Libya doesn't want to rush things, which could result in a system not meeting the 'minimum international standards.' Besides, why should Libya be told to hurry up, while the ICC itself, with 'its considerable resources' takes many years to bring accused persons to justice in 'significantly less complex' cases, quips the Libyan

203 Official transcript, ICC, 9 October 2012.

representative, who is asking the court for the 'necessary time' to build a national system and 'achieve justice.'

After his introduction El-Gehani gives the floor to Philippe Sands QC. The British lawyer, employed by the Libyan authorities to plead their case, is gifted with great rhetorical ability. He gives an overview of the investigations by the Libyan authorities. Sneeringly he gestures to the OPCD while explaining that Libya was 'deeply disappointed' when the defence's office – thus Keïta and Taylor – said that Saif Al-Islam Gaddafi is not being treated well. The national authorities were equally offended when the OPCD said that Libya only wanted to charge this high profile suspect with 'offences relating to camel licensing and the cleanliness of fish farms.'

While Sands is making his remarks, Keïta is consumed by anger. The flamboyant lawyer, with big rings on his fingers, a huge watch and a bunch of bracelets on his wrists, who usually wears a large Stetson hat outside the courtroom, is ready to get up and reply to Sands. But Taylor puts her hand lightly on his arm, calming him down. The relations between the Libyan representatives and the defence have plunged to their lowest point, as there have been the detention of Taylor and her colleagues, Libya's proceedings against the lawyer, and the ICC investigating her professional conduct. Later Keïta will tell me that at the time, his phone was illegally tapped by Libya. The head of the OPCD explains he simply had enough of the fact that the Libyan representatives continued to be campaigning against the defence and questioning the integrity of Gaddafi's lawyers.

With an ironic smile Taylor looks at her opponent, while Sands goes on to say that in Libya the 'false and inflammatory allegations and accusations' by the OPCD have started to undermine 'public confidence' in the ICC. The country is committed to do the Gaddafi case itself and is quite far along with its investigations into serious crimes, including murder and rape. Sands: 'We believe that the Libyan evidence is as comprehensive, if not more so, significantly more so, than that which has been gathered to date by the ICC prosecutor's office.'

With straight faces everybody is listening carefully to Sands submissions. But then he touches upon a very sensitive matter: the death penalty.

At the ICC the maximum punishment is basically 30 years, with a life sentence in extremely grave cases. The fact that the death penalty is not included in the Rome Statute reflects the global development towards abolishing this punishment. It would be a disgrace if the ICC allows a suspect to be prosecuted by national authorities who finally would decide to execute the defendant. But Sands reminds the court that this punishment isn't forbidden in international law. Besides, Libya applies restrictions. Capital punishment can't be carried out before the Libyan Supreme Court has considered the case, Sands explains. 'Libyan law also provides the important possibility of commutation of a death sentence to life imprisonment, where the family members of victims forgive the convicted person.'

But when he wants to discuss the question of who has control over Gaddafi's detention, presiding judge Silvia Fernández de Gurmendi intervenes. 'I'm sorry to interrupt you at this moment, but I'm afraid that we will need to suspend the session now because we have run out of the tape,' she says, referring to the reason why sessions can't last much longer than one and a half hours. The capacity of the tapes used for recording the hearing is limited. 'I would suggest that we suspend now and we will come back at twelve.'

'Absolutely,' agrees Sands, who adds that he needs less than a minute.

'Okay, you have a minute then,' responds judge Fernández.

'It is correct that he presently remains in the custody of the Zintan Brigade,' says Sands. Once the national prosecutor-general has been appointed by the new cabinet, he will be working with the Zintan Brigade to get Gaddafi transferred to the 'purpose-built trial and detention facilities' in Tripoli. 'This engagement with the Zintan Brigade will form part of the new government's commitment to demobilising the various militia groups which remain active across Libya.'

After the coffee break, the judges want to know whether the Libyan authorities are actually doing investigations. It is an important precondition before the ICC can transfer the Gaddafi case to Libya. 'The investigation is ongoing,' Sands answers.

'Continuing?' asks judge Fernández.

'Absolutely, the investigation is ongoing. I've shared with you what I'm able to share with you at this point. We've heard your question and we will reflect, both over the lunch break and over the course of the day, to see whether we can provide you with more specificity,' Sands adds rather vaguely.

The judges might only consider handing the case back to Tripoli if Libya and ICC's prosecutor are both charging Gaddafi with the same crimes, and if the national authorities are willing and able to handle the case. The next speaker Sara Criscitelli, representing the OTP, says the court's investigators have collected statements from crime-based witnesses and from insider witnesses. 'We see parallels in the way the investigations are proceeding,' she explains. At least 'on the face' of it, the prosecution has confidence that the Libyan authorities are investigating with the same 'serious approach,' although she has to admit that she doesn't have 'actual details' of what kind of material the Libyans have. 'We have not swapped evidence.' But the summaries of the evidence show that Tripoli 'has taken concrete steps to investigate the suspect for substantially the same conduct.'

Criscitelli agrees: 'This is sort of an odd case.' Because usually the defence wouldn't be pushing for a court case in The Hague, while the OTP 'would be a little bit more sceptical' about a state saying 'it has the right to have primary prosecution of the person.' But in this instance, she explains, 'we are confident that Libya is interested in prosecuting these crimes and this offender in the time period that we cover, and in fact beyond our time frame, and we are confident that it meets the admissibility standards.' She insists that Libya should have the chance to undertake the prosecution of Gaddafi. 'We are very sympathetic to the transitional justice issue and the need to give Libya a little bit more space.' Criscitelli adds that for the prosecution it is important that people are held 'criminally accountable', but 'not to push ourselves to the front and elbow aside the states that are genuinely able and willing to prosecute their nationals for their crimes.' Later prosecutor Fatou Bensouda will say that if Libya would try the persons that violently suppressed the uprising in a fair and transparent way, this could be a 'Nuremberg moment' for the country.

'Don't trust Libya'

But when it is Melinda Taylor's turn, she will say that Libya's admissibility challenge is 'a house of cards' built on 'false and misleading premises.' The national authorities lied with regard to the treatment of her client, she says, elaborating about matters such as incommunicado detention, family visits, charges, medical care and his rights. She attacks professor El-Gehani for mishandling her own visit to Gaddafi. Speaking about herself in the third person, she says: 'The defence accepted Libya's word they would be able to conduct a privileged visit which would respect international standards, and that it would not in any way be criminally sanctioned for its duty to represent the best interests of its client.' In fact, the professor had 'explicitly acknowledged' that the defence could transmit privileged documents to Gaddafi. 'As a result, counsel ended up spending 26 days in jail in Zintan and is still facing domestic prosecutions,' stresses Taylor. Referring to her failed visit to properly meet with her client, she says that the Libyan authorities 'happily broadcasted to the world that they had deliberately deceived the ICC delegation by placing someone in the room who pretended not to understand English, but actually speaks five languages, and that this was for the purpose of monitoring what was supposed to have been a privileged visit.' The meeting was even covertly filmed with 'a keyring camera.' After Taylor and her colleagues were detained, they were possibly used as blackmail material. The lawyer quotes former Australian foreign minister, senator Bob Carr, who had a meeting with members of the Libyan government during the detention crisis. In an interview with The Guardian, Carr said that the Libyan authorities had indicated that they would be likely to release the lawyer and the three other officials 'if the ICC agreed that Saif could be tried in Libya rather than The Hague.'

Don't trust Libya's promises, concludes Taylor, because the authorities are providing the court with 'misleading and contradictory information.' The judges should dismiss the admissibility challenge 'because the government has failed to establish that the domestic proceedings relate to the same conduct as the ICC case,' the defence lawyer says. The hearings in the Libyan case against Gaddafi are being postponed again and again. One of the reasons was that the authorities were waiting for the extradition by Mauritania of Al-Senussi, who is also demanded by the ICC, to be able to interrogate him and get more evidence against Gaddafi. The former chief of the military intelligence, who is suffering from a liver disease, had been too ill to travel, but when he arrived in Libya he was immediately questioned, without having had the opportunity to select a lawyer.

'A Libyan authority who was present during his initial interrogation noted that Mr Al-Senussi was in a complete state of shock during the interrogation' says Taylor, while her opponent Sands is suddenly yawning as she continues her long list of problems and abuses in Libya.

Taylor underlines that most witnesses in the Gaddafi case are detained officials from the former regime. She points out that there's been 'an extremely high incidence of mistreatment' of these persons while in detention. Their testimonies and those of others might have been procured under duress. Later she will say that in Libya 'confessions are routinely extracted by torture. Anyone captured and detained by rebels knows that they risk such mistreatment if they appear to sympathise with or exculpate the Gaddafi regime.'

In crafted sentences Taylor attacks the guarantees given by Tripoli. The atmosphere in the courtroom has changed. At first the Libyan delegation had looked satisfied with the presentation of their case, now the representatives are sitting tiredly in their chairs. The smiles have gone. Counsel Sands looks down, with a big frown on his face.

But then Taylor interrupts herself: 'Madam President, I see it is 4.30. Should we – '

'Yes, indeed, we have reached the end of our session,' says judge Fernández, 'so you may continue tomorrow.'

'Gaddafi is not a guinea pig'

The next morning, at the very last minute, Xavier-Jean Keïta comes hurrying into the courtroom. Quickly he puts his black robe on and sits down next to Taylor. After the opening of the hearing the defence counsel comes back to the issue of capital punishment. 'Although the government tried to diplomatically dance around the issue of the death penalty, let's be very clear. If convicted, Mr Gaddafi will be hanged,' Taylor insists.[204] Assurances that the death penalty could be commuted are false. The day before she had referred to Libyan law number 35 which says that 'no child of Muammar Gaddafi can ever benefit from any form of leniency or forgiveness.'

To add a universal dimension to her argument, she quotes Navi Pillay, former judge at the ICC and the International Criminal Tribunal for Rwanda (ICTR), who then still is United Nations High Commissioner for Human Rights: 'The death penalty cannot be reconciled with fundamental human rights values. It is an affront to human dignity; our shared human dignity. Every time the state drags a human being to the execution site and kills him in the name of the people, our name, a piece of our own human dignity, is shattered.'

---

204   Official transcript, ICC, 10 October 2012.

While the lawyer is in the midst of a next argument, presiding judge Fernández de Gurmendi says: 'I am sorry to interrupt you.'

'I'm sorry,' the counsel says, realising she is speaking too fast.

Judge Fernández de Gurmendi: 'I suggest that you try to slow down and also to take some space between sentences.'

Taylor: 'Thank you very much, Madam President, and I apologise sincerely to the interpreters.'

The usual guarantees in a country with a rule of law are absent in Libya, Taylor concludes, while trying to formulate her sentences more calmly. 'It is also unclear whether any lawyer would be willing to represent Mr Gaddafi, given that his defence counsel was arrested and detained by the very same persons prosecuting Mr Gaddafi's case,' she adds, explaining that it will be impossible for her client to prepare his defence without a lawyer or access to evidence.

But judge Fernández de Gurmendi will intervene again: 'Ms Taylor, you need to make a break between paragraphs. Maybe that is a better technique than trying to slow down completely.'

Taylor thanks the judge, while continuing her critical address crushing the image the Libyan authorities had tried to build. 'The ability of the present government to address this case in an impartial manner is also quite suspect in light of the fact that the current president was linked to several assassination attempts on the defendant's father,' the lawyer alleges. Even Libyan officials acknowledge there is no state, no security, no national army, no internal security agency, no police and a lack of expertise in certain judicial matters, says the counsel, who supports her arguments with many references. So how can witnesses, or even the judiciary, be safe? Libya is asking the ICC for some flexibility to set up proper institutions. But, says the lawyer, 'Mr Gaddafi is not a guinea pig. He is a person with rights. He shouldn't have to languish in detention whilst the Libyan government attempts to build a functioning system from scratch.' One month in isolation is hard, Taylor knows from experience. 'To that must be added the mental strain and frustration of knowing that he is facing the death penalty, whilst having no means to do anything to start preparing his defence.'

Sands, the lawyer for the Libyan delegation, is not impressed. He claims that the defence is creating 'a smoke screen' by listing 'minutiae' that don't reflect the reality of a post-conflict country in transition. If one compares it with Afghanistan or Iraq, then Libya is doing 'remarkably well after

42 years of dictatorship.' There is another matter he wants to raise. 'We do find the personalised attacks against professor El-Gehani to be really unacceptable.' The Libyan representative has been acting in 'good faith' and is 'entirely reliable,' says Sands, elaborating: 'I want to make sure in open court that everyone hears very clearly that professor El-Gehani, in the view of his counsel, is performing his functions admirably in very difficult circumstances.'

One more thing. Sarcastically he adds: 'You saw the remarkable spectacle of the same person acting as witness and counsel in her own defence. I need say nothing more about that.' With that attack on her position, wrapped in polite words, Sands wants to show that because of her detention and the Libyan accusations against her, Taylor has a double role and is not suitable as Gaddafi's counsel. But the hearing is not yet over. Judge Hans-Peter Kaul, who hasn't said a word during the status conference, wants to ask something. There is frustration in his voice. After two days of hearings of in total ten hours it is still not clear to him and the other judges how far Libya is with its case against Gaddafi. He wonders whether the Libyan authorities in Tripoli are aware they are obliged 'to provide concrete, tangible and pertinent evidence' to the chamber that 'proper investigations are currently ongoing, and proper and concrete preparations for the trial are ongoing?' And he adds the word: 'Please.'

Sands' reply is so vague that it provides an answer as well. 'I want to be very careful with what I say in open court,' he says. 'We are acutely aware and we remain absolutely committed to meeting Libya's full responsibilities in reaching the appropriate standard as determined by the pre-trial chamber.'

Half a year later Kaul's intervention proves to be a harbinger for the decision. On 31 May 2013 the judges reject Libya's claim to the prosecution of Gaddafi. They acknowledge the efforts by the state to 'improve security conditions, rebuild institutions and restore the rule of law.'[205] But the problems are too big and fundamental to transfer the case from the ICC to Libya. The national authorities are unable to get hold of Gaddafi who is still held by the Zintan militia, they don't have the capacity to obtain the necessary testimonies, nor to provide witness

---

205 Decision on the admissibility of the case against Saif Al-Islam Gaddafi,' ICC, 31 May 2013.

protection or to secure a lawyer for the suspect. The judges conclude that Tripoli is unable 'genuinely to carry out an investigation' against Gaddafi. It is also not clear whether the Libyan and the ICC investigations cover the same crimes. The government has lost the admissibility challenge. One year later, 21 May 2014, the appeals chamber confirms the decision.[206] Thus the case remains in the hands of the ICC, while Gaddafi remains in the hands of the Zintan Brigade.

The pre-trial chamber, presided by judge Fernández de Gurmendi, finds on 10 December 2014 that the Libyan government has not been complying with court orders to surrender Gaddafi and to return the defence's documents that were confiscated during the arrest of Taylor and her colleagues.[207] The judges refer the matter to the UN Security Council, which concludes in July 2015 that Libya immediately has to hand over the defendant to the ICC.

Another suspect, another outcome

Meanwhile the Libyan authorities have filed a second admissibility challenge. This time in the Abdullah Al-Senussi case. On 2 April 2013 Libya says it can manage the prosecution of the former head of the military intelligence at home. But the difficulties of building a proper state become clear while the judges are deciding about the Al-Senussi case. A day before the ICC ruling is made public, armed men entered at half past two in the morning the five star Corinthia Hotel in Tripoli where the Libyan prime minister Ali Zeidan stayed, for security reasons. The government leader is taken from his bed and kidnapped. After three hours he's released. The militia group that carried out the kidnapping is allegedly working for the ministry of interior, just as other government institutions are hiring armed groups to provide security as well. The kidnapping might have been an act of revenge for an earlier US raid seizing a senior al-Qaeda suspect.[208]

The incident, however, has no influence on the judges' decision. On 11 October 2013 they conclude that Libya is prosecuting Al-Senussi for the

---

206 Judgment on the Appeal of Libya against the decision of Pre-Trial Chamber I of 31 May 2013 entitled Decision on the admissibility of the case against Saif Al-Islam Gaddafi, ICC, 21 May 2014.

207 Decision on the non-compliance by Libya with requests for cooperation by the Court and referring the matter to the United Nations Security Council, ICC, 10 December 2014.

208 'Libyan PM Ali Zeidan detained by militia,' BBC, 10 October 2013.

same crimes as the ICC, and that the authorities are able to handle the case.[209] The fact that the suspect still has no lawyers is due to 'security challenges.' The judges assume this matter will be arranged. So they arrive at a completely opposite conclusion to that in the previous challenge: Libya can prosecute Al-Senussi.

'A shocking decision' reacts Ben Emmerson, counsel for the suspect. He underlines that the outcome of the trial against his client in Libya is already clear: the death penalty. Emmerson immediately appeals the decision. The Libyan system is collapsing, he says. His fears are supported by human rights organisations that are publishing worrying reports on armed groups threatening and attacking the national justice system. Human Rights Watch says that four judges and prosecutors have been killed.

The situation doesn't get better. The following months the conflicts between armed militia, radical Islamic groups and the weakened army only intensify. The airport in Tripoli is under fire. Several countries are closing their embassies. Amidst the growing lawlessness, the appeals chamber confirms on 24 July 2014 the earlier decision by the judges. The objections of the defence to a Libyan trial, such as the unlawful treatment of Al-Senussi, the absence of a lawyer and insecurity for witnesses, are swept aside. Tripoli can go ahead with the prosecution of the former head of the military intelligence.[210] Human Rights Watch has serious doubts. The decision in the Al-Senussi case 'comes out at a time when the challenges facing Libya's justice system continue to mount at an alarming pace,' reacts Richard Dicker, HRW's international justice director, in a press release.[211] He points out that the Libyan authorities have 'done little' to provide Al-Senussi 'with basic due process rights, like thousands of others detained across the country who remain without any meaningful access to a lawyer.' He adds: 'As the country enters another month of chaos, where judges, lawyers and prosecutors are being killed, it's hard to imagine that Libya can hold any fair trial, much less a trial of this sensitivity and significance.'

209 Decision on the admissibility of the case against Abdullah Al-Senussi, ICC, 11 October 2013.
210 Judgment on the appeal of Mr Abdullah Al-Senussi against the decision of Pre-Trial Chamber I of 11 October 2013 entitled Decision on the admissibility of the case against Abdullah Al-Senussi, ICC, 24 July 2014.
211 Libya: ICC Judges Reject Sanussi Appeal, Human Rights Watch, 24 July 2014.

The only person that might be able to change the situation is the prosecutor of the ICC. If new facts arise she could ask the judges to review their decision in the admissibility challenge. Given her office's previously stated opinion on the Libyan cases, that chance is not very big. However, Fatou Bensouda seems concerned about the general situation in Libya. On 25 July 2014, one day after the appeals decision, she issues a statement saying she is 'deeply troubled by the escalating violence' in Libya.[212] 'Recent reports of alleged attacks carried out against the civilian population and civilian objects in Tripoli and Benghazi are a cause for great concern,' she writes. Bensouda calls on all parties to 'refrain' from targeting civilians and warns she will 'not hesitate' to investigate and prosecute persons that commit international crimes – irrespective of their status, position or affiliation. She points to resolution 1970 of the UN Security Council that provided her office with jurisdiction over genocide, crimes against humanity or war crimes committed in Libya since 15 February 2011. Bensouda insists that her team has 'continued its investigative activities and has closely monitored the situation on the ground.' Many groups allegedly committed crimes, but so far the ICC seemed to limit itself to prosecuting leaders of the ousted Gaddafi regime.

Death penalty

The hostilities will result in the establishment of two governments. The internationally recognized government is based in the cities Tobruk and al-Bayda, controlling eastern parts of the country. In Tripoli sits an opposing self-declared authority, and that's where in March 2014 the trial against Gaddafi, Al-Senussi and 36 other suspects, charged with crimes committed during the uprising, starts. A few months earlier, in September 2013, Gaddafi was presented to the court via video-link, from the courtroom of Zintan. He was wearing a blue uniform and stood in a cage. But he wasn't brought to Tripoli to be physically present at the trial. The proceedings take place in the Al-Hadba corrections facility, controlled by the former deputy defence minister.[213] One year later, on 28 July 2015, the Tripoli court publishes the verdicts: 32 officials are convicted, while

---

212 Statement of the Prosecutor of the International Criminal Court, Fatou Bensouda, in relation to the escalating violence in the Situation in Libya, OTP, 25 July 2014.
213 Libya: Flawed Trial of Gaddafi Officials, Human Rights Watch, 28 July 2015.

four are acquitted and one person is sent to a medical facility. Gaddafi, al-Senussi and seven others are condemned to death, by firing squad. Exactly as their defence lawyers at the ICC predicted.

Human Rights Watch is deeply concerned about the way these sensitive trials have been conducted, as some defence lawyers were threatened and resigned, while some were not given the chance to speak with their clients in private. Hardly any evidence was presented, nor were prosecution witnesses brought in. The number of defence witnesses was limited. Although a video-link was established, Gaddafi appeared in only three of the 24 trial sessions, according to the human rights organisation. This means he has essentially been tried and convicted in absentia.

By 2016 Libya has two administrations, plus a government of national unity. The jihadi terror group Islamic State has taken advantage of the chaos and controls several coastal areas. In the meantime Al-Senussi has appealed his death penalty.[214] Nothing has been heard of Gaddafi. Then on 3 February 2016, John RWD Jones, who had become his ICC defence lawyer, requests the court to allow him to withdraw from the case, for reasons that were kept confidential.[215] Two months later, on 16 April, the counsel dies after being struck by a train at a London station.

Calling with Zintan

The ICC case against Saif Al-Islam Gaddafi is 'at an impasse' because Libya still hasn't surrendered the suspect to the court, the OTP writes on 26 April 2016 in a new filing to the judges.[216] For five years Gaddafi has been wanted by the court, but the national authorities confirm he is 'unavailable' to the Libyan state, so they are unable to do anything. He is in custody of al-Ajami Al-Atiri, commander of the Abu-Bakr al-Siddiq Battalion in Zintan. He is the local head of the judicial police and also of the guards controlling Gaddafi's detention.

Finally, the prosecution decides to give the commander a ring. During the telephone call, which takes place on 11 March 2016, the prosecution tells Al-Atiri that he has the obligation to hand Gaddafi over to the ICC. The Zintan commander, however, explains that the Libyan parliament

214 Profile: Abdullah al-Senussi, BBC, 16 October 2015.
215 Decision on Withdrawal of Counsel, ICC, 4 February 2016.
216 Request for an order directing the Registrar to transmit the request for arrest and surrender to Mr al-'Ajami Al-'Atiri, Commander of the Abu-Bakr al-Siddiq Battalion in Zintan, Libya, OTP 26 April 2016.

in Tobruk issued a general amnesty for all prisoners, including Gaddafi, back in 2015, somewhere around July or September. As a result, the ICC suspect is 'no longer wanted for any crimes' in Libya. Al-Atiri explains to the prosecutors that Gaddafi was still detained in Zintan, because the commander himself was 'awaiting instructions from the government, specifically the minister of justice who was based in Bayda.' He said that the suspect was in good health.

The ICC prosecution was however not going to let go Gaddafi just like that. In its briefing the OTP suggests to the judges they could send the arrest warrant for Gaddafi directly to Al-Atiri. But the chamber decides otherwise. On 2 June 2016 the judges order the registrar to check with the Libyan authorities whether they are in contact with Zintan, and if they would agree that the request to arrest and surrender the suspect be transmitted to the local militia and if they could facilitate such a manoeuvre.[217]

New lawyers

Meanwhile several lawyers have been working behind the scenes to constitute themselves as a whole new defence team. One of its members is the famous British counsel Karim Khan, who just got his client, the Kenyan deputy president William Ruto, off the hook. Well connected to the media, he sends an email to the 'Association of Journalists at the International Criminal Court,' inviting the press for a briefing at the luxurious Hilton Hotel in The Hague. 'You will be aware that this is also the first time Saif himself has selected his legal team,' Khan writes in his invitation, as 'previous lawyers were court-appointed.'

On Monday morning, 27 June 2016, in a windowless meeting room, the defence team welcomes a dozen journalists with coffee, tea and nice pastries. The lawyers have placed a roll up banner showing one photo featuring a broad smiling Saif Al-Islam Gaddafi putting his right hand in an at-your-service-gesture to his temples, while a second picture shows him behind bars wearing a blue prisoner's uniform.

---

217 Order to the Registrar with respect to the Request for an order directing the Registrar to transmit the request for arrest and surrender to Mr al– 'Ajami Al-'Atiri, Commander of the Abu-bakr al-Siddiq Battalion in Zintan, Libya, ICC, 2 June 2016.

After some informal chats and exchanges, the defence team takes its place behind a table to present itself. The Libyan lawyer Khaled Zaydi sits in the middle, flanked by Karim Khan and his colleague Dato Shyamala Alagendra. The big question is: how do they want to handle the case? But before that becomes clear, the media are invited to watch a video on Gaddafi's life. Images of their client on trial in Libya are followed by pictures of the suspect as a child, a student and an adult fighting for human rights. His outfits range from expensive suits to casual wear. Melancholic tunes come and go, invoking chuckling among the journalists, while the lawyers keep straight faces. Khan is making notes with an impressively large silver coloured pen. Gaddafi is presented as a person who wanted a united and peaceful Libya, and warned for mayhem if protesters would persist in pushing for a Libyan Spring. Towards the end the film is showing images of war with armed pickup trucks, men firing machine guns and destroyed buildings.

The first to speak is Khaled Zaydi. The lawyer is reading out a written statement. He explains that when Gaddafi tried to flee Libya in 2011, he became the target of an assassination attempt as the convoy he travelled in came under attack. Pictures show a car, hit by a rocket, lying on its side against a tree next to a large crater. Some 27 people died and just five survived, including his client, although he lost parts of his fingers. When he tried to seek medical treatment, Gaddafi was captured. Under promises of health care and a fair trial, he was flown to Zintan.

His case was referred to the court in Tripoli, which then convicted him on 28 July 2015. It is 'ironic', says Zaydi, getting to the point the defence wants to make, that the ICC wants to prosecute Gaddafi for the same charges as he faced at the Libyan court. Here the experienced Khan takes over from his colleague, answering questions from the media. The British lawyer stresses an ICC trial would amount to 'double jeopardy' which is 'absolutely prohibited' in law. One can't be prosecuted for the same crimes twice. Khan refers to article 17(1)(c) of the Rome Statute which says that when a suspect has 'already been tried for conduct which is the subject of the complaint' then an ICC trial 'is not permitted.'[218]

Indeed, such proceedings have taken place in Tripoli, Khan underlines. It would be 'cruel' to have a second trial at the ICC hanging as 'a sword

---

218 Rome Statute of the International Criminal Court.

of Damocles' above his client's head. Gaddafi 'is willing' to have his fate 'to be decided by the Libyan people, who suffered so much,' says Khan, pointing at the NATO actions in Libya, the collapse of the state and the rise of the jihadi terrorist organisation Islamic State. In a few weeks' time the defence will request the ICC judges to declare the Gaddafi-case inadmissible before the court in The Hague. The question of the fairness of the Libyan trial isn't relevant, stresses Khan, because the argument of 'double jeopardy' comes first. It is important to render 'sovereignty back to Libya,' the lawyer says, so that 'justice and peace can be reconciled.' This team is taking a complete different position from that of Melinda Taylor, who argued against Libyan proceedings, as her client would not get a fair trial and undoubtedly would be sentenced to the death penalty. She was right in her prediction. There are serious doubts about the fairness of that trial, and the Libyan court did condemn Gaddafi to death, although the sentence hasn't been executed.

It puzzles the journalists attending the press conference in the hotel's meeting room that the Zaydi-Khan-team seems to find an ICC case worse than the risk of capital punishment at home. Then a reporter of Libya 24 TV wants to know whether the new defence lawyers are sure Gaddafi would benefit from Libya's amnesty law. What follows is a long answer by Zaydi in Arabic, of which just tiny parts are translated. Apparently the Gaddafi family has requested to have the amnesty applied to Saif Al-Islam.

One source had approached me saying he doubted whether Khan possessed power of attorney, a written declaration by the client authorising the lawyer to represent him. The defence team explains today that the authorisation was given to Zaydi who has met Gaddafi. Although, when asked by the journalists, the Libyan lawyer has to admit that 'the last time' he saw his client 'was at the end of 2015.' This means the counsel hasn't seen Gaddafi for more than six months. He stresses though that his client's health was 'quite good.' When it comes to his morale, Gaddafi was mainly worried about the situation in his country. Then Khan steps in, clarifying: 'Everything Zaydi has said is based on instructions by Saif al-Islam Gaddafi.' But when asked how he communicates with his client, the Libyan lawyer says he will remain silent about that issue.

Despite the confusion, one thing is clear: there is something going on behind closed doors. The defence's strategy would be extremely reckless if these lawyers don't have assurances that the death penalty won't be carried out. Otherwise it would be better to go for an ICC trial where at least Gaddafi's life would be spared. A few days later there is breaking news that, in hindsight, turns the press conference into a bit of a show. The broadcast organisation France24 reports to have spoken to Khan, who says that Gaddafi 'was given his liberty' on 12 April under the amnesty law. This implies he has already been free for months.[219]

The Libyan authorities, however, insist he is still detained. The union government stresses he hasn't benefitted from the amnesty law.[220] The confusion about what exactly is going on with the ICC suspect only increases. The admissibility challenge hasn't yet been filed by Khan and his Libyan colleague. For the time being Gaddafi seems to be a pawn in the power struggle taking place in Libya. It is unlikely he will be handed over to the ICC any time soon.

On 24 April 2017 there is a press release from the court. The ICC is publishing a fourth warrant of arrest in the Libyan situation.[221] Al-Tuhamy Mohamed Khaled is wanted by the court since 18 April 2013. He was head of the Internal Security Agency (ISA) during the Gaddafi regime and is held responsible for crushing the Libyan Spring. He is charged with crimes against humanity and war crimes for arresting and detaining opponents, subjecting them to severe beatings, electrocution, rape, solitary confinement, deprivation of food and water, mock executions and threats of killing. Al-Tuhamy, who allegedly has at least ten passports, some issued under different identities, was believed to have been living in Egypt, but according to the prosecution he is now in Libya.

219 'Gaddafi son Saif al-Islam 'released' from Libya jail, his lawyer tells FRANCE 24,' France24, 7 July 2016.
220 'Libyan government says no amnesty for Saif al-Islam,' Africa News, 13 July 2016.
221 Warrant of Arrest for Al-Tuhamy Mohamed Khaled, ICC, 18 April 2013.

10

THE RIGHTS OF VICTIMS
Expectations and disappointment

'Ms Chana, how do you feel about starting with your opening statement?'
With professional courtesy, judge Ekaterina Trendafilova is looking to
her left. Sureta Chana nods and gets up. Then her deep voice sounds in
the courtroom. 'Madam President, members of the chamber, I am the
common representative of 327 victims,' she introduces herself.[222] Lawyer
Chana tells that her clients are all from the Rift Valley in Kenya. They are
victims of the post-election violence that erupted after the Kenyan vote in
December 2007.
She regrets not being able to introduce all her clients individually today,
1 September 2011, at the start of the confirmation of charges hearing
in the case against three Kenyan suspects: William Samoei Ruto, Joshua
Arap Sang and Henry Kiprono Kosgey. But she would like to share the
experiences of some victims with the court. 'Picture a man who for the
past 20 years has lived in Nandi Hills,' Chana begins, referring to a small
town in a region known for its green tea plantations and hills, where
many of Kenya's world-famous athletes originate from. A man who was a
farmer and the breadwinner of his family. A man who made sure that his
children went to school. Until his life completely changed on 18 January
2008, when violent youth attacked him. Chana quotes his words: 'It all
started with a cry for help and I attended, just to find that, in fact, it was
a plan to draw us close. Upon realising this, I took to my heels running
for my life, but unfortunately I was unable to outrun the youth coming
against me. I was shot down by an arrow to the leg. They caught up with
me and stoned me, leaving me for dead.'
He suffered spinal injuries. The rest of his life, Chana tells, he will remain
'paralysed and in the care of his wife, unable to work, to earn the funds

222 Official transcript, ICC, 1 September 2011.

for his own medication, let alone to provide for his wife and children. He has been transformed from a provider for his family to a burden to his family, in a country where social security, invalidity benefits, state-provided health care and compensation for victims of crimes are virtually unknown.'

Chana also tells about the fate of a Kenyan woman who had to flee with her child during the election violence. She sought refuge at 'the one place that is considered by most people as sacrosanct and consequently most secure: the church,' says Chana, who masters the art of oratory. The story resembles that of the first witness who would testify in the trial against vice president Ruto and broadcaster Sang.[223] 'A crowd of riotous youths viciously shouting slogans and brandishing crude weapons surrounded the church,' Chana explains. They sealed doors and windows, and set the place ablaze. The Kiambaa church was on fire. In a desperate attempt to save her child, she threw the child out of a window. 'She defied death but sustained burns to 80 percent of her body, and now she is scarred for life. Her child died, despite all her efforts to save him.'

Another victim lost her teenage son in the violence. The boy had just finished school examinations. 'I had great hopes and expectations of my son. Since his death during the violence I feel lost,' his deeply affected mother had told the lawyer.

Chana explains that virtually all her clients had their homes and property destroyed and looted. They had to flee. 'Many subsequently returned and have faced the heartbreaking prospect of seeking to rebuild all that was lost,' the lawyer says. 'They found themselves living in the same area as the people who were direct perpetrators of the violence.' Others can't return because they are still menaced or their properties are occupied.

Recognition for victims

Persons such as the paralysed farmer, the woman who was severely burned trying to save her child and the mother who lost her teenage son, all have, just like thousands of others, the status of victim with the ICC. The official recognition of victims is a novelty in the history of international criminal law. Although justice is carried out in their name, traditionally victims didn't have a specifique position and have been marginalised

---

223 The judges declined to confirm the charges against politician Henry Kiprono Kosgey, so he wasn't put on trial.

before international criminal courts and tribunals, which are primarily focused on the guilt or innocence of the accused. At the Nuremberg trials, where Nazi-leaders were prosecuted after the second World War, only a few victims were present. They participated solely in their capacities as witnesses. The same happened with the international criminal tribunals for the former Yugoslavia (ICTY) and Rwanda (ICTR), where victims only have been called as witnesses to give evidence. Their accounts are framed as testimonies that have to fit the case theory of the prosecution or defence. The questions they are asked in court about their experiences, having endured terrible atrocities or having seen pain inflicted on others, are limited to their relevance to the legal case against the suspect.

'With the ICC it is for the first time that victims have their own place in the proceedings. That is truly groundbreaking. They are not just a tool in the strategy of the prosecutor to achieve a conviction, but have their own status which recognizes their situation as a victim,' says Gaëlle Carayon, who worked as post-conflict policy advisor for Redress, an organisation that supports victims of torture, and also functions as the focal point of the Victims' Rights Working Group, a network of three hundred organisations and experts committed to the rights of victims at the ICC.[224]

The ICC still calls victims to give testimony as witnesses. But separate from that role, they have the right to be heard by the judges during all stages of the proceedings. Usually their legal representatives will perform that task for them by participating in the court cases, like Sureta Chana did. They have the right to express their views on matters such as the decision to open an investigation and the scope of the charges, to make submissions during trials, to question witnesses and also to comment on matters such as sentencing. Victims can be invited by the judges to come and tell the court about their experiences in their capacity as victims. And they can comment on reparations that can be awarded after a conviction. Despite this major progress in status, most aspects of this new position have proven to be problematic. It starts with the fact that they are often poorly informed. 'Most victim participants have insufficient knowledge to make informed decisions about their participation in ICC cases,' states

---

224 The views expressed by Gaëlle Carayon are her own, and don't necessarily reflect those of Redress. She worked for the organisation up until December 2016.

the study 'The Victims Court?' by the Human Rights Center (HRC) at the University of California, that interviewed 622 victim participants in Uganda, Democratic Republic of Congo, Kenya and Ivory Coast.[225] In rural areas of Uganda, DRC and Kenya participants often lacked access to information and had much less knowledge than those in cities. 'Few knew the location of the court's headquarters, and many believed the ICC was an aid organization rather than a criminal court,' the HRC study concludes.

Problems with registering

To become an officially recognized victim, a person needs to apply and register with the ICC. In the early days, this was a nightmarish exercise. The victims needed to fill in forms consisting of no less than eighteen pages. The difficulties for people living in poor rural areas in situation countries, many being illiterate, having to complete this paper work and to make sure the documents end up on time in The Hague, are huge. Intermediaries were called in to help the victims. 'Often intermediaries are simply persons already supporting victims in some capacity, who mean to help them seek justice,' says Carayon. But not all of these persons were truthful. There have been reports about intermediaries telling victims to claim more losses than they actually suffered, or even charging victims substantial sums of money for filling in forms. 'This might have been a problem in some cases, but it should not be generalised,' notes Carayon. The judges, who have been applying different rules in different cases, play a key role in the procedures. The chambers for instance set the deadlines for applications. The Victims Participation and Reparations Section (VPRS), a section that falls under the registry, is tasked to make sure victims can apply. When the long forms were filled in, the documents had to go to the judges, the prosecution and the defence. Every single application was discussed. Still, in the trial against the Congolese warlord Jean-Pierre Bemba Gombo, who has been found guilty of international crimes which his men committed in the Central African Republic (CAR), no fewer than 5229 victims were registered. In contrast, during the

---

225 The Victims' Court? A study of 622 victim participants at the International Criminal Court, by The Human Rights Center at the University of California, Berkeley, School of Law, 2015. The study was performed at the request of the ICC's registry.

aborted case against Callixte Mbarushimana – the Rwandan was released because the judges decided the evidence against him was not convincing – the ICC failed to handle hundreds of applications, due to a lack of manpower.

Over the years the process to register has been simplified. Currently victims need to fill in a one-page form. However, in the recent trial against Malian suspect Ahmad Al Faqi Al Mahdi, a jihadi found guilty of war crimes for destroying and attacking nine mausoleums and the door of a mosque in Timbuktu, at first no victims applied. Carayon: 'There was limited outreach by the ICC in Mali, so the victims didn't necessarily know they could apply with the court. There might have been security problems that prevented victims from registering as well. Also the timeline was very restricted. Victims could only register within the six months between the confirmation of charges that took place in March and the verdict in September 2016.' So far eight victims are participating. One might get the impression there is a lot of contact between victims and the court, but that would be a wrong assumption. According to the HRC report most victims said that although 'ICC staff treated them in a professional and respectful manner and genuinely cared about their suffering and loss,' almost all respondents wanted more interaction with court officials or their legal representatives with whom they usually had just one meeting. Only a few had met 'with ICC representatives or legal representatives more than three times,' the study says. The report added: 'Some had only interacted with court intermediaries, which gave them the impression that the ICC did not value their views and their testimony.'

A strict link with charges

Cases before the ICC focus on mass violence that victimizes many people. But not all of them will be accepted as official victims by the court. According to the rules, individuals can only participate as victims in cases if their suffering is directly linked to the charges against a suspect. This restriction has its consequences.

In the first trial, against the Congolese warlord Thomas Lubanga Dyilo, the scope of the charges was quite limited. The rebel leader was prosecuted for enlisting and conscripting child soldiers under the age of 15 years and using them to participate in the war in the Congolese district of Ituri, where some 50,000 people died in the ethnic conflict between Hema and Lendu. That's why primarily child soldiers were accepted as victims. Finally, just 146 people participated as victims in the trial.

The painful truth however is that child soldiers are not only victims. Many locals perceive them as perpetrators as well. The scope of the charges meant however that, legally speaking, the thousands of civilians who suffered at the hands of Lubanga's militia men and child soldiers, were not accepted as official victims in this ICC case. Another point was that the warlord mainly recruited child soldiers from his own ethnic Hema group, which means that the victims admitted to this case, are mostly Hema. Almost no one of the other ethnic groups fitted the victim criteria, because they weren't child soldiers in Lubanga's army.

His adversaries in the Ituri wars, Germain Katanga and Mathieu Ngudjolo Chui, were prosecuted by the ICC for attacking a Hema village in Ituri. The result of the prosecution's choices was that mainly people from the Hema community were recognized as victims in the Ituri trials before the court.

Apart from legal limitations, security can also be a barrier. Kenyan victims have been facing serious obstacles making it difficult for them to join in the cases against powerful suspects such as president Uhuru Kenyatta and deputy president William Ruto. Sureta Chana told the judges that her clients 'live in fear with particular trepidation that they may be recognised as participants in proceedings before the International Criminal Court.' In its study the HRC came to the same conclusion: 'Victim participants fear reprisals. Some participants, in Kenya and DRC especially, feared that they could be targeted for violence because of their association with the ICC and its representatives.' The intimidation and disappearance of –potential – witnesses in Kenya affected victims who feared 'that the accused could use the apparatus of the state to target them,' the HRC wrote. In the DRC victims were afraid of attacks by local warlords or hired thugs. In countries like Uganda and Ivory Coast, 'where violence had subsided and perpetrators lacked political power,' there were 'fewer concerns about reprisals,' the HRC report said.

Legal representation

Official victims have a lawyer representing them. 'The overwhelming majority reported that they were pleased to participate through intermediaries or their legal representatives who could convey their stories to the court,' the HRC stated. Usually these lawyers are working for a group of victims, because proceedings would become unmanageable if hundreds or thousands of victims would all want their individual lawyers. 'In theory victims can choose their own common lawyer, but that rarely happens. In most situations, the court appoints a legal representative,' says Carayon.

Take for example Sureta Chana, who had been presenting the stories of the Kenyan victims so convincingly in the proceedings against Ruto and Sang. These clients had, however, not always been hers. In fact, at the time she had been representing them for just a few weeks. There was a hidden drama behind her appointment. It was the Dutch lawyer Liesbeth Zegveld – famous in The Netherlands for defending victims in cases against the state – who had been travelling to Kenya to interview victims of the post-election violence together with her colleague Göran Sluiter and their Kenyan team. They registered victims and made sure the forms were filed on time so they could officially be recognized by the ICC. It had been a huge job. The Dutch lawyers had been financing these efforts out of their own pocket. They were ready for the confirmation of charges hearings taking place in September 2011. But a few weeks before the start of these sessions, they received a notice from the court. Judge Trendafilova had decided – after consulting the registrar – to push Zegveld and Sluiter aside. In her decision she quoted the registrar, who was not convinced that the Dutch lawyers had established 'meaningful relationships of trust with significant numbers of their clients' nor that 'counsel's representation to date in this case indicates a particular familiarity with ICC proceedings.'[226] The court felt free to look for another candidate. Chana was being appointed as formal legal representative of victims. But Dutch lawyer Sluiter says that he and Zegveld weren't accepted by the ICC because 'they weren't interested in active representation.' In other words, the court wasn't keen on counsels who would really fight for their clients. 'The ICC decided to not spend much time on victims. They are seen as an obstacle that can slow down cases,' Sluiter added.

But Chana wouldn't stay on the case either, as she was appointed just for the phase of the confirmation of charges. Kenyan newspapers described

226 Decision on Victims' Participation at the Confirmation of Charges Hearing and in the Related Proceedings, ICC, 5 August 2011.

how the lawyer was at odds with the court. There were conflicts about payments for her trips to Kenya, while Chana also complained that her staff was not paid sufficiently. [227] After the judges decided on 23 January 2012 that the evidence against the suspects Ruto and Sang was solid enough to commit them to trial, the court said a whole new era had begun, putting an end to Chana's mandate. The Kenyan lawyer Wilfred Nderitu became her successor, and so the third legal representative in a row was looking after the interests of these Kenyan victims.

In the case against the Congolese warlord Bosco Ntaganda victims had asked for six legal representatives. Judge Trendafilova didn't honour their request. On 2 December 2013 she decided to appoint two lawyers from the ICC's Office of the Public Counsel for Victims (OPCV) to represent two groups of victims.[228]

Recently in the case against Dominic Ongwen, a commander of the Lord's Resistance Army (LRA) who is on trial facing no fewer than seventy charges, the issue of representation came up again. In this case, more than 4100 victims have been registered. One group of 1502 victims is represented by Paolina Massidda, the principal counsel of the OPCV. The second group of 2601 victims chose Joseph Akwenyu Manoba and Francisco Cox as their lawyers. However, the single judge in this case decided that only the court appointed counsel is entitled to be paid by the ICC. The other legal team didn't receive a fee.

In an urgent letter to the court, five organisations including Redress, the International Bar Association and the human rights organisation FIDH wrote: 'It is unsustainable for a legal team to act pro bono from the opening of the trial onwards and for the entire duration of a case, which is likely to span many years. The workload involves, among other, consulting with and informing over 2,600 victims, reviewing evidence, attending trial sessions, questioning witnesses, preparing motions, and responding to filings.'[229] The organisations stressed that for twelve years the Ugandan victims have been waiting for this trial to start. They

---

227 Urgent Request by the Victims Representative for an order from the Chamber requiring the Registrar to provide appropriate resources for the current mission in Kenya, Victims' Representative, 29 February 2012. 'Victims' lawyer in Kenya case challenges ICC registrars decisions,' International Justice Monitor, 15 June 2012.
228 Decision Concerning the Organisation of Common Legal Representation of Victims, ICC, 2 December 2013.
229 'Legal Aid for Victims in the Ongwen case,' letter from Redress, FIDH, IBA, NPWJ, PGA, 17 November 2016.

have been mobilised and now made use of the right to select their own independent lawyer. 'We believe that listening to victims' choices of legal representation and supporting such choice, is a pre-condition for their genuine participation in the ICC proceedings,' the organisations wrote. Indeed, the ICC can't pay legal aid to five separate victims' teams, said Carayon. But she stresses the importance of the right of victims to choose their own legal representative. 'What is lacking,' she adds, 'is a clear and transparent model that is applicable to all cases.'

Tell their own story

Although usually the legal representatives will present the victims' views, there are specific moments in a trial when victims are offered the possibility to address the court. Pulchérie Makiandakama made use of this opportunity, stepping into the courtroom on 1 May 2012 to tell about her harrowing experiences. Even more remarkable was that she had decided to make her statement in full view of the public. Makiandakama, born on 17 April 1982 in the CAR, where she had been teaching traditional dance to young people, did not use a pseudonym. Her face and voice weren't broadcast in a distorted way. She had carefully put some modest make-up and was elegantly dressed, wearing an anthracite grey jacket and a grey shawl. When maître Marie-Edith Douzima-Lawson, the victims' lawyer, asked her why she hadn't chosen for anonymity, the young woman answered: 'I cannot ask for my voice or image to be distorted. I want it to be natural, be myself and say before the judges and before the whole world what I suffered,' she said. 'God is my witness.'[230]
I would follow her gripping account through a YouTube-clip. Mostly looking down she explained how she had been harmed, in March 2003, by Bemba's militia, the Mouvement de Libération du Congo (MLC), who were sent to the CAR to help quell a coup d'état, but would end up targeting ordinary citizens as well. Makiandakama told the judges how she had fled to a hospital, where Congolese militiamen discovered her. They took her with them, and forced her to put looted stuff on vehicles. After having loaded so many goods, she got tired and thirsty. 'I started to cry, and then at some point while I was still carrying those items, some of them dropped to the ground. A soldier who saw that happen was

230 Official transcript, ICC, 1 May 2012.

very furious and struck me with the butt of his weapon, so I dropped to the ground,' she told the judges, while bending her body slightly in an attempt to show what happened to her. 'At some point they sprinkled water on my face and then I came to.' It was just the beginning of the dramatic events that would ruin the life of this young woman, who was described by the judges as a 'very vulnerable person, illiterate, with no education at all.'

After she was beaten, the driver of the vehicle sped off, but ran into a tree and died on the spot. Makiandakama saw the accident happening before her eyes. While the militia drove to the riverbanks to put the body in a boat to take it to the other side, Makiandakama was ordered to offload goods from the vehicle. She refused. Then one of the soldiers threatened to kill her, saying: 'We will not spare your life, because if we spare your life you will betray us.' While the soldiers were 'joyfully' firing in the air, Makiandakama cried out of despair. Two soldiers came towards her. 'I was wondering whether my life was coming to an end this way, and how my children were going to fare. Those are the things that crossed my mind. Then one of them asked me to take off my clothes, and I refused to do so. Then he took two bottles and broke them before me in order to frighten me. Yes, I was indeed frightened,' she tells the judges. 'He took off my pair of trousers. All that was left on me were my undergarments and my panties. I tried to fight him off. Then one of them kicked my feet. I fell to the ground. Then one of them slept with me. Then another one slept with me again while the others looked on.' While shooting in the air, twenty bawling men watched how she was raped under a tree by two men. Only one soldier objected to the humiliations.

While the troops continued their raids, Makiandakama was forced to join them. She saw them slaughtering a Muslim man. Suddenly a soldier grabbed her at her hair. She was kicked again and fell on the ground. 'He used his knife to rip off my trousers and my shorts,' she says, while her face for a moment changes in a painful grimace. 'They started sleeping with me.' Just like other victims testifying before the court she spoke of 'sleeping', possibly because emotionally she wasn't able to utter the word 'rape', or because the term did not exist in her language.

She was taken by a third and a fourth soldier. The men held her, being naked, on the ground and brutally raped her. She reckons there were twelve of them, armed with rifles and arrows. 'They slept with me in the anus, in the vagina and even in the mouth, and it was after that, that I started vomiting and lost consciousness.'

When she came round, she got the impression that somebody gave her some Coca Cola. It was a soldier, who took her away, telling the other militia that she had to help him pillaging goods. It was a trick. They took a shortcut to the river where he told her: 'I'm freeing you here.' He warned her to stay away from the looting soldiers because next time he might not be there to save her. This was the man who had not participated in the pillaging, nor in the gang-rape, and who had held a rosary in his hand praying to Virgin Mary. 'He said to me that I should go away and that he was going to fire two shots into the air, and that I should not be afraid, and I should take advantage of the situation to flee.' He kept his promise and fired twice giving her the possibility to save herself. 'I know that my fate was not to die that day,' Makiandakama says. In the beginning she couldn't walk. She was bleeding and kept on throwing up. While Makiandakama crawled and hobbled she reached the bush where she fell on the ground. She made it through the night. Then she felt a presence. It was a pygmy. 'He saw me, he wanted to flee.' But she gestured with her hand. The pygmies agreed to help her and made a kind of stretcher to carry her to a camp, at quite a distance. 'There we saw the other inhabitants of the village who had taken refuge,' she tells. She stayed a few days at the pygmies' place where she ran into an acquaintance of her mother, who was alerted and came to pick her up and take her to a safe area on the border with Congo-Brazzaville. 'I was not feeling very well. I was tired, I had hallucinations. I could hear voices. So I did not feel well. Fortunately, Doctors Without Borders came to our help and treated me.'

They spent one week in the border-area, under very difficult conditions. 'We had no food. One could have spent an entire day without eating anything, just drinking some water.' Her mother decided to return home. But arriving in their town Mongoumba, they discovered their house had been pillaged. They spent the nights outside in open air, on mats and tarpaulins.

Makiandakama now has a twelve year old son, an eight year old daughter and another son of five. 'In my community I'm no longer considered a human person, and by extension in the whole of the CAR I'm not considered a human being,' she explained. 'I was a human being, but

I was treated like an animal, a burden, and that is why I cannot live normally. I cannot live calmly and live as all other girls of my age do.' She used to be 'a woman with dignity.' But the sexual violence made her an outcast, rejected by her community. 'And sometimes people spit on me, so that's how I'm stigmatised.'

The following day the defence would get the chance to question her. Bemba's lawyer Peter Haynes noted significant differences between her current statements and the initial report that was made after her first declaration in 2010, when a team of the legal representative of victims visited and interviewed her in her hometown. In her first account she left out several pillaging incidents, the gang-rape and two murders she witnessed. Makiandakama, officially referred to as V-1, blamed it on language problems – with her speaking Sango and the lawyers French. When Bemba was found guilty on 21 March 2016, the chamber noted that the 'inconsistencies and omissions do not undermine V1's testimony, which it considers to be generally reliable.'

Trust Fund for Victims

The rights of victims don't end there. The court is also committed to reparative justice, which is aimed at supporting victims to rebuild their lives. This is the main task of the Trust Fund for Victims (TFV), a separate organ that tries to operate as independently from the court as possible. 'Initially it wasn't self-evident. Not everybody was in favour of such a provision for victims,' explained Pieter de Baan, director of the TFV. Despite the resistance the fund was provided for in the Rome Statute.

The fund has two mandates: assistance (general support) and reparations (damages). In concrete terms the fund has until recently only been able to give assistance to victims. This ranges from mental and therapeutic support, medical help and plastic surgery, education for former child soldiers and micro credits. Local and international organisations can apply to carry out programmes formulated by the fund.

Assistance is provided to vulnerable groups, such as women, children, victims of sexual violence and former child soldiers living in situation countries where the ICC is investigating. The beneficiaries 'don't have to have a direct link with a specific court case,' director De Baan stressed. 'Take Uganda, where we do a lot of plastic surgery, treatment of burns and give medical help. The people who receive assistance can be victims of the LRA led by Joseph Kony, who himself and several commanders are charged by the ICC, as well as victims of government troops.' (The latter are not subject to investigations by the prosecution of the ICC.)

On its website the fund writes that over 300,000 people in the DRC and Northern Uganda have received assistance. The agency wanted to start in the CAR, where Pulchérie Makiandakama originates from, but continued violence has led to the postponement of these activities. In Kenya the political climate has been so hostile towards the ICC that the fund didn't start assistance activities there. For security reasons the TFV doesn't have projects in Sudan or Libya either. The possibility of activities in Ivory Coast is being looked at. Expansion of the work was also hampered by a lack of funds, De Baan pointed out.

Donations for the TFV come from governments and private contributors. From 2004 until 2014 the accumulated total of contributions from countries amounted to 20 million euros. However the annual income has been declining lately. From 5 million euros in 2013 and 2014, to around 2 million euros in 2016. Sweden is one of the most loyal donors, followed by the United Kingdom, Germany and The Netherlands. As of 2016 the fund had 12.8 million euro in its account. Most of that money was earmarked for projects, which means the fund had not much left for new activities, until Sweden granted a new 3-year commitment of 3 million euros.[231]

De Baan underlines the importance of the distinct and separate position the fund has from the court. Aid organisations cooperating with the TFV have to sign a contract that they don't work with other organs of the ICC, such as the office of the prosecutor. 'The court wasn't happy with that. And especially in the early years it was hard to convince people that the fund is independent from the court. Things were made even more difficult for us because of the flow of false rumours that we were collecting evidence for the prosecutors. Some organisations that were working with us have been threatened. A local partner was poisoned, but luckily survived. Other organisations don't want to be mentioned in our reports.'

231   TFV board: Closure for victims is the true measure of international justice, press release TFV, The Hague, 29 November 2016.

Not all projects are easily accepted. The word 'reconciliation' can be too sensitive to use. De Baan is proud that nevertheless in the east of the DRC, the fund made it possible to realise the 'Caravane de la Paix': meetings where sensitive matters such as violence and land issues were discussed among civilians, police and army. 'This had never happened before. During sessions civilians could present their complaints. They explained, for instance, that at certain checkpoints they always experienced problems. After that the police would look into the matter. Such meetings have to be built up slowly, and it is not an activity that leads to immediate results,' the director admits, 'but it is important such projects take place.' With support of the fund schools in eastern DRC were able to give peace education. Thousands of children were taught about the idea that communities can live together.

The first reparations

The other mandate of the TFV are reparations, which are directly linked to court cases. Only when a suspect is found guilty, with the conviction confirmed in appeal, can the judges order reparations, in the form of restitution, indemnification or rehabilitation. Reparations are often key for victims to join ICC cases, says the victims study by the HRC. 'In Uganda and DRC, the prospect of receiving reparations was the primary motivation for the overwhelming majority of victim participants,' the report states. Though in Kenya and Ivory Coast 'less than half' said that reparations were their main objective. 'Nearly all respondents, however, reported an interest in individualized reparations for themselves and others,' the researchers conclude.

'Reparations are a very strict judicial process,' TFV director De Baan explains. The proceedings take many years and demand tremendous patience. Only last year for the first time – symbolic – reparations were finally agreed upon, even though the first convict, Thomas Lubanga Dyilo, was found guilty back in 2012 (confirmed on appeal in December 2014). Explaining why things take so long, Gaëlle Carayon notes that 'initially the rules for reparations were very vague and nothing was settled. Only when Lubanga was found guilty, and the case entered the phase of reparations, the ICC started setting up a system. Some delays were legitimate, as it was the court's first reparation case, but things could have been prepared much better.'

Right after Lubanga was convicted, the judges who had been handling his trial, decided that his victims would be awarded collective forms of reparations, instead of individual damages. This had to do with the fact that the victims in this case were child soldiers. 'It could have a negative effect on affected communities if you give money to former child soldiers. People could become jealous and see it as a reward for violence, as many child soldiers are not only victims but also acted as perpetrators during the war in Ituri,' director De Baan explained. Indeed, during a trip in 2015 to Ituri the ICC's registry and TFV heard that many people were very negative about former child soldiers calling them 'thieves', 'drunks', 'drugs users' and said they were 'disrespectful' and 'violent.' They were seen as a 'lost generation' unable to return to civilian life. Their parents and communities feared them, because child soldiers 'think they can kill other people easily or sexually abuse women and think these are normal behaviours,' the TFV wrote in their report.[232]

Collective arrangements also have the advantage that a wider circle of victims could benefit from reparations, including girls who were sexually abused as child soldiers, a crime that was not included in the charges and thus formally reparations would not be apply. But not everybody was happy with the decision. 'Some victims were disappointed that they were not awarded the individual reparations they had requested through the proceedings. They didn't understand nor agree with the court's decision to only award collective reparations,' says Carayon.

Soon after the conviction of Lubanga two of the judges handling the trial had finished their mandate and new colleagues took over. Meanwhile the defence, victims' lawyers and the TFV were filing arguments and appeals. 'Most details of the reparations decision had to be tested in court,' says Carayon. In March 2015 the appeals chamber instructed the fund to prepare within six months a 'draft implementation plan.'[233] The judges formulated a long list with demands and said that the TFV had to identify the victims that potentially were eligible for reparations, assess their harm, come up with proposals with regard to the form of reparations

232 Filing regarding symbolic collective reparations projects, Trust Fund for Victims, 19 September 2016.
233 Lubanga case: ICC Appeals Chamber amends the Trial Chamber's order for reparations to victims, press release, ICC, 3 March 2015.

and to present the budget for reparations (Lubanga is considered indigent).

From May to July 2015 the TFV travelled several times to Ituri. The delegation visited 22 locations, meeting 1340 victims and affected families. The community explained that many child soldiers are in dire need. They couldn't catch up with school, found it hard to find work and haven't been able to build normal lives. Many became delinquents and got addicted to drugs and alcohol. The former female child soldiers were stigmatized as people said they had been raped and thus had lost their dignity, but also had to care now for the children born during that time. The child soldiers suffered physical disabilities (loss of limbs), psychological disorders, mental and physical harm because of drugs and alcohol addiction, ongoing medical problems because of lack of health care and previous malnutrition, and sexually transmitted diseases. It is hard to escape from the past and their families feel the burden as well. People remind them daily of the crimes committed by their children, accusing them and demanding fines.

The TFV submitted the draft implementation plan on 3 November 2015.[234] The fund proposed programmes that focus on the reintegration of former child soldiers (vocational training and literacy courses), training that encourages healing and the resolution of disputes between the victims, families and communities, and psychological support. But it had concluded that it would be impossible to make a full assessment of the number of potential eligible victims, due to a range of problems such as difficulties in establishing the age of individuals, the fact that the crimes happened long ago and former child soldiers were hard to trace as many were scattered throughout the area. 'The fund also had reservations about doing a full individual assessment of victims and their harm, which might re-traumatise them, for reparations that would be collective in nature,' says Carayon. Another issue was that the personal details of the victims could be sent to the defence, which might have put them at risk.

But the judges, who reacted three months later, weren't satisfied and said the report was 'incomplete.'[235] To their dismay the fund had 'not

---

234 Filing on reparations and draft implementation plan, TFV, 3 November 2015.
235 Order instructing the Trust Fund for Victims to supplement the draft implementation plan, ICC, 9 February 2016.

identified any potential victims.' The TFV was instructed 'to begin the process of locating and identifying victims potentially eligible to benefit from the reparations.' The judges also found that the fund had 'presented only a summary description of the prospective programmes.' The plans were not detailed enough. Tensions were running high. But the judges did not budge. They instructed the fund to propose 'a set of collective reparation programmes' which must 'be geared towards the direct and indirect victims' and 'designed so that as many victims as possible may participate.' Then, on 15 July 2016, the judges asked the fund to look at 'the feasibility of developing a concrete project aiming at providing prompt symbolic reparations.'

On 19 September 2016 the TFV sent the chamber an outline for such a project.[236] The plan is to build 'commemoration centres' in three localities in Ituri, which were kept confidential. The buildings offer a venue for symbolic activities such as exhibitions of artwork created by former child soldiers 'that depicts the past, present, and their hopes for the future,' the TFV writes. The centres could also host music events, dance and drama, as well as 'community dialogue concerning the crimes, the harms suffered, and reintegration efforts.'

In an additional five localities, community sensitization will take place about the harm caused by using child soldiers. The activities will include regular radio programmes and culminate in a 'commemoration week' taking place once a year. Local leaders will receive a special training about memorialization, reconciliation, children's rights and mediation. The TFV will ensure that women and girls are 'fairly represented and involved in all aspects.' The fund has a budget of 1 million euros for the reparations in this case, but the exact costs for these projects and its communication activities are kept confidential. It is also unclear how much all the preparations, proceedings, litigation, travels and studies have cost compared to what is actually spent on the reparations.

In its proposal the funds also explicitly addressed Lubanga, noting he hadn't accepted any responsibility for his crimes, nor had made an apology. Now was the time for him to play a role such as publicly supporting the symbolic reparations projects, reassuring victims or expressing regret, the TFV suggested. If only he would call on his militia

---

236 Filing regarding symbolic collective reparations projects, Trust Fund for Victims, 19 September 2016.

and the community 'to refrain from any negativity towards participants in reparations projects, this would, on its own, be a positive development that would increase the likelihood of reparation projects achieving their desired outcomes.'

The plan was approved by the judges on 21 October 2016.[237] The idea is that the symbolic reparations project 'paves the way' for acceptance of support for the affected communities and 'creates a safe environment for victims' so they can later join 'the service-based collective awards without undue fear for their safety or reputation.' In due course the judges will issue their decision on the collective reparations programmes, which are focused on vocational training for victims, reconstructive surgery, psychological help and livelihood support. Looking back Carayon notes: 'It took three years for the court and the other participants to get clarity on all of this.'

The victims of the crimes committed by Germain Katanga during the attack on 24 february 2003 on the village of Bogoro in the east of the DRC, also had to wait for three years. In March 2014 the Congolese warlord was convicted. Only on 24 March 2017 the judges awarded the 297 victims each a 'symbolic compensation' of 250 US dollars, and collective reparations such as support for housing, income-generating activities, education and psychological help.

In the Lubanga and Katanga trials only a limited group of victims are participating, although the collective reparations probably will reach more people in Ituri. 'Still, it's nowhere near the thousands of victims participating in the proceedings against Jean-Pierre Bemba and Dominic Ongwen. If they have so much difficulties in making it work in the Lubanga proceedings, how will they make it work in these cases,' Carayon wonders. The reparations phase has only just started in the Bemba case. Not only the high number of victims might pose challenges, but also the fact that the CAR is far from a peaceful place. Carayon: 'You can't travel beyond the capital city Bangui, because of the security situation. There have been multiple waves of violence and many people are displaced. How are you going to track down the victims?' The financial side of the process is not clear either. Bemba might be a multimillionaire, but he has

---

237 Order approving the proposed plan of the Trust Fund for Victims in relation to symbolic collective reparations, ICC, 21 October 2016.

to pay the fees of his legal teams. The question is, how much of his wealth will be left for the victims and will it be enough for reparations?

Rights on paper

Although reparations proceedings in trials where suspects have been convicted so far have proved to be extremely slow and bureaucratic, in the cases that ended in an acquittal or the withdrawal of charges, victims won't receive anything. This goes for no fewer than nine cases against Bahar Idriss Abu Garda, Callixte Mbarushimana, Mathieu Ngudjolo Chui, Mohammed Hussein Ali, Henry Kiprono Kosgey, Francis Kirimi Muthaura, Uhuru Muigai Kenyatta, William Samoei Ruto and Joshua Arap Sang.

On paper, victims have rights. But the reality is extremely complex. During a debate a few years ago in The Hague, in an outburst of indignation, ICC's senior lawyer Gilbert Bitti said that the rights of victims didn't meet the expectations at all. 'Victim participants express frustration at the length of trials, which, in turn, fosters distrust and disappointment,' notes the HRC report. The researchers continue to say that 'many victim participants were concerned that they would die before verdicts or reparations decisions, and some worried that delays in proceedings could compromise their personal information and cause them security problems. Some said that such delays signalled corruption at the court, and that infrequent updates about court developments damaged goodwill in their communities.'

'Not enough has been achieved,' agrees Carayon. 'It is not so much about the court doing more, but about the court doing better. Is the ICC doing what it can? It clearly hasn't reached its potential,' she says. Carayon concludes: 'There are days that I am cynical, and rightly so. But I have been working for ten years on the rights of victims before the ICC, because I believe the court can do better and has to do better. Victims are a constituency of the court, which claims to be doing justice in their name. The ICC simply can't afford to lose the support of victims and affected communities.'

11

REMARKABLE ASYLUM SEEKERS

Six sturdy guards in civilian clothes are sitting spread over the courtroom. Some have bold shaven skulls. All are provided with handcuffs and are wearing tiny earphones. On their bomber jackets is written in silver letters: 'justitie.' Apart from this Dutch law enforcement team there are another three uniformed policemen present in this courtroom of the district court in Amsterdam, the capital city of The Netherlands. The heavy security has to do with the three Congolese men, wearing dark suits, sitting quietly in a row next to each other. It is their asylum case that is being dealt with on this rainy day, 11 April 2013.

The Dutch judge, Jet van Gijn, checks their names and inquires about the health situation of one of the Congolese men, who has to take his medicine regularly. 'I hope you will say it when it is getting too much for you,' she tells him. Softly the voice of the interpreter buzzes, translating the Dutch words into French. Then Flip Schüller, the Dutch lawyer of the Congolese, walks with a pile of defence pleas to the front. He first hands over copies to the judges and then to his opponent in this case – the team of the Dutch immigration and naturalisation service (IND) of the ministry of security and justice. 'We have a long day ahead of us,' says presiding judge Van Gijn.

The hearing is part of a complex and lingering asylum case that takes place against the background of a deepening row between the International Criminal Court, The Netherlands and the Democratic Republic of Congo. How did the three men, the ICC and governments end up in this situation?

It all started on Sunday 27 March 2011, when the Congolese men are being flown from the Congolese capital city Kinshasa to The Netherlands. They are transported to the International Criminal Court in order to testify as witnesses for the defence of their comrades who are at trial in

The Hague.[238] The ICC has charged the warlords Mathieu Ngudjolo Chui and Germain Katanga with crimes against humanity and war crimes committed during the one-day attack on 24 February 2003 on the town of Bogoro in Ituri, in the east of the DRC.

The three Congolese men are special witnesses. For many years they had been jailed – without any form of trial – in the DRC. The Congolese government, The Netherlands and the ICC had agreed that the trio would be temporarily sent over to testify at the court, which would keep them in detention as well. After their testimony they would immediately be returned to Kinshasa. The arrangement was precise and mattered to the two countries involved, as well as to the ICC, that needs to keep good relations with governments, as it depends on state cooperation for many matters.

But their return became highly problematic after the three defence witnesses openly accused, in the ICC courtroom, the Congolese army of being involved in the attack on Bogoro.[239] According to the witnesses, the military had created a command centre in Ituri to regain control over the area and to train militia groups. Allegedly weapons and ammunition had been sent from Kinshasa to support the plans, which included the Bogoro assault. The Congolese president Joseph Kabila was aware of these operations, the witnesses said in open court. After these damning accusations, the three men feared their lives in the DRC would be in danger. On 12 May 2011, while in ICC detention, they applied for asylum in The Netherlands.

Sacred principles

The host state, however, wasn't prepared for the possibility of witnesses asking for asylum. While the Dutch authorities had made a lot of efforts setting up the ICC in The Netherlands, some key legal provisions still needed clarification, said a government source who wanted to stay anonymous. Matters that went to the heart of this case, such as how to deal with asylum applications and the question whether the ICC – like a foreign embassy – is located on its own territory or Dutch territory? The

238 'Urgent Request for Convening a Status Conference on the Detention of Witnesses DRC-D02-P-0236, DRC-D02-P-0228, and DRC-D02-P-0350, ICC, 30 January 2012.
239 'Third defence witness blames DRC government for attack on Bogoro,' International Justice Monitor, 29 April 2011. 'Floribert Njabu concludes his testimony,' International Justice Monitor, 27 April 2011.

latter would become one of the arguments for The Netherlands in the first phase of the legal battle. In 2011, the IND refused the men access to the asylum procedure on several grounds, including the argument that they weren't on Dutch soil.

Thus the three Congolese witnesses became pawns in an increasingly complicated joust between the ICC (that wanted to get rid of them – detention is terribly costly and state cooperation extremely valuable), Kinshasa (demanding the men back) and The Netherlands (that didn't want to take them).

One of the persons defending the position of the Congolese witnesses was Frans Timmermans, at the time member of the Dutch parliament. 'If a person comes with incriminating information about Kabila, one doesn't survive one day if returned to Congo,' he said. Timmermans feared the Dutch government was prepared to ignore the European Convention on Human Rights, which prohibits sending people back to countries where they run safety risks. 'That is a sacred principle for me,' the MP said. But later Timmermans became minister of foreign affairs in a cabinet that was keen on returning the Congolese as soon as possible.

After the IND had refused to allow the detained witnesses to file an asylum application, their lawyers had leaped into action. 'Denying a legal test by an independent judge and keeping these witnesses detained is reminiscent to Guantanamo Bay,' said counsel Schüller, in an interview with the Dutch daily De Telegraaf, comparing the situation of his clients with that of the American prison on Cuba where still dozens of terror suspects are detained without trial. 'And that in The Netherlands, the self-proclaimed legal capital of the world,' he added scornfully. Schüller suggested that The Netherlands was blocking access to the asylum procedure to discourage future ICC witnesses from asking for similar protection.

The lawyers won this part of the battle. On 28 December 2011 the district court decided that the Congolese witnesses were on Dutch territory and had the right to apply for asylum.[240]

---

240 Decision on the Urgent Request for Convening a Status Conference on the Detention of Witnesses DRC-D02-P-0236, DRC-D02-P-0228, and DRC-D02-P-0350, ICC, 1 March 2012.

War in Ituri

While formal asylum procedures were started, the state advocates representing the IND hinted that whatever happened, the fate of the Congolese men was actually a foregone conclusion. They pointed out that at least two of the three witnesses were suspected of being responsible for serious crimes such as rape, torture and murder in the DRC. 'The asylum request will probably be denied on those grounds,' the state advocate said. Indeed, on 31 October 2012, the witnesses received the news from the IND that their request was rejected. The immigration office referred to article 1(f) of the international 'Convention relating to the status of refugees' which says that protection for asylum seekers does not apply when there are 'serious reasons for considering' that a person has committed grave human rights violations. The IND stated there were indications the three 'had committed crimes against peace, war crimes or crimes against humanity,' and insisted that the DRC would be safe for the trio.

But the Dutch lawyers for the three men rejected all these arguments. 'There is no direct proof for their involvement with crimes,' they said in an interview. Neither would their safety be guaranteed in the DRC. Return was no option.

Who were the men who had spent so many years in jail without trial – first in the DRC and then in ICC detention? The three Congolese were part of the leadership of the same militia groups as to which belonged the two ICC suspects for whom they had come to testify: Ngudjolo (alleged leader of Front des Nationalistes et Intégrationnistes, FNI) and Katanga (commander of the Force de Résistance Patriotique en Ituri, FRPI). Since 1999 these groups had been involved in a bloody conflict in Ituri, where the Lendu and affiliated ethnic groups (represented by the FNI and FRPI) were at war with the Hema (represented by the Union des Patriotes Congolais (UPC) led by Thomas Lubanga Dyilo – see chapter 4). Anneke van Woudenberg, senior researcher with Human Rights Watch, knew two of the witnesses personally. Especially with Floribert Ndjabu Ngabu she shared many conversations. During the war, he was the leader of the much feared FNI. Although Van Woudenberg had insisted during their encounters time and again that Ndjabu should instruct his fighters to respect human rights, he didn't stop them from committing atrocities. 'He was not capable, or he closed his eyes and ignored it,' the human rights activist said in a telephone interview. How the militia leader actually viewed the actions by his fighters, became clear to her when in 2004 Van Woudenberg travelled, with his permission, to Mongbwalu in Ituri. Several months earlier his men had conquered this mining town, rich from gold, during an offensive. They had slaughtered five hundred people, mostly civilians. Now the town was preparing itself to celebrate international labour day on 1 May.

The official ceremony took place in the stadium of Mongbwalu. Ndjabu was glowing with pride, Van Woudenberg noted. The leader was wearing a suit, that was however way too big, with sloppy trousers and sleeves that were too long. From the stands the human rights activist watched a theatre piece by women and children reenacting the bloody battle for the gold town as an experience that gave them great pride. To her shock at the climax, the women imitated the attack with the children playing the civilian victims of Mongbwalu, falling on top of each other and forming a huge stack of bodies, to show how high the dead were piled up after the conquest. A bloodbath as victory drama. At the time, so many civilians were slaughtered that it had been impossible to bury them. The militia had seen only one solution: to set fire to the dead. The pyres would burn for three days.

Van Woudenberg also had met with another ICC witness in this case: Pierre-Célestin Mbodina Iribi, better known as Pichou. This former agent of the Congolese secret service became minister of defence of the FNI and also had a high position within the FRPI. He determined the military strategy of the rebel groups and gave orders to gather intelligence, to arrest people and torture prisoners, the HRW researcher tells. With the third witness, Sharif Manda Ndadza Dz'Na, she didn't have encounters like she had with the other two.

By 2005 the Congolese authorities had started to arrest these militia leaders. One of the accusations was that they allegedly were involved in the murder of nine UN peacekeepers. A trial against Ndjabu or Iribi however never took off. Not in the DRC, nor in The Hague.

Legal limbo

Meanwhile the detained men had requested the ICC to be set free because their imprisonment violated their human rights. But on 1 October 2013 the ICC judges decide they were 'not competent to rule on the release of the witnesses.'[241] They felt bound by the cooperation agreement with the DRC, which insisted the men had to be detained because of Congolese criminal proceedings against them and wanted them back. The judges noted that The Netherlands had adopted a 'particularly rigid approach', stressing that the witnesses 'were to remain in the custody of the court pending consideration of their asylum applications.' Things were stuck. The ICC saw no other option than to keep the three witnesses detained. But one of the judges disagreed. Christine Van den Wyngaert, who regularly differs from her colleagues, said that the witnesses' right to liberty was violated. She would have ordered their 'immediate release, possibly with conditions.'[242]

All parties were now eagerly waiting for the asylum decision by the Dutch district court. On 14 October 2013, the ruling is there. Jet van Gijn and her colleagues confirm that the IND's position to reject the asylum application was justified, because it is 'likely the three were themselves involved in committing crimes against humanity.' But this doesn't mean that the men can be sent back to their own country. In their decision the Dutch judges prohibit The Netherlands to return the men, saying: 'According to the court there is a serious risk that the three men will be detained in the DRC and won't have a fair trial. Moreover, there are insufficient guarantees the witnesses won't receive the death penalty.' With this decision, the Dutch court places the witnesses in a 'legal limbo: they may neither legally reside in the Netherlands, nor be deported to their country of origin,' states Joris van Wijk, director at the Center for International Criminal Justice at the Vrije Universiteit in Amsterdam, with fellow Marjolein Cupido in their article 'Testifying behind bars: Detained ICC witnesses and human rights protection.'[243]

Other cases

Up until January 2017 a total of 365 witnesses have testified before the court. So far six have applied for asylum. Apart from the three Congolese witnesses linked to the Ngudjolo and Katanga case, there was another Congolese man, Bède Djokaba Lambi Longa, who had requested

---

241 Decision on the application for the interim release of detained witnesses, ICC, 1 October 2013.
242 Dissenting opinion of Judge Christine Van den Wyngaert, ICC, 1 October 2013.
243 'Testifying behind Bars: Detained ICC Witnesses and Human Rights Protection,' Joris van Wijk and Marjolein Cupido, 23 January 2014.

protection in The Netherlands. This fourth person had also been a detainee in the DRC. He had been flown to the ICC together with the trio, but had testified for warlord Thomas Lubanga, whose spokesperson he had been. During his stay in The Netherlands, Longa appeared to be ill and was being treated for cancer in a local hospital. When he lost his legal fight against his 'illegal detention' in The Hague, he decided to return to the DRC, where Longa was initially detained and then released.

There are two other witnesses who asked for asylum in The Netherlands. However, they were not detained persons suspected of having committed crimes. To the contrary, they were human rights activists who came to The Netherlands to testify in another ICC case. Their identity has to remain confidential. But even in the case of these two human rights activists, the Dutch authorities at first denied them access to the asylum procedure. Their legal battle went all the way to the Dutch Council of State that decided they could apply for asylum, which they did. Finally these witnesses were given protection by the Dutch authorities.

The academics Van Wijk and Cupido point out that detained witnesses applying for asylum is not a new phenomenon. Other international tribunals have also been faced with detainees called to give testimony, who then wanted to apply for asylum. Dragan Opačić, a former camp guard, was serving his ten-year prison sentence in Bosnia when in 1997 he was called by the International Criminal Tribunal for the former Yugoslavia (ICTY) in The Hague to testify against Duško Tadić. Claiming his life was in danger back home, he first requested the ICTY to be allowed to stay in the tribunal's custody. Then he applied for asylum in The Netherlands, but that request was never considered. He was simply flown back to Sarajevo.

The former Rwandan minister of justice, Agnes Ntamabyariro, was being prosecuted for genocide in her country. In 2006 she was called by the International Criminal Tribunal for Rwanda (ICTR) in the Tanzanian city Arusha. Immediately after her testimony she wrote a request for asylum to the ICTR president, because she feared torture and the death penalty in Rwanda. The request was not even seriously looked at. With a chartered plane, she was returned to Rwanda, where she was found guilty of genocide and convicted to a life prison sentence.

After the former Liberian president Charles Taylor was convicted by the Special Court for Sierra Leone, he wanted to apply for asylum in The

Netherlands. His request was denied and he was flown to the United Kingdom, where a British cell was waiting for him.

Van Wijk and Cupido expect that in future other ICC suspects also might call their former comrades, detained at home or elsewhere, to testify in defence for them at trial. In their article the two academics look at the possibilities for the court to deal with such situations. The ICC could demand from national authorities to apply special protective measures to make sure that detained witnesses, once returned to their own countries, are treated well. For instance, by insisting that special guards will do extra surveillances in the prisons where they are jailed. But this option doesn't prevent witnesses from applying for asylum in The Netherlands.

The researchers also discuss the possibility whereby the witnesses don't have to come to the court, but the court comes to the witness. One could 'think of introducing ICC investigating judges who can issue 'rogatory commissions' which are mandated to take witness testimonies under oath and present written transcripts of these testimonies in court.' But this option comes with 'serious downsides' as well, Van Wijk and Cupido write. First of all, the rules at the ICC don't foresee in this solution, and it would require 'a complete paradigm shift in the existing legal culture of international criminal law.' Moreover, it will be 'difficult to find a venue which is truly conducive to truthful testimonies,' the academics note.

All options come with downsides. 'Although it is not likely that the ICC will be overwhelmed by detained witnesses applying for asylum in the Netherlands, the perceived threat alone will hamper the relationship between the ICC, states parties and The Netherlands as a host state,' Van Wijk and Cupido argue. But 'any solution that limits detained witnesses' access to human rights protection entails the risk that they for this very reason may not testify at all.' The two academics would like to raise another issue. The ICC, which praises itself on applying the highest standards of justice, can also lose some of that prestige. 'Because intuitively, it seems that something is not right if it would simply accept that material witnesses cannot testify in person for the mere reason that it may bring them in a rightful position to request for protection against persecution, acts of torture, illegal detention or the death penalty,' Van Wijk and Cupido state.

Impasse

How to find a solution for the three detained witnesses? A way out could have been to prosecute them. Apparently Ndjabu had been on the ICC list of suspects, but the prosecutor didn't proceed. The Dutch authorities weren't interested in a trial against the Congolese men, although they accused them of human rights violations. 'Considering the costs and the practical, legal and political complexities involved, it is, however, far from self-evident the Dutch prosecutor will start such investigations,' Van Wijk and Cupido note. But HRW-researcher Van Woudenberg argues that no matter what, Ndjabu and Iribi should be charged. 'It is a disdain for the victims if the FNI leaders are not being held accountable for their crimes.' In the meantime the men, after having spent years in illegal detention without trial in the DRC, were now detained by the ICC in The Hague, which proudly promotes itself as international city of peace and justice, not knowing what their fate would be. 'That's the problem of tribunals. Morally it all sounds wonderful and convincing. But the reality is far more complex and vague,' says lawyer Schüller. The academics Van Wijk and Cupido describe the rather desperate situation of the witnesses being detained probably far away from their families, 'caught up in many legal procedures' and confronted with 'a bleak perspective of eventually being granted an asylum status.'

On 20 January 2014 the appeals chamber of the ICC issues a new decision. Irritated, the judges note that 'the court cannot serve as an administrative detention unit for asylum seekers or persons otherwise involved in judicial proceedings with the host state or any other state.' The appeals chamber orders the registrar to take 'the necessary steps to return' the three witnesses 'without delay' to the DRC, thereby going against the position of the Dutch court that had ruled that the situation was not safe enough to send the men back home. The registrar will also have to contact the national authorities about the asylum proceedings. He has to check as well the promises made by the Congolese authrities to apply 'special protective measures' for these detainees upon their return. If these are no longer adequate, the appeals chamber needs to be informed and the DRC will have to be consulted. By this stage the detention of the three had cost the ICC about one million euros, as the court is paying The Netherlands rent for using the detention unit. The tension was building up.[244]

Hunger strike

'He is very weak,' says lawyer Göran Sluiter about his client Ndjabu, who had gone on hunger strike to protest against his desperate situation. His physical condition would quickly deteriorate. On 16 May 2014, the Congolese detained witness fainted and was brought to a penitentiary hospital. 'The way The Netherlands and the ICC are handling this case is a disgrace. If something happens to Ndjabu, this will be the direct consequence of their incompetence and the lack of courage and justice,' Sluiter underlines.

A few days later Ndjabu ends his hunger strike. Also to prepare himself for the last phase in his asylum procedure. By now the case has reached the Council of State. This is the highest legal institution in The Netherlands when it comes to asylum cases, and it has organised the final hearing on 5 June 2014.

But then there is an unexpected turn. Suddenly the deputy minister of the department for security and justice, Fred Teeven, is in a hurry. He has just filed summary proceedings with the same Council of State, demanding an immediate suspension of the ban that the national court had previously issued on returning the three witnesses to the DRC. If the deputy minister succeeds in his efforts, he could extradite the Congolese men. This would suit the ICC, the Dutch and the Congolese authorities. But it is a surprising step. If the judge rules in favour of the government, and if Teeven expels the men, then the Congolese witnesses won't be able to be present at the last hearing before the very same Council of State.

In the hypothetical situation that the Dutch legal system would grant them asylum, how will they then be flown back from the DRC to The Netherlands to enjoy their protection?

The atmosphere in the corridors of the palace of justice in The Hague is tense on 27 May 2014, just before the judge is going to hear the parties in the summary proceedings. The team of the state advocate and authorities consists of nine women and two men. The defence is represented by

---

244 Order on the implementation of the cooperation agreement between the Court and the Democratic Republic of the Congo, ICC, 20 January 2014.

two men – Göran Sluiter and Flip Schüller – balancing the gender ratio somewhat. Their three Congolese clients are not present. The Dutch authorities refuse to transport them from the ICC detention centre to the Dutch court down the road.

The case hasn't received much attention from national media, but now that the proceedings are reaching a climax, the current affairs TV programme Nieuwsuur is preparing an item. A camera team is following the two defence lawyers. With their legal papers loaded into wheeled suitcases they roll into the courtroom. Later that evening the item is on Dutch television. Not only are the lawyers given the opportunity to explain their position, but the registrar of the ICC as well. Herman von Hebel (coincidentally a Dutch national) reminds The Netherlands it has to keep its promises to the court. 'The obligation to cooperate with us is more important and has primacy over the obligation to respect national proceedings. We simply want to send these people back to the DRC in the next few days.' He warns: 'If it is impossible to get this case solved, than I am left with no other option then to open the door.' Registrar Von Hebel refers here to the entrance of the ICC detention centre, and threatens to set the witnesses free into Dutch territory. With this menace the public gets a glimpse of the conflict between the ICC and The Netherlands that is taking place. It is a clear sign that the court is increasing the pressure on the Dutch government to come up with a solution.

Inside the courtroom state advocate Elisabeth Pietermaat discloses that the national authorities have already ordered 'transport' that will take the men back to the DRC. The trip is planned between 30 May and 3 June. The timing is noteworthy. The date of transfer is right before the last and crucial hearing in the asylum case. But the state advocates see no problem, arguing that the Congolese trio can be sent back to the DRC, if only there wasn't that court ban on returning them. They underline that the men won't be in danger in the DRC. Kinshasa has promised that for instance the death penalty won't be applied and that the 'protective measures' will be in place as soon as the men have landed in their home country. The team of the state advocates refers to the situation of the fourth Congolese witness, who originally was in the same position. When Longa arrived in 2012 in Kinshasa, he was detained immediately. But by

September 2013 he had been released. He was doing fine now, the legal team for the state underlines.

But why the hurry? 'Do you have any idea why this sense of urgency to expel them now, while the very last hearing in the asylum case is next week?' asks judge M.G.J. Parkins-de Vin. She stresses that within a month the Council of State will take its final decision, which will be the absolute end of this dramatic case. So why, after all these years, do the Congolese suddenly have to be sent back 'while they are being kept here exactly because of their asylum proceedings?'

It is the ICC, the state advocates underline, that wants to see this matter closed. There is no room for negotiations anymore. The ICC doesn't want to wait for the last results in this asylum case. But why, insists judge Parkins, is there no possibility to wait, at maximum, for 'a month' until the national proceedings are finished? The judge doesn't get a satisfactory explanation. 'The space you suggest doesn't exist anymore,' reacts Pietermaat.

But judge Parkins just had a look at the 'Headquarters Agreement' which arranges the relationship between the ICC and The Netherlands. When there are problems between the court and the host state, there are several ways to resolve the matter: talks, negotiations and even arbitration. What power does the ICC have to force The Netherlands, the judge wonders. What would happen if the ICC opens itself the doors of the detention centre to let the men out? 'There is still, it seems to me, a long road ahead of us. And by that time there is a decision in the asylum case,' she says. Besides, the judge notes, it is doubtful whether these summary proceedings are suitable for such a complex case.

Calling with the registrar

Judge Parkins allows a short break so that the parties can discuss the situation and can seek extra information. When the parties have returned to the courtroom state advocate Pietermaat says that officials of the ministry of foreign affairs managed to contact the ICC registrar. In that phone conversation Herman von Hebel repeated he is bound by the order of the ICC's appeals chamber: the Congolese witnesses have to leave the detention centre now and be returned to the DRC. The case is deadlocked. But then Pietermaat suddenly comes with a proposal that offers a whole new perspective: 'The Netherlands can take the detainees from the ICC.' Judge Parkins is much interested in that option, that a few minutes ago didn't seem to exist. But Pietermaat adds immediately: 'If The Netherlands accepts the three men, the playing field changes drastically. Then a completely new situation arises.'

It remains unclear what kind of diplomatic and legal matters are being fought over behind the scenes. But Parkins closes the hearing. As is the practise with these summary proceedings, the next day, 28 May 2014, her decision is published. She says that deputy minister Teeven hasn't made it 'plausible' that The Netherlands is obliged to 'immediately' carry out ICC's request and transport the detained witnesses to the DRC. Anyhow, summary proceedings are not the right instrument for such a convoluted matter. More research is needed, concludes the judge, before all legal questions can be answered. And, guess what – a perfect opportunity offers itself for this purpose: the hearing which is planned the following week at the Council of State.

Before that day arrives, there are new moves in the chess game. The solution that for years seemed absent, that allegedly would totally change the legal playing field, all of a sudden seems to be possible. On 4 June The Netherlands agree to take over the three witnesses from the ICC. The Congolese are brought from the court's detention centre to the special immigration prison at Schiphol airport with its basic conditions. The next morning the Dutch authorities bring them back to The Hague for the last hearing in their asylum cases.

No costume, but a jacket

The Congolese witnesses no longer wear their smart suits like when they were ICC detainees. They are in cheap jackets. Ndjabu, who recently had been on hunger strike, looks remarkably well. Slightly slimmer in the face, but apart from that he makes an energetic impression. Iribi follows the pleas by the parties with much attention. But Manda looks sick and utterly depressed. During most of the session he leans forward with his head resting on his hands and arms.

The parties have crossed their swords. The legal battle between the witnesses' lawyers and the state advocates has lasted for three years. It is late in the afternoon when this final hearing in this dragging asylum case comes to an end. From their seats the three male judges watch how the legal teams and the Congolese detainees are getting ready to leave the courtroom. The state advocates quickly gather their documents and proceed to the door. The lawyers shake hands with their clients and the translator, and then leave.

A Dutch policeman suddenly sees that one of the three detained witnesses is holding a pen. 'That's not allowed,' the policeman says and immediately confiscates the writing tool. 'Are they already underway?' he asks in his walkie-talkie. The policeman is waiting for colleagues to take the Congolese back to the immigration prison at Schiphol. The interpreter, who has translated all what has been said this afternoon from Dutch into French, assists the three men with the last few words that are being said. A couple of guards are still spread over the courtroom. Until it is time to go. The first who is being led out is Manda. When it is Ndjabu's turn, he makes a solemn bow to the judges. His example is being followed by Iribi. These are like scenes from an absurdist theatre play. Stiff and formal the judges sit like official hosts seeing out a few unpopular guests. 'A good evening,' the policeman says to the judges, who stay behind in the empty courtroom. The show is over. Now all parties will await the ruling of the Council of State.

It takes the judges three weeks to come with a final decision. On 27 June 2014 the detained witnesses will know their fate. The Council of State arrives at a different conclusion than the three female judges at the district court a year before. The council supports the Dutch government in refusing the three men asylum, referring to agreements the ICC made with the Congolese authorities about their return. The judges attach 'great value' to the 'protective measures' the DRC has promised to apply.[245] These include the possibility for ICC officials to regularly visit the three men in their Congolese prison and check their safety. The ICC will also be able to follow legal procedures against them in the DRC. The Congolese authorities have also given other guarantees for the security of the witnesses. In case they receive the death penalty, this sentence will not be carried out. The Council of State stresses that the men previously also expressed accusations against the Congolese president, which didn't lead to problems. It is 'unlikely,' the judges summarize, that the three detained

---

245 'Congolese Strafhofgetuigen mogen worden teruggestuurd naar Congo,' press release Council of State, 27 June 2014.

witnesses will have to fear for 'poor treatment, an unfair trial or capital punishment.'

Human rights organisations and the lawyers of the witnesses hold a very different opinion. Amnesty International calls on the Dutch government not to send them back because of, indeed: the risk of receiving the death penalty, poor treatment and an unfair trial. Lawyer Schüller wonders how the ICC will be able to protect the men against such dangers. 'If there is a trial against my clients in the DRC, this will be before a military tribunal. How effectively will the ICC be able to monitor if procedures, because of national interests, partly take place behind closed doors? How will the ICC react if my clients are suddenly victims of a suspicious car accident or if they are slowly denied adequate health care?'

On 6 July 2014, the three Congolese witnesses are put on a plane and flown back to the DRC, from where they departed more than three years earlier.

'Unfortunately our fear is increasingly becoming reality,' says defence lawyer Göran Sluiter, two months after his clients arrived in the DRC. The Dutch legal team has only sporadic contact with its clients. The situation doesn't look good. 'Now their Congolese lawyer has fled himself, because the DRC wants to arrest him. Agreements about the use of medication are not being met,' Sluiter explains. For now, there are no signs that a trial is being prepared against them. 'We try to find out what exactly is going on, but it is very worrisome.' The Dutch lawyers are sending letters to the ICC, which is no longer responding.

Another asylum claim

The chapter on asylum requests wasn't closed however. The former Congolese warlord Mathieu Ngudjolo Chui, for whom the three witnesses had testified, would ask The Netherlands for protection as well. He had been acquitted by the ICC on 18 December 2012 because of a lack of evidence, although the judges added that if the chamber found an accused 'not guilty' this doesn't necessarily mean that they find him 'innocent.'[246] A few days after the acquittal the Congolese militia leader was released by the ICC from its detention centre.

---

246 ICC Trial Chamber II acquits Mathieu Ngudjolo Chui, ICC press release, 18 December 2012.

But Ngudjolo Chui would not enjoy freedom. His lawyer Jean-Pierre Kilenda Kakengi Basila, who had successfully defended him, had gone to the ICC detention centre to fetch his client. Upon arrival Kilenda was told by Dutch authorities they were taking Ngudjolo to a hotel near Schiphol airport. The lawyer accepted the proposal, not knowing that this solution would completely collapse. The national police transported Ngudjolo to the airport, where the ICC, following the advice of Dutch officials, was supposed to have reserved a room for him in a hotel located behind immigration lines. Arriving at the airport it turned out the court officials had made a mistake and had booked the wrong hotel, a source says. Faced with complete uncertainty, Ngudjolo feared he was going to be put on a plane and taken straight to the DRC. He quickly applied for asylum with the Dutch security officers, who took him to the immigration prison at Schiphol.

His Dutch lawyers – just like the three witnesses, Ngudjolo has counsels Schüller and Sluiter for his asylum case – objected. In May 2013, they won a victory when a Dutch court demanded the immediate release of the acquitted Congolese man. Moreover, the government was forced to pay Ngudjolo a compensation of 2400 euros. But, once released, where should he go? There was no other way for the ICC but to take care of Ngudjolo and lodge him in a proper hotel in The Hague.

The Dutch immigration and naturalisation service IND however rejected his asylum request and summoned Ngudjolo to leave the country immediately. His lawyers appealed and won, initially. The Dutch district court in Amsterdam decided on 28 May 2014 that deputy minister Teeven's research had been 'insufficient' to conclude that Ngudjolo had commanded militias who allegedly had committed war crimes.[247] 'The decision is also poorly motivated,' the Dutch judges said. The deputy minister had to re-do his work. 'He also has to check once more whether the man runs a real risk of inhumane treatment when returned to Congo,' the judges added. However, the deputy minister appealed to the Council of State, which on 15 October 2014 decided that the government had been correct in rejecting the asylum application.

There were several reasons why Ngudjolo wasn't deported. The travel ban the United Nations Security Council had previously ordered against him

---

247 'Asylum proceedings in the Ngudjolo case,' International Justice Monitor, 13 March 2015.

in his capacity as militia leader, was still active. His lawyers had launched a petition with the European Court of Human Rights. Meanwhile his ICC case was not yet completely over, as the ICC prosecutor had appealed against the acquittal, calling the judges' decision 'the result of fundamental legal procedural and factual errors which collectively amount to a miscarriage of justice.'[248] The prosecution was demanding a new trial against Ngudjolo.

But on 27 February 2015 the ICC's appeals chamber confirmed the acquittal.[249] It was with a narrow margin though. Two of the five judges were in favour of a retrial. The acquittal, however, again didn't make Ngudjolo a free man. Right after the decision, still in the ICC building and without his lawyers being informed, while the media were waiting outside to interview Ngudjolo, he was taken by Dutch police to Schiphol airport. Upon arrival he was put on a plane to the DRC.[250]

With no minute to lose, his Dutch lawyer Flip Schüller, who was driving home from holidays, managed to get permission to file a second asylum request. This led to the suspension of Ngudjolo's deportation. While already on the runway, the plane returned to the airport where the Congolese was again taken into the same immigration prison at the airport where he had stayed from December 2012 until May 2013.

The lawyers were left with one last chance to try to stop his expulsion, trying to convince the Dutch court that the IND had made mistakes in handling his asylum request. Again Ngudjolo appeared before a judge. 'The moment I return to the Democratic Republic of Congo I run the risk of persecution. I will disappear without a trace or be arrested,' he told a Dutch judge at the end of a long day, 16 April 2015, at the court in Amsterdam. He was wearing a small silver cross in the lapel buttonhole of his jacket, while holding a small dictionary, Dutch-French, in his hands. Despite the uncertain situation in which he found himself, he seemed mentally strong. 'I urgently request you to grant me protection,' he asked the court.

But this judge wouldn't fulfil his wishes and decided that the IND hadn't made an error in rejecting the second asylum request. His lawyers

248 Official transcript, ICC, 21 October 2014.
249 Case information sheet, ICC.
250 'Asylum proceedings in the Ngudjolo case,' International Justice Monitor, 13 March 2015.

launched a series of last minute legal and diplomatic actions, including requests for asylum in Switzerland, Belgium and Kenya. His ICC counsel Kilenda called upon the ICC member states to find a solution for his client 'materialised in the right to reside in a secure country where he will not fear for his safety.'[251] To no avail. On 11 May 2015 Ngudjolo was handcuffed and escorted by six policemen to the Belgian airport near Brussels and deported to Kinshasa.[252] During the first weeks after his return he was reportedly hiding in a safe place offered by friends and family. But after a while he returned to the infamous institution that had him employed at the time of his arrest back in 2008. Ngudjolo has rejoined the Congolese army, where he continued his training as a nurse, well informed sources confirm.

The three witnesses

And the three witnesses? They are still in a Congolese prison. On 19 December 2015, the other comrade for whom they had testified in The Hague returned to the DRC as a prisoner. Germain Katanga – nicknamed 'Simba' ('Lion') – had been convicted and sentenced by the ICC to a twelve-year imprisonment for his role in planning and supplying arms for the attack on Bogoro. While Ngudjolo had been acquitted, Katanga was found guilty as an accessory for murder as a crime against humanity and the war crimes of murder, attacking civilians, destruction of enemy property and pillaging. He was acquitted of rape, sexual slavery and using child soldiers. However one judge, Christine Van den Wyngaert, dissented, underlining the trial had been unfair and that Katanga's rights had been violated.[253]

The convict however would accept his ordeal, withdrew his appeal and expressed a strong desire to serve the rest of his prison time in the DRC. His defence lawyers worked hard to fulfil that request. Before he was transferred back home, the ICC judges decided it was appropriate to reduce his original sentence by three years and eight months. This implied he would only have to spend a month in the Congolese prison and would be set free on 18 January 2016.[254]

---

251 'Netherlands to deport Congolese militia leader Ngudjolo,' Coalition for the ICC, 1 May 2015.
252 'ICC Acquitted person sent back to Congo,' Hirondelle News, 12 May 2015.
253 Judgment pursuant to article 74 of the Statute, ICC, 7 March 2014.
254 Decision on the review concerning reduction of sentence of Mr Germain Katanga, ICC, 13 November 2015.

But the DRC authorities decided otherwise. Katanga would not enjoy freedom in his home country. Soon after his transfer to the DRC, the Congolese government made it clear that the 'Haute Cour Militaire' was planning to prosecute him for alleged international crimes committed between 2002 and 2006, including the killing of nine United Nations peacekeepers. After having spent four weeks in the Congolese jail, Katanga was not released.[255]

The ICC was not amused. The rules prescribe that in a situation like this, with the DRC enforcing the ICC prison sentence, the Congolese authorities are obliged to first ask permission from the court in The Hague before they can decide to prosecute Katanga, says Caroline Buisman, who has been part of his defence team in the ICC-trial. The court's presidency looked into the matter. Meanwhile Katanga's lawyers wrote to the judges protesting against the 'unlawful' detention of their client, stressing he would not get a fair trial in the DRC, nor have the means to pay for a counsel, while underlining there is no possibility to appeal a judgment of the Haute Cour Militaire. Nevertheless, the ICC presidency filed a decision on 7 April 2016 saying they saw no problem in a Congolese trial. The national authorities could go ahead.[256]

For many months, apart from a few preliminary hearings, not much happened. Until 10 February 2017, when the Congolese trial against Katanga and six others, charged with war crimes, crimes against humanity and participation in an insurrectional movement in Ituri, resumed.[257] Two of his co-accused are well known figures in this saga: the asylum-seeking witnesses Floribert Ndjabu and Pierre Celestin 'Pichou' Mbodina Iribi.

255 'Kinshasa: début du procès Germain Katanga et Cie,' Radio Okapi, 16 February 2016.
256 Decision pursuant to article 108(1) of the Rome Statute,' ICC, 7 April 2016.
257 'War crimes trial resumes for ex-warlord Katanga in DRC,' News24, 10 February 2017.

CONCLUSION
1.5 billion euros, four convictions, nine failed cases

With an open mind I had started, back in 2011, to closely follow the
International Criminal Court. It was of great value that persons who are
responsible for mass atrocity crimes, who ruthlessly sacrifice other people
and cause so much suffering and destruction, would be investigated,
prosecuted and punished by an international institution if national
courts aren't able or willing to do so. It was hopeful that the law could be
mobilised against the perpetrators of gross human rights violations.

The first testimony I followed, seated at the public gallery, made a deep
impression on me. Despite the fact that I could not see witness P-87, as
her identity needed to be protected. The woman was shielded by blinds
which were lowered against the bulletproof window separating the
courtroom and the public gallery. Her image was broadcast in pixelated
form on the screens. Her voice was distorted and sounded like that of a
robot in my headphones. Her words in Sango, the language she spoke,
were translated by an interpreter. That's how I heard her testimony about
the violence she experienced on that fatal day in 2002 in the Central
African Republic (CAR). P-87 told the court how her neighbourhood and
family house were pillaged. A few hours later she was savagely gang-raped
by three militiamen. But it was not over yet. When for a third time
fighters came to the house, P-87 heard how her brother was killed while
trying to protect a motorbike from being stolen.

At a few metres distance from where the witness was testifying, the
suspect sat in the dock. Jean-Pierre Bemba Gombo, a former businessman
and warlord who had made it to vice president of the Democratic
Republic of Congo (DRC), was charged with crimes against humanity
and war crimes for the rapes, murders and pillaging committed by
his soldiers in the neighbouring country. With the judges in their role
of courteous arbiters managing the case, the prosecutors and defence
counsels fought their legal, moral and strategic battles. But nothing could
more underline the importance of the International Criminal Court in
bringing justice, than the heartbreaking testimony by witness P-87.

The ICC began its work in July 2002, after sixty countries had ratified the Rome Statute. These nations were determined to put an end to impunity for the perpetrators of genocide, crimes against humanity and war crimes. The court would not so much target the executors of violence – the people with blood on their hands – but rather the persons most responsible for these crimes. The ICC was tasked to go after the leaders, creators, organisers, sponsors and commissioners of criminal plans to violently gain power or to stay in power by all means, attacking civilians and all the things they cherish, targeting peacekeepers and their missions, violating the international laws that prescribe the treatment of enemy soldiers and prohibit the use of certain weapons. The court would also prosecute the commanders who failed to prevent, stop and punish atrocities committed by their troops.

But how is the ICC doing, now fifteen years after its start? What are the results? Did the court manage to fulfil its noble task? What lessons are to be learnt?

Stagnating membership

The ICC hasn't become a truly global institute. In total 124 states – especially African, European and Latin-American countries – have acceded to the Rome Statute. The number of new members joining lately isn't very impressive. In 2014 no state became member. Palestine joined the court in 2015, and indeed, that membership created buzz and fury. El Salvador was the only country joining in 2016. Big powers such as the United States of America, China and Russia don't even consider membership. The Middle East is hardly represented.

The implications of so many absentees are huge, as the rules dictate that the ICC only has automatic jurisdiction in member states. This means the court doesn't have an immediate mandate in large parts of the world. If the United Nations Security Council doesn't refer situations in non-member states such as Syria, North Korea or South Sudan to the ICC, the court generally can't investigate the international crimes committed in these countries. It shows the limited power of an institution that was created to make a difference in exactly those situations of extreme violence and conflict.

When it comes to membership, 2016 was a disastrous year. The ICC suffered a massive blow when South Africa, Burundi and Gambia decided to withdraw from the court. These actions created a sense of existential crisis. In the case of Burundi its withdrawal was a clear attempt by the authorities to prevent the risk of being prosecuted, as the country is under preliminary examination by the ICC's prosecution. Although South Africa and Gambia's new president decided to revoke the decision to pull out, and more generally the withdrawals also spurred many governments to express their support for the court, there will always be the threat that states decide to leave when it suits them. Russia un-signing from the Rome Statute in November 2016 was a symbolic step because it was never a member of the court, but added to the feeling that the ICC is losing ground. With the rise of nationalism and calls for disengagement, also in the USA and Europe, the overall support for the court is likely to diminish.

Cooperation

This is highly problematic because the ICC can only function if countries are prepared to back and work with the court. The institution, which doesn't have its own police force, is depending on governments for crucial matters such as carrying out arrest warrants, permission to investigate crimes, handing over evidence, accepting witnesses who need protection, and the budget, which is paid for by the member states.

There are many positive examples of cooperation, but the ICC has also ample experience of how governments prioritize their own interests. While financial limitations have been a constant concern, during the last annual meeting of states parties in The Hague, a group of eleven countries – Canada, Colombia, Ecuador, France, Germany, Italy, Japan, Poland, Spain, United Kingdom and Venezuela – took the initiative to restrict funding.

Countries also actively campaign against the ICC. In the early days the United States undermined the court by signing bilateral non-cooperation agreements with other governments and by introducing the American Service-Members' Protection Act to shield US military and officials from being prosecuted by the ICC. More recently there are concerns that the USA and other countries are trying to influence Afghanistan to limit its cooperation with the court, in order to prevent possible investigations into alleged crimes by US forces, national Afghan security forces and the Taliban.

Kenya has been particularly active as well. For several years the Kenyan government has been involved in a crusade to convince African countries to withdraw from the ICC (although Nairobi hasn't pulled out itself). Kenyan authorities have been frustrating investigations in the case against president Uhuru Kenyatta by not handing over evidence. The presiding judge in the ICC trial against the Kenyan deputy president William Ruto and broadcaster Joshua Sang concluded that the case was probably weakened because of massive political meddling and witness intimidation. Many governments, including Ivory Coast, Kenya and Libya, refuse to hand over suspects. The Sudanese president Omar Hassan Ahmad Al-Bashir, charged by the ICC in 2009 with crimes against humanity and war crimes in Darfur, followed in 2010 with charges for genocide, has been touring dozens of countries, and was even welcomed by member states such as South Africa as an important guest with all immunities attached. When South Africa was criticized for not performing its duty by not arresting Al-Bashir, the government decided to leave the ICC (although there might have been other motives as well).

Even The Netherlands, being the host state, doesn't always present itself in the most gallant way. The government could have been more generous when there was a three years gap in the rent to be paid for the temporary court building until the permanent premises were ready. There have been problems with issuing visa for witnesses and even for a defence lawyer. The Dutch government refused to help the court out when detained defence witnesses from the DRC demanded asylum in The Netherlands, which led to a three year imprisonment of three Congolese men at the ICC detention centre. The detention costs amounted to about one million euros, to be paid by the court to the Dutch government. After the detained witnesses lost their asylum case, they were transferred back to the DRC.

It is telling that The Netherlands didn't want to grant asylum to a few human rights activists who had to testify before the ICC, but were in danger and asked for protection. Their case went all the way up to the Council of State, the highest national court for these matters in The Netherlands, which decided they should be granted asylum.

The Dutch authorities were slow to react when in 2016 a human rights lawyer, submitting materials to the ICC's prosecution for its preliminary examination into international crimes committed in Palestine, was receiving death threats. Amnesty International, which also felt targeted as an email account in relation to this case was hacked, decided to close its office in The Hague for security reasons. Three other NGOs did so as well. Only then the Dutch authorities understood the seriousness of the situation, and acted.

It would be wrong to conclude that the presence of the court in The Hague only comes with obligations and responsibilities. The host state is benefitting from having the ICC on its territory, not only in financial terms (according to the ICC the Dutch economy is making roughly 66 million euros per year, from expenditures by the court, its staff and visitors), but also in terms of prestige as the institution is contributing to the image of The Hague as international city of peace and justice.

Africans, rebels and political adversaries on trial

So far the ICC has only been prosecuting Africans. This focus has led to fierce criticism, anger and accusations of bias and even racism. However, in five of the eight African countries where the ICC is conducting full investigations, the governments themselves invited the court to become active on their territory (Uganda, CAR twice, DRC, Mali and also Ivory Coast). Recently, in September 2016, Gabon referred the post-election situation in its country to the ICC.

In 2016 the court opened its first non-African investigation: into the violent conflict between Georgia, South Ossetia and Russia that occurred in 2008. This could help to bring more balance in the geographical scope of its work, no matter how difficult investigations in this situation might prove to be. Besides, in its preliminary examinations for many years the prosecutors have been looking into situations beyond Africa, such as Colombia, Afghanistan, Ukraine, Palestine and Iraq, where the UK military is accused of having tortured and killed Iraqi detainees.

So far, the route of governments referring a situation to the ICC has also led to selectivity of another kind. It has kept national authorities, their security forces and allies conveniently free from being prosecuted by the court. This goes for the cases with regard to Uganda (only rebel leaders of the Lord's Resistance Army are charged), DRC (militia leaders are prosecuted), CAR (one Congolese warlord/opposition leader charged and convicted for the 2002-2003 violence) and Mali (one Tuareg-jihadi prosecuted and found guilty). Although Ivory Coast didn't file an official referral, the new government was in favour of the ICC investigating the post-election violence (three persons of the former Gbagbo-regime are being prosecuted). When the government of Gabon referred the recent election violence to the court, it explicitly pointed out to the prosecutor that its political opponents were to blame for the crimes. So far, self-referrals seem to have been a useful tool for states, as the ICC has a tendency to target their adversaries, politicians who lost elections and militia leaders.

It is noteworthy that the African protests against the ICC started when the court began targeting powerful members of governments in active duty. The first angry reactions came when Sudanese leaders were indicted (following a referral by the UN Security Council). The campaign grew stronger when The Ocampo Six, which included Kenyan leaders and officials, were charged (initiated 'proprio motu' by the prosecutor).

The prosecution hasn't been successful in these cases. Obstruction seems to pay off. Thanks to countries receiving them, the indicted Sudanese president and ministers are still walking free. Witness interference, politial meddling and non-cooperation were factors in the collapse of the Kenyan cases against 'The Ocampo Six.' Prosecutor Fatou Bensouda promised to investigate crimes committed by persons now in positions of power in Ivory Coast, but up until now this hasn't resulted in arrest warrants (as far as is publicly known). Burundi's withdrawal might be an example for other states to follow: pull out if there is a threat of investigations against political leaders, officials and military.

In conclusion, African governments largely owe it to themselves that the ICC became active on the continent. They also benefitted from their state-referrals as the court went after adversaries, leaders who lost power struggles and rebel leaders, which in turn has led to accusations that the ICC applies victor's justice. When the prosecution charges those in power, it faces strong protests and risks of obstruction, political meddling, witness interference, states withdrawing from the ICC and governments shielding suspects from facing justice. States are by no means powerless vis-à-vis the court. They support, use and obstruct the ICC when it suits them.

1.5 billion, four convictions, nine failed cases

By now the ICC has cost 1.5 billion euros (the total of the 2003–2017 budgets). Currently a total of 33 persons have been charged with international crimes. In the fifteen years of its existence the ICC convicted and sentenced four of these suspects: Thomas Lubanga Dyilo (14 years),

Germain Katanga (12 years), Jean-Pierre Bemba Gombo (18 years) and Ahmad Al Faqi al Mahdi (9 years).

However, the prosecutor failed in international crimes cases against nine persons, where evidence was lacking for a trial or conviction (Bahar Idriss Abu Garda, Callixte Mbarushimana, Mathieu Ngudjolo Chui, Henry Kiprono Kosgey, Mohamed Hussein Ali, Francis Kirimi Muthaura, Uhuru Muigai Kenyatta, William Samoei Ruto and Joshua Arap Sang). With such a limited result the ICC is not making a huge impression. This outcome has led to disappointment, doubts and debates about its relevance.

Separately, eight individuals have been charged with offences against the administration of justice, for bribing and intimidating witnesses, so-called Article 70 cases. In October 2016 the judges convicted five persons for corruptly influencing defence witnesses, and sentenced them five months later: Jean-Pierre Bemba (one extra year in prison and a fine of 300,000 euros), his lawyers Aimé Kilolo Musamba (2.5 years imprisonment, which is partly suspended, and a fine of 30,000 euros) and Jean-Jacques Mangenda Kabongo (prison term of 2 years, partly suspended), plus Fidèle Babala Wandu (6 months imprisonment) and Narcisse Arido (11 months imprisonment). The other three suspects (all Kenyans) are at large.

Office of the Prosecutor

The prosecution is operating in a complex context. Its task is to investigate international crimes, often in countries with a poor rule of law, that are unable or unwilling to carry out independent prosecutions. Moreover, the ICC isn't working in only one country or region, but is investigating in different countries where each time it will have to start from scratch. Adding to the complexity is that the Office of the Prosecutor (OTP) is tasked to target top-level perpetrators against whom it is usually more difficult to collect evidence, as they mostly not directly carry out the atrocities, but rather are initiators, planners, financiers and organisers of the crimes, who often make sure they cover their tracks.

The first chief prosecutor, Luis Moreno-Ocampo, saw setting up his office and starting the first cases as his main task. During this crucial initial period major mistakes have been made with regard to criminal investigations (policy, evidence, intermediaries, witnesses) and human resource management (work atmosphere, departure of top professionals, lack of quality), which contributed to failures and reputation loss. As the OTP works in a difficult environment, it will need top professionals, the highest quality and most intelligent policies.

Immediately after her appointment as chief prosecutor, Fatou Bensouda, who for eight years was Moreno-Ocampo's right hand and responsible for those prosecutions during his mandate as well, started to formulate new policies (the focus of investigations, other types of evidence than witness testimony, building cases by going after sub-top leaders, the possibility of prosecuting for instance environmental crimes), hiring new professionals and calling in the advice of experts. The changes the prosecutor announced are an implicit recognition of earlier problems and mistakes. Since Bensouda took office only two new arrest warrants have been issued against suspects of international crimes. It seems she wants to concentrate on the caseload – which included weak cases – she inherited from her predecessor. She also charged eight persons with witness interference. It is too early to tell whether Bensouda's new approach and policies will lead to better results. While the year 2016 saw the final collapse of the Kenyan cases, there were successes as well. With the conviction of Jean-Pierre Bemba Gombo, for the first time the court condemned a warlord in his capacity as commander and successfully prosecuted sexual crimes. In the case of the Malian Islamist, Ahmad Al Faqi Al Mahdi, the prosecution handled its first guilty plea, which saved the court lots of resources and time as the proceedings took just one year. The conviction of Al Mahdi highlighted the fact that destroying cultural and religious monuments that are part of the local and international heritage, is a serious crime, punishable with a severe sentence. 2016 also saw the first successful prosecution of offences against the administration of justice, as Bemba and four others were found guilty of bribing and coaching witnesses and presenting false evidence.

Conflict of interest

The ICC has been dealing with several cases where a conflict of interest is looming. While investigating the bribery case which involved Bemba and two of his lawyers, the prosecution was secretly investigating its adversaries in court. According to Bemba's defence team, this resulted in an unfair main trial, which dealt with international crimes in the CAR. This isn't a rare one-off case. The prosecution has been examining similar incidents with regard to the detained warlords Bosco Ntaganda,

Thomas Lubanga and Dominic Ongwen, who are accused of influencing witnesses, although they haven't been officially charged.

The prosecution did't hesitate to charge its former Kenyan intermediary Walter Barasa and two others for witness interference, which weakened its case against Kenya's deputy president William Ruto and broadcaster Joshua Sang.

It is striking that despite allegations by the judges and defence in the Lubanga trial and Kenyan cases, the OTP has been unwilling to investigate intermediaries and witnesses who have been accused of lying and fabricating evidence in support of prosecution cases. This suggests that the prosecution will go after persons who are weakening its cases, but refuses to investigate individuals who have been working in support of its cases.

One of the biggest ICC scandals has been the sexual abuse of four protected witnesses/victims by an official of the Victims and Witnesses Section in the DRC. The perpetrator was fired. An independent panel of external experts was called in by the court to analyse the situation. The experts concluded that the headquarters in The Hague mismanaged this abuse case which encompassed 'the whole of the structure and functioning' of the VWS. After the publication of the summary of the panel's report, the case went largely silent.

When such sensitive situations, with a possible conflict of interest, are left to be handled by the ICC, this leads to doubts about double hats and partiality. Indeed, in several cases independent experts were called in, to prevent a manifest conflict of interest or to give clarity. However, such cases should be handled from the start by external professionals, who can make their own decisions on taking action and informing the public. This matter has become even more urgent now that more suspects have been accused of witness interference. With so many different international courts and tribunals in existence, it should be possible and worthwhile to set up a separate mechanism for cases where these institutions are faced with a manifest conflict of interest.

Witnesses

For everybody it is stressful and difficult to give testimony – to be accurate and to give a good and detailed account. It requires enormous courage to testify before a court like the ICC, where most witnesses will speak about traumatic events, giving incriminating evidence against or exonerating evidence in favour of powerful people who are accused of being involved in criminal networks. They run risks and their safety is often at stake. Witness interference has been a problem in almost all cases. Witnesses have allegedly been intimidated and offered bribes, in order to pressure them to withdraw or change their testimony. The persons who are accused of such malpractices include suspects (Bemba, Ongwen, Ntaganda, Lubanga,), intermediaries (in the trials against Lubanga, Ruto & Sang), defence lawyers (Bemba-trial) and others (a politician and a witness in the Bemba-trial; social media in the trial against Gbagbo & Blé Goudé; a variety of individuals in the Kenyan cases). In the Kenyan cases the intimidation reached such levels – potential witnesses and a defence witness were even murdered – that it undermined the trials.

More than 650 witnesses and their families are included into the protection programme. This provides them with security, but it places them also in a very difficult position, as protected witnesses will have to cut all ties with their former lives – family, friends, acquaintances, work. There is however also another side to this matter. Defence lawyers, notably in the Kenyan cases, have accused witnesses of offering themselves to the prosecution by telling lies, for financial gains, inclusion in the ICC's protection programme and relocation outside Africa.

The pressure on witnesses is a deeply worrying development as the ICC depends on their testimony to build cases against suspects. Only in recent years the prosecution has intensified its efforts to gather a range of scientific evidence, such as electronic and digital information, video-footage and satellite images (the Malian Islamist Al Mahdi was caught on camera while ordering and participating in the destruction of cultural and religious heritage). Despite this type of evidence, most cases will continue to depend hugely on witness testimony.

Victims

For the first time in the history of international courts and tribunals, victims have a special status and their own rights at the ICC. This sounds better than it is. It has been difficult to register as victim. Especially in rural areas victims lack information. In several cases their right to choose their own lawyer was not respected by the judges. It is still relatively rare that victims themselves speak purely as victims before the court. The ICC is not a victim's court.

In several conflict situations where the court is actively investigating, the Trust Fund for Victims has been giving assistance to affected communities. The fund's second mandate is reparations for the harm victims suffered. This is however a limited right as reparations are strictly related to the charges. Besides, victims must be extremely patient and wait for many years, as reparations can only be awarded when a suspect is declared guilty. But even after conviction procedures take ages. The handling of reparations is a heavy legal process led by the judges, with limited room for victims' wishes. After the verdicts against Lubanga (convicted in 2012) and Katanga (convicted in 2014) it took the judges respectively four and three years to decide on reparations. It is doubtful whether the officially acknowledged victims in the Lubanga case all agree with the court's decision to apply collective forms of reparations, instead of individual compensation, and whether the victims in the Katanga case are satisfied with the 250 dollars they each receive to compensate the harm they personally suffered, while the whole reparations process must have cost a multitude of the total that is spent on victims individually.

Communication

The International Criminal Court has a complex relationship with the public. Obviously security measures are necessary, but in the permanent premises these have been stepped up to such a level that it has become a rather overwhelming feature causing queues, problems and irritation. Most people, however, will only 'visit' the court by logging in to its website. For years the website had been criticized as it was difficult to navigate and to find documents. Too often the web-streaming of public hearings failed.

After many promises, finally a new website was launched on 9 May 2016. Despite improvements, it also gave new trouble. NGOs, academics, media and bloggers noticed that hyperlinks in their work, connecting to online court documents, no longer worked as the codes had been changed. During the transfer from the old to the new website, documents disappeared altogether. The annual schedule for hearings seemed gone as well. Although several matters were fixed, it took a lot of complaining to the highest levels before action was taken.

This didn't mean all problems had vanished. For long the 'broadcasting' by the ICC of public hearings through the Internet continued to cause problems for audiences in Africa. Until very recently this web-streaming could only be followed in English and French, which meant that even when witnesses were testifying in their own language, the media and audience at home were getting a translation. Transcripts of hearings were often not registered on the day the sessions have taken place, but rather on the date the documents were uploaded, creating search problems. Visitors also have to do quite a bit of navigating to find the key figures of cases. (International crimes cases: a total of 33 suspects; 6 in ICC detention; judges evaluated evidence against 19 suspects; 4 suspects now at trial; 4 convictions; 9 failed cases; 9 at large; 2 kept in detention abroad despite an obligation to surrender them to the ICC; 4 deceased suspects. Witness interference cases: a total of 8 suspects; 5 convicted of whom 1 in ICC detention; 3 at large.)

There are questions about how much affected communities are kept informed. In situation countries where the ICC is actively investigating, the court usually has one official for outreach. In rural areas of Uganda, DRC and Kenya victims often lacked access to information and had much less knowledge than those in cities. Many didn't know the location of the court's headquarters, and believed the ICC was an aid organization rather than a criminal court. Only in April 2017 the ICC launched a free and interactive SMS platform to give victims and communities in Uganda the opportunity to follow the case against rebel leader Dominic Onwgen. The ICC is a 'sending' organisation – a bureaucracy distributing the messages it wants the audience to receive. However, being approachable for public and media, giving easy access to everyday information, making sure victims are well informed and affected communities can follow proceedings, is an essential part of the ICC's role in societies as well.

Effect

The ICC's task is to prosecute perpetrators of international crimes and to punish them if found guilty. The aim of the court is to render justice and to prevent future crimes. But what has been the effect so far?

One thing is certain, the court draws a lot of attention and is constantly in the news. The ICC generates debate, influences and shapes ideas about accountability and justice, and stimulates changes in national law and practice. The very fact that governments, politicians but also citizens have been rallying against the court, also shows that the ICC matters.

In The Hague I not only met Kenyans who were angry that their leaders were charged. I also spoke to a woman who stood squarely behind the prosecutions. The powerful, who were always seen as untouchable gods by ordinary Kenyans, suddenly had fallen from grace and appeared to be ordinary human beings who could be called by a court to account for their actions, she explained. A Kenyan sports teacher had taken the plane from London just to see with his own eyes how the Ocampo Six had to appear before the judges. Even among supporters of president Uhuru Muigai Kenyatta there were people who saw a role for the ICC (as long as it wasn't targeting Kenyatta, of course). Previous opinion polls by Ipsos Synovate in Kenya showed that the percentage of Kenyans in favour of the ICC would fluctuate between 40 and 50 percent.[258]

In the east of the DRC, where relatively speaking the court has been more successful, the ICC seems less popular. The court is largely seen as ineffective. Researchers of the Harvard Humanitarian Initiative & United Nations Development Programme concluded in their study 'Searching for Lasting Peace'[259] that most of the respondents (48 percent) agreed that the national court system (which has a bad reputation) 'is more appropriate to achieve justice for war-related crimes.' Just one in five respondents said the ICC had a positive impact on peace (20 percent) and/or justice (22 percent).

One of the most important aims of charging and punishing perpetrators is prevention. Former prosecutor Moreno-Ocampo claimed that the Kenyan cases sent out a warning to politicians that they could be prosecuted if they would again organise election violence, which resulted in a much more peaceful vote in Kenya in 2013. However, there weren't just positive results. Two Kenyan suspects managed to win those elections and become the country's top leaders by stirring emotions, exploiting anger among the population over the court's prosecutions and strategic manoeuvring. The cases also led to new crimes and offences such as the killing of potential witnesses, the intimidation of prosecution witnesses, victims and supporters of the court and the obstruction of handing over evidence by the national authorities to the OTP. Those factors most likely weakened the ICC cases.

Possibly a positive development took place in the DRC. Human rights activists say that after the conviction of Lubanga, several Congolese

---

258 'New opinion poll finds rise in support for ICC,' International Justice Monitor, 15 November 2013.
259 Searching for Lasting Peace, Harvard Humanitarian Initiative&United Nations Development Programme, 2014.

warlords started to worry about themselves as they had child soldiers in their ranks and decided to let these minors go. In other situations it is hard to see any preventive effect at all. Take Libya, that spiralled out of control during recent years. Despite arrest warrants for top government officials and the head of state of Sudan himself, large scale atrocities continue to be committed in Darfur. With regard to the violence that occurred in 2002-2003 in the Central African Republic, the prosecutor decided to go after Jean-Pierre Bemba Gombo, who is a 'neighbour' from the DRC – a choice that is unlikely to have had any effect on perpetrators in the CAR. In fact, while the Bemba trial was in full swing, a bloody civil war erupted in the country. The word 'genocide' was even mentioned to describe the violence in the CAR. So much for deterrence and prevention. And yet, a small glimpse of hope was provided in the small and isolated town of Bossemptele in the CAR, where the catholic mission was protecting hundreds of Muslims. When three refugees were abducted by a Christian militia group, a nun told the gang leader that the mission fell under the jurisdiction of the ICC and that he could be prosecuted by the court in The Hague if anything would happen to the abductees. It was not true, there was no special protection for the mission, but it worked. The three Muslims were set free. Their lives, and possibly that of other refugees, were spared thanks to the brave nun of that catholic mission, who decided to remind the militia leader of the ICC.

Too valuable to fail

The high expectations that existed in the early days have undergone a harsh reality check. The court hasn't become the strong and successful organisation many among the public hoped for. There are doubts about the court's impartiality, quality, impact and utility. Its image has been harmed – also by the ICC itself. Questions remain about the influence that countries have on the investigations; about the use of the court as a tool by the powerful; about the management and quality of the investigations; the position of victims and the way the institution is communicating with the public. The court could explain things better. Expectations should be managed.

In 2016 the ICC saw the final collapse of its most prominent case, the proceedings against the Kenyan suspects. Apart from this major setback, that same year there were also victories, as the judges convicted two suspects for international crimes, and five individuals for offences against the administration of justice. It is, however, too early to tell whether these latest successes mark a turning point. Will the court's new policies and approaches bear fruit? What will be the effect of rising nationalism and disengagement on – sensitive – investigations?

Despite all the criticism and concern, however, the creation of the International Criminal Court is an important step forward in the history of mankind. As a permanent institution, it is here to stay. With its important task of bringing justice, it is too valuable to fail.

APPENDIX I

Overview – Ten situations, nine countries and 40 suspects

The International Criminal Court is investigating ten 'situations' (in nine different countries). So far a total of 33 persons have been charged with international crimes. They are prosecuted for crimes against humanity and war crimes, while one person – the president of Sudan – is also charged with genocide. As the ICC targets the 'most responsible,' these suspects are usually not the direct perpetrators who themselves killed, raped, tortured, enslaved, looted and destroyed. Mostly they are the leaders who designed the criminal plans and gave orders for armed operations and violent actions. These suspects provided money, brainpower, manpower, arms and logistics. It is their leadership position that makes them responsible for the atrocities committed by armies, militia, rebels and supporters against civilians or for instance peace keepers. Commanders can also be charged for their inactivity – for not preventing, punishing and stopping crimes committed by their soldiers.

The court is also prosecuting a growing number of persons who are accused of corruptly influencing witnesses, in official terms: offences against the administration of justice. These suspects are charged with intimidating, pressuring and bribing witnesses and forcing them to recant their testimonies, to give false statements or withdraw from the case. By now 8 persons have been charged with these offences.

If all accused are counted, one comes to a total of 41 suspects, though in reality there are 40 individuals indicted. That is because the Congolese warlord and politician Jean-Pierre Bemba Gombo features in two trials: in the international crimes case and the case for offences against the administration of justice.

Who are these suspects? What were the circumstances under which they committed their crimes? What is the status of their case? Below you find an overview (last update April 2017).

Uganda (2004)

A war had been raging for many years between the Ugandan government
and the Lord's Resistance Army, when in January 2004 Uganda requested
the prosecutor of the ICC to start an investigation into the conflict in the
north of the country. The LRA is a militia group that was set up around
1986 in Northern Uganda and is led by its notorious commander-in-chief
Joseph Kony, who claims to possess spiritual powers. Although the LRA
initially had some support among ethnic Acholi communities who had
been suffering from oppression, this backing disappeared when the group
grew increasingly violent in the early nineties. The militia group became
notorious for its cruelties committed against the civilian population, such
as kidnapping children and adults to use them as fighters, porters, slaves
and sex-slaves. People who were suspected of supporting the government
were attacked, maimed, tortured, abused, enslaved, raped and killed by
the LRA. More than 1.9 million people fled their homes. Many were
forced to live in one of the two hundred terribly neglected government
camps, where in 2005 about one thousand people were dying weekly
because of malnutrition and disease. Civilians were not only victims of
the LRA, but also suffered at the hands of government troops.[260]
It has proved to be difficult to trace the LRA. The militia group is strong
in its tactics and strategies. The LRA moves constantly and in recent years
the fighters have been active in a large area stretching over remote parts
of the Democratic Republic of Congo, the Central African Republic and
South Sudan, committing atrocities against people there as well. The
LRA probably consists of some few hundred fighters, who have forced
kidnapped children and adults to join them. Despite military operations
(involving African countries, the United States of America and the United
Nations) to capture the militia, only one commander, Dominic Ongwen,
has surrendered and was then handed over to the ICC.
The ICC has accused five LRA fighters of atrocities against civilians
committed during the conflict with the Ugandan government and
military: Joseph Kony, Vincent Otti (possibly killed in 2007), Okot
Odhiambo (killed in 2013), Raska Lukwiya (killed in 2006) and Dominic

---

260 Q&A on Joseph Kony and the Lord's Resistance Army, Human Rights Watch, 21 March 2012.

Ongwen – all charged with war crimes and crimes against humanity, although between suspects the number and nature of the counts differ.

DOMINIC ONGWEN – former commander of the Sinia Brigade of the LRA. Arrest warrant: 8 July 2005. Transferred to the ICC detention centre on 21 January 2015. His initial appearance took place in The Hague on 26 January 2015. Confirmation of charges hearing: 21 – 27 January 2016. All seventy charges were confirmed on 26 March 2016. Trial started on 6 December 2016. Detained at the ICC detention centre in The Hague.

Ongwen was abducted himself as a young boy by the LRA, became a child soldier and climbed the ranks. Initially he was accused by the ICC of crimes against humanity and war crimes during the attack on one camp for internally displaced persons in Lukodi, northern Uganda. But after his surrender the charges were substantially increased as the prosecutor added other crimes such as the attacks on IDP camps in Pajule, Odek and Abok.[261]

The charges total seventy counts of crimes against humanity and war crimes. These relate to attacks on the four IDP camps and include: murder, attempted murder, torture, cruel treatment, other inhumane acts, enslavement, outrages upon personal dignity, pillaging, destruction of property, attacks on civilians and persecution. Ongwen is also accused of sexual and gender-based crimes: forced marriage, rape, torture, sexual slavery and enslavement. Finally he is prosecuted for the conscription and use of children under the age of fifteen, who were forced to participate actively in hostilities.

Democratic Republic of Congo (2004)

On 19 April 2004 the government of the Democratic Republic of Congo (DRC) referred the investigations into international crimes committed since 2002 on its territory, to the ICC. For many years the nation was ravaged by wars. Although the causes are extremely complex, the genocide in neighbouring Rwanda in 1994 can be seen as one of the triggers of

---

261 Case information sheet, ICC, January 2017.

these conflicts. After the mass killing of possibly 800.000 Tutsis and moderate Hutus, approximately one and a half million Hutus crossed the border into the DRC (then Zaire). There Hutu extremists continued their aggression, being hunted down by Rwandan forces that committed atrocities as well, while Zaire itself was facing huge tensions between ethnic groups, interest groups and political parties. In 1996 the armies of Rwanda and Uganda supported the Congolese rebel leader Laurent-Désiré Kabila, who toppled dictator Mobutu.

The regime change didn't bring peace though, but led to armed struggles between (ethnic) groups for power and natural resources (gold, copper, diamonds, coltan) in which eventually nine countries and dozens of militia groups were involved. During the series of wars between 1996 and 2008 possibly between 3.5 and 5 million people died.

The ICC investigations focus on two specific conflict areas in the east of the country: Ituri and Kivu. The court has indicted six Congolese and Rwandese militia leaders (some were briefly integrated in the DRC army). By contrast, the ICC has left the national authorities untouched. Government leaders, officials, politicians, staff of secret services and military leaders escaped prosecution.

ITURI – In the eastern district of Ituri an armed conflict flared up between the Hema (pastoralists) and the Lendu (mainly agriculturalists who felt discriminated against for a long time), which peaked from 1998 until 2003. Different militia groups were fighting each other, receiving weapons and other support such as logistics from the Congolese army, Rwanda and Uganda. The struggle was about power and natural resources and was extremely bloody. An estimated 50,000 to 60,000 people died during this conflict. Until today tensions and violence continue to exist.

THOMAS LUBANGA DYILO – Congolese leader of the Union des Patriotes Congolais (UPC) and its military wing Forces Patriotiques pour la Libération du Congo (FPLC). Charged with the war crimes of enlisting and conscripting children under the age of fifteen and using them to participate actively in hostilities. Arrest warrant: 10 February 2006, unsealed 17 March 2006. Detained at the ICC from 16 March 2006 until 19 December 2015, when he was transferred to a prison in the DRC. Found guilty on 14 March 2012 and later sentenced to 14 years imprisonment. Verdict confirmed by the appeals chamber on 1 December 2014. Lubanga serves his prison sentence in the DRC. On 21 October 2016 the judges approved a plan for symbolic collective reparations for his victims. A decision on non-symbolic collective reparations programmes will be made in due course.[262]

BOSCO NTAGANDA (NICKNAME: THE TERMINATOR / TERMINATOR TANGO) – originally Rwandan but became Congolese. Prosecuted in his capacity as former deputy chief of staff and commander of operations of the UPC/FPLC. Arrest warrant: 22 August 2006, unsealed 28 April 2008. Ntaganda surrendered voluntarily to the ICC on 22 March 2013. Currently detained in The Hague. On 9 June 2014, the pre-trial chamber confirmed the charges against him. Five counts of crimes against humanity: murder and attempted murder, rape, sexual slavery, persecution, and forcible transfer of population. Thirteen counts of war crimes: murder and attempted murder, attacking civilians, rape, sexual slavery of civilians, pillaging, displacement of civilians, attacking protected objects, destroying the enemy's property, and the rape, sexual slavery, enlistment and conscription of child soldiers under the age of fifteen years and using them to participate actively in hostilities. Trial started on 2 September 2015.[263]

GERMAIN KATANGA ('SIMBA' / 'LION') – commander Force de Résistance Patriotique en Ituri (FRPI). Arrest warrant: 2 July 2007, unsealed 18 October 2007. Transfer to ICC detention: 17 October 2007. He was charged for his role during a one-day attack on 24 February 2003 on the village of Bogoro, in Ituri, DRC. Found guilty by ICC judges (by majority) on 7 March 2014 of murder as crime against humanity, and also four counts of war crimes: murder, attacking a civilian population, destruction of property, and pillaging. He was acquitted for the crimes against humanity of rape and sexual slavery, and the war crimes of rape, sexual slavery and using child soldiers in hostilities. Katanga was sentenced to 12 years imprisonment. On 19 December 2015 he was transferred from The Hague to a prison in the DRC, where he is facing

262 Case information sheet, ICC, October 2016.
263 Case information sheet, ICC, January 2017.

a new trial on other charges.[264] On 24 March 2017 the ICC awarded 297 victims in this case an individual symbolic compensation of 250 US dollars and collective reparations.

MATHIEU NGUDJOLO CHUI – leader of the Front des Nationalistes et Intégrationnistes (FNI). Arrest warrant: 6 July 2007, unsealed 7 February 2008. Transfer to ICC detention: 7 February 2008. Accused of three crimes against humanity: murder, rape, and sexual slavery; and seven war crimes: wilful killing, rape, sexual slavery, using children under the age of fifteen to take part in hostilities, deliberately directing an attack on a civilian population, destruction of property, and pillaging. Acquitted on 18 December 2012. Released from ICC detention: 21 December 2012. Acquittal confirmed in appeal by majority on 27 February 2015. Ngudjolo applied for asylum in The Netherlands, but his request was denied. He was returned to the DRC in May 2015. He is back serving in the Congolese army, as a nurse.

KIVU – The second Congolese region where the ICC conducts investigations is Kivu, which was the scene of several conflicts in which militia groups and the armies of the DRC and Rwanda were fighting each other. One of the most powerful groups was the Forces Démocratiques pour la Libération du Rwanda (FDLR), founded by Hutus, among whom many génocidaires. These militia would cross the border from the DRC to attack Tutsis in Rwanda, but the group was also implicated in violence against civilians in Kivu. FDLR leaders in Europe, the USA and Canada are allegedly supporting the militia group with promotion work and the coordination of activities.
The government in Kinshasa had initially been using these Hutu militia in its conflict with Rwanda. However, in 2009 the two governments combined forces with UN troops to attack and dismantle the FDLR. The Hutu militia took revenge on villages suspected of supporting the military operation. The ICC has charged two FDLR leaders for violence against the population of Kivu-villages such as Busurungi, Manje, Malembe and Mianga.

---

264 Case information sheet, ICC, March 2015.

CALLIXTE MBARUSHIMANA – originally Rwandan, executive secretary of the Forces Démocratiques pour la Libération du Rwanda-Forces Combattantes Abacunguzi (FDLR-FCA). Charged with five counts of crimes against humanity: murder, torture, rape, inhumane acts and persecution; and eight counts of war crimes: attacks against the civilian population, murder, mutilation, torture, rape, inhuman treatment, destruction of property, and pillaging. Arrest warrant: 28 September 2010, unsealed 11 October 2010. Arrested by France on 11 October 2010. Transfer to ICC detention: 25 January 2011. Judges declined to confirm the charges on 16 December 2011 because of lack of evidence. Released from ICC custody: 23 December 2011.265

SYLVESTRE MUDACUMURA – supreme commander Forces Démocratiques pour la Libération du Rwanda (FDLR). Charged with nine counts of war crimes: attacking civilians, murder, mutilation, cruel treatment, rape, torture, destruction of property, pillaging, and outrages upon personal dignity. Arrest warrant: 13 July 2012. At large.

Central African Republic (2004)

The Central African Republic has a long history of violence and mutinies. In spring 2001, the elected president Ange-Félix Patassé was confronted with a coup attempt, which he managed to crush with the support of foreign troops. Subsequently Patassé dismissed and wanted to arrest army chief François Bozizé because he suspected him of having supported the putsch. (Both men had served under the ruthless dictatorship of 'emperor' Bokassa). The military commander however fled to Chad. From there Bozizé set up a power base, and in October 2002 he launched an attack on the capital city of Bangui trying to conquer the country. Again president Patassé turned to foreign allies: Libya, a militia leader from Chad, and the Congolese politician/warlord/businessman Jean-Pierre Bemba Gombo, who was the leader of the Mouvement de Libération du Congo (MLC). At first these forces seemed to quell the attack on Bangui, but in spring 2003 Bozizé seized power and became head of state.

---

265 Case information sheet, ICC, June 2012.

In December 2004 the new Bozizé government referred the conflict situation to the ICC. A few months later Bangui handed over to the ICC prosecutor the files with the national investigations into the atrocities committed between 2002 and 2003 during the violent takeover. The only person prosecuted by the ICC for the violence in the CAR is the Congolese leader Bemba. Initially he was charged as an indirect co-perpetrator (accused of having committed crimes with Patassé), but the pre-trial judges rejected this form of responsibility. The prosecutor then followed the chamber's advice and charged Bemba in his role as military commander for the crimes his MLC troops committed during the five months they had been fighting Bozizé's men.

On 30 May 2014 a new CAR government also turned to the ICC, this time referring the latest civil war (since 1 August 2012) to the court. A few months later, on 24 September 2014, prosecutor Fatou Bensouda announced that she had opened an investigation into the violence between Christian and Muslim militia. This second investigation, CAR II, hasn't led to arrest warrants yet, or at least nothing has been made public. The prosecutor believes crimes against humanity and war crimes have been committed, including murder, rape, forced displacement, persecution, pillaging, attacks against humanitarian missions and the use of children under fifteen in combat.[266]

JEAN-PIERRE BEMBA GOMBO – Congolese, president and military commander-in-chief of the MLC, former vice-president of the DRC. Charged with two crimes against humanity: murder and rape; and three war crimes: murder, rape and pillaging. These atrocities were committed by his troops. Arrest warrant 23 May 2008, which was replaced on 10 June 2008. Arrested by Belgian authorities on 24 May 2008. Transfer to ICC detention: 3 July 2008. Trial started on 22 November 2010. Verdict on 21 March 2016. The judges found Bemba guilty of all charges, because as a military commander he failed to prevent, punish or stop his troops committing the charged crimes. On 21 June 2016, Bemba was sentenced to 18 years of imprisonment. In appeals phase.[267]

---

266 Statement of ICC Prosecutor Fatou Bensouda on opening a second investigation in the Central African Republic, press release OTP, 24 September 2014.
267 Case information sheet, ICC, 26 July 2016.

On 20 November 2013 again an arrest warrant was filed against Bemba, charging him – plus two of his lawyers, a politician and a witness – with offences against the administration of justice. The five are being accused of corruptly influencing defence witnesses by giving them money and instructing them to give false testimony (the accusation of falsifying documents has been thrown out by the judges). The trial started 29 September 2015. On 19 October 2016 the judges found all five guilty, and they were sentenced on 22 March 2017.

Apart from Bemba the other four suspects in this case are:

AIMÉ KILOLO MUSAMBA – Congolese with Belgian nationality; lead counsel in Bemba's main case; arrest 23 November 2013; in ICC detention from 25 November 2013 until 21 October 2014, when he was granted interim release. [268]

JEAN-JACQUES MANGENDA KABONGO – Congolese, lawyer and case-manager in Bemba's main case; arrest 23 November 2013; transfer to ICC detention on 4 December 2013. The judge called for interim release on 21 October 2014, but the actual release took place somewhat later.

FIDÈLE BABALA WANDU – Congolese member of parliament for the MLC; arrest 24 November 2013; in ICC detention from 25 November until 21 October 2014, when he was granted interim release.

NARCISSE ARIDO – witness from the CAR; arrest 23 November 2013; in ICC detention from 18 March 2014 until 21 October 2014, when he was granted interim release.

The five convicts received different sentences. Bemba was punished with an extra year in prison (on top of his 18 years) and a fine of 300,000 euros. The other four saw the 11 months in detention deducted; Kilolo and Mangenda saw the remainder suspended. Kilolo was sentenced to 2.5 years in prison and a fine of 30,000 euros; Mangenda was sentenced to 2 years in prison; Arido got 11 months; and Babala 6 months.

---

268 Case information sheet, ICC, October 2016.

Mali (2012)

Early January 2012 ethnic Tuareg started an uprising against the Mali government in Bamako. Their goal was the independence of Azawad, the northern part of the country. Groups of heavily armed Tuareg had returned from the civil war in Libya, where they had fought at the side of the ousted Gaddafi regime. The Malian army was no match for the motivated fighters. Then in March 2012 disgruntled military mounted a coup and ousted the government in Bamako. The Tuareg benefitted from the power vacuum. They were supported by Ansar Eddine, a local Islamist group closely associated with Al Qaeda in the Islamic Maghreb (AQIM). While Tuareg and jihadi groups took control of large parts of the north, they committed massive human rights abuses. The Malian forces are also accused of committing atrocity crimes.

The government in Bamako requested military help. A French intervention force was deployed in the north in January 2013 to fight the Islamists. African forces joined the coalition. Since July 2013 the United Nations Multidimensional Integrated Stabilization Mission in Mali (Minusma) is active in a bid to restore stability in the country.

In July 2012 the Malian minister of justice visited the ICC with a request to start investigations into atrocities in the north where 'extrajudicial executions of soldiers of the Mali army, the rape of women and young girls, massacres of civilians and the conscription of child soldiers, torture, pillaging of state and civilian property and kidnapping' were taking place. The Malian government also asked the court to pay attention to attacks on hospitals, schools, courts, churches, mausoleums and mosques.

ICC prosecutor Bensouda declared on 16 January 2013 that her office had opened an investigation into international crimes committed in Mali since 2012. She said: 'At each stage during the conflict, different armed groups have caused havoc and human suffering through a range of alleged acts of extreme violence. I have determined that some of these deeds of brutality and destruction may constitute war crimes as defined by the Rome Statute.'[269] So far the ICC has prosecuted one Malian suspect.

---

269 ICC Prosecutor opens investigation into war crimes in Mali, press release 16 January 2013.

AHMAD AL FAQI AL MAHDI – Malian Tuareg, member of Ansar Eddine, head of 'Hisbah' (a body upholding public morals and preventing vice) and involved in the Islamic court in Timbuktu. Accused of war crimes for intentionally directing attacks against historic monuments and buildings dedicated to religion, including nine mausoleums and one mosque. Warrant of Arrest: 18 September 2015. Arrested in Niger (where he had been in detention) and transferred to ICC on 26 September 2015. First appearance on 30 September 2015. Confirmation of charges hearing on 1 March 2016. Charges confirmed on 24 March 2016. Al Mahdi pleaded guilty and made a deal with the prosecution. On 27 September 2016 the judges found him guilty and sentenced him to 9 years imprisonment.[270]

REFERRAL BY THE UNITED NATIONS SECURITY COUNCIL

Sudan/Darfur (2005)

For many years tensions had been growing in Darfur, a region of western Sudan bordering Chad. Ethnic groups accused the Khartoum authorities of discrimination, repression, creating an apartheid situation and stealing natural resources. Early 2003 the violent conflict erupted. Rebels decided to take up arms and attacked army and police posts. The regime responded with ground attacks and bombardments. Then it called for the mobilisation of the Arab Janjaweed militia to join a bloody counter offensive together with the army, secret services and police. During their offensive government troops and Janjaweed not only fought rebel groups such as the Sudan Liberation Movement/Army (SLM/A) and the Justice and Equality Movement (JEM), but also massively targeted civilians. Darfur, where more than six million people lived, became the scene of attacks, killings, sexual violence, torture, pillaging, enforced disappearances, forced displacement and ethnic cleansing. The regime has been accused of committing genocide. During the war possibly more than three hundred thousand people have died, hundreds of villages were destroyed and three million people were driven from their homes and land. Despite ceasefires and attempts to create peace, the violence continues. Amnesty International accused the regime of using chemical

270   Case information sheet, ICC, 7 October 2016.

weapons against civilians during thirty attacks in 2016.[271] There are also fights among the splintered rebel factions.

On 31 March 2005 the UN Security Council referred the situation in Darfur to the ICC. The court has indicted the Sudanese head of state, two ministers and the Janjaweed leader. For one specific attack the ICC charged three rebel leaders.

OMAR HASSAN AHMAD AL BASHIR – president of Sudan. Charged with three counts of genocide: killing, causing serious bodily or mental harm, and deliberately inflicting on each target group conditions of life calculated to bring about the group's physical destruction. Five counts of crimes against humanity: murder, extermination, forcible transfer, torture, and rape. Two counts of war crimes: intentionally directing attacks against a civilian population and pillaging. Arrest warrants: 4 March 2009 and 12 July 2010. At large.

AHMAD MUHAMMAD HARUN – former interior minister. Charged with twenty counts of crimes against humanity including: murder, persecution, forcible transfer of population, rape, inhumane acts, imprisonment or severe deprivation of liberty and torture; and twenty-two counts of war crimes including: murder, attacks against civilians, destruction of property, rape, pillaging and outrage upon personal dignity. Arrest warrant: 27 April 2007. At large.

ABDEL RAHEEM MUHAMMAD HUSSEIN – former minister of national defence, former minister of interior and former special representative of the president in Darfur. Charged with seven counts of crimes against humanity: persecution, murder, forcible transfer, rape, inhumane acts, imprisonment or severe deprivation of liberty, and torture; and six counts of war crimes: murder, attacks against a civilian population, destruction of property, rape, pillaging, and outrage upon personal dignity. Arrest warrant: 1 March 2012. At large

---

271 Scorched earth, poisoned air: Sudanese government forces ravage Jebel Marra, Darfur, Amnesty International, 2016.

ALI MUHAMMAD ALI ABD-AL-RAHMAN ('ALI KUSHAYB') – leader of
the Janjaweed militia. Charged with twenty-two counts of crimes
against humanity including: murder, deportation or forcible transfer of
population, imprisonment or other severe deprivation of physical liberty,
torture, persecution, inhumane acts of inflicting serious bodily injury and
suffering; and twenty eight counts of war crimes including: violence to life
and person, outrage upon personal dignity in particular humiliating and
degrading treatment, intentionally directing an attack against a civilian
population, pillaging, rape, destroying or seizing the property. Arrest
warrant: 27 April 2007. At large.

In 2004 the African Union had set up a peacekeeping mission (AMIS)
for Darfur. On 29 September 2007 a large and heavily armed rebel force
attacked an AMIS post, the Haskanita Military Group Site, in northern
Darfur. In the attack twelve soldiers were killed and eight were severely
wounded. The attackers pillaged and destroyed the site, stealing vehicles,
computers, ammunition, fuel, money and other belongings. For this
specific attack the ICC has charged three rebel leaders.

BAHAR IDRISS ABU GARDA – chairman and general coordinator of military
operations of the United Resistance Front. Charged with three counts
of war crimes: murder, intentionally directing attacks against personnel,
installations, material, units or vehicles involved in a peacekeeping
mission, and pillaging. Arrest warrant: 7 May 2009, unsealed 17 May
2009. Voluntary first appearance: 18 May 2009. Confirmation of charges
hearing: 19-30 October 2009. On 8 February 2010 the judges declined
to confirm the charges because of lack of proof. The prosecution has the
possibility to bring new evidence. Garda became minister of health with
the government in Khartoum.[272]

ABDALLAH BANDA ABAKAER NOURAIN – commander-in-chief of the
Justice and Equality Movement, one of the components of the United
Resistance Front. Charged with three war crimes: murder, intentionally
directing attacks against personnel, installations, material, units or
vehicles involved in a peacekeeping mission, and pillaging. Summons

---

272 Case information sheet, ICC, 15 June 2012.

to appear: 27 August 2009, unsealed 15 June 2010. First voluntary appearance: 17 June 2010. Confirmation of charges hearing: 8 December 2010. The judges confirmed the charges on 7 March 2011. The trial has been postponed several times, as the suspect didn't show up. Warrant of arrest: 11 September 2014. At large.[273]

SALEH MOHAMMED JERBO JAMUS (DECEASED) – chief of staff of SLA-unity. Charged with three war crimes: murder, intentionally directing attacks against personnel, installations, material, units or vehicles involved in a peacekeeping mission, and pillaging. Summons to appear in 2009. First voluntary appearance: 17 June 2010. Confirmation of charges hearing: 8 December 2010. The judges confirmed the charges on 7 March 2011, and committed the suspect to trial. Proceedings against Jerbo were terminated on 4 October 2013 after the ICC received information about his death.

Libya (2011)

For more than forty years the regime of Muammar Gaddafi ruled Libya with an iron fist, until in the east of the country an uprising started in February 2011. Tens of thousands of people took to the streets and demanded the departure of the Libyan leader, who then ordered his troops to fire on demonstrators. Soon an interim government was set up in the eastern city of Benghazi. The regime reacted with terror, ground offensives and bombardments. The uprising resulted in a bloody conflict between the Gaddafi regime, security forces and mercenaries on the one hand, and the opposition and several rebel groups on the other. In March 2011 the UN Security Council called for a ceasefire. From 19 March an international coalition, led by NATO, started a military intervention in Libya to enforce a no-fly zone and to curb the actions by the Libyan forces. After half a year, the opposition took Tripoli.
Already on 26 February 2011 the UN Security Council had decided unanimously to refer the situation in Libya to the ICC. On 3 March prosecutor Luis Moreno-Ocampo opened an investigation, and on 16 May he requested the judges to issue an arrest warrant against father and

273 Case information sheet, ICC, 23 March 2015.

son Gaddafi and the head of the military intelligence. The judges granted the request on 27 June 2011.[274] Then on 24 April 2017 the court unsealed an arrest warrant against the former head of the Internal Security Agency. After the fall of the Gaddafi regime the security situation in the country deteriorated, with scores of groups and militia competing for power and resources. ICC prosecutor Fatou Bensouda, expressing her concern about the high level of violence, announced in 2014 that her office is continuing investigations, but had to scale down operations and was limiting herself to mass crimes by rebel forces.[275] So far her efforts haven't resulted in arrest warrants against suspects from those groups (at least not publicly).

MUAMMAR MOHAMMED ABU MINYAR GADDAFI (KILLED IN 2011) – former head of state and commander of the armed forces. Charged with two counts of crimes against humanity: murder and persecution. Arrest warrant: 27 June 2011. Case withdrawn on 22 November 2011, after the Libyan leader was killed by rebels a month earlier, in October 2011. His killers are not prosecuted by the ICC.

SAIF AL-ISLAM GADDAFI – former de facto prime minister and son of the late Libyan leader. Charged with two counts of crimes against humanity: murder and persecution. Arrest warrant 27 June 2011. Gaddafi hasn't been surrendered to the ICC, but is being held by rebels in the town of Zintan. The Libyan authorities have prosecuted and convicted the former 'prime minister' in 2015. He received the death sentence, which so far hasn't been carried out.

ABDULLAH AL-SENUSSI – former head of the military intelligence and colonel in the Libyan army. Charged with two counts of crimes against humanity: murder and persecution. Arrest warrant: 27 June 2011. ICC proceedings ended 24 July 2014, when the appeals chamber confirmed that this case is inadmissible before the court in The Hague. Al-Senussi was prosecuted and convicted by Libyan authorities in 2015. His death sentence hasn't been carried out.

---

274 Case information sheet, ICC, 13 June 2016.
275 'Libya: ICC Prosecutor warns court's work faces 'deleterious impact' of ongoing instability,' UN News Centre, 11 November 2014.

AL-TUHAMY MOHAMED KHALED – former head of the Internal Security Agency (ISA) under the Gaddafi regime. Charged with crimes against humanity: imprisonment, torture, persecution and other inhumane acts; and war crimes: torture, cruel treatment and outrages upon dignity. Arrest warrant under seal: 18 April 2013. Unsealed: 24 April 2017. At large.

PROPRIO MOTU – CASES INITIATED BY THE ICC PROSECUTOR

Kenya (2009)

On 27 December 2007 elections for a new president and parliament were held in Kenya. The front runners were the leaders of the Party of National Unity (PNU) and opposition party Orange Democratic Movement (ODM). Politics in Kenya are closely related to ethnic groups. The PNU was seen as the party of the Kikuyu, while the ODM was seen as being supported by the Kalenjin, Luo and other ethnic groups.

When the results were published, the neck-and-neck race had been won by the PNU candidate. Subsequently massive fights broke out between ethnic groups which were connected to political parties. The violence that allegedly was organised by politicians and officials hit many parts of the country, especially in the Rift Valley and slums of cities such as Nairobi. In a few weeks' time at least 1100 people were killed and more than 600,000 persons were driven from their homes. Land disputes, that previously also had led to violence, are seen as one of the underlying causes.

Kofi Annan, the former secretary general of the United Nations, was appointed as mediator. His intervention resulted in a power-sharing government between the two parties PNU and ODM. Annan also worked on the creation of the Commission of Inquiry into Post-Election Violence (CIPEV), led by the Kenyan judge Philip Waki. In October 2008 Waki handed over his report to president Mwai Kibaki (PNU) and prime minister Raila Odinga (ODM). The names of possible perpetrators (it was said at least two ministers were named as suspects) were not disclosed, but the list was put in an envelope and given to Kofi Annan. In his turn, he handed the list in July 2009 to ICC's chief prosecutor Luis Moreno-Ocampo.

The Waki commission had given the Kenyan leaders one year to set up a special tribunal to prosecute perpetrators of the post-election violence. When that didn't seem to happen, Ocampo acted. On 5 November 2009 the prosecutor requested the judges' permission to start – proprio motu – an investigation. On 31 March 2010 the judges granted his request. On 15 December 2010 the prosecutor asked the judges to issue summons to appear for six Kenyans who represented the warring parties and were allegedly implicated in organising the violence. In Kenya they were called the 'Ocampo Six.' Because they appeared voluntarily before the judges, no one was detained.

WILLIAM SAMOEI RUTO – currently deputy president of Kenya. When he was indicted, he was a member of parliament and suspended minister of higher education, science and technology. Charged with three counts of crimes against humanity: murder, deportation and persecution. Summons to appear: 8 March 2011. Initial appearance: 7 April 2011. Confirmation of charges hearing: 1 - 8 September 2011. Charges confirmed on 23 January 2012. Start trial: 10 September 2013. On 5 April 2016 the judges (by majority) terminated the case, citing a lack of evidence. Because of the high incidence of witness interference, the suspect is not acquitted. The prosecutor can restart the case if she has new evidence.[276]

JOSHUA ARAP SANG – broadcaster with Kass FM. Charged with three counts of crimes against humanity: murder, deportation and persecution. Summons to appear: 8 March 2011. Initial appearance: 7 April 2011. Confirmation of charges hearing: 1 - 8 September 2011. Judges confirmed the charges on 23 January 2012. Start trial: 10 September 2013. On 5 April 2016 the judges terminated the case, because of a lack of evidence. The suspect is not acquitted because of the high incidence of witness interference. The prosecutor can re-start the case if she has new evidence.

HENRY KIPRONO KOSGEY – former minister of Industrialisation. Charged with three counts of crimes against humanity: murder, deportation and persecution. Summons to appear: 8 March 2011. Initial appearance: 7

---

276 Case information sheet, ICC, April 2106.

April 2011. Confirmation of charges hearing: 1 – 8 September 2011. The judges declined on 23 January 2012 to confirm the charges because of a lack of evidence. Kosgey went free.

UHURU MUIGAI KENYATTA – currently head of state. He was deputy prime minister when he was charged for five counts of crimes against humanity: murder, deportation, rape, persecution and other inhumane acts. Summons to appear: 8 March 2011. Initial appearance: 8 April 2011. Confirmation of charges hearing: 21 September – 5 October 2011. Judges confirmed the charges on 23 January 2012. The trial was postponed several times. Insufficient evidence forced the prosecutor on 5 December 2014 to withdraw the charges. The case is considered closed, but Kenyatta is not acquitted. If the prosecutor has new evidence she can again press charges and reopen the case.[277]

MOHAMMED HUSSEIN ALI – former police chief. Charged with five counts of crimes against humanity: murder, deportation, rape, persecution and other inhumane acts. Summons to appear: 8 March 2011. Initial appearance: 8 April 2011. Confirmation of charges hearing: 21 September – 5 October 2011. The judges decided on 23 January 2012 that the charges could not be confirmed. The case is closed.

FRANCIS KIRIMI MUTHAURA – former secretary to the cabinet and head of civil service. Charged with five counts of crimes against humanity: murder, deportation, rape, persecution and other inhumane acts. Summons to appear: 8 March 2011. Initial appearance: 8 April 2011. Confirmation of charges hearing: 21 September – 5 October 2011. Judges confirmed the charges on 23 January 2012. Prosecutor Bensouda withdrew the charges on 18 March 2013. The case collapsed when a crucial witness proved to have lied.

The prosecutor has also started investigations into the illegal interference with witnesses in the Ruto & Sang trial. This resulted in the arrest warrants for three Kenyans, accused of intimidating and bribing prosecution witnesses.

---

277 Case information sheet, ICC, 13 March 2015.

WALTER OSAPIRI BARASA – journalist and former intermediary of the ICC prosecution team. Charged with offences against the administration of justice for corruptly influencing three ICC witnesses. Arrest warrant under seal: 2 August 2013. Unsealed: 2 October 2013. At large.

PAUL GICHERU – a Kenyan lawyer. Charged with offences against the administration of justice for corruptly influencing prosecution witnesses of the ICC. Arrest warrant under seal: 10 March 2015. Unsealed: 10 September 2015. At large.

PHILIP KIPKOECH BETT – a casual labourer. Charged with offences against the administration of justice for corruptly influencing prosecution witnesses of the ICC. Arrest warrant under seal: 10 March 2015. Unsealed: 10 September 2015. At large.

Ivory Coast

After winning the elections in 2000 in Ivory Coast, protests helped Laurent Gbagbo to cash in his victory and become president. In 2002 troops mainly coming from the north mutinied. The civil war led to the division of the country. The north came in the hands of the rebels, while the government forces were controlling the south. But fighting continued. French and UN troops guarded and patrolled a buffer zone splitting the nation. In 2007 the north and south again signed an agreement. After the presidential elections in 2010 opposition candidate Alassane Ouattara, coming from the northern part of the country, was declared the winner. The constitutional council however claimed that Laurent Gbagbo had won the elections.

As the two sides couldn't come to an agreement, the power struggle became increasingly violent. Ouattara was supported by rebel forces from the north and mercenaries. Gbagbo relied on the security forces, militia, mercenaries and the youth groups. The latter were allegedly led by his co-accused Charles Blé Goudé. On 11 April 2011 former president Gbagbo, his wife and their entourage were overpowered by the French military who supported Ouattara's forces. The power struggle was won by Ouattara, who is currently president.

Both parties are accused of atrocities against each other's supporters. Troops and militia loyal to Gbagbo are blamed for killings, raping, harming demonstrators and shelling neighbourhoods. The militia that were fighting for Ouattara are accused of having abused and killed hundreds of citizens. They are allegedly responsible for a massacre that took place in the town of DuéKoué. It is estimated that during the post-election violence a total of three thousand people were killed, while a million people fled their homes.

In 2003, when Gbagbo was still president, the government of Ivory Coast had declared that the ICC had jurisdiction over crimes during the ongoing civil war. As new head of state Ouattara confirmed in 2010 and 2011 the ICC's mandate in his country. On 15 February 2013 Ivory Coast ratified the Rome Statute and became a full member of the court. Prior to that, on 3 October 2011, the judges had granted the prosecutor's request to open – proprio motu – an investigation. So far only leaders from the Gbagbo camp have been indicted by the court.

LAURENT GBAGBO – former head of state. Charged with four counts of crimes against humanity: murder, rape, persecution, and other inhumane acts/attempted murder. Warrant of arrest under seal: 23 November 2011. Unsealed: 30 November 2011. Transfer to ICC: 30 November 2011. Initial appearance: 5 December 2011. Confirmation of charges hearing: 19 – 28 February 2013. In 2013 the judges declined to confirm the charges, adjourned the hearing and gave the prosecution another chance to gather more evidence. On 12 June 2014 the charges were confirmed (by majority). Trial started on 28 January 2016.[278]

CHARLES BLÉ GOUDÉ – former youth minister and alleged militia leader. Charged with four counts of crimes against humanity: murder, rape, persecution, and other inhumane acts/attempted murder. Warrant of arrest under seal: 21 December 2011. Unsealed: 30 September 2013. Transfer to ICC: 22 March 2014. Initial appearance: 27 March 2014. Confirmation of charges hearing: 29 September – 2 October 2014. Charges confirmed: 11 December 2014. Trial started 28 January 2016.

SIMONE GBAGBO – former first lady. Charged with four counts of crimes against humanity: murder, rape and other sexual violence, persecution

---

278 Case information sheet, ICC, January 2016.

and other inhumane acts/attempted murder. Warrant of arrest under seal: 29 February 2012. Unsealed: 22 November 2012. Ivory Coast has filed an admissibility challenge which has been rejected by the ICC. In the meantime Simone Gbagbo has been prosecuted in Ivory Coast for attacks against the state and is serving a twenty years prison term. She faced a second trial for crimes against humanity before the national court, that started in May 2016. She was acquitted on 28 March 2017.

Georgia

Many years after the dismantling of the Soviet Union, a severe conflict broke out between Georgia and the breakaway region of South Ossetia. On 7 August 2008 Georgian troops launched an offensive to take control over the semi-autonomous area. Russia responded with a military operation supporting South Ossetia, entering Georgian territory. According to the Independent International Fact-Finding Mission on the Conflict in Georgia (IIFFMCG), established by the European Union, about 850 persons died, while more than 100,000 civilians fled their homes.

When the situation spiralled out of control, in August 2008 the ICC prosecutor immediately announced the start of a preliminary examination of the conflict. The court has jurisdiction as George is a member of the court. Although Russia and Georgia have been conducting investigations themselves, the ICC noted that national proceedings in Georgia were halted. On 13 October 2015 the ICC prosecutor requested authorisation from the judges to start – proprio motu – an investigation into crimes against humanity and war crimes.[279] This request was granted on 27 January 2016 for atrocities committed on the territory of Georgia between 1 July and 10 October 2008.

The ICC prosecutor is focusing her case on forcible displacements by South Ossetian authorities, with 'possible participation' of members of the Russian armed forces. During these operations between 51 and 113 ethnic Georgian civilians were killed, more than five thousand dwellings were reportedly destroyed and between 13,400 and 18,500 Georgians were forcibly displaced. According to the prosecutor, the Georgian

---

279   The Prosecutor of the International Criminal Court, Fatou Bensouda, requests judges for authorisation to open an investigation into the situation in Georgia, press release OTP, 13 October 2015.

population living in the conflict zone was reduced by at least 75 per cent. Russia has acknowledged South Ossetia's independence and has based Russian forces in the breakaway region.

The prosecutor also investigates war crimes allegedly committed by both parties attacking the peacekeeping mission. Georgian peacekeepers were the subject of heavily shelling from South Ossetian positions. Two Georgian peacekeepers were killed and five were injured. In another incident Georgian forces attacked a Russian base, reportedly killing ten Russian peacekeepers, wounding thirty soldiers and destroying the facility. These are the first criminal investigations by the ICC in a conflict situation outside Africa.

APPENDIX II International justice in twelve steps

1 The International Criminal Court comes into play when gross human rights violations can be categorized as international crimes over which the court has jurisdiction: genocide, crimes against humanity and war crimes. It is up to the judges to decide at what stage victims are entitled to participate in proceedings.

2 Criminal investigations into these crimes start when:
a a member state refers a situation to the ICC → prosecutor can start investigations.
b the UN Security Council refers a situation to the ICC → prosecutor can start investigations.
c the prosecutor requests permission from the ICC president to open a – proprio motu – investigation. Three judges of the pre-trial chamber study the request. If they agree → prosecutor can start investigations.

3 Investigations
Before the Office of the Prosecutor opens investigations, the OTP not only studies the alleged crimes, but also whether it has a mandate, whether the case would serve the interests of justice and whether the country is unable or unwilling to take up the case (complementarity). When the prosecutor decides to start an investigation, she will ask national authorities permission for her investigators to enter their territory to be able to do their work: visiting the crime scene, interviewing officials, NGOs, human rights organisations, victims and other potential witnesses. She will look for evidence such as documents, photos, videos, satellite images, digital information. Usually investigators work with intermediaries to contact witnesses.

4 Selection of suspects
The prosecution is tasked to prosecute individuals who are the most responsible for atrocity crimes – top leaders. However prosecutor Fatou Bensouda formulated also a 'strategy of gradually building upwards.' Her office could first investigate 'a limited number of mid- and high-level perpetrators' to have a 'reasonable prospect of conviction for those most responsible.' The OTP also considers

prosecuting lower level perpetrators 'where their conduct has been particularly grave and has acquired extensive notoriety.'

5   Arrest warrant
    The prosecutor requests the judges to issue (confidentially) an arrest warrant or summons to appear. In case a suspect is arrested, that person will be transferred to The Hague, where he or she will be detained. When suspects receive a summons to appear, they remain free during the proceedings as long as they cooperate. A team of defence lawyers will support the accused.

6   Initial appearance hearing
    The suspect is led before the judges of the pre-trial chamber, who check the identity of the accused and whether he/she has received and understood the charges. The prosecution and defence are present.

7   Confirmation of charges hearings
    The prosecutor, who has the burden of proof, presents her first evidence to the judges of a pre-trial chamber. She has the duty to look for incriminating as well as exonerating material. The defence and the legal representative of victims also present their case. After these hearings the judges analyse the evidence and decide (usually within a few months) whether the case is solid enough to start a full trial.

8   The pre-trial chamber can decide to:
a   confirm the charges, which means the case is committed to trial. The case is transferred from the pre-trial chamber to a trial chamber.
b   decline to confirm the charges, but to give the prosecution the possibility to present additional evidence and request for confirmation of the charges.
c   adjourn the hearing and ask the prosecution to consider to provide new evidence or conduct further investigations, or amend the charges because the evidence shows that a different crime was committed.

9   The trial
    Three judges of a trial chamber will lead the proceedings. An international crimes trial usually lasts several years. First the

prosecution presents its case and calls its witnesses. Then it is the defence's turn. The judges decide when the victims can present their views and concerns. Usually this is done by the legal representative of victims, but there are moments when victims themselves can address the court.

10 Verdict

The judges study the witness testimonies and other evidence (documents, logbooks, images, videos, audio recordings, digital information from computers and phones). It can take months, sometimes even more than a year, before the judges reach a conclusion. The suspect will be convicted or acquitted. Usually there is a separate sentencing hearing.

11 Appeal

The prosecution and defence have the right to challenge the verdict and sentence before the appeals chamber, which consists of five judges. It is possible that these judges come to a different decision and revise a conviction, acquittal or sentence.

12 Reparations for victims

In case of a conviction, the trial chamber can order a convicted person to pay reparations to the victims of his/her crimes. There must be a strict link with the charges. Reparations can be individual, collective and symbolic.

APPENDIX III Definitions of international crimes

Genocide is being described in Article 6 of the Rome Statute. It means carrying out acts with the 'intent' to destroy – in whole or in part – a national, ethnic, racial or religious group. Genocide can be committed through: killing members of the targeted group, causing serious bodily or mental harm, deliberately inflicting conditions of life calculated to bring about the group's physical destruction in whole or in part, imposing measures intended to prevent births, and forcibly transferring children to another group. So far the ICC has charged one person with genocide: the Sudanese president Omar Hassan Ahmad Al-Bashir.

Crimes against humanity are often committed during armed conflict, but these can also be perpetrated during peace time. Article 7 of the Rome Statute explains that atrocities will count as crimes against humanity if these are part of a widespread or systematic attack against a civilian population. These acts are not isolated events but perpetrated as part of a policy of a government or another organisation such as a rebel movement or a political grouping. When meeting these conditions, the following acts can fall under the category of crimes against humanity: murder; extermination; enslavement; deportation or forcible transfer of population; imprisonment or other severe deprivation of physical liberty; torture; rape, sexual slavery, enforced prostitution, forced pregnancy, enforced sterilization, or any other form of sexual violence of comparable gravity; persecution on political, racial, national, ethnic, cultural, religious or gender grounds; enforced disappearance; apartheid, and other inhumane acts intentionally causing great suffering, or serious injury to body or to mental or physical health.

War crimes – As such warfare is not forbidden, but the fighting parties should stick to the rules. War crimes are serious violations of these rules, which are laid down in treaties. The most well-known are the four Geneva Conventions, and their three additional protocols. Crucial in humanitarian law is the difference between civilians and soldiers/fighters. Soldiers are mandated to fight and can thus become a target. But when they are wounded, shipwrecked or taken as prisoner of war, they have the right to be treated well. Civilians are not allowed to fight (except during a spontaneous uprising to defend the country) and thus it is illegitimate to attack and target them.

Article 8 of the Rome Statute says that the ICC has jurisdiction over war crimes 'in particular when committed as part of a plan or policy or as part of a large-scale commission of such crimes.' The list with atrocities that can be characterised as war crimes is five pages long and includes: wilful killing; torture or inhuman treatment including biological experiments; wilfully causing great suffering or serious injury to body or health; extensive destruction and appropriation of property; compelling a prisoner of war or other protected person to serve in the forces of a hostile power; unlawful deportation or transfer or unlawful confinement; taking of hostages; intentionally directing attacks against the civilian population; intentionally directing attacks against civilian objects; intentionally directing attacks against personnel, installations, material, units or vehicles involved in a humanitarian assistance or peacekeeping mission; intentionally launching an attack in the knowledge that such attack will cause incidental loss of life or injury to civilians, or damage to civilian objects or widespread, long-term and severe damage to the natural environment; attacking or bombarding towns, villages, dwellings or buildings which are undefended and which are not military objectives; killing or wounding a combatant who laid down his arms; making improper use of a flag of truce, of the flag or of the military insignia and uniform of the enemy or of the United Nations, as well as of the distinctive emblems of the Geneva Conventions, resulting in death or serious personal injury; the occupying power transferring parts of its own civilian population into the territory it occupies, or the deportation or transfer of all or parts of the population of the occupied territory; intentionally directing attacks against buildings dedicated to religion, education, art, science or charitable purposes, historic monuments, hospitals; physical mutilation or medical or scientific experiments; pillaging a town or place; employing poison or poisoned weapons; employing asphyxiating, poisonous or other gases, and all analogous liquids, materials or devices; employing bullets which expand or flatten easily in the human body; outrages upon personal dignity, in particular humiliating and degrading treatment; rape, sexual slavery, enforced prostitution, forced pregnancy; enforced sterilization, or any other form of sexual violence; attacks against buildings, material, medical units and transport, and personnel using the distinctive emblems of the Geneva Conventions; using starvation of civilians; conscripting or enlisting children under the age of fifteen years or using them to participate actively in hostilities.

Aggression – In 2010 the member states of the ICC assembled in the Ugandan capital Kampala. One of the matters they discussed was the definition of the crime of aggression: the invasion or attack by the armed forces of one state against another state without the justification of self-defence or authorization by the United Nations Security Council. This includes acts such as an illegal military occupation, bombing or blockade. The court will only have the mandate to prosecute this crime if at least thirty member states ratified the text (by now this threshold is met, as 32 countries have done this), ánd if, after 1 January 2017, the Assembly of States Parties decides to activate that jurisdiction.

www.ingramcontent.com/pod-product-compliance
Lightning Source LLC
Chambersburg PA
CBHW060536220326
41599CB00022B/3513